Has Devolution Made a Difference?

Has Devolution Made a Difference?

The State of the Nations 2004

Edited by Alan Trench

IMPRINT ACADEMIC

The moral rights of the authors have been asserted
No part of any contribution may be reproduced in any form
without permission, except for the quotation of brief passages
in criticism and discussion.

Published in the UK by Imprint Academic
PO Box 200, Exeter EX5 5YX, UK

Published in the USA by Imprint Academic
Philosophy Documentation Center
PO Box 7147, Charlottesville, VA 22906-7147, USA

ISBN 0 907845 878

A CIP catalogue record for this book is available from the
British Library and US Library of Congress

www.imprint-academic.com

Contents

PART II
THE STATE

PART III
PUBLIC POLICY: THE EMERGENCE OF DIVERGENCE

List of Contributors

John Curtice is Deputy Director of the Centre for Research into Elections and Social Trends, and Professor of Politics at the University of Strathclyde. He has undertaken a particular interest in recent years in the impact of devolution on public opinion across the United Kingdom, most recently co-editing Devolution — Scottish Answers to Scottish Questions? (Edinburgh: Edinburgh University Press, 2003).

Helen Fawcett is Jean Monnet Fellow in European Public Policy at the University of Strathclyde. Her research focuses on comparative public policy. She has examined the impact of constitutional change on the welfare state, with special reference to social exclusion policy as part of the ESRC's Devolution and Constitutional Change Programme. She has recently edited a special issue of Political Quarterly on devolution and welfare reform.

Oonagh Gay has worked in the House of Commons Library for 20 years. She is currently senior researcher in the Parliament and Constitution Centre where she specialises in several aspects of parliamentary reform, parliamentary standards, electoral law, public administration and devolution. She has also published a number of articles in specialist journals and is a member of the Study of Parliament Group, and the Association of Electoral Administrators. She has completed an 18 month secondment to the Constitution Unit, University College London, where she was responsible for the Unit's Leverhulme funded work on Devolution and Westminster.

Robert Hazell is the Director of the Constitution Unit and Professor of Government and the Constitution in the School of Public Policy, University College London. Originally a barrister, he spent most of his working life at the Home Office. He left Whitehall to become director of the Nuffield Foundation and founded the Constitution Unit in 1995. He is the director of a five year research programme into the Dynamics of Devolution funded by the Leverhulme Trust.

Peter Hetherington is Regional Affairs Editor of The Guardian and a visiting professor at the Centre for Urban and Regional Development Studies.

Guy Lodge is a Research Assistant at the Constitution Unit, in the School of Public Policy, UCL. He works on a range of devolution projects as part of the Leverhulme Trust-funded Nations and Regions programme and the ESRC-funded Devolution and Constitutional Change programme. He writes the quarterly monitoring report on *Devolution and the Centre*.

John Osmond is Director of the Institute of Welsh Affairs, and has written widely on Welsh culture and politics. Recent edited volumes include: 'Birth of Welsh Democracy: The First Term of the National Assembly for Wales' and 'Second Term Challenge: Can the Welsh Assembly Government Hold its Course?', both published by the IWA in 2003. A former journalist and television producer, he is a Fellow of the University of Wales Institute, Cardiff, and a Honorary Senior Research Fellow with the Constitution Unit, University College, London.

Meg Russell has been Senior Research Fellow at the Constitution Unit, UCL, since 1998. She is author of various reports and briefings on parliament and its reform, and of *Reforming the House of Lords: Lessons from Overseas* (OUP, 2000). She is the lead researcher on the Leverhulme funded project 'The Impact of Devolution on Westminster'. She was seconded full time as an adviser to Robin Cook in his role as Leader of the House of Commons from June 2001 — March 2003, during which time Oonagh Gay led this project.

Mark Sandford is a Research Fellow at the Constitution Unit, University College London. He leads the Unit's research on regional government, and was co-author of the report *Unexplored Territory: Elected Regional Assemblies in England*. He has also researched aspects of strategy-making and civic engagement in the English regions. Mark also leads a substantial project examining scrutiny processes at all levels of government. He is a sociologist by training, with a BSc from the University of Bristol and an MA from Goldsmiths College.

John Tomaney is Co-Director of the Centre for Urban and Regional Development Studies at the University of Newcastle upon Tyne.

Alan Trench is a Senior Research Fellow at the Constitution Unit, working on intergovernmental relations both in the United Kingdom and comparatively. A solicitor by profession, he was specialist adviser to the House of Lords Select Committee on the Constitution for their inquiry into Devolution: Inter-Institutional Relations in the United Kingdom in 2001–03.

Rick Wilford is Professor of Politics at Queen's University, Belfast and co-leader with Robin Wilson of the Northern Ireland monitoring project team. He is the author of numerous articles and books on Northern Ireland politics and devolution.

Robin Wilson has been director of the think tank Democratic Dialogue since its foundation in 1995. Along with Prof Rick Wilford of Queen's University, he is co-leader of the Northern Ireland team in the devolution monitoring project co-ordinated by the Constitution Unit, of which they are both honorary senior research fellows. He is a member of the board of the Institute of Governance at Queen's University and of the advisory council of the Dublin-based think tank TASC. He chairs the policy committee of the Northern Ireland Community Relations Council and is an adviser to the Council of Europe project on intercultural dialogue and conflict prevention.

List of Figures

Chapter 5
ENGLISH REGIONS: THE QUIET REGIONAL REVOLUTION

Chapter 6
THE GOVERNANCE OF LONDON
STRATEGIC GOVERNANCE AND POLICY DIVERGENCE

Chapter 7
THE MORE THINGS CHANCE THE MORE THEY STAY THE SAME
INTERGOVERNMENTAL RELATIONS FOUR YEARS ON

Chapter 8
THE IMPACT OF DEVOLUTION ON WESTMINSTER
IF NOT NOW, WHEN?

Chapter 9
RESTORING CONFIDENCE AND LEGITIMACY?
DEVOLUTION AND PUBLIC OPINION

Chapter 11
CONCLUSION: THE UNFINSHED BUSINESS OF DEVOLUTION

Abbreviations

AM	Assembly Member
AMS	Additional Member Electoral System
ALG	Association of London Government
AV	Alternative Vote
BIC	British-Irish Council
BMA	British Medical Association
BSA	British Social Attitudes
CBI	Confederation of British Industry
CCN	County Council Network
CfER	Campaign for the English Regions
CPA	Comprehensive Performance Assessment
CRC	Community Relations Council
CSG	Constitutional Steering Group
CSR	Comprehensive Spending Reivew
DCA	Department for Constitutional Affairs
DHSS	Department of Health and Social Services
DHSSPS	Department of Health, Social Services and Public Safety
DEFRA	Department for Environment, Food and Rural Affairs
DETR	Department of Environment, Transport and Regions
DEL	Department Expenditure Limit
DGN	Devolution Guidance Note
DFM	Deputy First Minister
DTI	Department of Trade and Industry
DUP	Democratic Unionist Party
ESRC	Economic and Social Research Council
EPF	Executive Programme Funds
EU	European Union
FM	First Minister
GLA	Greater London Authority
GLC	Greater London Council
GLEB	Greater London Enterprise Board
GOs	Government Offices
GOL	Government Office for London
HIDB	Highlands and Lowlands Development Board
IGR	Intergovernmental Relations

IICD	Independent International Commission on Decommissioning
IMC	International Monitoring Commission
IRA	Irish Republican Party
IWA	Institute of Welsh Affairs
JMC	Joint Ministerial Committee
LFEPA	London Fire and Emergency Planning Authority
LDA	London Development Agency
MLA	Member of the Legislative Assembly
MPA	Metropolitan Police Authority
MoU	Memorandum of Understanding
MSP	Member of the Scottish Parliament
NAW	National Assembly for Wales
NGOs	Non-governmental organisations
NHS	National Health Service
NICS	Northern Ireland Civil Service
NILTS	Northern Ireland Life and Times Survey
NIO	Northern Ireland Office
NSMC	North-South Ministerial Council
NUT	National Union of Teachers
NWRA	North West Regional Assembly
ODPM	Office of the Deputy Prime Minister
OFMDFM	Office of the First Minister and Deputy First Minister
PC	Plaid Cymru
PIU	Performance and Innovation Unit (now Strategy Unit)
PLP	Parliamentary Labour Party
PPP	Public Private Partnership
PQ	Parti Quebecois
PSAs	Public Service Agreements
RA(P) Act	Regional Assemblies (Preparations) Act
RCU	Regional Coordination Unit
RFP	Regional Policy Forum
RDAs	Regional Development Agency
RPF	Regional Policy Forum
RUC	Royal Ulster Constabulary
SDA	Scottish Development Agency
SDLP	Social Democratic and Labour Party
SEU	Social Exclusion Unit
SF	Sinn Fein

SNP	Scottish National Party
SO	Scotland Office – check
SSA	Scottish Social Attitudes
SSP	Scottish Socialist Party
STV	Single Transferable Vote
TD	Member of the House (Republic of Ireland Parliamentarian)
TfL	Transport for London
WO	Wales Office
UKREP	UK's Permanent Representation
UUC	Ulster Unionist Council
UUP	Ulster Unionist Party
UU	University of Ulster
WFTC	Working Families Tax Credit
WGLA	Welsh Local Government Association
WLTS	Welsh Life and Times Survey
WO	Wales Office

Foreword

Regular readers of previous volumes in this series will find that this year's marks a departure in a number of respects. First, instead of seeking simply to chronicle the events of the last twelve months and relate those to what has happened in the past, this book asks a big question, and seeks from a variety of perspectives to answer it. That big question is in the title: has devolution made a difference? How has it affected politics and the constitution in Scotland, Wales and Northern Ireland? How have the UK Parliament at Westminster and the UK Government machine in Whitehall responded to it, and how do their responses affect the devolved institutions? How has devolution affected public policy — what sort of divergence has occurred, and to what extent is that attributable (directly or indirectly) to the establishment of devolved institutions? Where does England, and the ongoing debates about English regionalism, fit into the broader picture of a devolved UK? What does the experiment of the restoration of London-wide government have to say for England more generally? And how has public opinion changed in response to devolution, in Scotland and Wales and Great Britain as a whole? These are the sorts of questions with which this book is concerned.

That means that it is rather different to previous volumes in the series. Instead of looking back over one year, it looks back over four. Rather than try to find some sort of theme in what has happened over that year, this approach enables the contributors (in their various ways) to identify the more substantive changes that devolution has brought. This should make the book useful to a number of audiences and in a number of ways: it should help those interested in developments in Scotland, Wales or Northern Ireland see those in a broader UK-wide context, while as a whole the book constitutes a first stab at identifying the broader implications and ramifications of a particular form of constitutional and institutional change. The book as a whole draws on research done at the Constitution Unit as part of its five-year research programme on *Nations and Regions: the dynamics of devolution*, generously funded by the Leverhulme Trust. We are now entering the fifth year of that project, and can start to draw some meaningful conclusions from the eleven research projects within the programme. In particular it draws on the work of the monitoring teams covering Scotland, Wales, Northern Ireland, the English Regions and the Centre, who for the last four years have diligently prepared comprehensive accounts of events every three months. The full run of each set of quarterly reports is available on the Unit's website, at http://www.ucl.ac.uk/constitution-unit/leverh/monitoring.htm. We will be pleased to e-mail each quarter's report, as it appears, to anyone who wishes: please send an e-mail to constitution@ucl.ac.uk, indicating which report or reports you want.

Despite being produced with great speed, and with the ambitious aspiration of providing comprehensive coverage of events up to the date on which it went to press (17 November 2003), producing *The State of the Nations 2004* was made much easier by the expertise and helpfulness of all those involved. That includes not only the contributors (to whom I am most grateful), but also a large number of people working behind the scenes. I should therefore like to thank all the members of the monitoring teams whose quarterly reports have provided the backbone of work for this volume: in Scotland, James Mitchell and David Bell, John Curtice, Neil McGarvey, Philip Schlesinger, Mark Shephard, Barry Winetrobe and Alex Wright; in Wales, John Osmond and Sarah Beasley, Alys Thomas, Gerald Taylor, Mark Lang, Denis Balsom, Suzanne Grazier and Jessica Mugaseth; in Northern Ireland, Rick Wilford and Robin Wilson, and John Coakley, Lizanne Dowds, Greg McLaughlin, Elizabeth Meehan and Duncan Morrow; for the English Regions, John Tomaney, Peter Hetherington and Emma Pinkney; and for the Centre, Guy Lodge.

I should also like to thank all my colleagues in the Constitution Unit, many of whom have been involved in this book in some way. While it is invidious to single anyone out, I should record the great help provided by the Unit's Director, Robert Hazell and our wonderfully-capable administrators, Helen Daines and Matthew Butt. Particular thanks go to Guy Lodge, to whom fell the onerous task of copy-editing the book and turning the manuscript into printable text within a horrendously short period of time. And the speedy work and cheerfulness of our publisher, Keith Sutherland and his colleagues at Imprint Academic (notably Sandra Good) merit especial thanks.

Alan Trench	The Constitution Unit
17 November 2003	School of Public Policy
	University College London

1

Introduction: Has Devolution Made a Difference?

Alan Trench

Devolution is still new. After being discussed for more than a century, it has been part of the constitution of the United Kingdom for only five years. To try to reach a judgement about it after such a short time is a questionable undertaking. However, that is the task undertaken in this year's *State of the Nations*. Although it is rash and may be premature, it is also timely; we have now had two elections to the Scottish Parliament, National Assembly for Wales and Northern Ireland Assembly, as well as one Westminster general election, since the introduction of devolution. We have yet to see an alternation in power, producing governments of markedly different political complexions in London, Cardiff or Edinburgh (and may not for some years). But we do now know enough to form an interim assessment about devolution as Labour has brought it into being. Many questions remain, some of which will have to await that alternation of power and some of which will have to await access to official documents (still twenty-something years away). However, we do now have a reasonable sense of the subject-matter. If newspapers are the first rough draft of history (as journalists sometimes claim), this book is a second draft.

Assessing the impact of devolution is not straightforward. The changes devolution has brought about cannot be described in one or two neat phrases, but vary from territory to territory and according to the issue involved. Any serious evaluation has to be nuanced. Jumping to conclusions about whether devolution has been a success or not is even more problematic, not only because it is very early to make such a far-reaching judgement but also because deciding on 'success' involves deciding what devolution should have achieved, and views about what devolution's objectives were, or should have been, vary widely. This book shies away from such broad-brush judgements, and seeks to look at the nature of the changes devolution has already brought about. At the very least this should make political debates about devolution better informed.

Thinking about the changes devolution has wrought has to be done in the context of several propositions that have now gained the status of truisms.[1] The first is that devolution has quickly become a settled part of the UK's constitutional landscape, widely accepted across the UK as 'right' for Scotland and Wales. It commands broard political support from all major parties. The doubts about it that exist relate either to problems faced by the peace process in Northern Ireland or to its extension to the regions of England. Second, the predictions made before devolution by many figures, including notably Tam Dalyell and John Major but also such nationalists as Tom Nairn, that it would lead in short measure to constitutional chaos and the disintegration of the United Kingdom, have not been realised and now seem highly alarmist or optimistic, depending on one's point of view. Third, flowing from the first two, devolution has had a remarkably smooth ride so far. Fourth, because of that devolution remains essentially untested. Labour's control of the governments in London and Cardiff (since May 2003) and its dominance of those in Edinburgh and (between October 2000 and May 2003) in Cardiff means that serious intergovernmental tensions have not yet developed. Until there is real political conflict between administrations, which will require a change of government or serious pressure on their finances, hard questions about devolution will remain unanswered.

In the light of these propositions and despite a desire to maintain due academic caution, there are still some conclusions that can be reached about the record so far.

THE 2003 ELECTIONS: DEVOLUTION COMES OF AGE?

The most eye-catching event of 2003 was the May elections to the Scottish Parliament and National Assembly for Wales. The expected elections to the Northern Ireland Assembly were postponed, but eventually took place on 26 November even though the attempt to restart the peace process and resume devolution in October proved abortive. (That abortive restart is discussed in detail by Wilford and Wilson in chapter 4, and the election results — which appeared while the book was in press — are included as an annex.) The elections in Scotland and Wales and their implications are discussed in more detail in chapter 2 by Mitchell and chapter 3 by Osmond below. In Scotland, there were poor performances by Labour, the Liberal Democrats and the SNP, and strong ones by the Scottish Socialist Party (SSP) and Greens. Labour and the Lib Dems were still able to form a coalition, however, and were largely protected from serious attack by the fact that the SNP had done no better then they had. In Wales, a close result saw Labour gain 3 seats, and

---

[1] These have been discussed in earlier volumes in this series: Hazell, R., (ed.) *The State and the Nations: The First Year of Devolution in the United Kingdom* (Exeter: Imprint Academic, 2000); Trench, A., (ed.) *The State of the Nations 2001: The Second Year of Devolution in the United Kingdom* Exeter: Imprint Academic, 2001); and Hazell, R., (ed.) *The State of the Nations 2003: The Third Year of Devolution in the United Kingdom* (Exeter: Imprint Academic, 2003).

despite a suggestion from Rhodri Morgan before the election that he might continue with a coalition administration he took advantage of a bare majority (30 seats of 60, with the Presiding Officer drawn from the opposition's ranks) for Labour to govern alone.

From a UK-wide point of view, the most significant aspect of each was probably not the outcome, reinforcing Labour dominance in each case, but the low turn-out — a passable if poor 49.4 per cent in Scotland, but only 38.2 per cent in Wales. This suggests that devolved elections are indeed seen as 'second-order' elections by the electorate in general.[2] They may elect a government, but not *the* Government. That in turn suggests that the electorate do not see enough as being at stake in the devolved elections (whether in terms of the importance of the institutions elected or the likelihood of the election result leading to change in composition of the government) to justify people turning out to vote. This conclusion supports a broader one drawn by Curtice in chapter 9; that devolution has not succeeded — or not yet succeeded — in reconnecting voters with government. To what extent that was really a goal of devolution is another question, of course, as is whether it is in fact an appropriate standard by which to evaluate devolution.

However, the low turn-out and the rapid formation of governments substantially resembling the ones in office before the elections suggest that previous suggestions that these elections would mark devolution coming of age were overstated. (The present author eats humble pie as one of those who made such a suggestion.) They plainly have not transformed the nature of the devolved institutions or the process of devolution. They may yet mark the beginning of a transition, as First Ministers (neither of whom led their parties in the 1999 elections) now have their own mandates and may act in a more self-confident way as a result. The success of 'clear red water' in Wales, in contrast to Labour's experience in Scotland, may fuel that. But the real challenge will have to await real political differences between the UK Government and the devolved capitals, not merely differences of emphasis between Labour-dominated administrations.

NEW INSTITUTIONS, NEW POLITICS?

Devolution creates the space for different sorts of politics to develop in Scotland and Wales. The devolved institutions work in very different ways, and make different sorts of policy, to those at UK level. For example, they can involve a wider range of interest groups both through their formal procedures (such as the Public Petitions Committee in Scotland or the local government, business and voluntary sector partnership bodies in Wales) and

---

[2] For the importance of the distinction, see Jeffery, C., and Hough, D., 'Elections in Multi-level Systems: Lessons for the UK from Abroad' in Hazell, 2003.

informally, through their greater openness and their closeness to the electors. That does not stop problems arising or turning into scandals when they do (think of the rows about the new Scottish Parliament building at Holyrood, now the subject of a formal public inquiry, or mismanagement at Education and Learning Wales), but makes these different in nature when they do. The public inquiry into Holyrood chaired by Lord Fraser of Carmyllie QC contrasts with the lack of public investigation into the botched construction projects in London at Portcullis House in Westminster or the new British Library at St Pancras; the only detailed public investigation into either was carried out by the National Audit Office, gathering its evidence in private from a limited number of those involved.

With Northern Ireland, it is harder to form a view. This is not just because devolution as such (the institutions created under Strand 1 of the Belfast Agreement) has been subject to periodic suspensions, including the long suspension that started in October 2002, but because devolution has to be seen in the context of the 'north-south' and 'east-west' institutions created under Strands 2 and 3 of the Agreement. But even here devolution appears to have led to change, if only because policy issues (however defective, truncated or interrupted their development may be, as Wilson and Wilford point out in chapter 4) have started to become part of politics in Northern Ireland. They may only be a limited part, but they are now a part all the same. This 'new politics' may not match up to some of the aspirations of the early supporters of devolution. It is notable, for example, how quickly the National Assembly for Wales started to move away from the idea of an open and inclusive entity encompassing executive and deliberative or legislative functions, towards a more parliamentary model where the two were distinguished as clearly as they could be within the legal framework establishing the Assembly. All the same, it is a different approach to the sort of politics associated with Westminster.

MINIMAL ADJUSTMENT AT THE CENTRE

A further part of the picture is the minimal extent to which devolution has been accompanied by change at the centre of the UK state. Both so far as the civil service and the machinery of government in Whitehall and the UK Parliament at Westminster are concerned, little has altered since devolution. Lodge, Russell and Gay point out in chapter 8 that at Westminster, the Commons retains question-times for the territorial Secretaries of State, even though their functions are now largely limited to liaison behind the scenes with minimal responsibility for policy or programmes. The Commons also retains Select and Grand Committees for each territory, although these have little to do. Within the UK Government 2003 saw a partial change to the nature of the office of the territorial Secretaries of State — they became part-time posts, combined with other portfolios, but nonetheless Scotland and Wales retained their own seats in Cabinet. Likewise the Scotland and Wales Offices remained in existence, but moved under the umbrella of the Department for Constitutional Affairs. The implications of this minimalist approach to change at the centre are discussed by the editor in chapter 7.

There have been considerable pressures for change, including official reports calling for it, for example from the Commons Procedure Committee in 1998 and the Lords Constitution Committee in 2003.[3] By and large the action following such reports has been limited and grudging. The centre has made only those adjustments it has had to, rather than embraced devolution as an opportunity to re-think how UK Government operates or how to approach the government of England more systematically.

THE LOSS OF THE AWKWARD SQUAD

Devolution has however relieved the UK Government from the task of administering what had (under the Tories) been fractious parts of Great Britain which resented both the institutions administering them and the policies produced by those administrations. Resentment of the institutions of government has largely passed (Northern Ireland being a partial exception), and if it remains, it is no longer the UK Government's problem. The same largely applies to the policies made by the devolved institutions. At the very least, devolution has relieved the UK Government of a fair amount of onerous and politically unrewarding work. The same applies to Westminster; instead of incessant and time-consuming questions and debates initiated on the floor of the House by opposition parties about both institutional and policy matters, those issues have largely disappeared from the agenda. One might have expected the West Lothian question to serve as a partial replacement, but while it has occasionally reared its head (in 2003 more than ever, over Parliamentary votes on foundation hospitals for England and jury trials in England and Wales, and over Dr John Reid's appointment as Health Secretary) these have so far proved to short-lived episodes, not a sustained attempt to raise the constitutional issue.

THE IMPLICATIONS OF POLICY DIVERGENCE

As a result of these other factors, policy divergence is becoming increasingly a reality. That means that the UK now works in a different way. *The State of*

---

[3] House of Commons Procedure Committee, *The Procedural Consequences of Devolution*, Fourth Report Session 1998–99, (The Stationery Office: London, 1999); House of Lords Select Committee on the Constitution, *Devolution: Inter-institutional Relations in the United Kingdom*, Session 2002–03 2nd Report, HL Paper 28, (London: The Stationery Office, 2003).

the Nations 2003 contained chapters looking at the policy of free personal
care of the elderly in Scotland and at how health policy has started to develop
along very different lines since devolution.[4] It is too early to reach any sort of
conclusion, and the policy differences Greer noted are unlikely yet to have
had very marked effects that users of the NHS would notice. However, in an
area like health (which is devolved in all three territories) institutional
change has created, in effect, a laboratory for public policy that will enable
the devolved administrations to follow very different paths in the future.
How this works is likely to depend heavily on a variety of factors, including
the political will of the administrations involved and the sorts of competences and policy instruments available to them. Such policy areas provide a
testing-ground for how intergovernmental relations actually work. As the
editor shows in chapter 7, it is easy to overlook the background to this in the
structural characteristics of devolution — in particular its asymmetry and the
nature of the functions retained by the UK Parliament and Government.

The policy area considered in this volume is rather different to health. If
health is an area where conditions permit the maximum degree of policy
divergence, social exclusion is very different. Fawcett's discussion of social
policy in chapter 10 points out that during the 1980s and 1990s, one of the
ideas underlying demands for devolution in Scotland related to promoting a
vision of equity and social justice that was at adds with the policy and goals
of the Thatcher and Major administrations. It is therefore something of a
paradox that the functions of the Scottish Parliament and Executive in this
area are very limited. Policy regarding many matters — notably social security and the welfare state, and employment matters — is reserved to the UK
Government and Parliament. The range of policy instruments available to a
Scottish Executive wanting to make a major impact on social inclusion is
therefore restricted, even if a good deal is at stake politically — the Executive can use its influence in related areas such as housing, planning and local
government and criminal justice to influence what happens, but otherwise
has to rely on its ability to persuade the UK Government to adopt policies
that are compatible with the Scottish ones. The Executive has had some
successes, but these have derived from the fact that to a large degree Edinburgh and London want to do the same things, in largely similar ways.
Differences are in process (the way policy is made), or how arrangements
work on the ground.

One might characterise this as a common language spoken with different
accents, rather than different tongues altogether. It is hard to avoid the
conclusion that a large part of the reason is the nature of the powers available

---

[4] Greer, S., 'Policy Divergence: Will It Change Something in Greenock?' and Simeon, R., 'Free
Personal Care: Policy Divergence and Social Citizenship' in Hazell, R., (ed.) *The State of the Nations
2003: The Third Year of devolution in the United Kingdom* (Exeter: Imprint Academic, 2003).

to the Scottish Parliament and Executive. Sandford's conclusions about the Greater London Authority (GLA) in chapter 6 support this. The GLA, he finds, has been most effective where it has real powers, with funding to deliver them. It has made some impact with its 'strategic' functions, but this is limited in comparison to more substantive functions (or the expectations attached to the mere existence of a 'voice for London').

CONTINUING CONSTITUTIONAL DEBATES

Devolution has not put an end to constitutional debates, even if it has largely moved them out of Westminster. They continue in a number of diverse ways. The fact of devolution to Scotland or Wales is not part of them; as Curtice shows in chapter 9, while enthusiasm for the devolved institutions has declined following their establishment, and the general public regards them as having caused little improvement (if also no deterioration) in how well their territories are governed, there remains solid support for their existence. The new constitutional debates are about loose ends and unfinished business instead. One arises from the emergence of niggles in the settlement for Scotland, such as the size of the Scottish Parliament or the number of deputy presiding officers.[5] Another has been the ongoing debate about the powers of the National Assembly for Wales. As Osmond points out in chapter 3, these started in the National Assembly itself and have moved to centre state in the work of the Richard Commission, in the evidence given to it and the report it will produce (expected in February 2004, about when this book appears). A third has been debate about the appropriate institutional arrangements for devolution within Northern Ireland, which as Wilson and Wilford suggest in chapter 4 starts with questions about how appropriate the arrangements set out in the Good Friday Agreement were and the extent to which those reinforced rather than reduced communal divisions.

The last relates to England; whether there should be regional government for parts of England, what form that might take and what regions might be in line for it. Tomaney and Hetherington show in chapter 5 the extent to which this debate has been marked by ambivalence on the UK Government's part, characterised most clearly by the hurdle erected in the May 2002 White Paper that regional government could not be implemented without establishing single-tier local government in the regions affected (thus involving all the expense and complication of yet another local government reorganisation, less than ten years after the last one).[6] Another hurdle placed in the way

[5] Both are fixed by the Scotland Act 1998. The size of the Parliament is tied to the number of Scottish MPs at Westminster, which will be reduced following devolution to end the proportionate over-representation of Scotland that has lasted since Union in 1707. Neither is within the power of the Scottish Parliament to alter itself. See chapter 7 for further discussion.

[6] Office of the Deputy Prime Minister and Department for Transport, Local Government and the Regions, *Your Region Your Choice*, Cm 5511 (London: The Stationery Office, 2002).

has been the limited functions which elected regional assemblies would have; all the signs are that these will be strategic in nature, with assemblies having only limited powers to act or do things for themselves. The model for regional governments is clearly the new Greater London Authority, but Sandford shows in chapter 6 the limited value of such 'strategic' powers. In some cases they can combine with policy issues looking for an institutional home to increase the impact of an institutionally-weak organisation, but this is far less effective than the ability to make and deliver a real policy. Sandford's verdict about the overall success of the GLA is ambivalent; its entrepreneurial politicians and officers have been unable to overcome the obstacles of its limited legal powers and finance, and cumbersome internal arrangements.

The debate within the UK about how it should govern its territory is far from over, and can be expected to continue over the coming years if not decades. How that is likely to play out over the next few years is discussed by Hazell in chapter 11, where the issues of change for Wales and the English Regions are identified as the key areas of change and the many obstacles in their path considered in detail. If devolution has a political and institutional dynamic that has not reached its conclusion but which is going to be interrupted or constrained, major questions arise for the future of devolution.

THE CHALLENGES FOR POLITICIANS

Devolution creates major challenges for the political parties in Scotland and Wales. The Conservatives and the Liberal Democrats appear to have dealt with these best. Both have created structures that allow the Scottish and Welsh parties considerable autonomy. Both have managed to develop distinctive identities that are not tied so closely to the UK party that they are seen as local clones of the UK politicians. Both have been substantial beneficiaries of the voting systems used, allowing a substantial measure of proportional representation. Labour has faced the challenge in different ways — in Wales by taking a very different tack to the UK party, following an 'old Labour' approach with 'clear red water' to distinguish it from 'new Labour'. In Scotland, under Jack McConnell Labour has cleaved more closely to the 'new Labour' approach. This has partly been an attempt to have a lower profile and have an Executive that does less, better, rather than to ape London Labour, but to judge from the 2003 election results the Welsh strategy has been more successful than the Scottish. While Labour in Wales held its share of the vote on a reduced turnout, won back constituency seats it had lost in 1999 and secured half of the Assembly seats as a result, in Scotland Labour lost votes and seats, and found opposition growing to its left in the form of the Scottish Socialist Party and the Greens. The challenge Labour faces is how to respond when it has to deal with voters wanting more radical government then new Labour offers them, in territories where there are parties that challenge Labour from the left as well as the right.

The parties with the largest problems, however, are the nationalist parties. Neither Plaid Cymru nor the SNP have yet found a clear way of stating what they stand for after devolution — what the relationship is between the constitutional elements of their stance and their approach to more bread-and-butter policy matters. In addition, they have not succeeded in making it clear to the electorate what difference independence rather than devolution would mean. Internal debates continue within both parties, in Plaid Cymru's case resulting in a new leader with a commitment to 'independence' rather than merely 'full national status'. As Curtice shows in chapter 9, around a quarter of the Scottish electorate support independence, and a solid majority supports remaining in the UK with a Parliament (which may or may not have powers over taxes). In Wales, remaining in the UK with a parliament or assembly also commands support from a very solid majority of the electorate, while only 12 per cent of the electorate support independence.[7] Those figures have remained largely constant since 1997 (with a small upward blip for Scottish independence in 1997, at the time of the referendum on devolution). Despite their support for it, devolution has not helped the nationalist parties at all. To make progress, they need to find a programme that will attract broader appeal than they have since 1999. One temptation may be to occupy space to the left of Labour, and seek to build support on the basis of a firm commitment to progressive social policies. Given the control of a number of key functions in this area at UK level, that creates a way to combine a popular political position with a reason for needing further, large-scale, constitutional change.

However, that approach contains a major hazard. This is the sort of approach taken in the recent past by the secessionist Parti Québécois (PQ) in Quebec. The PQ has long been committed to a progressive social programme. Through the 1980s and 1990s, its position was that Quebec needed to become independent in order to deliver that programme, which (it was said) was not possible within the framework of the federation; key areas of policy were beyond Quebec's control, in the hands of the Parliament and Government of Canada. The PQ needed to show that it could make a real difference to the lives of its electorate and so did its best, sometimes going beyond Provincial powers but not facing legal challenges from a prudent federal government. By the time the April 2003 Provincial elections came, the PQ lacked an answer to the question of why independence was needed; it had delivered its social programme, within the constraint of Provincial competences and the framework of a federal Canada. It could no longer

---

[7] See Table 9.2, page 222.

sustain the argument that independence was necessary for Quebec to have its $5-a-day childcare, the Quebec Pension Plan, good-quality healthcare or support for students at university. True, there was also a strong sense that it was running out of steam as a government, and that the people of Quebec were fed up with incessant debates about independence and secession. Change was in the air. But the lack of a credible intellectual argument for separation fatally undermined the PQ, not despite but because of its policy success.

For the SNP and Plaid Cymru the need to map out a new agenda is a real challenge. They need to steer between the Scylla of appealing to their own members with an appeal to independence as soon as possible and the Charybdis of diluting that commitment for other policies that turn them into a replica of other parties. That is a tough balancing act, but they need to find an answer to it if they are to disprove Labour's belief that devolution would kill nationalism dead. So far, for practical purposes Labour's belief seems to be winning.

QUESTIONS FOR THE FUTURE

In this context, devolution appears to be a reform half-completed. On one hand it is accepted widely, by elected politicians and political parties, the public and civil servants. It has very rapidly become part of the furniture of the British constitution. On the other, it still awaits its biggest challenges — large-scale divergence in policy, nationalist parties offering real alternatives to Labour, institutional change that is really disruptive to existing political or administrative arrangements. There is also the prospect, lying behind those factors, of a real political challenge, which will only occur when different parties are in office in UK Government and one or more of the devolved capitals. How devolution develops over the next few years will be intriguing to watch.

Part I

The Nations

2

Scotland: Expectations, Policy Types and Devolution

James Mitchell[1]

After four years of Scottish devolution, its contours are becoming clear. The Scotland Act 1998 and the formal institutional structures have been analysed in detail in numerous works. Students of political institutions have long recognised, however, that institutions need to be understood as incorporating both formal and informal dimensions. Peters, for example, distinguished between *formal institutions* as, for example legislatures, agencies in the public bureaucracy and the legal framework, and *informal institutions* such as a network of interacting organisations or a set of shared norms.[2] The latter only become clear as a new institution beds down and starts to operate. It is widely acknowledged that decisions and practices determined in the early life of an institution (or indeed a policy) can have profound long-term implications. Institutional change becomes difficult, though not impossible, as 'the formal rules, compliance procedures, and the standard operating practices that structure the relationship between individuals in various units of the polity and economy' settle.[3] The first four years of the Scottish Parliament and Scottish Executive are not only interesting in understanding the establishment of these new formal institutions but also to identify the informal institutions — the practices and procedures — which are likely to remain largely intact well into the future.

While much effort was put into determining aspects of devolved government by supporters of Scottish home rule prior to devolution during the long years of Conservative rule before 1997, much was neglected. Both the Constitutional Convention before 1997 and Constitutional Steering Group (CSG) thereafter played parts in putting flesh on the bones of devolution, but much was left implicit or could only be left to be determined with the establishment of devolution. Many home rulers had wished to see a form of 'new politics', however vaguely conceived, which informed the work of those

[1] I am grateful to colleagues with whom I work monitoring devolution: David Bell, John Curtice, Neil McGarvey, Philip Schlesinger, Mark Shephard, Barry Winetrobe, Alex Wright. I would also like to thank Dan Wincott for helpful comments on an earlier draft.

[2] Peters, G.B., *Institutional Theory in Political Science: The New Institutionalism* (London: Pinter: 1999), p. 18.

[3] Hall, P., *Governing the Economy: The Politics of State Intervention in Britain and France* (Oxford: Oxford University Press, 1986), p. 19.

planning devolution and four principles — participation, accountability, equal opportunities, and power sharing — were set out by the CSG in 1998.[4] After four years, it is worth considering the extent to which Scottish devolution has involved not only an alteration in the formal institutions, which seems undeniable, but the informal institutions.

We should not be surprised to find that the informal institutions that have grown up with devolution owe much to those that existed pre-devolution. Some of the hopes and expectations that a new form of politics would emerge around the new formal institutions were unrealistic. Nonetheless, devolution has brought significant change to politics in Scotland. The structure adopted in this chapter focuses mainly upon public policies. But instead of the familiar journalistic approach that views these through departmental structures — looking in turn at education, health, etc — public policies are discussed in the terms used in academic public policy analysis. Four distinct headings are adopted: Redistributive Policies; Distributive Policies; Regulatory Policies; and Process.[5]

This is important for two reasons. First, it allows us to relate public expectations to the policy options available under devolution. Second, as students of public policy have long noted, 'policies determine politics' and the types of policies discussed give rise to different types of politics.[6] The nature of the devolved polity will, therefore, in part be determined by the relative importance of each policy type.

Redistributive policies involve redistribution between classes of people. Examples of these types of policies include taxation and social security policies. However, the arrangements for Scottish devolution have involved retaining the range of policy tools necessary for redistribution in London, and this presents a problem in terms of what people in Scotland had expected of devolution. Supporters of a Scottish Parliament hoped to see it deliver on a redistributive agenda of public policies.[7] Distributive policies are those

[4] The Constitutional Steering Group of the Scottish Parliament 1999 stated, 'We adopted the following key principles to guide our work: the Scottish Parliament should embody and reflect the sharing of power between the people of Scotland, the legislators and the Scottish Executive; the Scottish Executive should be accountable to the Scottish Parliament and the Parliament and Executive should be accountable to the people of Scotland; the Scottish Parliament should be accessible, open, responsive, and develop procedures which make possible a participative approach to the development, consideration and scrutiny of policy and legislation; the Scottish Parliament in its operation and its appointments should recognise the need to promote equal opportunities for all.'

[5] See Lowi, T., 'American business, public policy, case studies, and political theory', *World Politics*, 16, pp. 677–715, (1964); Lowi, T., 'Four Systems of policy, politics and choice', *Public Administration Review*, 32, pp. 298–310, (1972). For an early application of this typology to understanding Scottish devolution see Mitchell, J., 'What Could a Scottish Parliament Do?', *Federal and Regional Studies*, 8 (1), Spring, pp. 68–85, (1998).

[6] Lowi, 1972, p. 299.

[7] Mitchell, J., 'Devolution and the end of Britain', *Contemporary British History*, 14, pp. 61–82, (2000) at pp. 68–70.

policies which involve public expenditure on groups rather than individuals. This would include grants to farmers or local government as well as the funding of schools and hospitals. These are often associated with patronage, and 'pork barrel' politics.[8] Regulatory policies are policies involving public control over private activities in the public interest for example consumer protection as well as social and economic regulation. Much of contemporary public policy in liberal democracy is concerned with regulatory policy-making. By process is meant the procedures established to make decisions from agenda setting to implementation.

Much of the emphasis among the elites who supported devolution was a concern that devolution would alter the informal as well as the formal institutions of Scottish politics. The Scottish Constitutional Convention, for example, in 1995 maintained that the creation of a new parliament was a 'rare and exciting moment, one which affords unique opportunity for change and renewal . . . a chance to effect fundamental improvements in the way Scotland is governed' and was an early statement of the principles of accountability, accessibility, openness, and responsiveness with which the Constitutional Steering Group operated.[9] This was, notably, more a concern of the elites who supported devolution. The wider public appears to have had more interest in the policy outputs that would flow from devolution. This is not to suggest that the elites campaigning for devolution were unconcerned with outputs, rather that they placed considerable weight on the role of processes on policy outputs.

The relationships between the different types of policies are complex. Distributive policies, over time, may have redistributive consequences. Public funding of education, for example, will provide the means through which individuals improve their socio-economic standing. The process through which policy is made can have a real impact on policy outputs. The very existence of a Scottish Parliament, especially one with an electoral system different from that used in elections to the House of Commons, could be anticipated to result in a different type of politics but the further hope of greater accessibility, accountability, openness and responsiveness raised other expectations. But policy types are not simply a useful way of simplifying and making sense of the world. These policy types give rise to distinct types of politics. The politics of distributive policies in nineteenth-century USA 'became dominated by localized, logrolling, non-ideological parties'.[10] They are also prone to *sub rosa* politics. Lowi's comment that 'nothing open and democratic can come of [distributive policies]' may be an exaggeration

---

[8] Lowi, 1964, p.690.

[9] Scottish Constitutional Convention, *Scotland's Parliament. Scotland's Right* (Edinburgh: Scottish Constitutional Convention, 1995).

[10] Lowi 1972, p. 300.

but is a cautionary observation from an authoritative source.[11] This presents serious challenges to those who argued for devolution on the grounds that it would open up policy-making. Redistributive policies give rise to more cosmopolitan ideologies and usually involve strong executive government. The rise of regulatory politics has been associated with a shift towards a less ideological politics or at least, the ideologies of new social movements as distinct from the old forms of politics.

One of the key problems identified pre-devolution was the existence of a capability-expectations gap, that is that Scottish devolution was not capable of delivery all that was expected of it.[12] This gap was sharpened by the quite normal tendency to exaggerate the merits of devolution on the part of its supporters in the run up to and during the devolution referendum in 1997. The absence of a strong opposition counterbalancing these claims predicting exaggerated dire consequences of devolution meant that little was done to close the capability-expectations gap. Understanding devolution in operation requires taking account of expectations, capabilities, policy types and related politics. Together these provide a useful way of making sense of the politics of Scottish devolution.

Figure 2.1: Chronology of Events August 2002–October 2003

2002	
4 October	Scottish Parliament Corporate Body estimated cost of Holyrood building at £29.5 million.
16 October	Jack McConnell met representatives of Celtic and Rangers football clubs to discuss sectarianism.
30 October	Launch of Parliament's annual report
19 November	Announcement of delay in opening of Holyrood building.
22 November	Beginning of firemen's strike
26 November	Richard Simpson resigned as Deputy Minister for Justice following allegations that he made scurrilous comments about firemen.
27 November	Ross Finnie, Minister responsible for fisheries in cabinet, announced European Commission proposals to cut drastically North Sea fishing.

[11] Lowi, 1972.

[12] The term is derived from Hill, C., 'The Capability-Expectations Gap, or Conceptualizing Europe's International Role', *Journal of Common Market Studies*, 31, pp. 305–328, (1993). In the context of Scottish devolution it was first adopted in a series of papers by Mitchell before devolution and in published work subsequently. See Mitchell, J., 'Towards a New Constitutional Settlement', in Hay, C., (ed.) *British Politics Today* (Cambridge: Polity, 2002), pp. 237–258.

4 December	Three-year financial settlement for local government announced.
18 December	Helen Liddell, Scottish Secretary, announced that Scottish Parliament will continue to have 129 members.
20 December	Ross Finnie, Minister responsible for fisheries, expressed frustration at inability to get better deal for Scotland on fisheries from Brussels.

2003

7 January	Jack McConnell launched a healthy eating campaign.
8 January	Ross Finnie announced Executive is considering financial package of support for fishing communities that will lose out under EU fisheries policy.
9 January	Executive attempted to amend legislation allowing it to close fire stations without taking it to the Parliament. Executive defeated on casting vote of Deputy Presiding Officer.
17 January	Scottish Parliament debated Iraq. Labour rely on Conservatives to win victory.
3 February	Ross Finnie announced programme of support for fishing communities at cost of £3.2 million.
4 March	Robin Cook MP, Leader of the House of Commons, visited the Parliament to consider electronic voting system and Public Petitions Committee.
4 March	Iain Gray, Minister for Transport announced £375 million investment in public transport in Edinburgh.
5 March	Jack McConnell announced transfer of Glasgow's 81,000 council houses to not-for-profit Glasgow Housing Association (see April 2002 referendum of tenants).
6 March	Launch of consultation on future of regional policy in Europe.
31 March	First four-year session of Scottish Parliament ended officially at midnight.
1 May	Scottish Parliament elections
7 May	George Reid elected Presiding Officer.
9 May	Jack McConnell wrote to George Reid indicating preference for more spontaneity, more time for back-bench contributions and flexibility in the Parliament's working hours.
15 May	Jack McConnell re-elected First Minister. *A Partnership for a Better Scotland* (the coalition agreement between Labour and LibDems) published.

20 May	McConnell announced his new cabinet and Ministers:
3 June	The Queen addressed second session of Scottish Parliament
5 June	Parliamentary Corporate Body received report suggesting Holyrood project could cost £375 million.
10 June	Holyrood project consultants agreed to cap fees.
25 June	Parliament's annual report issued – 22 bills passed and 40 enquiries completed.
26 June	Tavish Scott, Deputy Finance Minister, attended Ministerial European Co-ordination Committee (MINECOR) in Downing Street.
10 July	Decommissioning grants offered to Scottish fishing boats.
29 August	Executive responded to proposal to extend First Minister's Question Time from 20 to 30 minutes and change of time to noon.
2 September	Executive ordered Scottish Natural Heritage staff to proceed with controversial plans to disperse jobs from Edinburgh.
17 September	Transport Minister Nicol Stephen announced the creation of Transport Scotland, a new agency.
27 September	John Swinney defeated challenger for leadership of SNP at annual conference by 577 (84 per cent) votes to 111.
8 October	John Elvidge, new Permanent Secretary of Scottish Executive, held first media briefing and discussed restructuring of office. Called for a less adversarial relationship between Executive officials and MSPs.
30 October	Jim Wallace, Deputy First Minister and Enterprise Minister, reiterated Executive opposition to top-up fees for universities.

CREATING THE CAPABILITY–EXPECTATIONS GAP

There was no single argument for a Scottish Parliament, and in fact some of the cases made were mutually incompatible. Most often noted was the support for devolution as a means of strengthening the Union against support for devolution as a stepping-stone to independence. But there were many other arguments in favour of devolution some of which had elite support while others had more popular support. In crude terms, arguments focussing on process — creating more openness, democracy, participation — tended to be articulated among the elites. Arguments that focused on public policy outputs and greater Scottish control of Scottish affairs to this end tended to have greater appeal to the public at large. This was not, however, primarily support for innovation in policy but the reverse. Conditioned by the context of eighteen years of Conservative rule, this might best be described as the poll tax argument. A summary of research for *Scotland Forward*, the pro-devolution campaign group that operate during the referendum campaign, noted that the poll tax 'remains an emotive issue' and was cited by members of focus groups as a reason for wanting devolution.[13] Many Scots came to support devolution from the late 1980s as a way of preventing, as they saw it, the imposition of unwanted policies. There were other more positive arguments for devolution. It is likely that these gained force as devolution drew nearer and in particular during the referendum campaign (see Figure 2.2 below for findings of pro-devolution campaign group). In November 1996, research was carried out for supporters of devolution that gave an indication of what voters expected would follow after devolution.

Peter Kellner (who had been commissioned to conduct the research) concluded from this and a set of responses to 'negative' statements about devolution that, 'economic issues drive the 'double no' vote, while governance issues drive the 'double yes' vote' — or that this was a 'thistle in your kilt, versus pound in your sporran divide'.[14] Kellner's use of the over-used term 'governance' merged with notions of national identity fails to dissect the explanations adequately. An alternative interpretation of the data is that the public were interested in the output of devolution and sought to 'improve the quality of public welfare in Scotland'.[15] Surridge and McCrone expressed this well, ' . . . those who have argued that people are much more interested in 'real' politics — the delivery of services — than in purely constitutional politics are correct. On the other hand, they are wrong insofar as the distinction between these two realms is artificial, because they are linked together in the minds of the electorate'.[16]

Scots did expect taxes to rise under devolution but still voted for a Parliament with tax-varying powers. While issues of 'governance' may have motivated activists campaigning for a Parliament, more prosaic matters motivated the public. In large measure devolution was a conservative measure — a means of blocking unwanted policies from London — but also a moderately progressive measure — a means of improving welfare services and life chances across a range of public policies. The public may have appeared unconcerned with the details or even which matters would be retained and devolved. The need to ensure convincing endorsement in a referendum, coming when opponents of devolution had recently been routed in the UK general election, ensured that voters went to the polls in September 1997 with unrealistic expectations. Having played a significant part in

[13] 'Pre-Testing Slogans for Scotland Forward', *Scotland Forward papers*, Vol. 10, 31 July 1997.

[14] Kellner, P., *Report on Devolution Poll* (London: Political Context, 1996), p. 5.

[15] Surridge, P., and McCrone, D., 'The 1997 Scottish referendum vote', in Taylor, B., and Thomson, K., (eds.) *Scotland and Wales: Nations Again?* (Cardiff: University of Wales, 1999), p. 47.

[16] Surridge and McCrone, 1999, p. 54.

building up these expectations, sections of the media attempted, with only limited success, over the succeeding years to undermine devolution.

Figure 2.2: Public Views on 'Positive' Aspects of Devolution, November 1996[17]

'Positive statements'	Agree %	Dis-agree %	Net
1. It's about time important decisions affecting Scotland were made by a Scottish Parliament, elected by Scottish people, rather than hundreds of miles away in England.	86	9	+ 77
2. Scotland needs to take more control and stop blaming other people for its problems.	80	11	+ 69
3. A Scottish Parliament would strengthen Scotland's pride in itself.	80	12	+ 68
4. Money for Scotland's public services such as schools and hospitals would be spent more wisely if the decisions about it were made by a Scottish Parliament	80	12	+ 68
5. A Scottish Parliament would be able to do much more to boost jobs and investment in Scotland.	79	13	+ 66
6. A Scottish Parliament within the United Kingdom would be able to bring out the best of the talents of the Scottish people.	77	12	+ 65
7. It is vital for a Scottish Parliament to have the power to vary income tax up or down to make the right decisions about public spending in Scotland.	76	12	+ 64
8. Scotland's interests in Europe would be better represented if there was a Scottish Parliament.	77	13	+ 64
9. A Scottish Parliament would be able to make sure that the British Government in London takes notice of Scotland when deciding policies for Britain as a whole.	76	13	+ 63

[17] Source: Scotland Forward Papers, access to papers kindly provided by Nigel Smith.

'Positive statements'	Agree %	Dis-agree %	Net
10. A Scottish Parliament elected by a fair voting system would encourage politicians from different parties to work together for the good of Scotland as a whole.	67	20	+ 47
11. The plans to make sure that roughly equal numbers of men and women make up a Scottish Parliament would help it to make better decisions.	56	21	+ 35

Figure 2.3: Expectations of Scottish Parliament, 1997[18]

The Scottish Parliament would:	A lot %	A little %	Total %1
Increase unemployment	2	9	11
Increase taxes	2	68	70
Improve the economy	26	60	86
Improve the standard of the NHS	36	46	82
Improve the quality of education	39	50	89
Improve the standard of social welfare	19	52	71

REDISTRIBUTIVE POLICIES

The most politically sensitive aspect of the devolution scheme was its tax-varying power: there was an extreme imbalance between the fiscal feebleness and the political salience of these powers. Tax was given a second question in the 1997 referendum and was the focus of much of the opposition's attacks on devolution in the years leading up to devolution. At the first elections to the Scottish Parliament in 1999, the SNP proposed to use the very limited tax power and was attacked by all other parties and most of the media for doing so. This marked a remarkable change from two years before when those arguing for a Yes-Yes vote in the referendum had insisted that

[18] Ns varied between 311 and 314. Source: CREST in Denver, D., Mitchell, J., Pattie, C., and Bochel, C., *Scotland Decides: The Devolution issue and the 1997 referendum* (London: Frank Cass, 2000), p. 200.

use of the tax power could have little, if any, adverse impact. Many voters may have supported use of the tax and there was evidence that, however poorly articulated by the SNP leadership who had focussed on using the tax rather than what it would be used for, this was not altogether unpopular. Nonetheless, this first election marked a watershed in making it unlikely that into the foreseeable future any of the established parties would campaign to increase taxes to improve services. The politics of tax-and-spend appears in decline in 'radical Scotland'.

As new leader of the Scottish National Party, John Swinney moved his party away from its image as a 'tax-and-spend' party that some concluded had damaged it in 1999. By the second elections to the Scottish Parliament in May 2003 the SNP had abandoned support for using the tax power. Indeed, redistributive politics were absent from the agendas of the main parties in the election. There had been speculation that the Conservatives might attempt to distinguish themselves from the pack by arguing in favour of using the tax-varying power to lower taxation. In the event, the Conservatives proved as conservative as the other main parties, leaving it to the smaller parties to cut out a distinct position.

The party which most fervently argued on a redistributive agenda was the Scottish Socialist Party, providing a home for voters who supported old style 'tax-and-spend'. This probably accounts for the SSP's performance in May 2003 through the image it created as an alternative, radical party though other policies (including its opposition to the war in Iraq) helped it harness support. The SSP emerged during the first Scottish Parliament with Tommy Sheridan, its leader and only MSP elected in 1999, cutting out a niche in the electoral market place which had opened up with both Labour and SNP turning their backs on 'tax-and-spend'. Indeed, *reinforcing* the SSP's support for a redistributive agenda, the party had argued in the lead up to the 2003 elections for a local income tax which the party saw as not only providing a basis for funding local government but a vehicle for redistribution of wealth. In its 2003 manifesto, the SSP included the local income tax, but called it a Scottish Service Tax in order to emphasise that this was a proposal to reform local government finance (which under the terms of the Scotland Act 1998 was devolved) rather than other forms of tax (which are reserved to Westminster).[19] The Greens too were in favour of redistribution but a problem with the Green manifesto was that it failed to distinguish either between priorities or matters that were devolved and retained.[20] Additionally, it seems unlikely that voters perceived the Greens as a party with a clear redistributive agenda given the prominence given to environmentalism.

[19] Scottish Socialist Party, *another Scotland is possible*, Holyrood Election Manifesto 2003, (Scottish Socialist Party, 2003).

[20] Scottish Green Party, *reach for the future*, Scottish Green Party 2003 Scottish Manifesto, (Scottish Green Party, 2003).

Though these are not incompatible, indeed some would argue that redistributive policies are a prerequisite of environmentalism, that is unlikely to be appreciated by the electorate. Redistribution was certainly not a major issue at the launch of the Green manifesto.

While the four main parties were lowering expectations, whether deliberately or otherwise, the minor parties and others were seeking to do the opposite. Under a first-past-the-post system, the dominance of the four main parties might have contributed to the closure of the expectations gap, but the rise of the others has made that more difficult. A Pensioners Party member was elected in Central Scotland, seeking to increase the state pension prominent among his objectives. Pensions are, of course, retained at Westminster. Public opinion may play its part in shaping party policies but party loyalties and policy leadership may equally shape public opinion. Significantly, the existence of the SSP ensured that expectations of redistribution have been kept alive and continue to trouble the two main parties. The shift away from tax-and-spend inside the SNP has removed one pressure on Labour only to be replaced by another in the shape of the SSP.

Figure 2.4: Results of Scottish Parliament Elections, 1 May 2003

Labour	50 seats	(-6);
SNP	27 seats	(-8);
Conservatives	18 seats	(-);
LibDems	17 seats	(-);
Greens	7 seats	(+6);
SSP	6 seats	(+5);
Others	4 seats	(+3).

DISTRIBUTIVE POLICIES

The Parliament and Executive inherited the old Scottish Office's powers regarding the distribution of public spending in Scotland. The Scottish Parliament is a spending rather than a revenue-raising body. It also inherited the limitations placed on the Scottish Office in this regard. The increased visibility and salience of territorial public spending matters across the UK has been an important backdrop against which the Parliament has operated (see chapter 7). In crude terms, the total amount available to the Scottish Parliament and Executive is determined by the Treasury but with relatively more autonomy given to the Scottish institutions than offered by the normal constraints of a spending department in Whitehall. The devolved government has more scope to determine its own priorities. Other than the Treasury setting the budget, the main limitations, as always, are past and long-term commitments. So long as there is a legal obligation to provide full-time school education for all between the ages of five and sixteen, for example, this will take up a considerable part of the budget available. Such commitments exist across the range of devolved services and commonplace in public policy. This does not remove scope for changing priorities, merely limits its scope. There have been occasions in the past when the Scottish Office has approached the Treasury with a 'special case' arguing for special assistance, usually ad hoc support, to deal with a particular problem.

The experience of devolution to date does not suggest that the new formal institutions have altered this dramatically. Throughout its relations with the Scottish Office, the Treasury was consistently careful to take account not only of any Scottish special pleading but also the implications this might have elsewhere in the UK, in particular the danger of provoking equivalent demands from other Whitehall departments.[21] This remains a concern of the Treasury and has frustrated the Scottish devolved institutions. The new formal institutions appear to have little impact in this respect on the informal rules governing relations with the Treasury. The key difference post-devolution is that the Treasury and other Whitehall departments continue to view the devolved institutions much as they viewed the Scottish Office while the new devolved bodies assume they have greater leeway at least in setting priorities if not in demanding more resources. There is an imbalance in understandings of devolution north and south of the border. This has created tensions around such Scottish initiatives such as care for the elderly and tuition fees. The Executive's spending priorities and plans have followed those of Whitehall remarkably. This shadowing of distributive priorities may be explained by Scottish Labour following London Labour's lead or reflect what we should expect in the early days of devolution.

The most significant policy divergence has been care for the elderly, a policy which initially was set to apply uniformly across the UK. The intervention of Henry McLeish, who as the new First Minister insisted on a change of policy (despite strong pressure from the UK Prime Minister, Chancellor of the Exchequer and Social Security Minister)and so led Scotland down a different path.[22] Backed by the majority report of the Royal Commission on the subject and with the Parliament falling into line (especially as the issue gained prominence in the media), an uncosted policy was adopted. The Executive appealed for financial support from London. This differed from the many previous Scottish Office approaches to the Treasury for special assistance in important respects. The policy had been confirmed and very publicly announced *before* an approach was made to the Treasury.

[21] Mitchell, J., *Governing Scotland* (Basingstoke: Palgrave Macmillan, 2003), pp. 149–181.

[22] For more on this see Simeon, R., 'Free Personal Care: Policy Divergence and Social Citizenship', in Hazell, R., (ed.) *The State of the Nations 2003: The Third Year of Devolution in the United Kingdom* (Exeter: Imprint Academic, 2003).

Also, and related to its high public profile, the Scottish policy was bound to lead to pressure for similar treatment elsewhere in the UK. The 'spill-over' effect had always been a concern of the Treasury in its dealing with the Scottish Office.[23]

Changes that occur in distributive policies are likely to be gradual unless there is a dramatic change in the total budget available. Notably, there was an increase in public spending after New Labour's spending purdah after coming to power in 1997. The new devolved institutions benefited from this, but the operation of the Barnett formula meant that the share of this increase accruing to the Scottish Executive was relatively smaller as compared to that awarded to England.[24] Nonetheless, devolution's greatest test, even more than different parties holding power in London and Edinburgh, will be when public spending comes under pressure, and that has yet to occur. Scottish devolution has so far operated in the benign context of increasing public spending in real terms and compatible regimes operating in London and Edinburgh. The capability-expectations gap has at least not been growing and may even be closing. These aspects of context are related. Pressures on public spending are likely to increase in difficult economic times when demands increase for welfare services (especially those which are the responsibility of local government and so funded by the Scottish Executive) that Scottish devolution is most capable of delivering. This may create its own capability-expectations gap. Added to this is the consequent increased prospect of incompatible goals and approaches on the part of governments in London and Edinburgh, whether of the same party or otherwise.

Jack McConnell's tenure as First Minister began with criticisms of his removal of senior Labour colleagues. Having no electoral mandate of his own and being the third First Minister within the first Parliament, McConnell's authority was initially weak as compared with his predecessors. However, his strategy was unmistakably that of lowering expectations and closing the gap between what devolution could and would deliver. His focus was on public welfare delivery. Labour's poor performance in the 2003 election has not harmed McConnell partly because Labour's manifesto was so unexceptional and no particular item can be seen to have been undermined — but largely because the SNP's performance was even less impressive.[25]

In the run-up to and during the 2003 elections, the two main parties moved increasingly towards each other in terms of distributive policies. Differences

---

[23] For a discussion of earlier examples see Mitchell, 2003, pp. 149–181.

[24] For more on this see Bell,. D, and Christie, A., 'Finance — The Barnett Formula: Nobody's Child' in Trench, A., (ed.) *The State of the Nations 2002: The Second Year of Devolution in the United Kingdom* (Exeter: Imprint Academic, 2002).

[25] Scottish Labour, *On your side*, Scottish Labour's Manifesto 2003, (Glasgow: Scottish Labour Party, 2003).

between the parties were given prominence in news releases and party literature. This was exemplified in the difference over school class sizes. Labour
wanted to concentrate resources on reducing secondary class sizes while the
SNP sought to concentrate on reducing primary class sizes. Both parties
have set out to create or maintain images as paragons of fiscal responsibility.
Each had costed its programme so that it could not be accused of being prof-
ligate, possibly at the cost of removing the excitement from political battle
and inducing apathy.

The most heated debates between the two main parties over distributive
policies arose over the role and extent of private finance and details of
service delivery. The Treasury had forced the Executive to adopt Public
Private Partnerships for capital projects, which have proved controversial
with the SNP leading attacks inside the Parliament and the trade unions
among the main critics outside. There has been a significant difference in the
presentation of private finance in Scotland where the Executive has been
disinclined to make as much of these as equivalent departments in England.[26]
Neither Labour nor SNP oppose private finance being used in the provision
of welfare services and the differences between them are likely to have been
seen as technical to most users of these services or the media. Once more, the
SSP may have managed to cut out a distinct position on this given its very
clear opposition to private finance. Far more heat was generated in parliamentary and media clashes on individual cases. Towards the end of 2002,
John Swinney brought cases of individuals who had suffered poor quality
public service delivery, especially in health policy. While this heat may have
generated interest in politics, it amounted to little in distinguishing the SNP
from Labour in strict public policy terms. Altogether, the poses as responsible government and its alternative struck by the two main parties (as well as
the Liberal Democrats) contributed to dealing with the capability–
expectations gap.

However, it would be wrong to assume that devolution has given rise to
stale responsible politics with a rush towards the safe, centre ground. The
electoral system has helped to ensure that ground vacated by Labour and the
SNP is fertile for those setting up stalls beyond the centre. During the course
of the last Parliament, the SSP and Greens cut out niches for themselves in
the electoral marketplace. The SSP appeared more adept at exploiting the
new institutions though it won six MSPs in 2003, one fewer seat than the
Greens. The SSP once more set out a distinct position on the distributive
agenda. It has become adept in identifying and exploiting opportunities to
climb onto issues and create campaigns allowing it to position itself as

[26] Bell, D., 'Public Private Partnerships' in *Devolution and Scotland: Monitoring Report February
2003* (London: The Constitution Unit), pp. 36–37. See http://www.ucl.ac.uk/constitution-unit/monrep
/scotland/scotland_february_2003.pdf.

distinct. Among the issues it has exploited well has been free school meals. Campaigning in favour of a policy with a populist edge as well as winning support from various specialist interest groups, the SSP has been able to attract considerable media attention. The SSP has had no worries about the capability-expectations gap for a number of reasons. First, it was explicit in arguing during the election campaign that if people voted for the SSP and its policies then London would be obliged to fund these. It was, essentially, adopting a confrontational stance reminiscent of past battles between local authorities and central government, most notably those associated with Militant in Liverpool in the 1980s but also between some Scottish local authorities and the Scottish Office in the early 1980s. Second, there was little prospect of the SSP forming or being part of an administration in Edinburgh. The SNP leader ruled out the prospect of an SNP-SSP coalition at the launch of his party's manifesto and, in launching its manifesto, the SSP ruled out any prospect of forming a coalition but instead preferred to consider issues on an *ad hoc* basis. The SSP did, nonetheless, offer a home to those seeking to widen the capability-expectations gap who saw it as a way of provoking political change, whether socio-economic policy change or constitutional change, both of which are supported by the party.

At the start of the 2003 Scottish election, the BBC drew up a list of policies that they deemed significant and asked electors to prioritise these. Unfortunately, the BBC's advisers appear to have both a limited understanding of the issues being pursued by the parties and, indeed, devolved responsibilities. Nonetheless, the poll indicated the kind of matters that electors prioritised at the start of the campaign. Distributive matters dominated the top positions. The top priorities reflected public service provision — distributive policies in the main. Policing and law and order in general had been a theme that was frequently raised in the Parliament and the media as was more pay for nurses. The decline of fishing communities in particular, and also farming, had been highlighted in the run-up to the elections.[27] Even more extraordinary, there was no mention in the BBC's list of economic growth or business matters despite both Labour and SNP having growth as the opening issue in their manifestos.

---

[27] Electors were shown a list of 21 policies that might be introduced by the new Parliament and asked to give their priorities marks out of ten to come up with the most popular policies.

Figure 2.5: Scottish Voters' Priorities 2003, BBC Scotland Poll[28]

1. More police on the streets

2. Pay nurses more

3. More money for farming and fishing communities

4. Ensure all state schools and hospitals are built and run publicly, not privately

5. Let some 14-year-olds stop studying academic subjects and study a trade

6. Take tougher action against nuisance neighbours

7. Cut class sizes in primary and secondary schools

8. Phase out nuclear power stations and replace with wind and wave power

9. Change electoral system for councils to reflect better the number of seats compared to the number of votes

10. Give private firms more money to start businesses

11. Give free school meals to all school children

12. Reduce taxes on business

13. Cut number of MSPs in Parliament

14. Spend more on health promotion rather than hospital treatment

15. Hold a referendum on independence for Scotland

16. Spend more on helping heroin addicts come off drugs

17. Encourage more people to live in Scotland to stop population falling

18. Phase out public funding of Catholic schools

19. Charge drivers for bringing vehicles into city centres

20. Substantially increase spending on the arts

21. Allow universities to charge students higher fees.

[28] Source: http://news.bbc.co.uk/1/hi/scotland/2889089.stm

REGULATORY POLICIES

The scope for innovation that arises in regulatory policies was always going to be considerable — especially as the legal system, the ultimate horizontal regulatory policy area, was devolved. These types of policies cover a vast array of possibilities for innovation. The appeal of regulatory politics to a government with limited public spending is that costs involved can be transferred to consumers or others. The main costs may be the regulatory agencies themselves. Much social, environmental and economic policy-making is regulatory. It has been argued, most notably by Majone, that we are witnessing a dramatic increase in regulatory politics in Europe as traditional Keynesian policy-making, associated with taxing and spending, has declined. Making and enforcing rules which are regulated by specialist agencies are part of change from traditional welfare states to regulatory states.[29] If correct, the lack of strong redistributive powers and limited scope in devising new streams of spending should not be too worrying. The European Commission has built up a vast armoury of policy tools with extremely limited redistributive and distributive policies. The challenge for the Scottish Executive lies in finding imaginative regulatory policies. The particular challenge, in light of public perceptions, will be to use regulatory policies for redistributive ends. Many policies under this heading could be described as symbolic. The policy change in itself may have limited effect but what make them significant is what they signal.

The main tools for regulating the Scottish economy have not been devolved but a range of powers have been entrusted to the devolved institutions. Frenetic activity marked Wendy Alexander's period as Enterprise Minister between 2000 and 2002. This was followed by a more sober approach under Iain Gray, who lost his Edinburgh Pentlands seat to Tory leader David McLetchie in 2003. It was frequently suggested in the media that Alexander had resigned from the Executive in part because she felt that the economy was not given the place it deserved in Jack McConnell's priorities. McConnell had set out his priorities early in his period as First Minister but neglected to mention economic affairs. In an attempt to assure the business community that their interests were central to his incumbency, he subsequently admitted to the Institute of Directors in September 2002 that having, 'relentlessly [talked] about the priority of our key public services — health, education, crime, and transport . . . Somewhere along the way though, there has been the impression that my fifth priority — jobs — has somehow been downgraded.' He was then attacked for talking about jobs rather than growth.[30]

---

[29] Majone, G., *Regulating Europe* (London: Routledge, 1996).
[30] Young, A., *The Herald*, 12 September 2002.

The SNP made much of Scotland's poor economic growth record and attempted to turn this into an issue before the 2003 election but with very limited success. Almost unnoticed by the media, the SNP had shifted its emphasis over the course of the Parliament away from its argument that Scotland subsidised the rest of the UK.[31] This shift from distributive matters was toward regulatory matters and in particular economic growth. Top of the priorities was more police patrolling the streets followed by better pay for nurses and extra help for farming and fishing communities. Unfortunately, the aforementioned BBC list of policies did not include an option asking whether electors would support using its limited tax-raising power. The absence of economic growth suggests that the SNP failed to make much of an impact on the electors or, at least, on most sections of the media.

Alexander's main contribution in the economic field had been the 'Smart, Successful Scotland' campaign. Though presented as a policy, it amounted to little more than an attempt at rebranding a symbolic policy. In large measure this reflects the limited economic powers of the Parliament. Part of the continuing problem inherited from pre-devolution times has been the expectations invested in government in Scotland on economic matters. Within the limited scope available, the Smart, Successful Scotland campaign has merit in terms of policy prescriptions in recognising these limitations, though it might be criticised for doing little to close the capability-expectations gap. McConnell's early refusal to emphasise business and economic matters might be seen as lacking ambition but equally might be deemed as based on an appreciation of devolved powers. However, Labour's manifesto in 2003 started with a chapter entitled 'Building Scotland's Economy' with the opening line, 'Labour's number one priority for Scotland is a growing economy.'[32] However, economic affairs were far from dominant at its launch — greater emphasis was placed on McConnell's earlier priorities of improving welfare services. Confirming this, Liberal Democrat leader Jim Wallace was given the Enterprise portfolio following the 2003 election. Given that this portfolio had been held by a Labour Minister during the last Parliament, this was a decidedly odd decision given the prominence that McConnell had claimed was attached to economic affairs.

The Smart Successful Scotland campaign has been criticised by the SNP for lacking the full panoply of policy tools available to an independent state, most notably fiscal powers, though the nationalists have supported particular policies under the umbrella. The Smart, Successful Scotland campaign represents a form of symbolic politics in that it attempts to provide an over-arching framework for existing policies. Critics would have difficulty

[31] The *Financial Times* was the exception here. See for example, Firn, D., and Nicholson, M., 'A Scottish nationalist policy that is not just about oil', *Financial Times*, 25 April 2003. The FT's coverage of Scottish politics is limited but nonetheless far more perceptive than any other paper's.

[32] Scottish Labour, 2003.

opposing a smart and successful Scotland but there has been much criticism of its elements. The *Scotsman* has been among the strongest critics. An article written by Sharon Ward, formerly an employee in Donald Dewar's private office, for the *Scotsman* in February 2003 sparked off a stream of criticisms based on leaked Scottish Enterprise documents which suggested the agency was failing to meet most of its own targets. One of the most significant aspects of the ensuing debate was the lack of support given to the agency by the Scottish Executive fuelling speculation that there were serious divisions between the agency and the Executive. This made the position of the agency's chief executive, Robert Crawford, untenable.

The issues surrounding Scottish Enterprise show that devolution has failed to confront underlying issues of accountability inherent in much regulatory policy-making. It would be wrong to suggest that devolution has made the situation worse. Devolution appears to have been largely irrelevant. Greater attention needs to be paid to this. One response that has emerged from the Parliament has been a set of proposals to increase scrutiny of membership of agencies. Efforts to respond have been limited.

Among the most controversial policies pursued by the Scottish Executive in the last Parliament was the decision to reverse the clause in local government legislation prohibiting positive portrayals of homosexuality (Section 28 as it came, erroneously, to be known). It was announced in October 1999 in a speech at Glasgow University by Wendy Alexander, then Communities Minister. Research has shown that Scotland is becoming a increasingly liberal and tolerant society but there was clearly a strong backlash against the proposals.[33] Sections of the media, the head of Scotland's Catholic community and individuals such as Brian Souter (reputedly Scotland's richest man at the time) put up a vigorous, populist defence of the clause. Souter financed an unofficial referendum in May 2000 on the issue which saw the devolution establishment ranged against popular Scotland. The reaction caused internal difficulties among the Labour members of the Executive. Jack McConnell and Henry McLeish were among those members who were keen to reach a compromise and focus on other matters. A lesson was learned. Patrick Harvie, a newly elected Green MSP, proposed a Civil Registered Partnerships (Scotland) Bill including the extension of rights to gay couples in May 2003. This was broadly in line with proposals being proposed by Tony Blair's Government in London. The Executive decided to make use of a Sewel motion to avoid confronting the issue. Sewel motions allow the Executive, with the Parliament's support, to delegate responsibility for legislating back to London, a devolution rebound. After the experience of Section 28, confronting Scotland's illiberal demons head-on appears less likely.

[33] Bromley, C., Curtice, J., Hinds, K., and Parks, A., *Devolution — Scottish Answers to Scottish Questions?* (Edinburgh: Edinburgh University Press, 2003), p.108.

Jack McConnell has instead chosen to challenge a different type of demon in the shape of sectarianism. McConnell's decision to launch a campaign against sectarianism was believed in some circles to have been motivated by a need to shift attention away from the First Minister's difficulties when he came under fire for 'Wishawgate', issues surrounding the financial affairs of his constituency office. A campaign against racism in Scotland supported by advertising billboards has also been given prominence by the Scottish Executive. These may not have an obvious immediate impact but backed with laws prohibiting anti-social behaviour send out clear signals. Removing Section 28, anti-sectarianism and anti-racism were all regulatory symbolic. The impact on behaviour could only be indirect, as is often the case with regulatory policies, even if backed by legislation. Nonetheless, these have been important initiatives aimed at underlying cultural norms in Scottish society.

One criticism voiced by the director of the Confederation of British Industry (Scotland) was that the Scottish Parliament had been 'self-indulgent', ignoring economic growth and instead focusing on banning fox-hunting, encouraging breastfeeding and liberalizing the law on homosexuality. This charge provoked a response from Sir David Steel, the Parliament's Presiding Officer (and erstwhile leader of the Liberal Democrats) who noted that only 9 hours 48 minutes had been spent on fox-hunting, 9 hours 45 minutes on repealing Section 28 (reforming the law on homosexuality) and 130 hours had been spent on issues relating to Scottish industry and commerce.[34] Public perceptions and media coverage were not the same as Parliamentary time. Significantly, there was no voice arguing that these other matters were legitimate issues for the Scottish Parliament to address. Nor was the point made that the CBI had long argued against devolution and had sought to ensure that matters affecting business should be retained at Westminster. In a curious way, the CBI's criticism were a back-handed compliment.

Most MSPs burst into spontaneous applause when final approval was given to reform of Scotland's antiquated land laws. The measure passed was limited but, again, signified a change which had long been sought by land reform campaigners. It was frequently asserted that such legislation could never have passed through Westminster, especially the Lords. There was an element of truth in this claim though it needs to be set alongside three observations. First, the legislation is probably no more radical for its time than earlier land legislation such as that concerning the Crofting counties in the nineteenth century, the Sinclair Landholding legislation early in the twentieth century or the establishment of the Highlands and Islands Development Board in 1965.[35] Second, Lords reform under the Blair Government has

---

[34] *The Scotsman*, 3 October 2002.
[35] Small Landholders (Scotland) Act, 1911.

removed many peers who might otherwise have acted as a block on legislation. Third, the legislation's aims need to be seen in conjunction with the financial powers associated with it and the prospect of transfers of land with state financial support is limited.

PROCESS

The term 'process' is used to refer to the institutional arrangements — formal and informal — within which policy-making occurs. Crucial to any understanding of Scottish devolution is that it is not independence. This needs emphasis as much of the discussion of devolution fails to adequately take account of the UK dimension. Redistributive policies are retained at Westminster. The moderately (and stealthily) redistributive nature of public policy under Labour at the centre is important in understanding attitudes devolution and its functioning in Scotland. Labour at Westminster, especially the Treasury, is maintaining a firm grip of redistributive policies. Though the rise of the SSP might suggest some disillusionment with the established parties on the redistributive agenda, the fact that a moderately redistributive government at the centre is pursuing this agenda will go some way towards satisfying voters. As rational actors, voters are unlikely to care where policies come from but are concerned with policy outputs.

The Treasury also still retains considerable control over distributive policies. The operation of the Barnett formula has an effect in Scotland but this is incremental and the real increases in levels of public spending have meant that the devolved administration's share of spending has still been rising, only not as much as elsewhere. Once more, the operation of devolution and satisfaction levels — at least measured by support for the existing arrangements and lack of serious support for the status quo ante — is notable. The public may well be taking account of what is happening in London in expressing opinions on devolution. Surridge and McCrone's point about 'real politics' can be expanded. Not only does the public's view of policy outputs elide easily into policy processes, but given the emphasis in public expectations on outputs, it may not matter which level or levels deliver so long as improved policy outputs are delivered. The Scottish public appear to approach these matters in a fairly rational and comprehensive manner. Similarly with the vast array of regulatory policies. Many regulations come from London but also from Europe as well as from Edinburgh.

However, the main concerns of this chapter are with devolution *in* Scotland. The delivery of public services usually involves some role for Westminster, often Europe and almost invariably local government. Devolution's success or failure in the public mind will in part focus on how policies are delivered and this requires a significant local authority involvement. Local government is also important in reflecting some of the changes in party political support. Labour's strength in local government is evident but so too is the extent of multi-party politics. Coalition has been the norm in local government for a long time and may offer parallels to those observing the Scottish Executive. Local authority elections were held on the same day in 2003 as those for the Scottish Parliament. At these elections, Labour ended up with outright control of 13 of Scotland's 32 authorities (down two). Labour had lost control of a number of authorities over the previous four years through by-election losses — Aberdeen City, Fife, Inverclyde, Renfrewshire, and West Dunbartonshire. Labour regained control of Stirling, Renfrewshire and West Dunbartonshire. There was no overall control of eleven councils with six under the control of Independents and SNP and Liberal Democrats in control of one council each (Angus under the SNP and Inverclyde under Liberal Democrats). The multi-party nature of Scottish policies at local level and the variety of coalitions perhaps gives a truer indication of contemporary Scottish politics than would be gained from looking only at the Scottish Parliament. Labour formed minority administrations in three councils (East Renfrewshire, Fife and South Ayrshire) and went into coalition in Dundee with the Liberal Democrats and in Perth with Conservatives, Liberal Democrats and Independents. The Liberal Democrats are in coalition in five councils and formed a minority administration in one (East Dunbartonshire). In Dumfries and Galloway a coalition of Liberal Democrat, SNP and Independents has been formed. With the exception of Perth — where an anti-SNP coalition has been struck — and Aberdeen City (with the Liberal Democrats), the Tories are out of power, remaining at local level the pariahs of Scottish politics. Paralleling developments in the Scottish Parliament, Independents did well in local elections. All of this may change with a move towards using the single transferable vote in local elections. The likeliest outcome is that the Labour heartlands will see more variety, so that overall at local level the process of breaking down the dominance of the large parties will continue. This may prove a development that has wider implications for Scottish politics.

The existence of the Scottish Office made devolution relatively easy to introduce. Though it did not amount to a separate Scottish civil service, it has long been noted that Scottish Office civil servants were predominantly Scottish.[36] Devolution has altered the work of the civil service and has raised questions about a separate civil service, possibly along the lines of the Northern Ireland Civil Service. This continues to be an issue that rumbles below the surface though, unsurprisingly, it attracts little public interest. *Holyrood*, the nearest equivalent to Westminster's *House* magazine, carried

---

[36] Kellas, J., *The Scottish Political System* (Cambridge: Cambridge University Press, 1973), pp. 72–84.

an article by Susan Deacon, former Minister, in which she argued for an open debate on the subject, and it later surveyed MSPs for views on the subject.[37] While much attention has been paid to changes in the office of First Minister, less attention has focused on change at the top of the civil service in Scotland. In August 2002, after a relatively short period as Scotland's top civil servant, Sir Muir Russell announced that he would be leaving to take up post as Principal of Glasgow University. His replacement was John Elvidge who took up post in July 2003. There was much media speculation as to the reasons behind Russell's departure and the implications of Elvidge's appointment for Scottish devolution. Though none of this speculation quoted Bagehot's comment on the impact of the 1832 Great Reform Act it contains the essentials of much speculation, 'A new Constitution does not produce its full effect as long as all its subjects were reared under an old Constitution, as long as its statesmen were trained by that old Constitution. It is not really tested till it comes to be worked by statesmen and among its people neither of whom are guided by a different experience'.[38] This comment could apply to politicians as well as civil servants but suggests that the implications of change will only be felt long-term. As a new generation of politicians and civil servants schooled increasingly in the ways of devolution emerge and as others depart from office, then it is conceivable that long-term, incremental change will occur. The past is important and constrains future action though this need not be a straightjacket.

Throughout its existence, the Parliament has kept an eye on its operations in relation to its founding principles (discussed above). In March 2003, the Procedures Committee published its findings following a review, listing 135 recommendations: 21 to improve accessibility, 13 to improve equal opportunities, 34 to improve accountability, and 60 to improve power sharing.[39] The emphasis was on power-sharing, largely in relations with the Executive. It is no surprise to find the legislature attempting to cut out a greater role for itself, especially in its relations with the executive branch of government. The Scottish Parliament has the founding principles as a basis for making its case.

The Parliament has been a success as an institution. Expectations that it should be markedly different from Westminster raise questions as to how much different. Having grown out of the Westminster system, it is hardly surprising that the Scottish Parliament looks more like Westminster than any other legislature. Indeed, the negative templating involved in efforts to ensure that it differs from Westminster has meant that the starting point remained Westminster. Many features of the Westminster system which are deemed odd by students of comparative legislative studies — most

---

[37] *Holyrood*, issue 97, 20 October 2003.

[38] Bagehot, W., *The English Constitution* (London: Fontana / Collins, 1981), p.268.

[39] Scottish Parliament Paper 818.

obviously Question Time — were imported into Holyrood largely because of this starting point, and the lack of expert knowledge on the part of those involved in the Constitutional Steering Group which met prior to the Parliament's establishment. Much faith has been placed in the committee system and claims are frequently made about its superiority as compared with Westminster. Yet none of the Scottish Parliament's committees compare in expertise or impact to Westminster committees such as the Commons Treasury Select Committee or Public Accounts Committee or the Lords Select Committees on European Union, Science and Technology or the Constitution. This is not so much a weakness of the committees themselves but of the unrealistic hype that surrounds them. Indeed, if the Parliament has had a problem in terms of expectations it has been a result of its supporters, especially those involved in its foundation, making unrealistic claims based on limited knowledge of legislatures. Measured against other criteria, the Parliament as a legislature has been a remarkably stable, professionally-run body.

The experience of coalition government has been a novelty in Scotland where one party dominance has been normal in recent decades. The Labour-Liberal Democrat coalition has operated reasonably well, especially when Scotland's confrontational political culture is taken into account. The discussions after the 2003 elections were less difficult than those after 1999. At the 1999 election, the Liberal Democrats had made much of their opposition to tuition fees and finding some means of creating a consensus around this proved tricky. The lesson for the coalition partners appears to have been to avoid contentious matters though the Liberal Democrats insisted on single transferable vote for local elections. This may prove a thorny issue for Jack McConnell who has agreed to this policy. Coalition has, probably inevitably, forced the governing parties towards the centre ground, a phenomenon that devolution as a whole has facilitated.

The Partnership Agreement for the second session differed from that for the first in a number of respects.[40] It was the culmination of discussions that had been going on within the Labour-Liberal Democrat coalition for some time. In the months preceding the election, the two parties had been discussing policy matters. This was reflected in the length of the document. The 52-page document covered the range of responsibilities of the Scottish Parliament. Matters which might have caused difficulty were known well in advance. At Scottish level, coalition formation is proving remarkably easy given the oppositional and confrontational nature of Scottish politics.

---

[40] Scottish Labour Party and Scottish Liberal Democrats, *A Partnership for a better Scotland: Partnership Agreement* http://www.scotland.gov.uk/library5/government/pfbs–00.asp.

Figure 2.6: The Scottish Executive, May 2003

Jack McConnell	First Minister
Jim Wallace	Deputy First Minister and Minister for Enterprise and Lifelong Learning
Cathy Jamieson	Minister for Justice
Peter Peacock	Minister for Education and Young People
Malcolm Chisholm	Minister for Health and Community Care
Ross Finnie	Minister for Environment and Rural Development
Andy Kerr	Minister for Finance and Public Services
Margaret Curran	Minister for Communities
Patricia Ferguson	Minister for Parliamentary Business
Ministers attending Cabinet but receiving Deputy Ministers' salaries:	
Frank McAveety	Minister for Tourism, Culture and Sport
Nicol Stephen	Minister for Transport
Law Officers:	
Colin Boyd	Lord Advocate
Elish Angiolini	Solicitor General

The issue which has come to dominate media attention was the cost of the new Parliament building. For sections of the media and consequently perhaps also for a sizeable section of the public, the new Parliament has come to symbolise the extravagance of devolution. The key decisions to build the Holyrood Parliament were made prior to the first elections in 1999. Despite this it has been the Parliament, rather than the Executive or White-hall, that has been under attack, a classic case of blame displacement. Part of the reason for this was the expectation of elites that devolution's new politics would involve a shift of power towards legislative at the expense of executive power. Devolved government was never likely to involve an institutional year zero, shaking off institutional continuities from the UK system of government, as some hoped. Indeed, even formal independence would likely have involved considerable institutional inheritance from the UK system of government. The expectation that a new electoral system would have fundamentally altered the nature of politics rested on an understanding of institutional politics in which informal institutions were directly and immediately affected by formal institutions. In other words, changing the electoral system was unlikely to have the transformative effects that were anticipated in some quarters. However, in the early months and years of devolution, the myth of a strong legislature was a useful means of the Executive shifting responsibility for the Holyrood project. Having started as an executive-controlled matter, devolution allowed it to be transformed into a legislative responsibility. Traditional opponents of devolution — whether hardline nationalists or the *Scotsman* newspaper — used the project as a proxy for continuing the devolution argument. The Holyrood project featured prominently during the 2003 election. After the SNP effectively deselected Margo MacDonald, the erstwhile SNP MSP stood as an independent principally on an anti-Holyrood project platform, gaining massive media attention. Jack McConnell recognised the value of MacDonald as an Independent candidate to damage the SNP and provided her campaign with media coverage and credibility. Ironically, Holyrood had initially been chosen in preference to redeveloping the Old Royal High School building on Edinburgh's Calton Hill, initially proposed to home the ill-fated Scottish Assembly in the 1970s. It has been suggested that the Calton Hill site was as a 'nationalist shibboleth' (though the origins of the phrase are unclear).[41]

Despite unrealistic expectations that the Scottish Parliament would be different from Westminster, from which tradition it emerged, the Parliament has succeeded in becoming a professionally operated and relatively efficient legislature. There were inevitably some changes in working practices reflecting the process of bedding down but for the most part the Parliament qua parliament has been successful. The absence of expert advice on legislatures, other than that from extremely well informed Westminster insiders, was a remarkable feature of the process of establishing the institution given the claims and hopes that it would be different. Much has been made of features which distinguish the Parliament from the Westminster Parliament and little of what makes it unusually similar.

Having played a significant role in the creation of the Scottish Parliament, the media contributed to growing disillusionment with devolution.[42] This disillusionment did not, however, amount to support for the Parliament's abolition and tended to be evident among the elites. In fact, support for the status quo ante has fallen and even the Conservatives have attempted to redefine themselves as the true party of Scottish devolution. However, media coverage of devolution and Scottish politics has been significant in at least two important respects over the period of the first Parliament and in both respects this was most obvious in the last year. First, Scottish politics has come to be defined in media terms as synonymous with the politics of the Scottish Parliament and Executive. Scottish MPs in the Commons have

---

[41] Black, D., *All the First Minister's men: the truth behind Holyrood* (Edinburgh: Birlinn, 2001), pp. 84–92.
[42] Denver, D., Mitchell, J., Pattie, C., and Bochel., 2000, pp. 78–100.

complained bitterly at the lack of Scottish media interest in their activities. This has found expression among the many Labour MPs opposed to the 'Scottish Six', the idea of replacing network BBC news at 6 o'clock with a Scottish news programme. Less commented upon, but also significant, has been the emphasis on party politics in and around the Holyrood village, the Upas tree effect of devolution, at the expense of other types of politics in Scotland.[43] Local government has continued its long decline towards insignificance as viewed by most sections of the media. Instead of challenging the obsessive centralisation and parochialism of UK politics obsessed with the Westminster village, devolution has replicated this with a focus on Holyrood.

Concern with media coverage of Scottish politics and a desire to reinvigorate the idealism that informed the campaign for devolution has resulted in the Scottish Civic Forum proposing the establishment of a Scottish Media Commission. This idea emerged from meetings in 2002 at which concern had been expressed about media coverage and was taken up by the Forum which produced a document in May 2003.[44] Its recommendations are unlikely to win the support of the Scottish media but they are an indication of a deep concern in Scotland as to the nature of media coverage of politics.

CONCLUSION

When the Scottish Office was founded in 1885, Prime Minister Lord Salisbury remarked in private correspondence with the first holder of the office that, 'The work is not very hard — the dignity (measured by salary) is the same as your present office — but measured by the expectations of the people of Scotland is approaching the Arch-angelic'. Salisbury went on in a further communication, 'the whole object of the move is to redress the wounded dignities of the Scotch or a section of them who think that enough is not made of Scotland'.[45] Much the same could be said of devolution. The Scottish Office managed expectations reasonably well though, by the end of the twentieth century, the perceived differences between what Scotland wanted and London delivered was the motor for constitutional change.

The expectations gap which had been identified at the Scottish Parliament's inception had lessened by the time of the 2003 elections. Most notably, the expectations around a redistributive agenda had altered as a consequence of the main parties placing far less emphasis, perhaps no

[43] The Upas tree tends to kill off all that tries to grow underneath it.

[44] Schlesinger, P., 'Stirrings in civil society', in *Devolution and Scotland: Monitoring Report August 2003* (London: The Constitution Unit), p.14. See http://www.ucl.ac.uk/constitution-unit /monrep/scotland/scotland_august_2003.pdf.

[45] Quoted in Hanham, H., J., 'The creation of the Scottish Office, 1881 — 87', in *Juridical Review*, pp. 229–30, (1965).

emphasis, on this as compared to the past though this opened up space for the SSP to exploit this agenda. There has been some disillusionment surrounding distributive and regulatory policies though it should be remembered that there were both negative and positive reasons for devolution's support. The poll tax argument may be less significant post-devolution, especially with a Labour Government at Westminster, but may well explain continuing high levels of support for devolution. The hopes that devolution would improve welfare services were dependent in part on the funding arrangements.

One significant change has been the volume of legislation that has been passed. In its first term the Scottish Parliament has passed over 60 Acts, a vast increase in legislation compared with pre-devolution days ensuring that the potential for policy initiative has emerged. Agenda-setting has changed and issues that were excluded simply through lack of time have managed to find legislative time. Indeed, much of the legislation passed appears to be of the kind produced by the Scottish Law Commission — extremely important but often non-controversial and, from the media and public's perspective, unexceptional. The extent to which the system has opened up and allowed other issues which had been deliberately excluded — which would otherwise not have emerged on the institutional agenda — is more difficult to detect. Tommy Sheridan's successful bill to get rid of warrant sales is an example, though even it was watered down by subsequent legislation. The land reform legislation perhaps sums up the situation well — claimed to be a policy that would have been inconceivable without devolution has some validity but is probably an exaggeration.

The Parliament's redistributive powers were limited by the statutory constraints and while the gap that existed at the outset between what people wanted and what could be delivered has narrowed at least as far as the main parties are concerned, the rise of new parties has ensured that redistributive issues remain significant. It may well be the case that in time Scottish expectations on redistribution during the long years in Opposition will give way to more conservatism though it seems probable that such a drift among the main parties will leave open space for success on the fringe. It may even result in the fringe becoming more significant.

Distributive policies have remained largely extensions of pre-devolution policies. This reflects the dominant incrementalism of public policy combined with the common ideological framework within which Labour in London and Labour-Liberal Democrats in Scotland operate within as well as the funding arrangements. Those instances of distinctive positions may in the fullness of time prove problematic. Unless Gordon Brown's predictions that the days of boom and bust are over are correct, then difficulties will set in when, as may happen sooner rather than later, difficult choices are forced on the Executive as a result of financial constraints.

The range of regulatory powers available to the Parliament is immense and here perhaps the Parliament or, more accurately, the Executive, has been least impressive. The position of what were once called quangos, and their relationship to the devolved institutions has been paid little attention. The Executive has at times behaved as if economic and business issues were not its responsibility. While in part true, as most matters of this kind are retained at Westminster, there has been a reluctance to engage with these matters. Scotland's economic growth record has hardly registered on the devolutionary radar, despite frequent nods in that direction.

The existence of the Parliament has inevitably increased the scrutiny of the Executive. However, the extent to which much of this, based on the Westminster model, has been effective in terms of improving accountability is less certain. First Minister's Questions offer the theatre of Prime Minister's Questions with about the same amount of serious accountability. It seems unlikely that such practices — so engrained a part of the Westminster system but deemed mildly amusing in many other liberal democracies — will disappear. Much has been made of engagement with civic Scotland through the Petitions Committee, the use of modern technology and the Civic Forum. Measured in terms of political power — the essential test in politics — these appear more symbolic than effective.

Michael Forsyth, the last Conservative Secretary of State for Scotland frequently remarked that devolution was 'not just for Christmas'. All that can be said with confidence after its first four year is that it works well in good times. However, the bad times which Forsyth warned would highlight its deficiencies have yet to put devolution to the test. The expectations, capabilities, policy types and related politics associated with devolution suggest that much more has remained as before — through no fault of the institutions or the personnel operating within them. In particular conditions, these created a dynamic which led to devolution but it remains unclear whether, under similar conditions which have yet to arise, will lead to disillusionment with devolution and looking for non-constitutional alternatives or whether people will again will see further constitutional change as the way forward. The jury is still out as to whether devolution will undermine or underline the union.

BIBLIOGRAPHY

Primary and Official Documents

Constitutional Steering Group, *Shaping Scotland's Parliament* (Edinburgh: The Scotland Office, 1998).

Scottish Constitutional Convention, *Scotland's Parliament. Scotland's Right* (Edinburgh: Scottish Constitutional Convention, 1995).

Scottish Green Party, *reach for the future*, Scottish Green Party 2003 Scottish Manifesto, (Scottish Green Party, 2003).

Scottish Labour, *On your side*, Scottish Labour's Manifesto 2003, (Glasgow: Scottish Labour Party, 2003).

Scottish Labour Party and Scottish Liberal Democrats, *A Partnership for a better Scotland: Partnership Agreement*, 2003. Available at http://www.scotland.gov.uk/library5/government/pfbs-00.asp.

Scottish Socialist Party, *another Scotland is possible*, Holyrood Election Manifesto 2003, (Scottish Socialist Party, 2003).

Secondary Sources

Bagehot, W., The English Constitution (London: Fontana / Collins, 1981), p.268.

Bell,. D, and Christie, A., 'Finance — The Barnett Formula: Nobody's Child' in Trench, A., (ed.) *The State of the Nations 2002: The Second Year of Devolution in the United Kingdom* (Exeter: Imprint Academic, 2002).

Bell, D., 'Public Private Partnerships' in *Devolution and Scotland: Monitoring Report February 2003* (London: The Constitution Unit). See http://www.ucl.ac.uk/constitution-unit/monrep/scotland/scotland_february_2003.pdf.

Black, D., *All the First Minister's men: the truth behind Holyrood* (Edinburgh: Birlinn, 2001).

Bromley, C., Curtice, J., Hinds, K., and Parks, A., *Devolution — Scottish Answers to Scottish Questions?*, (Edinburgh: Edinburgh University Press, 2003), p.108.Denver, D., Mitchell, J., Pattie, C., and Bochel, C., *Scotland Decides: The Devolution issue and the 1997 referendum* (London: Frank Cass, 2000).

Hall, P., *Governing the Economy: The Politics of State Intervention in Britain and France* (Oxford: Oxford University Press, 1986).

Hanham, H.J., 'The creation of the Scottish Office, 1881–87', in *Juridical Review*, pp. 229–30, (1965).

Hill, C., 'The Capability-Expectations Gap, or Conceptualizing Europe's International Role', *Journal of Common Market Studies*, 31, pp. 305–328, (1993).

Kellas, J., *The Scottish Political System* (Cambridge: Cambridge University Press, 1973).

Kellner, P., *Report on Devolution Poll* (London: Political Context, 1996).

Lowi, T., 'American business, public policy, case studies, and political theory', *World Politics*, 16, pp. 677–715, (1964);

Lowi, T., 'Four Systems of policy, politics and choice', *Public Administration Review*, 32, pp. 298–310, (1972).

Majone, G., *Regulating Europe* (London: Routledge, 1996).

Mitchell, J., 'What Could a Scottish Parliament Do?', *Federal and Regional Studies*, 8 (1), Spring, pp. 68–85, (1998).

Mitchell, J., 'Devolution and the end of Britain', *Contemporary British History*, 14, pp. 61– 82, (2000).

Mitchell, J., 'Towards a New Constitutional Settlement', in Hay, C., (ed.) *British Politics Today* (Cambridge: Polity, 2002).

Mitchell, J., *Governing Scotland* (Basingstoke: Palgrave Macmillan, 2003).

Peters, G., B., *Institutional Theory in Political Science: The New Institutionalism* (London: Pinter: 1999).

Ross, William, (1978), 'Approaching the Archangelic ?', *Scottish Government Yearbook 1978* (1978).

Schattschneider, E.E., *The Semi-Sovereign People* (Hinsdale, Ill., The Dryden Press, 1975).

Schlesinger, P., 'Stirrings in civil society', in *Devolution and Scotland: Monitoring Report August 2003* (London: The Constitution Unit), p.14. See http://www.ucl. ac.uk/constitution-unit/monrep/scotland/scotland_august_2003.pdf.

Simeon, R., 'Free Personal Care: Policy Divergence and Social Citizenship', in Hazell, R., (ed.) *The State of the Nations 2003: The Third Year of Devolution in the United Kingdom* (Exeter: Imprint Academic, 2003).

Surridge, P., and McCrone, D., 'The 1997 Scottish referendum vote', in Taylor, B., and Thomson, K., (eds.) *Scotland and Wales: Nations Again?* (Cardiff: University of Wales, 1999).

3

Nation Building and the Assembly
The Emergence of a Welsh Civic Consciousness

John Osmond

The Welsh experience of devolution since the creation of the National Assembly in 1999 can be best summarised by contrasting it with the Scottish. In 1999 Scotland's new Parliament took charge of a pre-existing array of civic institutions that had survived and flourished beyond the 1707 parliamentary union with England. These included a distinctive legal system, a separate structure for education, and the Scottish Kirk. Later were added Scottish financial institutions, a mature system of administration from the 1880s, and a highly developed press and media. To a great extent Scottish identity revolved around these institutions. They supported a middle-class leadership for Scottish society, a class whose own interests and future were tied closely to the success of their distinctive institutions. They also provided Scots with a civic sense of their nationality which served as a unifying factor. Consequently, when the Scottish Parliament met in 1999 it was as though a keystone was placed in an arch of an already-existing structure.

In Wales the position was very different. Apart from a much shorter experience of separate administration, by the Welsh Office from 1964, the idea of a civic identity embracing the whole of Wales was foreign to the sensibility of the Welsh. Instead, their identity relied upon a much more fractious sense of locality, language and culture. This was one reason why, in contrast to the Scots, the idea of a National Assembly was so controversial and only narrowly achieved. When it came, far from completing an institutional structure, the Assembly had to set about building one. Before it could become the keystone it had to construct the arch.

At the same time the significance of what took place in the 1997 referendum should not be underestimated. The result represented a remarkable 30 per cent increase in votes for the Yes side, or a 15 per cent swing, compared with 1979.[1] How can we account for this very large movement in opinion? Eighteen years may be a long time in politics, but in the history of a nation it is a short period for such a significant shift in opinion to occur.

---

[1] The more emphatic two-to-one majority in the Scottish referendum actually produced a smaller swing compared with the 1979 result, of 11.5 per cent.

Figure 3.1: Chronology of Events in the National Assembly's Fourth Year 2002–2003

2002	
18 September	Civil service review of Wales's largest Quango, Education and Learning Wales (ELWa), recommends splitting the management of its two constituent organisations, the National Council for Education and the Higher Education Funding Council for Wales.
24 October	Neath MP Peter Hain appointed Secretary of State for Wales in place of Paul Murphy who moves to the Northern Ireland Office.
29 October	Assembly Government published its plans for 14–19 education in *Learning Country: Learning Pathways 14–19.*
27 November	Assembly Government launches *Iaith Pawb* ('Everybody's language'), an action plan aimed at producing a bilingual Wales.
11 December	First Minister Rhodri Morgan delivers his 'Clear Red Water' speech, redefining Welsh Labour's philosophy and programme.
13 December	Permanent Secretary Sir Jon Shortridge tells the Richard Commission that the acquisition of primary powers would 'represent a manageable progression, not a major step change' for the civil service. Counsel-General Winston Roddick advocates primary powers and says the Assembly as a 'corporate body' has 'in practice evolved into a parliamentary body'.
2003	
4 March	Assembly Government launches *Wales for Innovation,* a £260 million three year innovation action plan.
9 March	Ron Davies, Secretary of State for Wales at the time of the devolution referendum, announces he will not be standing in the forthcoming Assembly elections, following further newspaper revelations about his private life.
14 March	Education Minister Jane Davidson announces that top-up fees for students attending universities in Wales will not be introduced within the life of the next Assembly government, up to May 2007.
1 April	22 new Local Health Boards, replacing the five former Health Authorities, are established.

1 May | National Assembly elections. Labour wins 30 seats in the second Assembly elections, one short of a majority, but resolves to dispense with a coalition and govern alone. Half the Assembly seats are held by women.

7 May | Rhodri Morgan announces Cabinet with a new portfolio of Minister for Social Justice and Regeneration given to Edwina Hart.

8 May | Ieuan Wyn Jones resigns as President of Plaid Cymru.

13 June | UK Cabinet reshuffle: Peter Hain becomes Leader of the House of Commons while holding on to his position as Secretary of State for Wales. The reshuffle also sees the creation of the Department for Constitutional Affairs.

30 June | Announcement that fire services are to be devolved from the Office of the Deputy Prime Minister to the National Assembly.

1 July | Assembly Government agrees a fixed £41 million contract for the new National Assembly building with Taylor Woodrow which has the Richard Rogers Partnership, the original designers, as part of its consortium.

9 July | *The Review of Health and Social Care*, advised by former NatWest chief executive Derek Wanless, finds that excessive emergency admissions are clogging up acute hospitals and contributing to Wales's high waiting lists.

20 September | At its annual conference Plaid Cymru elects Dafydd Iwan as its new President of the Party. Ieuan Wyn Jones returns as Leader of the Assembly Group, narrowly beating off a challenge from Mid and West Wales AM Helen Mary Jones.

23 September | *Wales: A Better Country*, Labour's programme for the second term, includes commitments to abolish prescription charges and provide free breakfasts in primary schools.

30 September | Assembly Government launches *The Wales Spatial Plan*, a 20-year planning framework document.

2 October | Assembly Government establishes an Advisory Group to examine the role of its proposed Commissioner for Older People in Wales.

14 October | Finance Minister Sue Essex's 2004-05 budget takes the Administration's spending to £11.9 billion. This is a 6 per cent increase on 2003-04 and £4.5 billion higher than the 1999-2000 budget inherited by the Assembly from the Welsh Office.

Of course, the 1997 referendum took place in strikingly different political circumstances from the one held in 1979. It was promoted by a popular Labour government at the beginning rather than at the end of its mandate. Moreover, it was a government that was anxious for its policy to succeed. There was an effective Labour Yes campaign, led with energy by the then Secretary of State for Wales, Ron Davies and his deputy Peter Hain. Although there were still Welsh Labour backbenchers opposed to the policy, they lacked coherence and charisma, when compared with the Labour Vote No Campaign in 1979 led by Neil Kinnock.

Yet the changes that took place in Wales between the 1970s and 1990s were the result of deeper forces than those determining the immediate political circumstances of the campaigns. Most important was a shift in the generations. A survey of 700 people throughout Wales within three weeks of the 1997 referendum underlined the importance of generational factors in determining the way people had voted. Those under 45 were more likely to vote Yes by a margin of 3:2, while those over 45 indicated they were more likely to have voted No by a similar margin.[2] So far as the actual referendum result was concerned these figures require a health warning. That is to say, the younger age group failed to turn out and vote to a much greater extent than the older. In itself, this contributed a great deal to the narrowness of the result.

Nonetheless, the split was revealing about the changes that took place in Wales between 1979 and 1997. In fact, the stark contrast in the divide said as much, perhaps more, about the way Britain was perceived as it did about Wales itself. During the 1980s and 1990s attitudes to Britain changed as markedly as attitudes to Wales. In 1979 the dominant generation was one that had grown up through the Second World War, and in its wake, the creation of a nationalised economy and the welfare state. For those who lived through it, the Second World War was a defining experience both in personal and collective terms. After 1945 the nationalised industries were hugely influential in the Welsh economy for some 40 years. The welfare state, and particularly the creation of the National Health Service, became embedded in the affections of the Welsh people. These were all distinctively British institutions and experiences. For a generation they described a framework of priorities and common-sense within which Welsh politics and political identity were understood. In 1979 they were still determining what really mattered.

Yet in less than two decades virtually the whole of this landscape, much of what had described the previous contours of Welsh political and economic life, had changed fundamentally. A generation was assuming influence for whom the Second World War was either history or something that had been experienced directly only by their parents. Along with that memory the British Empire had also slid beneath the horizon. Under the feet of this

---

[2] *1997 Welsh Referendum Survey*, Institute of Welsh Politics, University of Wales, Aberystwyth.

generation, too, the nationalised industries largely disappeared. In place of British Coal and much of British Steel (now Corus) were multinational manufacturing firms. Their main reason for being in Wales, apart from a relatively cheap and well-educated labour force, was that it was a handy location within the European Union. In short, between 1979 and 1997 a shift in generations took place that resulted in the Welsh becoming palpably and self-confidently, indeed patriotically, more Welsh. They were still British, though this was felt less strongly. At the same time they were also becoming European, an identity that, with the Maastricht Treaty, afforded them with constitutional citizenship for the first time.

The majority for the National Assembly in the 1997 referendum, albeit wafer-thin, demonstrated how far the notion of Welsh citizenship had advanced. This process was reinforced by the experience of the referendum itself and its aftermath. Certainly, the outcome of the first elections to the significantly termed *National* Assembly, confirmed that a profound shift had taken place in the way Welsh people understood who they were and their place in the world. Britain remained important to them, and in British elections for the Westminster Parliament they vote differently to the way they vote in Assembly elections.

At the same time Britain continues to change. It no longer provides the only, or perhaps even the essential, lens through which Wales and what it means to be Welsh has to be viewed. So far as Welsh politics and identity are concerned the key reference point is now an autonomous civic institution, embracing Wales as a whole. Welsh identity is no longer to be 'nationalised' within Britain. Nor is it something to be felt primarily as an intensely local-ised experience, with the language bearing an undue weight. The coming of the National Assembly has opened up a civic space for a truly Welsh politics to occur for the first time.

AN UNFINISHED CONSTITUTION

Unlike Scotland, Wales did not have the benefit of a Constitutional Conven-tion to hammer out cross-party agreement before the onset of democratic devolution. Instead, the National Assembly was the best compromise that Ron Davies, as Shadow Welsh Secretary, could push through the Wales Labour Party ahead of the 1997 general election. Left to his own devices he would have produced a Scottish-style Parliament. As it was, he was forced to appease devolution-sceptics within his own party and settle for a minimalist Assembly based on a local government model. This inheritance inevitably cast a shadow across the National Assembly's first four-year term. Insofar as it could within the framework of the Government of Wales Act 1998, the new institution immediately set about digging up its constitutional foundations. The Assembly was established as a single corporate body. That is to say, its legislative and executive functions were combined along local government lines rather than separated, as is normal in parliamentary institutions. By the end of the first term it had re-laid them in such a way that they now had the potential of carrying the full weight of a parliament with legislative powers.

The powers of the Assembly are derived from those previously exercised by the Secretary of State for Wales and comprise specific ministerial functions named in pieces of primary and secondary legislation. Those 5,000 functions are set out in the first Transfer of Functions Order, made under the Government of Wales Act, and detail the exact functions the Assembly may carry out. Within the Act these functions had to be transferred to some authority. In the absence of legislative powers, and hence a clearly defined, separate Administration, the drafters of the Government of Wales Bill came up with the notion of the Assembly as a whole, as a corporate body, to which the powers would be transferred.

The constitutional history of the Assembly's opening period was dominated by an emphatic rejection of this mode of operation. Instead, the Assembly moved as far as it possibly could in the direction of separating its administrative and legislative roles. By the time of the establishment of the coalition between Labour and Liberal Democrats in October 2000 these two elements had developed highly distinctive personalities. Representing the legislative side was the Presiding Office, with its own budget. Representing the executive was what became known as the Welsh Assembly Government, supported by the bulk of the civil service. Each acquired separate identities symbolised by distinctive logos.

The main force driving the split in the first period of the Assembly's life was the Presiding Officer, Lord Elis-Thomas.[3] Thereafter, however, it was the Assembly Government, led by the First Minister, that was most anxious to define and emphasise the difference. Part of the motivation was a widespread anxiety that its decisions were being interpreted by the media as coming from the Assembly as a whole. Both Government and Opposition in the Assembly shared an interest in avoiding such confusion. This development was highly significant, not just because the practical functioning of the Assembly made it inevitable, but because it also confirmed the Assembly was moving in a parliamentary direction. As the Assembly's chief legal officer, the Counsel-General Winston Roddick QC, put it in his written evidence to the Richard Commission on the Assembly's powers:

> The legislature and the executive have been living apart for more than three years. They remain married but only legally. So far apart have they grown, they have

---

[3] See Osmond, J., 'In Search of Stability: Coalition Politics in the Second Year of the National Assembly' in Trench, A., (ed.) *The State of the Nations 2001: The Second Year of Devolution in the United Kingdom* (Exeter: Imprint Academic, 2001), pp. 26-31.

taken different names and different identities. If they were human beings the law would permit them to divorce and thereby formalise the separation.[4]

However, to make the separation legal, so to speak, would mean further legislation, with the Government of Wales Act 1998 either being amended or replaced. The Richard Commission, established as part of the Partnership Agreement between Labour and the Liberal Democrats, began its work against this background in September 2002. The logic of the Assembly's constitutional progression pointed toward a new Westminster Act that would reconstitute the Assembly as a Parliament. In this sense the Richard Commission was but another stage in an ongoing debate that characterised the first term of the National Assembly as a constitutional convention by other means.[5] The key moments of this debate during the first term are shown in Figure 3.2.

Figure 3.2: Key Moments in the First Term's Debates on the Constitution

- The enforced resignation of Alun Michael as First Secretary in February 2000.
- Creation of the majority Coalition government in October 2000.
- Report of the cross-party Assembly Review of Procedure.[6]
- Establishment of the Richard Commission in July 2002.

These episodes were disruptive to varying degrees. It is noteworthy, therefore, that the Assembly came into being so smoothly and experienced relatively little conflict in its first term, not least with Westminster and Whitehall. That this was the case was due, in large part, to the two considerable advantages delineated in Figure 3.3.

---

[4] Roddick, W., Counsel-General of the National Assembly for Wales, *Evidence to the Richard Commission*, December 2002, para. 85. Available at http://www.richardcommission.gov.uk/content/evidence/index.htm

[5] This notion was first explored in the first volume of this series. See Osmond, J., 'A Constitutional Convention By other Means — The First year of the National Assembly for Wales' in Hazell, R., (ed.) *The State and the Nations: The First Year of Devolution in the United Kingdom* (Exeter: Imprint Academic, 2000), pp. 37-77.

[6] See Osmond, J., 'Constitution Building on the Hoof: the Assembly's Procedural Review' in Jones, J. B., and Osmond, J., (eds.) *Building a Civic Culture: Institutional Change, Policy Development and Political Dynamics in the National Assembly for Wales* (Cardiff: Institute of Welsh Affairs, 2002). It is argued there (p. 69) that for much of the time, '... the Review took on the character of an informal Constitutional Convention ...'

**Figure 3.3: Political Advantages Enjoyed by the
First-Term National Assembly**

- An ever-rising budget. This central fact contributed more than anything else to the stability of the new institution and its relative harmony with Westminster and Whitehall. It more than counter-balanced the generally acknowledged constitutional inadequacies in the Government of Wales Act, exemplified by frustrations that surfaced from time to time over the lack of clarity of the Assembly's powers.
- Maintenance of Labour-dominated administrations in London and Cardiff. This was an important stabilising influence, notwithstanding underlying tensions that occasionally occurred in relation to specific policy issues such as free personal care for the elderly and student fees.

Imagine the difficulties that would have arisen if these circumstances were different, if say the Assembly had been established in the early 1980s. At that time there was a stridently right-wing Conservative administration in Westminster, public expenditure was being cut, and major Welsh industries were being dismantled. How would the Assembly and its present constitutional arrangements fare if the going became a good deal rougher? How would it manage a combination of falling UK public expenditure and party political competition between London and Cardiff? Such questions were also raised by the House of Lords Select Committee on the Constitution, commenting on the legislative relationship between Cardiff and Westminster. Its report, following a lengthy inquiry during 2002, put forward a number of constructive suggestions how these might be improved within the present arrangements, but concluded:

> The problems arising over Westminster legislation cause us to doubt whether the form executive devolution has taken in Wales is sustainable in the long term . . . [Underlying the difficulties] is the reliance of the Welsh arrangements on mutually sympathetic administrations in London and Cardiff. We find it hard to see how such arrangements could work satisfactorily if there were major policy differences between the two governments.[7]

RE-DEFINING WELSH POLITICS

The National Assembly has provided an arena for a re-definition of Welsh politics. Arguably it has allowed a truly Welsh politics to develop for the first time. Certainly so far as the political parties are concerned, the Assembly has had a transforming and on the whole liberating impact on their activities. During the first term the character and strategies of all of them

[7] House of Lords Select Committee on the Constitution, *Devolution: Inter-Institutional Relations in the United Kingdom*, HL Paper 28, (London: The Stationery Office, 2003), p. 37.

underwent substantial change. Each had to cope with different challenges, many emanating from the results of the first two elections in 1999 and 2003 (see Figure 3.4). In just over four years the Assembly moved from being run by a minority Labour administration, to a coalition between Labour and the Liberal Democrats, and finally to a de facto majority Labour administration following the May 2003 election.

These changes resulted in many tensions and strains, not least for the leading personalities concerned. For instance, only the Liberal Democrats approached the 2003 Assembly elections with the same leader as at the beginning of Assembly's life. Labour had to deal with the fall-out from the enforced resignation of Ron Davies as Secretary of State for Wales even before the first elections. The perceived imposition by Tony Blair of Alun Michael, as Davies's successor as first Secretary of State for Wales and then as First Secretary in the Assembly, led directly to the vote of no confidence in February 2000 and the election of Rhodri Morgan as First Minister.

Figure 3.4: Vote Shares and Seats (change from 1999), 2003 Election[8]

Party	1st Vote	2nd Vote	Seats
Labour	40.0% (+2.4%)	36.6% (+1.1%)	30 (+2)
Plaid Cymru	21.2% (-7.2%)	19.7% (-10.8%)	12 (-5)
Conservatives	19.9% (+4.0%)	19.2% (+3.2%)	11 (+2)
Lib. Dems	14.1% (+0.6%)	12.7% (+0.1%)	6 (-)
Others	4.8% (+.0.1%)	11.8% (+6.9%)	1 (+1)
Turnout = 38.2% (-7.7%)			

The Conservatives lost their first leader, Rod Richards, within months of the establishment of the Assembly, following his involvement in a court case. Plaid Cymru lost their leader, Dafydd Wigley, due to illness in early 2001 and have since struggled to re-establish their profile under Ieuan Wyn Jones. Even the Liberal Democrats saw their leader, Mike German, temporarily forced out of the coalition Cabinet for a year from July 2001 because of a police investigation into his former role at the Welsh Joint Education Committee.[9]

[8] Source: Institute of Welsh Politics, University of Wales, Aberystwyt. See Richard Wyn Jones and Roger Scully's analysis of the 2003 election in Wyn Jones, R., and Scully, R., 'The Importance of Welshness', *Agenda* Summer 2003, (Cardiff: Institute of Welsh Affairs).

[9] For a comprehensive account see chapters on each of the parties in Osmond, J., and Jones, J.B., (eds.) *Birth of Welsh Democracy: The First Term of the National Assembly for Wales* (Cardiff: Institute of Welsh Affairs, 2003).

However, from the point of view of the long-term development of the Assembly, the most interesting aspect is the way devolution has re-defined the culture of the parties. This can be seen in their approaches to policy-making, their relations with the rest of the UK, and their constitutional aspirations.

Welsh Labour

The onset of devolution has had a profound impact on the Welsh Labour Party. In the first place it changed its name to the *Welsh* Labour Party, from Labour Party Wales (and before that the Labour Party in Wales). This registered an important emblematic and tonal change. There is a recognition by all the parties, but especially Labour, that identifying with the national dimension can bring political rewards in post-devolution Wales. There is now a recognisably nationalist (with a small 'n' wing) within the Labour Group in the Assembly that remains in the ascendant under Rhodri Morgan's leadership. To a large extent this Group is defining itself against the policy profile being developed by Labour at Westminster. A classic expression of this view was First Minister Rhodri Morgan's so-called 'Clear Red Water' speech delivered in December 2002. This set out his aspirations for the Assembly's second term, emphasising the philosophical distinctiveness of *Welsh* from *New* Labour. The most quoted passage reiterated his opposition to Foundation hospitals:

> . . . our commitment to equality leads directly to a model of the relationship between the government and the individual which regards that individual as a citizen rather than as a consumer. Approaches which prioritise choice over equality of outcome rest, in the end, upon a market approach to public services, in which individual economic actors pursue their own best interests with little regard for wider considerations . . . My objection to the idea of Foundation Hospitals within the NHS is not simply that they will be accessed by those public service consumers who are already the most articulate and advantaged, and who can specify where they want to be treated, but that the experiment will end, not with patients choosing hospitals, but with hospitals choosing patients. The well-resourced producer will be choosing the well-resourced consumer as the kind of patient they want — the grammar school equivalent in hospitals.[10]

He continued that free entitlements, such as free prescription charges for all, free bus travel for people over 60, and free breakfasts at school for primary schoolchildren — all commitments made by Welsh Labour at the 2003 Assembly election — stressed the individual's position as a citizen rather than consumer. In a later speech Morgan said Wales also needed a different

[10] Morgan, R., *Clear, red water* Speech to the National Centre for Public Policy, University of Wales, Swansea, 11 December 2002.

approach because of the scattered nature of its communities, with 70 per cent of the Welsh population living in settlements of less than 30,000 people:

> The key point is that the way we organise ourselves and the values that we hold are shaped by this experience of living in relatively small settlements and medium sized villages, towns, valley agglomerates and cities. The consumerist approach to choice in public services that stresses differentiation may fit best the practicalities and the expectations of those metropolitan settlements of a million or several million people that are a feature of countries that are urbanised in a different way to Wales. As an Assembly Government we have given higher priority to the provision of high quality, community based, comprehensive secondary schools than we have to the development of a choice of specialist schools. This does not mean that we are against choice and diversity. We are, in fact, creating parallel systems of Welsh and English medium schools in most parts of Wales. We have faith-based schools. In fact, taking together our differentiation according to language and faith we have as our base-line fewer undifferentiated comprehensives than in England. But it seems to me that our values and our geography lead us to stress the community basis of our schools. Research on the performance of different schools in Wales is indicating that the most successful schools in our poorer areas are those that develop the fullest links with their communities — involving parents, families and community groups in the life of the schools.[11]

Such statements are not especially radical in terms of the traditional Welsh attitudes to politics. It is difficult to imagine them being articulated by a New Labour politician in England, however. What devolution has allowed is the emergence of a distinctive Welsh Labour approach, distinctive because it has refused to depart from previous mainstream Labour party thinking.

In itself this reflects a fundamental shift. Prior to devolution the Labour party in Wales was widely regarded as a vote-gathering machine as opposed to a policy-making organisation.[12] Although new policy initiatives have so far emanated from the top rather than the grass roots, the 'top' in question is now authentically Welsh-based in the Assembly Cabinet. This has been acknowledged by the UK Prime Minister. Questioned at the time of the 2002 UK party conference whether, so far as health and education policy was concerned, he was now effectively premier for England, Tony Blair replied:

> I agree with him [Rhodri Morgan] that the Welsh health service and schools are matters for the Assembly and the Welsh executive. If people in Wales want to do it in a different way they can — and it will be the people of Wales that will be the judge of that.[13]

---

[11] Morgan, R., *Delivering for Wales: The Implementation of Public Policy in a Small Country*, Annual Lecture, Welsh Governance Centre, Cardiff University, March 2003.

[12] A quotation attributed to the late Val Feld, Labour AM for Swansea East during the early years of the Assembly's first term. See Williams, P., *The Psychology of Distance* (Cardiff: Institute of Welsh Affairs, 2003), p. 39.

[13] *Western Mail*, 4 October 2002.

However, problems in the relations between Westminster and Welsh-based Labour politicians, reflected in arguments over further constitutional change, have been harder to resolve. Regular contacts take place between the First Minister and the Secretary of State for Wales, usually in Cardiff every Monday. This aside, however, Welsh Labour AMs have little contact with backbench Welsh Labour MPs at Westminster, most of whom remain disengaged from the devolution process. Many are against any early constitutional advance, regarding the Assembly as either so far failing in key policy areas such as health service delivery, or as not yet sufficiently mature to acquire more powers. Many are also concerned that increased powers for the Assembly would be likely to be accompanied by a diminution of their own numbers and influence.[14]

Carwyn Jones, a leading Labour Cabinet exponent of primary powers, has pressed the case for greater cohesion between the party's representatives at local, Assembly, Westminster and European levels. He argues that they should provide a united front in representing Wales's interests within the UK and the European Union.[15] This might sound like so much common sense, and indeed would only follow what already is largely the case so far as Scotland as concerned. In the Welsh context, however, Labour politics have not been characteristically undertaken in this way, either historically or in contemporary practice. Instead, they have been far more intertwined with a British perspective, and far less comfortable with emphasising the Welsh national dimension. Nonetheless, until and unless real change along these lines begins to happen, it will be exceedingly difficult to pursue constitutional change at Westminster. Certainly, it will be hard to persuade the UK Labour party generally that further concessions to Wales are needed if they are opposed by Wales's own Labour MPs at Westminster.

Plaid Cymru

The onset of the National Assembly also radically changed the character of Plaid Cymru. For the first time it has a relatively large and cohesive group of full-time, professional politicians within its ranks, the elected Members in the Assembly together with their support staff. These have altered the balance of forces within the party's traditional structure. At the same time the party's focus of attention has shifted decisively from Westminster to Cardiff Bay. For the first time in its history, too, the party has a sense that it

---

[14] See, for example, the evidence of the ten-strong Group of North Wales Labour MPs to the Richard Commission: 'We do not believe that the case for major change at present has been made, but even if it had, it would require specific endorsement by the people of Wales through a further referendum.' North Wales Labour Group of MPs, *Evidence to the Richard Commission*, 12 June 2003. Available at http://www.richardcommission.gov.uk/content/evidence/index.htm.

[15] Jones, C., *Future of the Welsh Labour Party*, Gregynog Papers (Cardiff: Institute of Welsh Affairs, 2004).

could be a party of government. These changes have created new problems of communication and increased the potential for divisions between the leadership and the wider membership, not least over the party's objectives and how they are articulated.

These divisions were fully exposed in the wake of the 2003 election in which the party lost five of its seats. It immediately jettisoned its leader, the Anglesey AM Ieuan Wyn Jones, and embarked on a period of soul searching about its objectives and the strategy for achieving them. Events rapidly overtook an orderly debate, however. Ieuan Wyn Jones resigned as President of the party, not as Leader of the Group in the Assembly. In the contest that followed no-one emerged from the Group to contest the Presidency. Consequently, the position of Group leader also became vacant since that post is automatically held by the President only if he or she is also an Assembly member. Accordingly Ieuan Wyn Jones announced that he would remain in contention for leadership of the Group. In the elections that followed, in late September 2003, the veteran nationalist Dafydd Iwan, a folk singer and long-standing Gwynedd councillor, best known for his campaigns on behalf of the Welsh language, won the presidency. Meanwhile Ieuan Wyn Jones held on to the Group leadership, against a close and determined challenge from the more radical former Llanelli AM, Helen Mary Jones, who since May 2003 represents Mid and West Wales on the list. In many ways this was the worst possible result for the party, leaving unresolved many of the organisational and policy difficulties that had accumulated in the first term.

As a first constitutional step Plaid Cymru wishes to achieve parity with the Scottish Parliament, with primary legislative and some tax-varying powers. This would involve a reduction in the number of Welsh MPs at Westminster and a corresponding increase in Assembly Members in Cardiff. Development beyond this stage is what was at issue in the debate that engulfed the party following May 2003. To some extent the options available depend on what happens elsewhere, for instance whether England evolves regional government with significant powers, and the progress made with European integration and enlargement. In a policy document published early in the Assembly's first term the party envisaged two scenarios: a democratic, federal 'Europe of the Regions' with a greatly empowered European Parliament and a written constitution, within which Wales could find a role; or, failing that, full national status for Wales as a member-state within a confederal European Union.[16]

In the wake of its setback in the Assembly election in May 2003, Plaid Cymru re-focused its thinking around the second scenario, amidst pressure to simplify its message to more straightforwardly call for Welsh independence. The party had to decide on broadly two choices. Was it to be essentially

---

[16] Plaid Cymru, *Towards Full National Status: Stages on the Journey*, December 2000.

a regionalist movement operating within a British / European framework, seeking perhaps to emulate what Catalunya has achieved within Spain? Alternatively, should it opt for a more conventional approach to autonomy by demanding independence? Some in the party, notably Ieuan Wyn Jones, regarded this as a needless or false choice. Independence was seen as a chimera. Within the globalised economy of the twenty first century even large states were interdependent one with another. Others attributed the party's loss of momentum to a failure to clarify its constitutional objectives in terms of independence. It was noteworthy that — citing such small applicant states as Lithuania and Estonia — the former President, Dafydd Wigley, pronounced that since independence was what was required to join the European Union, Wales had no other choice if it wished to do so. Another argument was to say that Plaid Cymru should adopt a more extreme position to leave greater space for other parties more moderate on the constitutional question to occupy. In the event, at its Autumn 2003 conference, and led by its new President Dafydd Iwan, the party swung decisively in favour of independence.

Shortly before his early death in June 2003, the figure most associated with aligning Plaid Cymru with independence, Phil Williams, articulated a continuing dilemma for Plaid Cymru in the following terms:

> Within the Party of Wales there is a recurring debate as to whether an essential pre-requisite for self-government is that Plaid Cymru replaces the Labour Party as the mainstream, dominant party in Wales. Alternatively, is it possible for a single-minded and uncompromising Plaid Cymru to create the conditions whereby other parties deliver self-government, albeit step-by-step and with some reluctance. Progress over the past forty years, and especially the establishment of the National Assembly, point to the latter strategy.[17]

In other words, is Plaid Cymru to think of itself as primarily a pressure group, forcing the British parties, and particularly Labour, to address the Welsh constitutional question? Or is it to be a mainstream party seeking a role in the government of Wales? To say it should be both is not as straightforward as it might seem. During the first term Plaid Cymru concentrated on making the Assembly work while preparing a raft of policy positions to allow it to present itself as an alternative party of government. Some argued that this had diluted its message and image, making it seem a pale version of Welsh Labour. In turn, it was argued, this contributed to its relatively poor performance in the May 2003 elections.

[17] Williams, 2003, p. 41.

Welsh Liberal Democrats

For the Welsh Liberal Democrats the advent of devolution had the potential for bringing their constitution to life.[18] That is to say, it made a reality of their long-standing federal relationship with the wider party within the United Kingdom. As a party policy document put it in the wake of the first elections:

> Many voters switched to the Liberal Democrats in the Assembly elections. However, the reasons for switching did not include a recognition that the Liberal Democrats were a party which could take decisions in Wales. This belief is totally at odds with the reality of our federal party, and clearly demonstrates that we must make more effort to demonstrate that we are a Party for Wales.[19]

Welsh Liberal Democrats have an identity problem in more ways than one. It is not just a question of their identification with Wales, as the above quotation underlines, or their centre position at a shifting point between the other parties. Rather it is a lack of correlation between the generally conservative inclinations of their supporters and the radical positions of the party, especially on constitutional matters.[20] Moreover, survey evidence suggests that the party draws its support and activist base from people originating from outside Wales. For example, of the candidates standing in 1999 Assembly election, only 38 per cent were born in Wales. This contrasted with 64 per cent for Labour, 68 per cent for the Conservatives, and 79 per cent for Plaid Cymru.[21]

Consequently the likelihood that a proportionally-elected Assembly would introduce Wales to coalition politics was a tremendous opportunity for the Welsh Liberal Democrats. For the first time they had the chance of moving from the fringes to literally the centre ground promoting their electoral prospects in the process. And, undoubtedly, their coalition with Labour in the first term gave them a good deal of influence on policy development. However, in the election that followed, in May 2003, though the party kept its six seats, the overall electoral arithmetic meant Labour could govern on its own without them. Arguably this was a fluke result. If Plaid Cymru had held on to Llanelli or Conwy, seats it lost by the narrowest of margins, the outcome might have

---

[18] Chris Lines, Chief Executive of the Welsh Liberal Democrats, quoted in Thomas, A., 'Liberal Democrats' in Osmond, J., and Jones, J.B., (eds.) *Birth of Welsh Democracy: The First term of the National Assembly for Wales* (Cardiff: Institute of Welsh Affairs, 2003).

[19] Welsh Liberal Democrats, *Building Community Politics: Liberal Democrats Wales's Party Strategy into the Millennium*, 1999.

[20] For example, a majority of Liberal Democrat voters opposed the Assembly in the 1997 referendum. See Wynn Jones, R., and Trystan, D., 'The 1997 Welsh Referendum Vote', in Taylor, B., and Thomson, K., (eds.) *Scotland and Wales Nations Again* (Cardiff: University of Wales Press, 1999).

[21] Bradbury, J., Bennie, L., Denver, D., and Mitchell, J., *Party Attitudes and the Politics of Devolution: An Analysis of Candidates at the 1999 Scottish Parliament and Welsh Assembly Elections*, Paper to Political Studies Association Territorial Politics Workshop, Cardiff, January 2001.

been different. [22] Equally, Labour was highly vulnerable to Plaid Cymru in Carmarthen West and to the Conservatives in Clwyd West and Cardiff North.

What the electoral arithmetic points to is the probability that coalition politics will return, perhaps even before the next election in 2007. As it is, Labour's majority relies on the fact that both the Presiding Officer and his deputy come from opposition parties. The question for the Liberal Democrats is how they are to keep themselves in the limelight of frontline Assembly politics in the absence of holding on to Cabinet positions. The answer is that it is probably an impossible task. They have to bide their time.

Meanwhile, the party lacks focus on policy issues. Whose interest does it most clearly represent? Even on the constitutional question, where it has a relatively high profile in calling for primary powers, this remains the case. Here it is partially because the Liberal Democrats' constitutional objective of achieving a federation within the UK creates an inherently weak position. As a result of devolution Britain may be moving in a quasi-federal direction. However, the contrasting size and populations of England, Scotland and Wales, coupled with the peculiar character of the UK state apparatus itself, mean that devolution is likely to continue to be both asymmetrical and ungoverned by the written constitution as a fully-fledged federation would require. Meanwhile, in Wales the future salience and impact of the Liberal Democrats remains contingent upon the return of coalition politics.

Welsh Conservatives

Electorally the Conservatives have benefited most from devolution, achieving significant representation in the Assembly through the operation of the regional list proportional system. Moreover, it improved its position significantly between 1999 and 2003, moving from nine to eleven AMs (see Figure 3.4). There is also a determination on the part of the leadership to identify more with Welsh concerns and develop a distinctive Welsh identity and policy profile. As Nick Bourne, the Conservatives' leader in Wales put it:

[22] It is worth following the analysis provided by Paul Wilder, Director of the McDougall Trust — in its journal *Representation*, No 4, 2003 — as to what would have happened in the 2003 election if the Plaid Cymru candidate in the Conwy constituency had polled an extra 73 votes. In that event the constituency seat would have been held against Labour, with the Conwy constituency seat in effect being exchanged by Plaid Cymru for its North Wales regional list seat. Labour, on the other hand, having lost the Conwy seat, would not have been compensated by a North Wales regional list seat. Instead, the d'Hondt formula used to distribute top-up regional lists seats would have awarded the spare regional list seat to the Conservatives. In other words, 73 extra votes for Plaid Cymru in Conwy would have increased Conservative representation in the National Assembly from 11 seats to 12. Labour would have seen its representation fall from 30 seats out of 60 to a minority of 29. Plaid Cymru's overall representation would have been unchanged. The result would have been another Labour Liberal Democrat coalition, with Plaid Cymru and the Conservatives fighting it out to be the lead opposition party.

Before the ink was dry on the 1997 referendum result, close as it was, there was no doubt in my mind that the political topography in Wales was changing, and changing forever. The Welsh Conservative Party — not a body that then existed in reality — would need to accept these results and move forward. It was obvious to me that we would need to establish clear Welsh water between Conservatism in Westminster and Welsh Conservatism in Cardiff.[23]

What this may imply for the party's constitutional thinking has been speculated upon by a number of its politicians. For example, David Melding, AM for South Wales Central, declared:

The party least sympathetic to devolution needs to become its most conspicuous supporter. I believe we have reached a stage where the British state can only survive with devolution. Commentators should not rule out, therefore, the possibility that the next and most vital advance for devolution in Wales will be instigated by the Conservative Party.[24]

In the wake of the 2003 election it was noteworthy that Melding eschewed a front-bench position as a spokesman for his party to free him to campaign for a constitutional advance for Wales. As he put it, 'There is a coherent, centre-right argument for a federal Britain with primary law-making powers for the Welsh Assembly'.[25] Melding is well ahead of most of his party in embracing constitutional change. However, the logic of its position makes it likely that he is merely in the vanguard. This applies just as much, and perhaps more importantly to the party's organisation, with pressure for it to become more autonomous. As one senior figure, Jonathan Evans MEP, has argued:

. . . further organisational changes will be required if we are to meet the challenge of making the Conservatives the leading force in Welsh politics. Central to this project must be the organisation of the way the Party is run from within Wales. Ron Davies has rightly pointed out the contradiction of Labour facilitating the transfer of powers from Westminster to Cardiff and then not exercising parallel decision-making in respect of its own party organisation. Conservative Central Office in London appears to have adopted a somewhat ambivalent approach towards autonomy in the party structure in Wales and the English regions. For many years the party organisation was run on a regional basis with strong regional offices. As the Party finances have contracted and the Party machine in London has grown, we have gradually seen the erosion of the Conservative Party's regional structures. I believe that we are now at the time when Central Office staff in Wales must come fully under the control and remit of the Welsh Conservative Party.[26]

[23] Bourne, N., 'Clear Welsh Water', *Agenda* Winter 2003 / 04, (Cardiff: Institute of Welsh Affairs).
[24] Melding, D., 'Conservatives should finish the job', *Agenda* Autumn 2001, (Cardiff: Institute of Welsh Affairs).
[25] *Western Mail* 14 May 2003. He elaborated his position in 'New Dawn or Sunset Boulevard — What Role for the Welsh Conservative Party?' Annual Lecture, Institute of Welsh Politics, University of Wales, Abserystwyth, 27 October 2003.
[26] Evans, J., *The Future of Welsh Conservatism* (Cardiff: Institute of Welsh Affairs, 2002).

Welsh Conservatives face a prospect analogous to that facing Anglican-
ism in Wales in the early twentieth century. In order to separate itself from its
English parent and establish itself as an authentically Welsh institution it
must go through a process of dis-establishment. It needs to adopt a set of
specifically Welsh policies, which a growing number of its leaders and intel-
lectuals wish to see developed. However, this may not go down well with
many of the party's traditional supporters who are yet to be reconciled with
devolution. Motivating its traditional supporters while simultaneously
emphasising a stronger Welsh identity remains a challenge for the Welsh
Conservative Party.

CIVIC INSTITUTIONS

The coming of the National Assembly provided an entirely new political
context for each of the political parties and, as we have seen, each has
responded in distinctive ways. Significant developments have taken place to
the structures and aspirations of all four political parties within the Assembly. The notion that devolution is a process rather than an event applies as
much to political cultures as to political institutions.

And, of course, the process applies just as much to the wider civic society
within which the political parties have to negotiate their programmes and
identity. This can be demonstrated by an account of important developments
in response to devolution that have occurred in the six related fields shown in
Figure 3.5. A political culture is produced by far more than the political
parties. The civil service, press and media, lobbyists, think tanks and other
organisations combine to produce a political milieu that is distinctive to a
greater or less extent, depending on the dynamic guiding the direction of the
institutions to which they relate.

Figure 3.5: Developing Dimensions of Welsh Civic Society

- Moves towards a Welsh public service
- Emergence of a distinctive Welsh legal system
- Partnerships
- Press and Media
- Greater representation of women
- Assembly provides a focus for lobbyists

A Welsh Public Service

The clearest manifestation of the distinctive civic culture that began to
emerge during the first term was the changes that took place within the civil

service, alongside the definition of the Welsh Assembly Government. It was widely acknowledged at the outset of democratic devolution that the National Assembly would create a demand for a new breed of civil servants. To begin with they would have to respond to a more public and politicised environment. A further reason was the political change involved in the removal of UK Cabinet collective responsibility from the Welsh political leadership. It is perhaps too soon to judge whether the onset of democratic devolution has resulted in a different kind of civil servant working in Cathays Park and Cardiff Bay. But certainly there are more of them: over the first term their number increased by about 1,500, or 63 per cent, to around 3,800 full-time equivalents.[27]

Whether they are a new 'breed' is another matter. They have inevitably been engaged in more autonomous policy-making that in previous Welsh Office days and they have more contact with politicians. Undoubtedly they are becoming more Welsh, in the sense that a cadre of officials is building up whose roots are firmly in Wales. This has the obvious advantage of promoting commitment and loyalty. At the same time, however, it holds out dangers that the service might offer too narrow a career path for aspiring civil servants and become inward-looking. To address this an effort is underway to widen the recruitment pool within Wales through the Assembly Government's 'public service management initiative'. This entails the creation of common leadership and management training for staff working in all parts of the public sector in Wales — the Assembly civil service, the National Health Service, Local Authorities, and the sponsored bodies. As the Permanent Secretary Sir Jon Shortridge put it, in effect describing an embryonic Welsh public service:

> This should mean that over time Wales will develop its own cadre of public servants with experience in and understanding of different parts of the public sector in Wales. They should also have an established network of contacts in different parts of the Welsh public sector. This, coupled with the policy on open recruitment, should mean that there will increasingly be a common set of values and experiences amongst staff in the Welsh public sector.[28]

And looking ahead to the Assembly's second term First Minister Rhodri Morgan declared:

> We need to invent a new form of public service in Wales, in which individuals are able to move far more easily than now between one form of organisation and another. Local government employees, Assembly civil servants, health service

---

[27] Shortridge, Sir J., Permanent Secretary of the National Assembly for Wales, *Evidence to the Richard Commission*, 13 December 2002, para. 5. Available at http://www.richardcommission.gov.uk/content/evidence/full-libevidence-e.htm.

[28] Shortridge, Sir J., Permanent Secretary of the National Assembly for Wales, *Evidence to the Richard Commission*, 13 December 2002, para. 22.

administrators, staff from the Assembly Sponsored Public Bodies should all be able to map out career paths which move between these bodies, developing expertise and cross-fertilising from one place to another . . . We need a Welsh public service, rather than a Welsh civil service.[29]

Such a development would be a striking confirmation that an autonomous structure of civic institutions was being put in place. The pace of such changes will depend on the recommendations that emerge from the Richard Commission in March 2004. In his evidence to the Commission the Permanent Secretary made it clear that the civil service, as it had developed during the first term, could cope with primary legislative powers. As he put it:

. . . compared with the changes that have already taken place, the acquisition of further powers, including those of primary legislation, would represent a manageable progression, not a major step change, in terms of the demands made upon us . . .[30]

This statement was testimony to how far the Administration had travelled in the first four-year term. It had inherited a junior Department of the UK state, fully integrated into a Whitehall milieu, with little experience of policy-making and without the means of driving forward a distinctive agenda. In just four years a transformation had taken place as far as was possible within the constraints of the Government of Wales Act. In place was a growing parliamentary system, a separation of powers, and an increasingly confident policy-making machine ready to take on board the acquisition of more powers. Not only that, but in the words of the Permanent Secretary, the major changes to make this possible had already happened. For the Assembly's civil service the acquisition of legislative powers would entail a 'manageable progression' rather than a 'step change' in its operation.

A Distinctive Legal System

Perhaps the most important expression of the new civic society is the growing development of distinctively Welsh legal institutions since the onset of democratic devolution. As one observer has put it:

The proposition is that the development of law and legal institutions in Wales is an essential part of a trajectory towards nationhood, in which the 1998 settlement constituted the most significant step in centuries and provided a particular opportunity for the legal profession both to contribute to and benefit from that process. [31]

[29] Morgan, 2002.

[30] Shortridge, Sir J., Permanent Secretary of the National Assembly for Wales, *Memorandum to the Richard Commission*, 13 December 2002, para. 33.

[31] Williams, J., 'Legal Wales' in Osmond, J., and Jones, J.B., (eds.) *Birth of Welsh Democracy: The First Term of the National Assembly for Wales* (Cardiff: Institute of Welsh Affairs, 2003). She was

Sir Roderick Evans, Wales' only fully bilingual High Court Judge, has identified five essential components of the Welsh legal system — set out in Figure 3.6. [32]

Figure 3.6: Components of the Welsh Legal System

1.	The repatriation to Wales of law making functions.
2.	The development in Wales of a system for the administration of justice in all its forms which is tailored to the social and economic needs of Wales.
3.	The development of institutions and professional bodies which will provide a proper career structure in Wales for those who want to follow a career in those fields.
4.	Making the law accessible to, and readily understood, by the people of Wales.
5.	The development of a system which can accommodate the use of either the English or Welsh languages with equal ease so that in the administration of justice within Wales, the English and Welsh languages really are treated on the basis of equality.

Undoubtedly the most important component is the first. Notwithstanding the many and diverse difficulties for the National Assembly's law-making competence resulting from the Government of Wales Act 1998, Assembly Government policies *are* being given effect using both primary and subordinate legislation. As a result, gradually and over time, a distinctive body of Welsh law is being accumulated. A notable example was the Assembly Government's radical changes to the health service that required distinctive Welsh legislation during 2002 (see Figure 3.7).

Putting these changes through Parliament involved Assembly Government officials in detailed negotiations with Whitehall civil servants. In the process the Assembly Government engaged directly with the preparation of primary legislation. As Simon McCann, leader of the Assembly team of lawyers responsible, put it in his account of the exercise:

> . . . the Assembly has no power to introduce primary legislation to Parliament, yet the vast majority of the policy and legal expertise required to prepare it and ensure its passage resides in the Assembly.[33]

commenting on a lecture given at the University of Wales Swansea, October 2000, by Lord Morris of Borth-Y-Gest: *Legal Wales: Its Modern Origins and its Role after Devolution: National Identity, the Welsh Language and Parochialism.*

[32] Evans, R., Lord Morris lecture, University of Wales, Aberystwyth, 2002.

[33] McCann, S., 'Permissive Powers are Good for the Health: The Health Reforms in Wales', *Wales Law Journal*, 2 (2), p. 81, 2003.

He argues that a constitutional precedent was set with this bill whereby Parliament allowed the Assembly broad enabling or permissive secondary powers within the context of framework legislation. The mechanism was a formal agreement between the Wales Office and the Assembly Government under Section 41 of the Government of Wales Act 1998.[34] This enabled Assembly Government policy officials and lawyers to exercise the functions of the Wales Office in advising Ministers, drawing up the policy, instructing Counsel, managing the pre-legislative scrutiny process, and supporting the Wales Office Ministers in securing the passage of the Bill. As Simon McCann concluded:

> The Assembly was thus entrusted with the powers which it lacked, to exercise them on a quasi-agency basis on behalf of the Wales Office, whilst benefiting hugely from the very considerable political experience and influence which the Wales Office can provide. This is not only an excellent example of devolved and central government working together to achieve a shared goal, but also powerful evidence that the Assembly is coming of age and is ready, willing and able to exercise primary legislative powers of its own.[35]

Figure 3.7: Assembly Government NHS (Wales) Plan

1.	The abolition of the five Health Authorities and the establishment of 22 Local Health Boards.
2.	A duty on Local Health Boards and local authorities to prepare a joint health and well being strategy.
3.	Reform of the Community Health Councils.
4.	A new body to accredit training of nurses, midwives and other health-related professions.
5.	A Wales Centre for Health to bring together expertise in public health and provide a focus for health research.

Such developments have far reaching consequences for the administration of justice and the legal profession in Wales. The establishment of the Office of the Counsel General within the National Assembly has also had a significant impact. Associated developments have been :

• A panel of counsel chosen from the Wales and Chester Circuit to represent the Assembly on Public Law Matters.

---

[34] The residue of the former Welsh Office, the Wales Office — with bases in London and Cardiff — serves the Secretary of State for Wales. Following the June 2003 UK Cabinet re-shuffle, in which the Secretary of State for Wales Peter Hain also became Leader of the House of Commons, the 55 Wales Office staff became part of the new Department of Constitutional Affairs, headed by Lord Falconer. Despite this shift they continued to work directly to the Secretary of State for Wales.

[35] McCann, 2003.

- A Welsh Public Law and Human Rights Association, established in 1999.
- The Centre for Welsh Legal Affairs at the Department of Law, University of Wales, Aberystwyth, established in 1999. It is noteworthy that the Centre acknowledges its creation was prompted by 'the setting up of the National Assembly for Wales and the emergence of a more distinct Welsh legal order'.[36]
- Associations for Personal Injury Lawyers, established in 1999, and Commercial Lawyers, established in 2000.
- The Welsh Legal History Society, established in 2000.
- Establishment of a *Wales Law Journal*.

Alongside all of this the Assembly is making bilingual legislation. That is to say, it is making legislation bilingually rather than first making it in English and then translating it into Welsh. This is a reflection of the equal status accorded both languages, with far reaching consequences for the administration of justice and the legal profession. There have been other institutional changes as well, shown in Figure 3.8.

Figure 3.8: Developments in Welsh Legal Institutions Since 1999

- Establishment of the Administrative, Chancery, and Mercantile Courts in Wales.
- Regular sittings of the Court of Appeal Civil and Criminal Divisions in Cardiff.
- Hearings in Wales rather than in London — as was invariably the case before the establishment of the Assembly — of judicial review cases involving public bodies in Wales.
- Appointment of a High Court Judge whose fluency in Welsh enables him to conduct trials bilingually or entirely in Welsh, according to the wishes of the parties, without translation.

As the Counsel-General Winston Roddick QC has put it:

It would not be correct historically to say that we are seeing the creation of Legal Wales but it is undoubtedly the case that since the National Assembly for Wales was established we are seeing the reawakening of it after centuries of slumber . . . The administration of justice in Wales is closer to the people now than at any time during the 19th and 20th Centuries.[37]

[36] McCann, 2003, p. 219.
[37] Roddick, W., 'Creating Legal Wales', *Agenda* Spring 2002 (Cardiff: Institute of Welsh Affairs).

Partnerships

The National Assembly's reach into Welsh civic life has been enhanced and intensified by the establishment of formal partnerships in three key areas: with the business community, local government and the voluntary sector. The active promotion of partnership working was a requirement in the Government of Wales Act 1998, reflecting much of the rhetoric of the time about pursuing a new politics of inclusivity in Wales.[38] At a national level three partnership councils have been established, between the Assembly and the Welsh Local Government Association; with the business community — the Wales CBI, Wales TUC and Business Wales; and with the Wales Council of Voluntary Action. Other statutory, strategic partnerships have been established by Assembly Government since 1999. Some of these, operating in the main with local authority and local health organisations are listed in Figure 3.9.

Figure 3.9: Welsh Assembly Government Sponsored Statutory Partnerships

> - Local Health Alliances (1999)
> - EU Structural Fund Partnerships (2000 onwards)
> - Alcohol and Drugs Action Teams (2000)
> - Community Strategies (2001)
> - Communities First (2002 onwards)
> - Health, Social Care and Well Being (2003)
> - Children and Young People (2003)

Partnerships also reach down to the regional level within Wales, especially through the operation of two major initiatives, the European Union Objective 1 regeneration programme for west Wales and the Valleys, and the Communities First initiative. Objective 1 entails the expenditure of some £1.2 billion of EU regional aid over seven years to 2006. Its administration has entailed the formation of an elaborate array of partnerships — four at the all-Wales level, ten regional partnerships, and 15 for each of the local authority areas within the Objective 1 region. In addition around 700 individual Objective 1 projects display varying degrees of partnership activity. In pursuit of inclusiveness, the Assembly Government has required that membership of Objective 1 partnerships be made up on the basis of the so-called 'three-thirds principle' — that is to say, the public, private, and voluntary sectors have equal representation.

With a budget of £83 million between 2002-05, Communities First aims to regenerate 132 of the most disadvantaged communities defined by ward boundaries, with ten further 'communities of interest' spread over wider

---

[38] Government of Wales Act 1998, Part V.

geographical areas. By the end of 2003 there were approaching 100 Communities First partnerships overseeing the delivery of the programme. Again, the 'three-thirds' membership principle has been applied.

Finally, the 22 unitary authorities themselves have spawned a wide range of partnerships with other agencies in their areas, most notably in the health field. It has been estimated that there are as many as 2,000 loosely defined local partnerships operating across Wales. Assuming that each of these has around 20 places, this implies that there could be as many as 40,000 'seats' on local partnerships.[39]

The objective of all these various partnerships is to promote inclusiveness, increase efficiency and achieve greater administrative integration, what is often termed 'joined-up' government. Obviously, the extent to which the huge range of partnerships operating across Wales achieve these aspirations varies a great deal. There are complaints, especially from the business sector, at the effectiveness of their operation in many instances. Some from the voluntary sector feel that they are there simply to make up the numbers, to fulfil the 'three-thirds' requirement. In general it has been the public sector membership that has driven many of the partnerships. That said, many of the participants value the involvement and access to decision making, and at the national level the decision-makers, that partnership working entails. What is not in doubt is that the huge growth of partnerships since the Assembly was established in 1999 has involved a much larger range of people and organisations in the country's civic infrastructure than was previously the case.

Press and Media

One of the main difficulties that faces the National Assembly in establishing itself in the minds and affections of the Welsh people has been a sense of its detachment from their everyday concerns. In part this must be because, in contrast to Scotland, for example, Wales has a much smaller national press to report and give a context and explanation to its proceedings. Nonetheless, the press and media that does exist in Wales are an extremely important part of the civil society infrastructure. Since the establishment of the Assembly Welsh-based newspapers and broadcast media have responded by significantly increasing their political coverage. And at key moments the impact has been remarkable. For example, the BBC's *Wales Today* evening news bulletin achieved one of the highest recorded ratings for a Welsh television programme on the day Alun Michael resigned, in February 2000. About half the available audience, some 450,000 people, tuned in.

In terms of an indigenous daily press Wales has only two morning newspapers — *The Western Mail*, weekday circulation of around 50,000 in

---

[39] This estimate is quoted in a report prepared for the Welsh Assembly Government by the Centre for Local and Regional Government Research at Cardiff University, see Bristow, G., et al, *Partnerships between the public, private and voluntary sectors in Wales*, May 2003.

southern Wales, and the *Daily Post*, weekday circulation in north Wales of about 40,000. In the capital city the *Western Mail's* circulation is thought to be no more than 5,000. The London press, especially the tabloids which rarely mention Wales at all, and more seldom yet the workings of the National Assembly, account for the bulk of newspaper sales in Wales. The launch of the *Welsh Mirror* in September 1999 added considerably to the range of indigenous reporting. However, the Welsh edition, which achieved some notoriety for its intemperate attacks on Plaid Cymru and what it saw as a linguistic élite in Wales, folded in September 2003.

In any event it cannot be said that the Assembly is covered by a newspaper that gives a sense of a 'paper of record' being at work. The *Western Mail* comes closest, often devoting a great deal of space to proceedings and events at the Assembly. Generally, however, stories are personality led and given prominence in response to their human interest. Relatively little space is allowed for reflective analysis or commentary.

The three television channels in Wales — BBC Wales, S4C and HTV have a much bigger audience and greater geographical coverage than the press. This is despite the 40 per cent of north-eastern and south-eastern Wales in the so-called overlap areas where viewers can tune into signals coming from both sides of the border. The Welsh-based television channels have also invested heavily in their coverage of the Assembly. Each have established new studios in the Assembly itself and the news bulletins on radio and television, on all channels, are full of reportage from the Assembly's proceedings. S4C has digital space for a completely new channel, part of which is being devoted to live coverage of the Assembly's proceedings. In addition, in 2001 there was a small increase in the amount of media made in Wales with the launch of BBC Wales's 2W digital service. Despite limited audience penetration, 2W is the first dedicated English language programme zone for Wales. With a regular place in the schedule, it offers a range of programmes including for the first time a nightly international and national news bulletin for Wales.

A rare snapshot of the media sources from which people in Wales obtain political information was provided by a BBC Wales poll commissioned from Beaufort in the immediate aftermath of the May 2003 Assembly elections (see Figure 3.10).[40]

Among other issues this probed where people obtained information about the Assembly election during the campaign. As would be expected it showed that television — BBC1 Wales mentioned by 42 per cent, followed by HTV with 25 per cent — was overwhelmingly dominant. In the survey the lack of penetration of the Welsh-based press to the mass of the population was

---

[40] For the full details see Williams, D., 'Stirring Up Apathy', *Agenda* Summer 2003, (Cardiff: Institute of Welsh Affairs).

painfully exposed. The *Western Mail*, for example, was mentioned by only 7 per cent, only a little way ahead of teletext's 4 per cent.

Undoubtedly, the Welsh press, and in particular the *Western Mail*, is extremely important for decision makers, opinion formers and other activists. At the same time its lack of penetration to the mass of the people demonstrates the weakness of Welsh civil society, certainly compared with Scotland.

Figure 3.10: May 2003 Election: Sources of Information
(percentage points are each equivalent to about 25,000 adults)

Main Sources: candidate leaflets, mentioned by 71 per cent; polling card delivered to all homes, 55 per cent.

BBC Wales sources: BBC1 Wales 42 per cent; BBC2 Wales 9 per cent; Radio Wales 6 per cent; S4C 4 per cent; Ceefax 4 per cent; Radio Cymru 3 per cent.

Other sources: HTV Wales 25 per cent; Welsh Mirror 9 per cent; Western Mail 7 per cent; Daily Post 5 per cent; Teletext 4 per cent.

Representation of Women

One of the most significant and visible changes the National Assembly has brought to the political culture of Wales was been the better representation of women. The 1999 Assembly election produced the second highest proportion (46 per cent) of women elected to a national body in Europe. The second election, in May 2003, saw the proportion rise to 50 per cent. Not only that, but the Cabinet has a female majority, with five out of the nine Ministers (Figure 3.11).

These developments were hugely important for the potential political engagement and civic consciousness of the women of Wales. Until this point they had been largely invisible in Welsh political life. Relatively few were elected to local government, and over the last century only a handful have been elected to the House of Commons. Of the present 40 Westminster MPs from Wales, only four are women.[41]

This transformation of the Welsh political scene, which was previously dominated by men at every level, was the result of two initiatives: the introduction of proportional representation, and the use of 'twinning' by the Labour party. Proportional representation allowed the parties to manipulate their regional lists to allow women candidates to be placed at the top. Plaid Cymru, for instance, placed women alternately on their regional lists of candidates. The Liberal Democrats shied away from adopting a formal

[41] Ann Clwyd (Cynon Valley), Jackie Lawrence (Preseli Pembrokeshire), Julie Morgan (Cardiff North), and Betty Williams (Conwy).

method of promoting women candidates arguing that it went against their 'liberal' values. However, they offered training days for women only and emphasised an informal route in order to encourage female applications.[42]

Apart from the impact on Wales's civic culture, there is no doubt that the critical mass of women in the Assembly has brought a different tone to its proceedings than otherwise would have been the case. Debates have been less adversarial than at Westminster and topics such as family welfare, the rights and wrongs of smacking children and equal opportunities have been given a higher priority. The women members also added more weight behind the implementation of family-friendly working hours.

Figure 3.11: The Cabinet of the Assembly Government Following May 2003 Election

Rhodri Morgan	(63)	First Minister	(Cardiff West)
Sue Essex	(57)	Finance, Local Government and Public Services	(Cardiff North)
Karen Sinclair	(50)	Assembly Business	(Clwyd South)
Edwina Hart	(46)	Social Justice and Regeneration	(Gower)
Jane Hutt	(53)	Health and Social Services	(Vale of Glamorgan)
Andrew Davies	(50)	Economic Development and Transport	(Swansea West)
Jane Davidson	(46)	Education and Life-Long Learning	(Pontypridd)
Carwyn Jones	(36)	Environment, Planning and Countryside	(Bridgend)
Alun Pugh	(47)	Culture, the Welsh Language and Sports	(Clwyd West)

The New Lobbyists

Another obvious expression of Wales's emerging civic society has been the way a growing number of organisations are recasting their structures to reflect the new Welsh polity, and often appointing National Assembly

---

[42] See Chaney, P., 'An Absolute Duty' in Osmond, J., and Jones, J.B., (eds.) *Building a Civic Culture: Institutional Change, Policy Development and Political Dynamics in the National Assembly for Wales* (Cardiff: Institute of Welsh Affairs, 2002).

Liaison Officers in the process. As the late Professor Phil Williams, a Plaid Cymru AM during the first term, observed:

> For the first time ever we see the growth of an all-Wales civic society. The National Assembly has become the focus for all public and voluntary bodies depending on — or seeking — support from the Assembly. My diary was filled during the four years of the first term with meetings where such bodies — often in co-operation with other organisations working in related fields — gathered together on an all-Wales basis to present their case to AMs. This brought active members of such organisations to Cardiff from all over Wales, often for the first time.[43]

Cardiff is now rarely seen as a branch office for London-based organisations. Instead, organisations are progressively establishing more autonomous Welsh structures to more effectively interact with and influence National Assembly politicians. Examples range from the British Medical Association and the Country Landowners Association to the National Union of Teachers, Confederation of British Industry, Federation of Small Businesses, and the Royal Society for the Protection of Birds. By now more than 30 such organisations have appointed Assembly Liaison Officers. In addition the advent of the Assembly has seen the spawning of a growing number of Welsh-based political consultancies.[44]

A WELSH CIVIC CONSCIOUSNESS

An impressive indication of the number of all-Wales organisations now actively engaged in Welsh political debate can be see from the analysis of those which gave evidence to the Richard Commission on the Assembly's powers during the 12 months from September 2002 (Figure 3.12). Before the Assembly was established in 1999 it would have been impossible to imagine such a civic involvement in a debate on Wales's constitutional future. The nearest equivalent was the evidence collected by the Crowther-Hunt / Kilbrandon Royal Commission on the Constitution, which reported in 1974. Then views from Wales were limited to the political parties and a handful of academics.

---

[43] Williams, 2003, p. 49.

[44] See, for example, Phipps, S., and Owens, C., 'The New Lobbyists', *Agenda* Summer 1999, (Cardiff: Institute of Welsh Affairs).

Figure 3.12: Evidence Given to the Richard Commission	
Assembly Government	First Minister; Deputy First Minister; Culture, Health, Environment, Education, Finance, Economic Development, and Rural Affairs Ministers; Permanent Secretary; Counsel-General; staff representatives
Presiding Office	Presiding Officer, Deputy Presiding Officer and officials; Chairs of Subject Committees and Chairs of the European, Legislation and Audit Committees
Wales Office	Secretary of State for Wales
AMs and Former AMs	David Melding; Brian Hancock; Delyth Evans; Gareth Jones; Alison Halford; Ron Davies; Dr Brian Gibbons; Mark Isherwood; John Griffiths; Laura Ann Jones
Welsh MPs	Wayne David; Gareth Thomas; Donald Anderson; Ian Lucas; Betty Williams; Llew Smith; Hywel Williams; Wyn Griffiths; Jon Owen Jones; Denzil Davies; Kevin Brennan; Alan Williams; Huw Iranca-Davies
Welsh MEPs	Jill Evans; Eurig Wyn
Welsh Peers	Lord Thomas of Gresford; Lord Roberts of Conwy; Lord Livsey; Lord Prys Davies; Lord Carlisle; Lord Kenneth Morgan
Political Parties	Plaid Cymru; Welsh Liberal Democrats; Wales Green Party; UK Independence Party; Wales Council of the Co-operative Party; Welsh Labour and eleven Welsh Labour Party branches; Welsh Conservatives
Scottish Executive	Deputy First Minister; Lord Advocate; Permanent Secretary; Head of Legal and Parliamentary Services; Minister for Parliamentary Business, Minister for Finance
Scottish Parliament and Northern Ireland Assembly	Presiding Officer; Deputy Presiding Officer; Clerk/Chief Executive of the Scottish Parliamentary Corporate Body; Scottish Parliament Committee Convenors; Shadow First Minister and SNP Parliament Minister; Conservative Spokesperson on Justice and Home Affairs Lord Alderdice, Speaker of the NI Assembly
Assembly Sponsored Public Bodies	National Council for Education and Training; Welsh Development Agency; Wales Tourist Board; Countryside Council for Wales; Environment Agency Wales; Arts Council of Wales; Welsh Language Board; Higher Education Funding Council for Wales; Sports Council of Wales; National Museums and Galleries of Wales; Care Council for Wales

Statutory Organisations	Equal Opportunities Commission; Disability Rights Commission; Auditor General for Wales; Audit Commission in Wales; Children's Commissioner for Wales; Youth Justice Board; Commission for Racial Equality; Forestry Commission; Wales Youth Agency
Education	Fforwm; UCAC; University of Wales, Bangor; Institute of Welsh Politics
Health and Social Services	North East Wales NHS trust; Welsh Ambulance Services NHS Trust; Royal College of Nursing; Care Council for Wales; Chartered Institute of Environmental Health
County Councils	Powys; Gwynedd; Pembrokeshire; Newport; Bridgend
Community Councils	Gowerton; Llwchwr; Coedffranc; Graig; Ferwig (written opinion to public meeting); Ruabon (written opinion to public meeting)
Police	Police Authorities in Wales; North Wales Police Authority; Dyfed-Powys Police Authority; Police Federation of England and Wales
Fire Authorities	North Wales Fire Service; Mid and West Wales Fire Service
National organisations	Welsh Local Government Association; Wales TUC; Wales CBI; Wales Council for Voluntary Action; Chamber Wales; Engineers Employers Federation; Institute of Chartered Accountants in England and Wales Chartered Institute of Housing; Royal Town Planning Institute in Wales; Association of National Park Authorities; Community Enterprise Wales; Institute of Welsh Affairs; Council for Wales Voluntary Youth Services; Welsh Overseas Agencies Group; Voluntary Arts Wales; Royal Institution for Chartered Surveyors
Regional representative organisations	Powys Association of Voluntary Organisations; South and West Wales Fishing Communities; Newport Crossroads
Rural representative organisations	NFU Cymru; Farmers Union of Wales; Country Landowners and Business Association; Royal Welsh Agricultural Society; Countryside Alliance Wales; Young Farmers Clubs; Meat Promotion Wales
Trade Unions	Unison
Environmental groups	RSPB Cymru; National Trust Wales; Newport and Valleys Branch of the Campaign for the Protection of Rural Wales; National Botanic Garden of Wales

Youth organisations	Urdd Gobaith Cymru; National Union of Students in Wales; Girl Guides Cymru; Boys and Girls Clubs of Wales; Young People's Forum; Canllaw Online; Fairbridge de Cymru
Church organisations	CYTUN; Faith Council; The Congregational Federation in Wales.
Legal	Law Society; Mr Justice Thomas; Milwan Jarman QC, Phillip Howell Richardson; Huw Williams; Clive Lewis; Nicholas Neal; Nicholas Cooke QC; Mr Justice Roderick Evans and Professor Iwan Davies; The Incorporated Law Society for Cardiff and District; Standing Committee on Legal Wales
Campaigning Groups	Parliament for Wales Campaign; Cymdeithas yr Iaith Gymraeg; Cymuned; Electoral Reform Society; Wales Women's National Coalition; Welsh Food Alliance; Help the Aged; Age Concern Cymru; Anti-Poverty Network Cymru; Disability Wales; Stonewall Cymru; Joint Committee for Ethnic Minorities in Wales; All Wales Ethnic Minorities Association; Wales Transport Research Centre; CPT Wales; Anti Poverty Network Cymru
Constitutional, academic and other experts	Professor David McCrone; Professor David Bell; Professor Alan Page; David Lambert; Professor David Miers; Dr Denis Balsom; Professor Vernon Bogdanor; Professor David Butler; Dr Simon King; Professor Richard Rawlings; Geraint Talfan Davies; Professor Kevin Morgan; Professor Robert Hazell; Professor Martin Laffin; Mari James; Robert Buckland; John Osmond; Professor Keith Patchett
Individuals	98

At the same time a large caveat needs to be set against this chapter's account of the growth of civic consciousness in Wales since the establishment the National Assembly. This is, quite simply, that by and large it has been confined to an élite strata in Welsh society, the political class. So far the Welsh devolution experience has been characterised by its weak engagement with the wider electorate. Turn-out in the two elections held so far is testimony to that: falling from 46 per cent in 1999 to 38 per cent in 2003. In general, the verdict from the polls is that the Assembly has made little impact on the lives of ordinary people and there has been disappointment at its record, whether it be in health, education or economic development.[45]

---

[45] See Wyn Jones, R., and Scully, R., 'Public Engagement' in Osmond, J., and Jones, J.B., (eds.) *Birth of Welsh Democracy: The First Term of the National Assembly for Wales* (Cardiff: Institute of Welsh Affairs, 2003).

However, the response has not been a rejection of devolution. Instead, the polls have shown a remarkable shift in favour of greater powers for the Assembly. Now close to 40 per cent favour a Parliament for Wales with powers equivalent to those enjoyed by the Scots (see Figure 3.13). The sentiment appears to be, if we are to have an Assembly, let's make it work effectively.

Of course, the notion of Wales having a civic culture is novel to a society with such little experience of its own institutions. Before the onset of the National Assembly it could be fairly said that there was a *civil society in Wales* rather than a *Welsh civil society*. This was simply because there was an under-developed civic infrastructure to which Welsh organisations and society more generally could respond.

Figure 3.13: Constitutional Preferences (%) in Wales, 1997–2003[46]

Constitutional Preference	1997	1999	2001	2003
Independence	14.1	9.6	12.3	13.9
Parliament	19.6	29.9	38.8	37.8
Assembly	26.8	35.3	25.5	27.1
No elected body	39.5	25.3	24.0	21.2

Undeniably this position has now changed. The onset of democratic devolution revolutionised the prospects for a Welsh civic consciousness to emerge. Despite so far being confined to those most immediately engaged in the political life of the country, the civic dimension of Welsh identity is surely destined to grow. After all, as this chapter has reported, remarkable transformations have already occurred in the short time the Assembly has been in existence. This has been especially the case with the political parties; developments within the civil service and notions around building a distinctively Welsh public service; the growth of the legal system and the emergence of the idea of 'Legal Wales'; the large multiplication of partnerships across all levels of Welsh government and the public, private and voluntary sectors; the response of the media; and the truly remarkable rise of women's representation in political life. If all this can happen in five short years, what may we expect from five decades?

[46] Source: Institute of Welsh Politics, University of Wales, Aberystwyth

BIBLIOGRAPHY

Primary and Official Documents

Evidence to the Richard Commission. Available at http://www.richardcommission. gov.uk/content/evidence/index.htm.
  House of Lords Select Committee on the Constitution, *Devolution: Inter-Institutional Relations in the United Kingdom*, Session 2002–3, Second Report, HL Paper 28, (London: The Stationery Office, 2003).
Plaid Cymru, *Towards Full National Status: Stages on the Journey*, 2000.
Welsh Assembly Government, *Iaith Pawb* ('Everybody's language'), (Cardiff: The Stationery Office, 2002).
Welsh Assembly Government, *Learning Country: Learning Pathways 14–19* (Cardiff: The Stationery Office, 2002).
Welsh Assembly Government, *People, Places Futures — The Wales Spatial Plan* (Cardiff: The Stationery Office, 2003).
Welsh Assembly Government, *The Review of Health and Social Care* (Cardiff: The Stationery Office, 2003).
Welsh Assembly Government, *Wales for Innovation* (Cardiff: The Stationery Office, 2003).
Welsh Assembly Government, *Wales: A Better Country* (Cardiff: The Stationery Office, 2003).
Welsh Liberal Democrats, *Building Community Politics: Liberal Democrats Wales's Party Strategy into the Millennium*, 1999.

Secondary Sources

Bradbury, J., Bennie, L., Denver, D., and Mitchell, J., *Party Attitudes and the Politics of Devolution: An Analysis of Candidates at the 1999 Scottish Parliament and Welsh Assembly Elections*, Paper to Political Studies Association Territorial Politics Workshop, Cardiff, January 2001.
Bristow, G., et al, *Partnerships between the public, private and voluntary sectors in Wales*, May 2003.
Chaney, P., 'An Absolute Duty' in Osmond, J., and Jones, J.B., (eds.) *Building a Civic Culture: Institutional Change, Policy Development and Political Dynamics in the National Assembly for Wales* (Cardiff: Institute of Welsh Affairs, 2002).
Evans, J., *The Future of Welsh Conservatism* (Cardiff: Institute of Welsh Affairs, 2002).
Jones, C., *Future of the Welsh Labour Party*, Gregynog Papers, (Cardiff: Institute of Welsh Affairs, 2004).
McCann, S., 'Permissive Powers are Good for the Health: The Health Reforms in Wales', *Wales Law Journal*, 2 (2), p.81, 2003.
Osmond, J., 'A Constitutional Convention By other Means — The First year of the National Assembly for Wales' in Hazell, R., (ed.) *The State and the Nations: The First Year of Devolution in the United Kingdom* (Exeter: Imprint Academic, 2000).

Osmond, J., 'In Search of Stability: Coalition Politics in the Second Year of the National Assembly' in Trench, A., (ed.) *The State of the Nations 2001: The Second Year of Devolution in the United Kingdom* (Exeter: Imprint Academic, 2001).

Osmond, J., 'Constitution Building on the Hoof: the Assembly's Procedural Review' in Jones, J.B., and Osmond, J., (eds.) *Building a Civic Culture: Institutional Change, Policy Development and Political Dynamics in the National Assembly for Wales* (Cardiff: Institute of Welsh Affairs, 2002).

Osmond, J., *Divided We Fall: The Politics of Geography in Wales* (Cardiff: Institute of Welsh Affairs).

Osmond, J., (ed.) *Devolution and Wales Monitoring Report: Dragon Takes a Different Route September 2002* (London: The Constitution Unit and the Institute of Welsh Affairs). All monitoring reports are available at http://www.ucl.ac.uk/constitution-unit/leverh/monitoring.htm.

Osmond, J., (ed.) *Devolution and Wales Monitoring Report: Dragon Debates its Future February 2003* (London: The Constitution Unit and the Institute of Welsh Affairs).

Osmond, J., (ed.) *Devolution and Wales Monitoring Report: Welsh Labour Takes Control June 2003* (London: The Constitution Unit and the Institute of Welsh Affairs).

Osmond, J. (ed.) *Devolution and Wales Monitoring Report: Wales Unplugged August 2003* (London: The Constitution Unit and the Institute of Welsh Affairs).

Osmond, J., (ed.), *Second Term Challenge: Can the Welsh Assembly Government Hold its Course?* (Cardiff: Institute of Welsh Affairs and The Constitution Unit, UCL, 2003).

Osmond, J., and Jones, J.B., (eds.) *Birth of Welsh Democracy: The First Term of the National Assembly for Wales* (Cardiff: Institute of Welsh Affairs, 2003).

Prosser, S., *The Case for a Welsh Public Service* (Cardiff: Institute of Welsh Affairs, 2003).

Rawlings, R., *Delineating Wales: Constitutional, Legal and Administrative Aspects of National Devolution* (Cardiff: University of Wales Press, 2003).

Thomas, A., 'Liberal Democrats' in Osmond, J., and Jones, J.B., (eds.) *Birth of Welsh Democracy: The First term of the National Assembly for Wales* (Cardiff: Institute of Welsh Affairs, 2003).

Williams, J., 'Legal Wales' in Osmond, J., and Jones, J.B., (eds.) *Birth of Welsh Democracy: The First Term of the National Assembly for Wales* (Cardiff: Institute of Welsh Affairs, 2003). Evans, R., Lord Morris lecture University of Wales, Aberystwyth, 2002.

Williams, P., *The Psychology of Distance* (Cardiff: Institute of Welsh Affairs, 2003).

Wyn Jones, R., and Scully, R., 'Public Engagement' in Osmond, J., and Jones, J.B., (eds.) *Birth of Welsh Democracy: The First Term of the National Assembly for Wales* (Cardiff: Institute of Welsh Affairs, 2003).

Wynn Jones, R., and Trystan, D., 'The 1997 Welsh Referendum Vote', in Taylor, B., and Thomson, K., (eds.) *Scotland and Wales Nations Again* (Cardiff: University of Wales Press, 1999).

4

Northern Ireland: Renascent?

Robin Wilson and Rick Wilford[1]

INTRODUCTION

Northern Ireland's experience of devolution has been fitful and for some, even many, dispiriting. Two long and two short suspensions, the postponement, twice, of the second Assembly election, the serial disruptions of the confederal dimensions of the Belfast Agreement, the lack of Executive focus and coherence, and a less-than-legislatively-active Assembly have each dimmed the dawn's early light that broke metaphorically on Good Friday 1998 and flickered more luminously at the subsequent referendum.

Over a period that has seen four Northern Ireland Secretaries in office, the trust necessary to sustain the stable outworking of the devolution 'settlement' has diminished progressively. The catalogue of proven and alleged breaches of its ceasefire by the IRA has exacted a heavy toll on Protestant attitudes in particular. A poll conducted in the immediate aftermath of the announcement of the October 2002 suspension indicated that, overall, support for the Agreement had fallen to its lowest level since the 1998 referendum, largely because only one third of those (overwhelmingly Protestant) respondents supporting 'unionist' parties still endorsed the accord.[2] Thus, the expectation which some harboured at the time of the Agreement that a cross-cutting political cleavage, turning on a pro- and anti-agreement axis, could emerge in the context of a new political dispensation faded from view.

In retrospect, the die was cast at the 1998 Assembly election. Even discounting the first-preference votes cast for successful Ulster Unionist Party (UUP) candidates who had voted against the Agreement, the candidates from the overtly anti-agreement unionist parties (and independents) secured a marginal lead of first-preference votes, though not seats, over their pro-agreement unionist opponents. This lent real delicacy to the balance of unionist forces within the Assembly, given the 'parallel consent' voting

---

[1] As ever, we are indebted to the rest of the Northern Ireland ESRC / Leverhulme devolution monitoring team — John Coakley, Lizanne Dowds, Greg McLaughlin, Elizabeth Meehan and Duncan Morrow — for their valuable contributions to the quarterly reports on which this chapter is based, though the authors are of course entirely responsible for its content.

[2] Wilford, R., and Wilson, R., 'Northern Ireland: valedictory?', in Hazell, R., (ed.) *The State of the Nations 2003: The Third Year of Devolution in the United Kingdom* (Exeter: Imprint Academic, 2003a), p. 88.

procedure for the election of the First and Deputy First Minister (which requires concurrent majorities of 'unionist' and 'nationalist' Assembly members for success). It was eventually to lead to parity in numbers of pro- and anti-agreement unionist Members of the Legislative Assembly (MLAs), and the somewhat improvised (not to say unseemly) sequence of events that led to the re-election of the UUP leader, David Trimble, and election of his Social Democratic and Labour Party counterpart, Mark Durkan, to the top posts in November 2001.

The devolution experience in Northern Ireland has in short been a case of 'arrested development': unlike in Scotland and Wales, it is still in its infancy. There was, at the time of writing, no second set of election results to analyse, and no new process of Executive formation to reflect upon. Nor, indeed, have a seamless or bountiful record of distinctive legislation and policy initiatives unfolded since the first transfer of powers in December 1999. That, however, is not to claim that devolution has made no difference to Northern Ireland: it has, and can still.

That tangible improvements have been made to the lives of many is testa- ment to the persistence of regional politicians in what at times has been a decidedly inauspicious context. In addition, during the latest and most protracted suspension the expanded team of direct-rule Ministers has been active, expediting legislative proposals bequeathed by their devolved prede- cessors and taking forward new, though well-flagged, policy initiatives. Thus, any assessment of devolution has, perversely perhaps, to include deci- sions made by the five Northern Ireland Office (NIO) Ministers during 2002 and 2003.

It is unlikely that devolution will be restored in the foreseeable future. But if it should be, a question mark hovers over whether the 1998 template can, or should, be sustained in unamended form. That is not to imply any qualifi- cation to its underpinning plural philosophy, but rather to suggest that some of the procedural rigidities created by the Agreement do need to be addressed in the full-blown review scheduled to begin in December 2003.[3]

The shared aspiration of most of the key players, including London and Dublin, is that the Agreement should be 'implemented in full'.[4] As an earnest of their commitment to this objective, the two governments published a 'Joint Declaration' on 1 May 2003, setting out how they, especially London, would contribute to its realisation, a process in part contingent upon 'acts of

---

[3] Wilford, R., and Wilson, R., *Northern Ireland: A Route to Stability* (Swindon: ESRC, 2003b).

[4] One of the authors (Wilson) must take responsibility for putting this phrase into the public domain. At a private conference attended by all the principal protagonists in 1999, before devolution was secured, he suggested that the then impasse over weapons decommissioning could be resolved by all parties agreeing to 'implement the Agreement in full', as mandated by the 71 per 'yes' referendum vote, rather than pursuing their partisan, more restrictively mandated, positions on the arms issue. In retrospect, this was stunningly naïve, since the upshot was merely to transfer the antagonism to the domain of which party was truly 'implementing the Agreement in full'.

completion' being carried out by the republican movement.[5] The declaration was, however, seized upon immediately by anti-agreement unionists, including within the UUP, as a litany of 'concessions' to republicanism, and threatened to split Mr Trimble's party asunder.

For anti-agreement unionists, not least the Democratic Unionist Party (DUP), the declaration underlined the need for a new agreement, not a tweaking (however extensive) of the original. Intense efforts were made by the UUP, Sinn Fein (SF) and the two governments to achieve a deal involving the full implementation of both the Agreement and the Joint Declaration, thereby creating what Mr Blair had called the 'positive atmosphere' conducive to the restoration of devolution, but they came to nought.

On 21 October those deemed the key players — London, Dublin, the UUP, SF, the IRA and the Independent International Commission on Decommissioning (IICD) — were to unfold a series of events paving the way to an election in November *and* the return of a stable devolved administration. The day began with the announcement from Downing Street that the election would be held on 26 November, followed in turn by a speech by the SF President, Gerry Adams, a statement from the IRA endorsing his speech and an announcement by the head of the IICD, John de Chastelain, that a further stockpile of the IRA's weapons had been put 'beyond use' — to be confirmed by a second IRA statement. Next should have come a statement from Mr Trimble that these steps had created the trust necessary to enable him to commit his party to Executive formation and to a set of reforms to the devolved administration. That process would culminate with the Prime Minister and the Taoiseach, Tony Blair and Bertie Ahern, setting their joint seal on the deal, including the pledge to implement the Joint Declaration in full. According to Downing Street, this was to be Northern Ireland's most historic day since Good Friday 1998. It was not, however, to be.

As these events unfurled all seemed to be going well, until General de Chastelain's statement. Following a longer-than-expected meeting with the two Premiers, the clearly exhausted IICD head appeared in front of the cameras — a rare event itself — at Hillsborough to present his report on the third act of IRA decommissioning. Everything hung on his words, more precisely on the extent of transparent detail he would convey to an expectant audience, chief among whom was the UUP leader, tucked away in the folds of his party's HQ. Confirming that a third event at which IRA arms were put beyond use had occurred in accordance with the decommissioning scheme, the normally tight-lipped general conveyed in broad terms the nature of the weapons that had been decommissioned. They included 'light, medium and heavy ordnance and associated munitions, automatic weapons, ammunition, explosives and explosive materiel' that in aggregate 'was larger than the

---

[5] Text available at www.nio.gov.uk/pdf/joint2003.pdf.

quantity put beyond use in the previous event'.[6] While the assembled journalists sought to extract more detail from General de Chastelain, all that was
forthcoming was a statement from his colleague on the IICD, Andrew Sens,
that 'the material put beyond use this morning could have [caused] death or
destruction on a huge scale had it been put to use'. The statement had some
(limited) breadth but lacked the necessary depth because the IRA had
insisted that its confidentiality be respected, thereby preventing the General
from presenting anything that resembled an inventory of the destroyed
weaponry, let alone any photographic evidence confirming that parts of its
arsenal had been put beyond use.

This proved insufficiently expansive for Mr Trimble. While commending
Mr Adams's speech earlier in the day, he made it clear that the de Chastelain
report lacked the transparency needed to have a significant impact on public
opinion. He continued: 'In view of the failure of the IICD to create the necessary confidence — and because of what the IICD has done we probably have
less confidence than we had an hour ago — because of that I regret [that] . . .
we are putting the sequence on hold'.[7]

Thus, when Messrs Blair and Ahern appeared to make their statements,
the planned celebration became a hastily-improvised exercise in damage
limitation. Over the following week, while efforts continued in private —
including further face-to-face meetings between Mr Trimble and Mr Adams
— to restore at least the outline of an agreed deal between SF and the UUP,
these failed. In the interim, and despite some prospect that it could be further
postponed, the Northern Ireland Secretary, Paul Murphy, announced in the
Commons on 22 October that the election order had been made to enable the
poll to take place on 26 November, even if the nature of the election was
transformed. It would be an election 'to process' and not an election to
government, thereby controverting the oft-stated remarks by London and
Dublin that it would be pointless to hold an election that did not result in the
creation of stable devolved institutions. Certainly for the short run, direct
rule will continue.

In the wake of the election two related, and possibly conflated, processes
will ensue. First, it will lead to the review of the Agreement as provided for
within the accord, four years after 'it comes into effect'.[8] Second, it will pave
the way to further negotiations that in the words of Mr Blair are intended 'to

---

[6] *BBC News Online*, 21 October 2003.

[7] *UUP press release*, 21 October 2003. The text of Gerry Adams's speech is available at
www.sinnfein.ie/news.

[8] *The Agreement: Agreement Reached in the Multi-party Negotiations* (Belfast and London:
Northern Ireland Office, 1999), p. 26. The review can only occur if there is an Assembly in place.
However, with little or no immediate prospect of an Executive being nominated nor of First and Deputy
First Ministers being elected on a cross-community basis, it seems that the newly elected Assembly will
have only shadow status, as was the case between 1 July 1998 and 2 December 1999 when the
direct-rule régime continued to administer the region.

create the conditions which will enable a working Executive to be formed', rendering the contest akin to the 1996 Forum / Entry into Negotiations election that paved the way to the 1998 Agreement.[9]

Clearly, all hinges on the relative fortunes of the parties at what will be a first-order election.[10] The prospect having finally been dashed that a potential partnership among the pro-agreement parties could have developed in the run-up to the contest, it now seems likely that the election will revert to type, with three concurrent major battles raging: that between the UUP and the DUP, the SF-SDLP contest and the wider unionist-nationalist party competition.

Turnout will be critical, all the more so in the dark of late November. Anti-agreement unionist voters will be more disposed to trek to the polls than their pro-agreement counterparts: the failure of the planned deal lends some force to the DUP's argument that the 1998 template is irredeemably broken and that Northern Ireland requires a new 'agreement'. Countering this with a 'let David Trimble finish the job' platform on the part of the (internally divided) UUP is less likely to persuade middle unionism to venture to the polling stations. While the SDLP and SF share the determination to implement the Agreement, their contest will be no less keenly fought, with Mr Adams's party expected to consolidate the lead it gained at the 2001 local and general elections. The major outcome could be what Mr Trimble once described as the 'nightmare scenario' — the emergence of the DUP and SF as the two largest parties.

The immediate period under review thus ends as it began 12 months ago — shrouded in uncertainty. *Plus ça change!* Such insecurity and instability has been a chronic feature of Northern Ireland's venture into devolution from the first. The initial delay of 20 months between the signing of the Belfast Agreement and the formal transfer of powers and, thereafter, the discontinuous experience of devolution have always had the potential to render it an event rather than a process. Between December 1999 and October 2002, when the fourth suspension was imposed — a calendar total of 35 months — all three institutional strands of the Agreement operated in tandem for just 19 months. Between July and October 2001, there was no First or Deputy First Minister, following Mr Trimble's resignation on 1 July and, throughout the entire period, the DUP boycotted all Executive Committee meetings, all plenary and sectoral meetings of the North/South Ministerial Council and each of the meetings of the British-Irish Council. The Civic Forum, the other institutional expression of the Agreement, did not convene

---

[9] *BBC News Online*, 28 October 2003; Elliott, S., 'The Northern Ireland Forum / Entry to Negotiations election 1996', *Irish Political Studies*, 12, pp. 111–112, (1997).

[10] Hough, D., and Jeffrey, C., 'Elections in Multi-Level Systems: Lessons for the UK from Abroad', in Hazell, R., (ed.) *The State of the Nations 2003: The Third Year of Devolution in the United Kingdom* (Exeter: Imprint Academic, 2003), pp. 239–262.

until October 2000 and was suspended *sine die* along with the other devolved institutions two years later.

Such institutional instability has limited the potential to 'make a difference'. To arrive at an assessment of the extent to which devolution has served this broad objective, we address four major questions. Has it:

- engendered political stability
- facilitated policy innovation
- enhanced accountability, and
- improved 'community relations'?

THE PURSUIT OF STABILITY

As we intimated in *State of the Nations 2003* when the then Northern Ireland Secretary, John Reid, again raised the curtain on direct rule on 14 October 2002, the signs were that the fourth suspension of devolution was likely to be prolonged — and so it has proved.[11] It has become the longest sustained period of direct rule since the first transfer of powers and, somewhat ironically, succeeded the longest uninterrupted period when the institutions of all three strands of the Agreement were operating concurrently.[12]

It has, of course, fallen to Dr Reid's successor, Mr Murphy (who returned to Northern Ireland on 24 October), and his Dublin counterpart, the Minister for Foreign Affairs, Brian Cowen, together with Messrs Blair and Ahern, to try to put the political process back on the rails.[13] In addition, of course, the already expanded Northern Ireland Office (NIO) team has had to keep the (formerly devolved) legislative and policy wheels turning.[14]

Between Dr Reid's departure and Mr Murphy's arrival, the Prime Minister made a flying visit to Belfast to deliver a speech that was designed to

---

[11] Wilford and Wilson, 2003a.

[12] From the round of talks led by the then Northern Ireland Secretary, Peter Brooke, in 1991, successive UK governments have subscribed to the theory of the former SDLP leader, John Hume, that there are three sets of 'relationships' involved in resolving the Northern Ireland 'problem': 'internal' to the region, between north and south in Ireland and between Britain and Ireland. This formulation, emanating from the nationalist leader, excluded the relationship between Belfast and London which is key for unionists but, since unionist affections have tended to be unrequited in this regard, Mr Hume's approach was accepted by Tory and Labour administrations. The 'three-stranded' talks led ultimately to the tripartite architecture of the Belfast Agreement: the Assembly and Executive, the north-south bodies and the rather aetiolated British-Irish Council. The upshot has been a tendency to reinforce Northern Ireland provincialism, as devolution gravitated towards *involution* in many policy respects and progressive initiatives in Britain, as in childcare matters, for instance, have been ignored by Northern Ireland's more conservative political élite.

[13] Mr Murphy had been Minister of State in the Northern Ireland Office at the time of the Belfast Agreement.

[14] Wilford and Wilson, 2003a, p. 103. In the 2003 summer reshuffle of the UK Government, Des Browne left the NIO to take up a post at the Department of Work and Pensions and was replaced by John Spellar, who took on the brief of political development among other things.

inject momentum into a severely ailing political process, the terms of which have structured the continuing efforts to revive self-government. Mr Blair set out what in his view lay at the heart of the present crisis: 'We cannot carry on with the IRA half in, half out of this process . . . Remove the threat of violence and the peace process is on an unstoppable path. That threat, no matter how damped down, is no longer reinforcing the political, it is actually destroying it.' The Prime Minister was blunt in driving the point home, insisting that it was time for the IRA to engage in 'acts of completion'.[15]

This last phrase has dominated the agenda over 2003. Until the publication of the Joint Declaration on 1 May — though available to all the key players, including the IRA, beforehand — when Mr Blair also announced the indefinite postponement of the election, its exact meaning was unclear. The required 'acts' were, however, spelled out in paragraph 13 of the declaration. The exhaustive list included military attacks, training, targeting, intelligence-gathering, the acquisition or development of arms or weapons, other preparations for terrorist campaigns, 'punishment' beatings and attacks and involvement in riots. In addition, the practice of 'exiling' had to cease, those who had already fled had to be free to return and sectarian attacks and intimidation aimed at vulnerable communities had to end. Such activities had to be brought to an 'unambiguous and definitive conclusion', 'immediately', and 'in a manner that is conducive to creating public confidence'. Moreover, paramilitaries had to make it clear that they had made such an historic act of completion, and that it was 'reflected in reality on the ground' — in effect, that, respectively, their 'war' was over and that their organisation had to all intents and purposes been disbanded.

Up to mid-March 2003, against a background of negotiations that had continued over the autumn, winter and early spring, the original date scheduled for the election — also 1 May — was still in play. But, as a signal of the continuing difficulties, this had been put back to 29 May, to create more time and space for a resolution of the continuing difficulties to be sought. An earlier exchange of documents between the IRA and the two governments had, it transpired, failed to provide sufficient clarity on the part of armed republicans that they were, in word and in deed, committed to exclusively peaceful and democratic means.

As for the incentives, both governments reiterated their commitment to the Agreement, which they described as 'the template for political progress'. London undertook to play its full part by engaging in a reciprocal and clearly timetabled process of security normalisation ('demilitarisation' to republicans) and in undertaking measures intended to enable 'on the run' paramilitaries to return to Northern Ireland in an essentially judicially unhindered way. To reassure all parts, but especially unionists, that paramilitarism

---

[15] Available at www.nio.gov.uk/press/021017pm.htm.

was ending or, ideally, had ended, and republicans that the British Army's presence was on schedule to be reduced over two years to that required 'in any peaceful society', the Joint Declaration proposed to create an independent monitoring body to oversee both processes. This idea was originally canvassed by the Alliance Party in 2002 to address the fact that it was not in the political interests of the Northern Ireland Secretary to admit that paramilitary activity was continuing. However, during the process of putting the required legislation together, this ceasefire-monitor proposal was extended to include within its remit whether the parties were fulfilling their obligations under the terms of the Agreement. So, while the body would enable unionists to complain about alleged republican infractions, it would also enable republicans to respond to unionist reluctance to share power with them.

This body, the International Monitoring Commission (IMC), was duly legislated for at Westminster, with at the time of writing ratification awaited in the Dáil.[16] The four-member IMC held its first meeting (in shadow form) in Belfast on 12 October 2003. Its members, nominated by their respective governments but thereafter wholly independent, reflect the key stakeholders to the wider process: Lord Alderdice (Northern Ireland), John Grieve (Britain), Joe Brosnan (Republic of Ireland) and Richard Kerr (USA), although only the two UK members will examine whether and how any future devolved Ministers and the Northern Ireland parties are honouring their commitments under the terms of the Agreement.[17]

While a consolation for the UUP leadership, the establishment of the IMC was and continues to be resisted by SF as outwith the terms of the 1998 Agreement — although, more accurately, it reflects the failure of the Agreement to generate the necessary solid political centre that can hold on the basis of mutual trust and so obviate reliance on external supervision and sanction.[18] For SF, as the only party in the Executive with direct paramilitary links, any prospect of sanctions being imposed upon it, whether a mere fine or exclusion from government, offended two of its operating principles: first, that it should not be held accountable for the actions of the IRA and, second, that it had a legitimate right to serve those whom its MLAs were elected to represent.[19] However, the rather generous proposals to deal with the 'on the runs' were a quid pro quo for the IMC, and thereby provoked the ire of many unionist politicians as well as offending surviving victims of

[16] The Northern Ireland (Monitoring Commission etc) Act 2003 received Royal Assent on 18 September.

[17] As usual, the EU, despite its financial commitment to Northern Ireland via the 'PEACE' programmes, was ignored.

[18] This reliance on external actors has led one former devolved Minister to characterise Northern Ireland's politicians, himself included, as among the most 'indulged' in the world.

[19] The fact that authority to impose sanctions was vested, ultimately, in the Secretary of State also offended republicans because it was further proof positive of British sovereignty.

republican violence and the families of those maimed or killed. More broadly, the declaration was perceived by many unionists, including within the UUP, as further evidence of the 'appeasement' of republicans. The inclusion of a nominee of the Republic's government on the proposed IMC, the perceived threat to the home battalions of the Royal Irish Regiment occasioned by the proposed run-down of the Army's presence, and the prospect — no matter how remote — of an SF Minister to preside over the proposed devolved department of policing and criminal justice were all anathema.

The leading voice within the UUP opposing the declaration was Jeffrey Donaldson, who claimed it was 'a non-starter'. Amid speculation stoked by the Lagan Valley MP that he would leave the party, the UUP was thrown into disarray and yet another attempt to oust Mr Trimble ensued. It was, however, again to fail. At a meeting of the ruling Ulster Unionist Council (UUC) in June, the UUP leader secured a 54 to 46 per cent victory over his opponents, prompting Mr Donaldson and two fellow MPs, Martin Smyth and David Burnside, to resign the whip at Westminster, effectively halving the party's presence in the Commons.

An abortive attempt to expel the three from the party followed, succeeded by a further meeting of the council in September at which members voted in favour of Mr Trimble's motion (55 to 45 per cent) calling for the three rebels to retake the parliamentary whip, an offer they refused. Despite the subsequent unanimous adoption of a resolution by the party's Executive which concluded that 'the Joint Declaration does not provide a satisfactory basis for progress', the three MPs chose to remain outside the party fold. [20] Their decision was prompted by Mr Trimble's insistence that the party had not, as the rebels sought to claim, 'rejected' the declaration.

The UUP's continuing internecine strife thus conjures up an unsettling prospect for the party. Had a deal been struck on 21 October 2003, Mr Trimble's hand would have been strengthened vis-à-vis his internal critics. After that however, the party stands on the brink of a bruising defeat at the hands of the DUP and his position could become untenable. Though to date Mr Trimble has successfully fought off serial attempts on his position as party leader, he thus enters the election at some real risk. Even if the UUP maintains its position as the larger of the two major unionist parties its relative strength is likely to be weakened, and the composition of the party bloc within the (virtual) Assembly is likely to include Messrs Donaldson and Burnside, making its management a much more problematic enterprise than has previously been the case.

Given that London, Dublin, Washington and at least parts of the political class in Belfast remain wedded to the Agreement, much now turns on the acceptability or otherwise of the Joint Declaration. Thus, plotting the pursuit

---

[20] *UUP press release*, 6 October 2003.

of stability means that one has now to understand not just the 1998 Agreement but also the declaration. Of course, the DUP and the smaller, flanking anti-agreement unionist parties are equally opposed to both, believing that nothing short of a new agreement acceptable to nationalists and unionists alike will realise the goal of a stable, democratic model of governance. Though this alternative is as yet unstated, the likelihood is that it will resemble an inflated form of local authority governance in which committee chairs, allocated via d'Hondt, would govern without an over-arching Executive — the model which Mr Trimble had initially adopted in 1997 during the talks that led eventually to the 1998 Agreement. This would generate joint-less rather than joined-up 'government'; it would be an administration akin to an archipelago with little to connect its constituent islands. Though this would appeal to some, even many unionists, it would be rejected utterly by nationalists — as it was by their representatives when first mooted.

The latest, failed episode in the pursuit of régime and political stability has by no means been restricted to players drawn from what some term 'the British Isles'. Direct American involvement in the painstaking efforts to create, sustain and renew devolution has been a particular feature of the past five years, and the past 12 months have been no exception. On 7 April 2003 the US President, George W Bush, flew into Northern Ireland for an overnight visit accompanied by, among others, Richard Haass, his envoy to the region. While Messrs Bush and Blair were preoccupied with two major items, the war in Iraq and the 'road map' for peace in the middle east, they, together with the Taoiseach who paid a flying visit to Hillsborough on 8 April, took the opportunity to reaffirm their shared commitment to the Agreement and its complete implementation.[21]

The intense secret diplomacy involving London, Dublin, Washington, the UUP, SF and the IRA continued throughout April but to no immediate effect. On 1 May Mr Blair postponed the election 'until the autumn' and he and Mr Ahern took the decision to publish the Joint Declaration so that the wider public could have a clear understanding of the measures each government — particularly London — proposed to take to implement the Agreement in full.[22] There was, in short, a literal war of words under way.[23]

---

[21] The text of the joint statement is available at www.nio.gov.uk/press/030408a.htm.

[22] The two governments had intended to publish the Joint Declaration on 10 April, two days after Mr Bush's departure. The initial postponement signalled the extent of continuing difficulties caused by a lack of clarity on the part of the IRA about its intentions. In a joint statement issued by the two premiers, the operative cause of the problem was said to be that this opacity was failing to provide 'the necessary confidence which is the life-blood of the process'. See Joint statement, *BBC News Online*, 10 April 2003.

[23] It emerged later that on 13 April the IRA had conveyed its secret response to the Joint Declaration to London, Dublin and Washington, but that response failed to convince the three governments. The failure of subsequent efforts to achieve clarity on the part of the IRA led a frustrated Mr Blair to hold a press conference at which he spelled out three questions to which its answers had been unclear and

In the event, the election campaign did get started on 29 April, only to be halted by Mr Blair two days later. The ensuing months culminated in intense efforts during September and through October to enable an election to government to take place in November. The Joint Declaration and the IRA's written response issued in early May, together with a supplementary state-ment issued alongside it, were to hand and provided the bases for the negoti-ations. [24] Mr Haass returned to Belfast in mid-October for his third visit of the year to assist with the talks and General de Chastelain arrived back in the region on 14 October 2003, prompting well-founded speculation that the IRA was about to embark on a further round of putting arms 'beyond use'.

Readers can be forgiven if, having followed this tumult of events, they experience a sense of déjà-vu. Trilateral crisis management in both pre- and post-devolution Northern Ireland has become a chronic condition of its political (half-)life, characterised since 1998 by perpetual negotiation, and renegotiation, of the devolution arrangement. Throughout, the sticking point has been and remains the decommissioning of weapons, primarily those in the IRA's arsenal since it alone has a direct link to a party of government. For those with a slightly longer memory the sense of déjà-vu will be more acutely felt. A decade ago, in an earlier 'Joint Declaration', the then London and Dublin premiers called for 'a permanent end to the use of, or support for, paramilitary violence', if SF was to be accepted as a legitimate player in the democratic process.[25]

Familiar though such phrases, objectives and aspirations are, the adminis-trative landscape has been transformed over the past five years, as have many personal relationships. One of the more positive features of the recent efforts to strike a new political bargain over the terms of the Agreement and the declaration was a series of face-to-face meetings between Mr Trimble and Mr Adams between late September and early-mid October 2003. Though not entirely new, their frequency was significant, as was the fact that they were bilaterally engaged rather than appealing over one another's heads to their respective political patrons.

There was, though, a negative dimension to this aspect of the new relation-ship. The talks excluded all the other key players, including the other

unambiguous. In order, they were: 'When the IRA say that their strategies and disciplines will not be inconsistent with the Good Friday Agreement, does that mean an end to all activities inconsistent with the Good Friday Agreement, including targeting, procurement of weapons, so-called punishment beatings and so forth? Secondly, when they say they are committed to putting arms beyond use through the Decommissioning Commission, does that mean all arms so the process is complete? And, thirdly, when they say that they support the Good Friday Agreement and want it to work, does that mean that if the two Governments and the other parties fulfil their obligations under the Good Friday Agreement and the Joint Declaration, that that means the complete and final closure of the conflict?' *Downing Street press release*, 23 April 2003.

[24] See *BBC News Online*, 6 May 2003, for the IRA statements.

[25] The text of the 1993 declaration can be found at http://cain.ulst.ac.uk/events/peace/docs/dsd151293.htm.

pro-agreement parties: the SDLP, Alliance, Progressive Unionists and Women's Coalition functioned to all intents and purposes as spear carriers in the political drama. To that extent, while it can be argued that such bilateralism was an exercise of *Realpolitik*, it nevertheless jarred against the inclusivity that the Agreement is founded upon. Such inclusiveness will be a necessary condition of the review of the Agreement and, more to the point, the efforts actually to restore stable devolved government if and when the opportunity arises.

One lesson that has emerged from the experience of devolution in Northern Ireland is the abiding truth of the conclusion drawn in the magisterial survey of the literature on the conflict by the late John Whyte — that the Northern Ireland problem is essentially 'internal'. Ironically, nationalists and unionists traditionally shared the same 'paradigm' — that what mattered was the region's external relationships. On the contrary, Whyte argued:

> [T]he crucial conflict is between the communities in Northern Ireland. Though this conflict is influenced by the relations which Northern Ireland has with Britain on the one hand and the Republic on the other, those relations are not the heart of it. There would still be tensions between the two communities no matter what wider framework was adopted for the region.[26]

Whyte contended that this paradigm had become dominant over the preceding two decades of the 'troubles', and his thesis finds powerful confirmation in the fate of intergovernmental relations since the Agreement. The recurrent tensions associated with devolution have, for the most part, not had utterly deleterious spill-over effects on the north-south, intra-UK, or London-Dublin axes. Apart from the period when the First Minister — illegally, according to a judicial review — suspended participation by SF Ministers in the North/South Ministerial Council (NSMC) in 2000–01, intergovernmental relations have been insulated from what Churchill famously called the 'integrity' of the Ulster 'quarrel'. Even after the suspension in October 2002, the two governments were at pains to ensure, via a new treaty, that the six north-south 'implementation bodies' would remain in operation, albeit on a care-and-maintenance basis.[27] The bodies, in terms of political supervision, had in effect been moved on to an 'east-west' axis. Whatever the fate of the devolved aspect of the Agreement, the north-south dimension is not going to go away. If nothing else, the pull of pragmatic co-operation will ensure that this is so.

---

[26] Whyte, J.H., *Interpreting Northern Ireland* (Oxford: Clarendon Press, 1990), p. 258.

[27] The British-Irish Agreement (Amendment) Bill implementing the new Anglo-Irish treaty came into effect on 27 November 2002. See *Devolution and Northern Ireland Monitoring Report February 2003* (London: The Constitution Unit), p. 23.

Figure 4.1: Chronology of Events 2002–2003

2002	
30 October	The IRA ends its contact with the IICD. Army Council member Martin McGuinness, speaking in a BBC documentary, states 'my war is over. My job as a political leader is to prevent war.'
4 November	The Lord Mayor of Belfast, Alec Maskey (SF), hosts a civic reception for the Royal British Legion.
7 November	A civil servant with access to David Trimble's Stormont office is arrested in connection with allegations of an IRA spy ring.
27 November	A new Anglo-Irish treaty enabling the north-south bodies to continue on a 'care and maintenance' basis comes into effect.
13 December	Mr Trimble walks out of multi-party talks at Stormont following the discovery there of an Irish Government document saying that the IRA was still active.
2003	
5 January	Jeffrey Donaldson says the Protestant community 'has lost all confidence in the process . . . The only way this will work is if the republican movement disbands.' The SDLP leader, Mark Durkan, attacks the UUP and SF — for engaging in 'the same old blame game'.
9 January	The IRA says the peace process is under threat from 'the British military establishment, its intelligence agencies and loyalist murder gangs'.
10 January	The Northern Ireland Secretary, Paul Murphy, revokes Johnny Adair's licence and the loyalist paramilitary is returned to prison.
14 January	Sir Edward Heath appears before the 'Bloody Sunday' inquiry.
17 January	The UVF and Red Hand Commando break contact with the IICD and David Ervine (PUP) ends contact with SF, saying he does not know the intentions of the IRA towards his community.
22 January	Growing evidence emerges of a loyalist feud in Belfast.
24 January	Gerry Adams says in a BBC interview that if the UK Government is 'serious about its obligation [to implement the Agreement in full] then it puts a huge onus on republicans to be imaginative'.

25 January	The SF President adds 'when I say the IRA is not the cause of the crisis, this is not to suggest that IRA activities do not cause political difficulties in the unionist constituency. They do, of course; and, regardless of whether they are real or unfounded, Irish republicans know that.'
30 January	The UUP and PUP boycott multi-party talks at Stormont to discuss equality and human-rights issues.
1/2 February	Two leading loyalists, John Gregg of the UDA and Robert Carson, are murdered in Belfast, signifying increasing tension among loyalist paramilitaries. Supporters of Johnny Adair are blamed. The Red Hand Commando admits killing Mr Gregg.
6 February	Supporters of Mr Adair, his family and friends flee Northern Ireland after a warning from the UDA leadership.
22 February	The UDA announces a 12-month ceasefire and says only the Ulster Political Research Group has authority to issue statements on its behalf.
3/5 March	Bertie Ahern and Tony Blair host talks at Hillsborough with the pro-Agreement parties. Mr Blair announces that the election scheduled for 1 May has been put back four weeks because no breakthrough has been achieved.
10 March	Mr Trimble says republicans can save the process by stating that the 'war' is over, engaging in visible decommissioning and ending all paramilitary activities.
29 March	Mr Adams says he can envisage a situation where SF joins the Policing Board.
7 April	George Bush arrives in Northern Ireland for the 'war-peace summit' and talks designed to hasten a deal enabling the election to proceed.
8 April	Together with Messrs Blair and Ahern, Mr Bush issues a statement reaffirming shared commitment to the Agreement and insisting there must be an end to paramilitarism.
10 April	Messrs Blair and Ahern postpone publication of the Anglo-Irish Joint Declaration following the breakdown of talks.
14 April	The UK and Irish governments seek clarification of a secret IRA statement.
15 April	The IRA says it has clarified the statement.

23 April	Mr Blair publicly poses three questions to the IRA to which there must be clear and unambiguous answers
27 April	Mr Adams says the IRA's statement is of 'completely peaceful intent' and if the parties and the governments 'fulfil their commitments . . . this will provide the basis for the complete and final closure of the conflict'.
29 April	The Assembly election campaign begins.
1 May	Mr Blair postpones the election 'until the autumn' because of a lack of clarity over the IRA's position. The two governments publish the Joint Declaration.
6 May	The IRA publishes its secret paper of 13 April and an accompanying statement on its view of the peace process.
11 May	Newspapers publish the identity of the alleged British agent 'Stakeknife', naming him as Freddie Scappaticci. Mr Scappaticci denies the allegation and launches a legal attempt to force the UK Government to say that he is not the agent.
21 May	The inaugural meeting of Omagh's District Policing Partnership is abandoned following protests by republicans who drown out the proceedings.
25 May	Mr Adams says republicans 'need to approach northern Protestants in the language of invitation ... Sinn Féin's engagement with the unionist community is a sincere effort to listen to and understand unionist concerns.'
27 May	Mr Trimble says the IRA should spend the summer preparing for its acts of completion, thereby enabling devolution to be restored in the autumn.
6 June	The body of Alan McCullough, another victim of the loyalist feud, is found by police. The UDA says it carried out the killing, linking it to the earlier murder of Mr Gregg.
17 June	Mr Trimble wins the backing of the UUC for the proposals from London and Dublin to break the political impasse. Three UUP MPs, Jeffrey Donaldson, David Burnside and Martin Smyth, resign the whip.
27 June	Messrs Donaldson, Burnside and Smyth are suspended from the UUP.
12 July	The annual Orange Order marches pass off peacefully.

7 August	Michael McKevitt is convicted in Dublin of directing terrorism as leader of the Real IRA and is sentenced to 20 years.
8 August	The UK Government provides £800,000 to enable the relatives of the Omagh bombing to pursue a private prosecution against those they believe were responsible for the 1998 atrocity.
26 August	Remains, believed to be those of Jean McConville, murdered by the IRA in 1972, are unearthed at a beach near Carlingford, Co Louth.
4 September	The names of the members of the International Monitoring Commission (IMC) are released: Lord Alderdice, John Grieve, Joe Brosnan and Richard Kerr.
6 September	Mr Trimble wins another UUC vote, inviting the three rebel MPs to retake the party whip. The three reject the offer.
15 September	Mr Trimble meets Mr Ahern in Dublin. Mr Murphy says the IMC can restore confidence among the parties.
16 September	Tom Constantine, the Policing Oversight Commissioner, says deaths threats issued by dissident republicans against members of the district policing partnerships and Policing Board are a major threat. Two DPP members resign following intimidation.
18 September	UK legislation establishing the IMC completes its Parliamentary passage.
14 October	Richard Haass, Mr Bush's Northern Ireland envoy, returns to Belfast, as does John de Chastelain, head of the IICD.
18 October	Mr Trimble tells his party's annual conference that republicans must demonstrate a commitment to ending paramilitarism for good. Mr Donaldson boycotts the speech.
21 October	The UK Government announces that the Assembly election will take place on 26 November. At Hillsborough Castle the key players assemble to unfold what Downing Street calls Northern Ireland's 'most historic day' since Good Friday 1998. The choreographed sequence of events paving the way to the restoration of devolution, which includes statements from Mr Adams and the IRA, falls apart following Mr Trimble's reaction to the lack of detail and transparency in General de Chastelain's statement on a third act of IRA decommissioning.
22 October	Mr Murphy announces in the Commons that the order has been made for the election to occur on 26 November
23 October	Talks resume to rescue a deal before the election.

27 October	Mr Trimble confirms that the renewed talks have failed to resolve the impasse. It is clear that the election will be 'to process' rather than to government.
4 November	Nominations of candidates for the election close, revealing a total of 256 candidates for the 108 seats.
4 November	Mr McGuinness appears for the first of two days of testimony at the Bloody Sunday inquiry in Derry. During questions he confirms that he was the IRA's second-in-command in the city at the time and became commander two weeks later.

POLICY INNOVATION

It was made apparent by Mr Murphy, and his immediate predecessor, that the period of direct rule would not see the incumbents at Stormont Castle simply twiddling their collective thumbs. In a statement to the Commons on 15 October 2002, Dr Reid set the tone that characterised the NIO's approach over the succeeding 12 months:

> [W]e will carry on the process of government in Northern Ireland proactively . . .
> this cannot be a matter of mere care and maintenance. We owe it to the people of
> Northern Ireland that effective government should be moved forward. We will
> not duck the difficult issues.[28]

Whilst the energies of key players in Belfast, Dublin, London and Washington have been directed towards restoring devolution, the survey period has been one of active rather than passive direct rule. A key example, discussed in more detail below, is the crunch issue of 'community relations'.

Another, more conventional, political concern — the rationalisation of acute hospitals — provides a revealing insight into the dysfunctional character of Northern Ireland's political system, including its parties and its devolved arrangements, when confronting the challenges of modern regional governance. No politician likes telling constituents that the optimal array of hospital services may not mean that the one around the corner has to be able to perform every surgical function (witness the success of the Kidderminster hospital campaigner in the 2001 UK general election), but Northern Ireland faces some particular difficulties in this regard.

The combination of a generation of direct rule before devolution and Northern Ireland's self-contained, sectarian politics, lubricated by significant public expenditure largesse from London — throwing money at the problem — resulted in an entrenched political culture based on clientelism and oppositionalism. As Scott Greer has observed, 'the structure of devolved

[28] Text available at www.nio.gov.uk/press/proct02.htm 15 October 2002.

government' under the Agreement, notably the allocation of ministries via the d'Hondt rule, was 'designed to induce parties to take office rather than to produce responsibility for policy'.[29] A context less conducive to the making of 'hard choices' would be hard to imagine. And the impoverished political debate during devolution about finance — the rates review, water charges, the Barnett formula and public-private partnerships — has borne this out.[30]

Northern Ireland has a significantly higher number of hospitals with acute functions per head than the rest of the UK. All logic pointed to a rationalisation that would guarantee higher-quality, specialist expertise at fewer sites. This was the conclusion drawn by an official report by the old Department of Health and Social Services (DHSSNI), written before devolution in apocalyptic tone and describing a system in a very acute crisis.[31] However, a source close to the direct-rule health Minister at the time, George Howarth, indicated that such decisions would be left for the in-tray of the devolved administration, when it was established.

The party manifestoes for the 1998 Assembly elections showed that only the small centre parties had anything significant to say on health: Alliance's manifesto displayed a close understanding of the issues, while the Women's Coalition proposed a radical restructuring of the department. Of the main ethno-nationalist parties, the DUP managed just two sentences on health.

After the election, Assembly members were offered by the NIO a crash course in the governance of Northern Ireland, grandiloquently styled the 'Transitions Programme'. A series of seminars, some very poorly attended, covered the various departmental responsibilities, including two on health. One senior official involved described participants as 'a blank sheet' except on local issues, when 'one by one these angry men got up to criticise civil servants for closing their hospitals'.

In the absence of a more considered debate about the potential of health policy to improve health outcomes, the Minister allocated what was deemed to be a 'poisoned chalice' was, it transpired, Bairbre de Brún of SF, though as likely as not a minister of another of the four main parties would have behaved similarly. Ms de Brún commissioned a fresh review, under the former departmental permanent secretary Maurice Hayes who unsurprisingly was driven to similar conclusions to those in the 1998 report, complete with the same urgency of tone, when his review was published in 2001.[32] The Minister thereafter embarked on a prolonged public consultation

[29] Greer, S., 'Policy Divergence: Will it Change Something in Greenock?', in Hazell, R., (ed.) *The State of the Nations 2003: The Third Year of Devolution in the United Kingdom* (Exeter: Imprint Academic, 2003), pp. 202–203.

[30] Wilford and Wilson, 2003a, pp. 104–106.

[31] Department of Health and Social Services, *Putting it Right: The Case for Change in Northern Ireland's Health Service* (Belfast: DHSS, 1998).

[32] Acute Hospitals Review Group, *Report, June 2001* (Belfast: DHSSPS, 2001).

on Hayes and published a departmental paper deriving from that consultation — yes, this was for further consultation — a year later.[33] A regional
strategy incorporating the proposal, was promised for sometime in 2003.
Meantime, even the Leninist party discipline of SF proved vulnerable to
old-fashioned Irish clientelism. Two SF MPs who won their seats in 2001,
Pat Doherty in Mid-Ulster and Michelle Gildernew in Fermanagh and South
Tyrone, also wearing MLA hats, lined up behind respective local hospital
campaigns in a battle over where the one new facility proposed by Hayes for
the west of the region should be sited. That was a *very* hard choice for which
the Minister showed no obvious enthusiasm.

Suspension took matters from her hands. Despite having year on year
extracted big budget increases from her ministerial colleague (from the rival
SDLP) at the Finance and Personnel Department, she bequeathed an unre-
formed system marked by the longest waiting lists in the UK — even, the
BBC Northern Ireland health correspondent claimed, the longest in western
Europe. The British Medical Association (BMA) bemoaned 'a total lack of
decision-making within the healthcare system', a phrase echoed in an
unprecedented joint UUP-SDLP amendment in a debate at Stormont on
waiting lists the month before suspension.[34]

The anxiety of official tone soon returned and in February 2003 the then
direct-rule Minister, Des Browne, in line with both the 1998 document and
the Hayes review, announced the anticipated rationalisation of acute functions, to be concentrated at nine hospitals rather than 15 and with a new facility, as Hayes had recommended, in Fermanagh. Mr Browne said everyone
had pressed on him the 'urgent need to end further deliberation'.[35] While
party-political reaction reflected parish-pump concerns, the BMA welcomed
an end to 'seemingly endless consultations'.[36]

In fairness to Ms de Brún, she did during her tenure oversee the elabora-
tion of a public-health strategy for Northern Ireland, *Investing for Health*.[37]
If she failed to move the argument on to a health, rather than service-focused,
agenda, she was no more at fault than successive (de facto) English health
Ministers under New Labour.

There were genuine policy innovations during the first, and aborted, term
of the Assembly, although they tended to reflect the populism of a politics
attenuated by ethno-nationalism. A 'Children's Commissioner' was
appointed in 2003 (an idea imported from Wales) to act as an advocate for

[33] Department of Health, Social Services and Public Safety, *Developing Better Services:
Modernising Hospitals and Reforming Structures* (Belfast: DHSSPS, 2002).

[34] *Irish News*, 6 and 18 September 2002.

[35] Department of Health, Social Services and Public Safety, *'Developing Better Services
Ministerial announcement'*, 24 February 2003.

[36] *Belfast Telegraph*, 25 February 2003.

[37] Department of Health, Social Services and Public Safety, *Investing for Health* (Belfast:
DHSSPS, 2002).

the rights of children and young people.[38] School 'league tables' were abolished (a measure exported to Wales) — though this means educationalists have no output data by individual schools to assess their 'value added' in relation to their catchment area.[39] Free 'nursing' care (but, unlike in Scotland, not free 'personal' care) for the elderly was confirmed, while (as in the Republic of Ireland) free travel for senior citizens were introduced on public transport, although recent evidence indicates that elderly people are more likely to be excluded by lack of access than by cost.[40]

An interesting exception to this trend was the more progressive (in the sense of needs- and ability-to-pay-based) régime on student finance established by the then SDLP Minister for Employment and Learning, Séan Farren. Dr Farren avoided the temptation of 'no fees' grandstanding, in the context of a finite budget and the absence of tax-raising powers, appreciating that within these constraints the latter would have actually sustained subsidies to the middle class. His efforts were not, however, endorsed by the Assembly committee monitoring his department and it was ironically only as a result of the Executive domination of Northern Ireland's top-heavy devolved system that he was able to get his way.

A bad political taste was left by the decision of the outgoing education Minister, Martin McGuinness of SF, to announce on the eve of suspension that the discredited '11+' examination would no longer be held beyond 2004. While the substance of his action was unchallengeable (although there was strong resistance from Northern Ireland's powerful, mainly Protestant, grammar-school lobby), he had no alternative to put in its place. While cocking a snook at his Executive colleagues from rival parties he left the direct-rule Minister, Jane Kennedy, with a hot potato.[41] Ms Kennedy might have hoped it would cool but in April 2003 the *Belfast Telegraph* led with a report that no work had been done on an alternative arrangement and that teachers were predicting 'classroom chaos'.[42] Amid evident alarm among the parents of primary-school children, Ms Kennedy passed the issue on to a 'working group' comprised of individuals drawn from across the education sector, which was due to report by the end of October 2003.

[38] This had been debated by the Assembly but was enacted by a UK order-in-council after suspension: see The Commissioner for Children and Young People (Northern Ireland) Order 2003, SI 2003 No. 439 (N.I. 11).

[39] Thus, for example, it is impossible to assess the current performance of integrated schools as against their segregated counterparts — an important dimension of the policy debate on the issue.

[40] Hillyard, P., Kelly, G., McLaughlin, E., Patsios, D., and Tomlinson, M., *Bare Necessities: Poverty and Social Exclusion in Northern Ireland — key findings* (Belfast: Democratic Dialogue, 2003), p. 58. The decision was not without controversy. Unveiled by the then Minister for Regional Development, Gregory Campbell, he claimed the policy as his party's (DUP) own, whereas the other Executive parties registered it as a collective decision. Thus, a squabble over policy paternity erupted among the Ministers, underlining the absence of collegiality within the administration.

[41] Wilford and Wilson, 2003a, pp. 98–99.

[42] '11–PLUS FEARS: schools braced for classroom chaos', *Belfast Telegraph*, 18 April 2003.

Inevitably, the group sought and secured an extension. It was claimed by a source close to it that the grammar schools were blocking the widely-canvassed alternative, promoted by Northern Ireland's official educational advisory body, the Council on the Curriculum, Examinations and Assessment, of common schooling to 14 with individual choice from a broad curriculum thereafter. The source warned that 'it now looks like we are going to end up with the status quo, or worse'.[43] Ironically, the 'emerging consensus' — including some cross-community support — Mr McGuinness had (rightly) detected around the 14+ option has been stymied by the fresh polarisation occasioned by his pre-suspension exercise of political pique.

ACCOUNTABILITY

Before devolution, a perennial complaint by politicians of all hues, not least unionists, was that the direct-rule régime was largely unaccountable to the people of Northern Ireland. While time and space were created on the Westminster agenda to address law and policy within the region, the opportunities afforded to discuss its 'low' politics were severely limited. This was especially apparent in relation to the legislative process, whereby the bulk of business was dealt with by blunt order-in-council procedures.

To the extent that Northern Ireland featured at Westminster it was invariably in relation to two 'high' politics matters: its constitutional status and 'security'. Their predominance skewed the perception of the region, inducing at least weariness and at worst alienation, especially in the wake of atrocities perpetrated by the IRA and other republican paramilitaries in Britain.

Ritualised debate about these issues also generated a habit of oppositionalism among the region's MPs. Unionist MPs were fearful that perfidious Albion would 'betray Ulster', a mood particularly apparent after the 1985 Anglo-Irish Agreement, while after 1979 the SDLP's representatives set their faces resolutely against any initiative that did not accommodate the 'Irish dimension'. Drawn inexorably to the high ground of politics, Northern Ireland's MPs largely ignored the more mundane, 'bread-and-butter' nature of politics, preferring to remain alert to any hint of betrayal — either, as far as unionists were concerned, among themselves or, whether unionist or nationalist, on the part of the UK Government.

During the Major years there was something of an improvement in the procedures to scrutinise Northern Ireland matters, namely the creation of a Northern Ireland Affairs Select Committee, a full 15 years after its Scottish and Welsh equivalents.[44] The performance of the select committee was,

---

[43] '11–plus could stay in place until 2010', *Belfast Telegraph*, 3 October 2003.

[44] On the circumstances surrounding the committee's creation see Wilford, R., and Elliott, S., 'The Northern Ireland Affairs Select Committee', *Irish Political Studies*, 10, pp. 216–224, (1995).

however, less than inspiring.[45] Along with the Northern Ireland Grand Committee, it laboured on in a largely unremarked way, and the quality of the scrutiny of Northern Ireland's domestic governance left an enormous amount to be desired. For that reason alone, devolution offered the opportunity for a leap in the accountability afforded to regional politicians and the wider population. Yet this promise has been only partially fulfilled.[46] The reasons for such incompleteness are threefold: structure, agency and individual.

The *structural* reason lies in the very consociational architecture of the Agreement. The inclusive nature, though not obligation, of Executive formation, allied to the requirement of all MLAs to designate themselves as 'unionist', 'nationalist' or 'other', has entrenched rather than ameliorated communal identity. Moreover, the fact that all bar 18 of the MLAs elected in 1998 belonged to the four governing parties has reinforced party and communal attachments, a nexus that has been strengthened by the continual travails, and mounting mistrust, that have attended the outworking of devolution. Members, many of whom were suspicious of both inter- and intra-communal rivals from the outset, increasingly exhibited a felt loyalty to 'their' Ministers rather than 'our' Executive that has tended to militate against joint ownership of the self-governing project.

Such a predisposition was accentuated by the attitude and behaviour of the DUP. Its boycott of Executive meetings from the first and its subsequent decision to rotate its Ministers on two occasions has enabled it to operate in a semi-detached manner throughout. This stance placed its MLAs on a war footing in relation to the other Executive parties whilst ensuring the lionisation of their own ministerial incumbents, behaviour that was also evidenced by SF members towards their two Ministers.

In effect, the method of Executive formation (d'Hondt) consolidated the exclusivity of government — a bewildering, but predictable, paradox of the 'inclusive' design of the Agreement, given the divided nature of Northern Ireland's society. Moreover, the provision in the Northern Ireland Act 1998 vesting ministerial responsibility in individual Ministers, rather than in the Executive, gave textual licence to the temptation of Ministers to treat their departments as their own party's property, further strengthening the bonds

[45] For an assessment of the committee during its first term see Wilford, R., and Elliott, S., 'Small earthquake in Chile: the first Northern Ireland Affairs Select Committee', *Irish Political Studies*, 14, pp. 23–42, (1999). The creation of the committee did concentrate the minds of Northern Ireland's civil servants. Though some would have appeared before the Commons Public Accounts Committee, a small number before other select committees and others before the scrutiny committees of the 1982–1986 Northern Ireland Assembly, an impending appearance before the NIASC was viewed with some trepidation by officials. On the 1982–86 Assembly, see O'Leary, C., Elliott, S., and Wilford, R., *The Northern Ireland Assembly 1982–1986: A Constitutional Experiment* (London: Hurst, 1988).

[46] See Wilford, R., and Wilson, R., *A Democratic Design? The Political Style of the Northern Ireland Assembly* (London: The Constitution Unit, 2001).

between each incumbent and his / her party bloc in the Assembly, and thereby constraining the exercise of critical independence among their respective members. Indeed, as the wider political process waned, the need for party solidarity between Ministers and their MLAs waxed, inhibiting the exercise of more muscular overall scrutiny within the legislature.

This situation also allowed governing parties if they so chose (and the DUP and SF did) to have the best of all possible worlds — simultaneously to be both government and opposition. Within the 'British Isles' Northern Ireland is unique in having no formal opposition within its legislature, another check on the quality of scrutiny. Of course, one doesn't have to be a party in opposition to ensure scrutiny and accountability, but the dominance of the Executive parties in the chamber and their consequent in-built majorities on the Assembly's statutory committees was, among other things, an inherent potential obstacle in the path of committee unity and consensus. The party card could always be played to frustrate an agreed, critical report, whether on policy or legislation. This enabled Ministers to exploit such dissensus to their advantage, as Dr Farren did in relation to student finance and Ms de Brún did over maternity provision in Belfast.[47]

The compliance of *individual* MLAs with the dictates of ministerial or communal loyalty thus had a negative impact on the key *agencies* designed to carry out the scrutiny function, the statutory committees. Behaviourally, MLAs belonging to the Executive parties who served on the committees — that is, the majority on all ten of them — were too submissive; they acted primarily as party animals rather than committee creatures.

The committees were also handicapped as key agents of scrutiny because they were overloaded, being something of a hybrid of Westminster's select and standing committees. In addition to the task of scrutinising the policy, administration and expenditure of their associated departments, they also took the committee stage of all Executive Bills. While there were periods of legislative famine in the Assembly, there were also phases of legislative feast, especially in the months leading to the latest suspension. But, whether lean or fat, the legislative load was Executive-driven and the weight of proposed legislation tended to squeeze out the time available to exert scrutiny over other departmental activities, besides leaving little scope — if members were inclined, which in practice they weren't — to table committee bills.

Scrutiny and the holding of Ministers to account was not confined to the activities of the committees, whether statutory or standing. Members had the opportunity of a weekly question time when three Ministers in succession

---

[47] See our last quarterly monitoring reports for the Devolution and Health project funded by the Nuffield Foundation, *Devolution and Health: The Northern Ireland Experience March 2002* (London: The Constitution Unit), available at www.ucl.ac.uk/constitution-unit/files/devolution_and_health/ni_mar_ 2002.pdf.

would each make themselves available for half-an-hour for oral questions — occasions that all too often descended into ritual abuse, especially when SF Ministers came to the despatch box. Members' use of written questions suggests on a preliminary and partial analysis that there was an unhealthy tendency among unionist, especially DUP, members to clog the in-trays of the SF Ministers, Mr McGuinness and Ms de Brún.

For unionist MLAs, certainly those opposed to the Agreement, perhaps the most resented lacunae in Executive accountability related to 'strand two', the north-south dimension. The periodic appearance in the Assembly of Ministers — the DUP excepted — to make a statement on the activities of the relevant north-south body was greeted by anti-Agreement parties with disdain. More generally, the time-limited, set-piece nature of these statements curtailed the extent to which the actions of the six cross-border 'implementation bodies' and the further six areas of policy co-operation could be held properly to account.[48]

This lack of scrutiny also extended to the Office of the First Minister and Deputy First Minister (OFMDFM). Early in the life of the Assembly, members voted to create two standing committees respectively to scrutinise the European affairs and the equality, human rights and community relations dimensions of the office, and were on the verge of voting for a third to examine all its remaining functions (26 in total).[49] However, the then First and Deputy First Ministers, Messrs Trimble and Mallon, brought forward their own proposal to create a single, but not all-purpose committee, the 'committee of the centre', to scrutinise some of its responsibilities. This motion succeeded on a whipped vote of all SDLP and UUP members and meant that the 'external' activities of the office, including relations with the Republic of Ireland, Britain and the wider world, were dealt with by way of statements to the Assembly by the First and Deputy First Ministers or their two junior Ministers (one UUP, the other SDLP).

The Committee of the Centre, which at 17-strong is a highly unwieldy creation, struggled to come to terms with its remit. With the DUP's Gregory Campbell initially in the chair, it failed to operate at all because Mr Campbell refused to acknowledge the presence, let alone the legitimacy, of its SF members. Even under the more enlightened chairmanship of Edwin Poots (also DUP), it cannot be said to have unduly exercised OFMDFM's Ministers.

The performance of the scrutiny function, and thereby the level and quality of Ministerial and Executive accountability, has also been hindered by

---

[48] Both set out in the *Report from the First Minister (Designate) and Deputy First Minister (Designate)*, New Northern Ireland Assembly report NNIA 7, of 15 February 1999, following post-agreement negotiations between Messrs Trimble and Mallon on the structure of departments in Northern Ireland and the detail of the north-south architecture.

[49] *Ibid.*

the character of many MLAs. On the face of it, the pool of talent available to the parties in selecting prospective members seems shallow. There are, of course, exceptions but, by and large, the calibre of members does not command overwhelming confidence. In part, this is because the 30 years of 'troubles' that preceded devolution acted as a deterrent to many who might otherwise have contemplated a political career. Also, the habit of oppositionalism was not a sound preparation for prospective legislators and policy makers.

In addition to the 'democratic deficit' caused by a generation of direct rule, this also created a 'policy deficit'.[50] The parties were simply not accustomed to constructive thinking about day-and-daily political issues. The only tier of government that functioned continuously pre-devolution was the policy-impoverished sphere of local government, and this was where the Assembly parties found the majority of all MLAs.[51] Of the 108 members elected in 1998, 60 were serving councillors who brought with them relative inexperience, old (and, in some cases, sectarian) habits and, of course, a dual mandate.

The latter has been a particular operational problem. It was not uncommon for Assembly committees to be left inquorate as councillors deserted Parliament Buildings to attend council sub-committees elsewhere. The extent of 'double-jobbing' on the part of most MLAs is not a feature of their counterparts in the Scottish Parliament or the Welsh Assembly, even if a number of MSPs and AMs did cut their political teeth in local government. Given a period of sustained, stable government, Northern Ireland would do well to emulate the models provided by its legislative cousins, no matter how distant, and end the dual mandate norm among its MLAs. Abandoning other, competing representative roles — whether councillor, MP or MEP — would signal investment in, and commitment to, the Assembly, and indicate to the wider community that devolution is being taken seriously by all parties.[52]

On a more positive note, the procedures for scrutinising the Executive's draft budget proposals have been improved over the devolution period. The timetable for the consideration of the proposals and the co-ordination of committee responses to them has become more efficient, due largely to the energy and industry of the Finance and Personnel Committee, chaired by Francie Molloy (SF).

[50] A phrase coined by a former public-health administrator in Northern Ireland, Dr Gabriel Scally, in his submission to an independent international commission on ways forward for the region, Pollak, A., (ed.) *A Citizens' Inquiry: The Opsahl Report on Northern Ireland* (Dublin: Lilliput Press, 1993), p. 319.

[51] A 1969–70 review and the pressures of the civil-rights movement led to the removal of all but the most modest of functions from local government, restructured in 1973 as a single tier of 26 district councils.

[52] In addition 60 outgoing MLAs being councillors, 12 were MPs, one was an MEP and two were peers.

As suspension loomed, there had been growing evidence of 'joined-up' scrutiny on the part of the statutory committees and, for the most part, working relations within them had become more businesslike. One standing committee, Standards and Privileges Committee, had tabled a Bill prior to the October 2002 suspension and, for only the second time in the life of the Assembly, a private member's Bill had also been tabled.[53] But, as they were beginning to find their feet, devolution once again stumbled.

Nevertheless, evidence of a developing committee 'system' had grown over the devolved period and the statutory committees in particular were beginning experiments to improve the efficiency of conducting their business, notably by 'conferencing' as an alternative to the routine of taking evidence with single or small numbers of witnesses at oral sessions in Parliament Buildings.[54] Some committees have held joint evidence-taking sessions and an informal liaison committee of committee chairs was established to provide a forum within which matters of common concern could be discussed.[55] However, as yet, there seems to be insufficient inter-party trust to enable the adoption of rapporteurs as evidence-gatherers, as an alternative to oral hearings involving whole committees.

COMMUNITY RELATIONS

In the preamble to the Belfast Agreement, the parties declared: 'We acknowledge the substantial differences between our continuing, and equally legitimate, political aspirations.'[56] By legitimating 'nationalism' and 'unionism' — mutually exclusive political philosophies marked by a desire to treat the Agreement *not* as a settlement but as a staging post to a united

---

[53] The committee Bill (NIA 25/01) was to create the office of the Assembly Commissioner for Standards following the committee's report of April 2002. The committee's view, endorsed by the Assembly, was to graft the functions of the Commissioner on to the existing remit of the Office of the Ombudsman for Northern Ireland. The primary function of the Commissioner will be to investigate complaints against MLAs and to submit any report to the committee on standards and privileges. The second private member's Bill — the first, to create the office of Children's Commissioner, was superseded by an Executive Bill — was the Agriculture Amendment Bill, whose major purpose was to include horses within the definition of agricultural animals. It became dubbed the 'let horses be cows' bill.

[54] In September 2002, the Enterprise, Trade and Investment Committee held two conferences as evidence-gathering exercises to conduct its inquiry into the tourism industry. This experiment was monitored closely by officials in the Assembly's Committee Office, who were well disposed to its wider adoption. Such a *modus operandi* had, in addition to efficiency savings, another attraction: it encouraged committees to hold sessions outside Parliament Buildings where they have tended to be firmly rooted from the first, thereby countering their sedentary character.

[55] Because the liaison committee has no statutory basis, it has been boycotted by the DUP. The parties, including the DUP, in the shape of the whips do routinely attend the standing Business Committee, charged to set the Assembly's agenda for plenary sessions on a weekly basis. Chaired by the Speaker, and with senior Assembly officials in attendance, it has operated as a constructive and efficient means of managing the business of the chamber.

[56] *The Agreement*, p. 1.

Ireland or to be interpreted only in such a fashion as would copper-fasten Northern Ireland's position in the United Kingdom — the Agreement ensured that the nationalist-unionist antagonism would be perpetuated and Northern Ireland would remain a deeply divided society. As a recent assessment concludes, 'the fundamental conflict between the proponents of two competing visions of national belonging is far from over; (some of) the conflict parties have merely agreed on a new framework in which they want to pursue these distinct visions.'[57]

This led to the post-agreement paradox that 'community relations' between Protestants and Catholics were widely perceived subsequently to have steadily deteriorated.[58] This flew in the face of 'a widespread desire', detected in focus groups conducted in 1999, 'to see politicians take a lead in defusing this oppressive atmosphere of partisan belligerence, by adopting more open, constructive, and less emotional terminology and debate'.[59]

The first two iterations of the Programme for Government (PfG) of the devolved administration, however, contained no substantive measures to improve community relations. One official close to the drafting of the PfG dryly suggested that the relevant section, 'Growing as a community', should be renamed 'Withering as a community'. Insofar as the grand coalition of the ethno-nationalist parties faced any opposition in the Assembly, principally from the non-sectarian Alliance Party, it was on the failure of successive programmes to tackle communal division.

The first (March 2001) PfG promised by 2002 to 'review and put in place a cross-departmental strategy for the promotion of community relations, leading to measurable improvements'.[60] The review, due for completion by the end of the year, was promptly delivered to Ministers in mid-January 2002.[61] Yet the commitment felt by its author, the retiring liberal-minded civil servant Jeremy Harbison, was not reflected by his political masters. Indeed, Dr Harbison found it extremely difficult even to get to meet the First Minister, Mr Trimble, to discuss the report. And the Executive did not discuss it before suspension, leaving NIO Ministers frustrated by the parties' inaction.[62]

Direct rule duly saw movement. In January 2003, the relevant Minister, Des Browne, issued a consultation paper, *A Shared Future*, based on the

---

[57] Wolff, S., 'Conclusion: the peace process in Northern Ireland since 1998', in Neuheiser, J., and Wolff, S., (eds.) *Peace at Last? The Impact of the Good Friday Agreement on Northern Ireland* (New York and Oxford: Berghahn Books, 2002), p. 205.

[58] Wilford and Wilson, 2003a, p. 100.

[59] Wilford, R. and Wilson, R., 'A "bare knuckle ride": Northern Ireland', in Hazell, R., (ed.) *The State and the Nations: The First Year of Devolution in the United Kingdom* (Exeter: Imprint Academic, 2001), p. 114.

[60] Northern Ireland Executive, *Making a Difference: Programme for Government 2001–2004* (Belfast: Office of the First Minister and Deputy First Minister, 2001).

[61] Available at www.ofmdfmni.gov.uk/communityrelationsunit/harbisonreport.pdf.

[62] Wilford and Wilson, 2003a, p. 101.

Harbison review.[63] For the first time in any government document it was officially declared that the vision for Northern Ireland had to be based on sharing rather than separation between its two so-called 'communities' — finally echoing a case made by the veteran civil-rights duo of Tom Hadden and Kevin Boyle nearly a decade earlier in an under-appreciated book, *Northern Ireland: The Choice*.[64] It was a choice the Agreement had effectively flunked, in deference to its ethno-nationalist negotiators, yet *A Shared Future* — note the absence of a question-mark, the head of the Community Relations Council (CRC), Duncan Morrow, insisted — highlighted evidence of deep segregation.

The consultation stirred substantial interest within civil society, stimulated in particular by the CRC, a body funded by but independent of government. And Alliance, which had already generated a policy paper on the subject, submitted a substantial and positive response, as did the Women's Coalition.[65] But the main parties were less forthcoming. In particular, the Ulster Unionist Party eventually called for the CRC to be wound up in favour of a board under the aegis of the Office of the First Minister and Deputy First Minister, with a majority of political appointees, and with the focus shifted to the funding of work by district councils.[66] The underlying philosophy was that sectarianism was a localised social problem, rather than an endemically dysfunctional feature of Northern Ireland's political culture.

What would happen to community-relations policy thus depended, as 2003 closed, on what happened to the political institutions. While a return of devolution was devoutly awaited by democrats, the nagging concern among the civic-minded was that it could be associated with renewed inertia in this policy domain.

Such concerns were not assuaged by the behaviour of the ethno-nationalist parties towards the Northern Ireland Human Rights Commission during the survey period. The Commission had already come under attack in 2001 when it published its initial proposals on a bill of rights for Northern Ireland (over and above the European Convention on Human Rights), on which it was mandated to advise by the Belfast Agreement under which it was established.[67] Despite the independence ascribed to the body under the Agreement, and the fact that this policy domain is 'reserved', Esmond Birnie (UUP) felt free to condemn the commission in an Assembly debate — his

[63] Community Relations Unit, *A Shared Future: A Consultation Paper on Improving Community Relations in Northern Ireland* (Belfast: Office of the First Minister and Deputy First Minister, 2003), available at www.asharedfutureni.gov.uk/

[64] Boyle, K., and Hadden, T., *Northern Ireland: The Choice* (London: Penguin Books, 1994).

[65] The Alliance party's available at www.allianceparty.org/showpaper.asp?id=10 .

[66] See www.uup.org/current/displayfullpress.asp?pressid=1144.

[67] See Northern Ireland Human Rights Commission, *Making a Bill of Rights for Northern Ireland: A Consultation by the Northern Ireland Human Rights Commission* (Belfast: NIHRC, 2001) and *The Agreement*, pp. 16–17.

motion passed on a sectarian headcount, opposed by the SDLP and SF — for allegedly over-stepping its remit in proposing an extensive range of measures.[68]

If, at that time, nationalists rose to the defence of the commission in the face of unionist assault, that didn't stop them turning *volte-face* following the resignations of three commission members in 2002 and 2003. While the issues at stake were oblique, the chapter of the 2001 document on 'Rights concerning identity and communities' had provoked division in the Commission, starting as it did from the individualist assumptions of existing international minority-rights standards, such as the 1995 Council of Europe Framework Convention on the Rights of National Minorities. These rights attach to 'persons belonging to' such minorities, not groups as such, and include the right not to wish to be so identified at all.

This civic-pluralist approach, while endorsed by the small centre parties in Northern Ireland, is anathema to the communalist thinking of the SDLP and SF. They were also angered by the handling by the Chief Commissioner, Brice Dickson, of a case arising from the Holy Cross school intimidation affair of 2001, which had also divided the commission. Following the third resignation in July 2003 the nationalist parties clamoured for the head of Professor Dickson who, while accepting criticism on Holy Cross, has indicated every intention of standing his ground.[69] Unspecified radical change to the commission was added to SF's ever-updated wish-list of demands, in its recurrent negotiations with London and Dublin — with no sense of irony, given the IRA has been the single most egregious source of human-rights violations in the last three decades in Northern Ireland. The tables now having been turned, the DUP attacked the nationalist parties for attacking the commission — only to add, in a fashion typical of the region's chronic lack of public political generosity, that nothing it was saying should be interpreted as lending support to the commission.[70]

The greatest irony, however, was that a bill of rights for Northern Ireland had originally been conceived by the civil-rights movement in the 1960s as a means to level the political playing-field after decades of unionist oppression, and so make possible a politics that *transcended* the unionist-nationalist antagonism.[71] The name of today's main 'nationalist' party, the Social Democratic and Labour Party, founded by civil-rights activists in 1970, is a reminder of a more idealistic period before the brutalising violence of subsequent decades took hold — a reminder which the 'war by other means' atmosphere of post-agreement politics might be thought to require.

---

[68] See *Devolution and Northern Ireland Monitoring Report November 2002* (London: The Constitution Unit, 2002), available at www.ucl.ac.uk/constitution-unit/monrep/ni/ninov01.pdf.

[69] 'SF and SDLP criticise rights leader', *Irish Times*, 31 July 2003.

[70] 'DUP slams body's critics but fails to back it', *Irish News*, 1 August 2003.

[71] Professor Hadden is a stalwart of the current commission.

There was some evidence during 2003, however, that community relations on the ground were beginning to improve. The 'marching season' did not witness the bitter clashes of previous summers, notably over the Drumcree Orange Order parade in Portadown, Co Armagh, while the main 12 July march in Belfast was attended by only 2,800 Orangemen.[72] Hard work on the ground by community activists helped contain tensions at interfaces.

The Chief Constable's report showed a welcome downturn in paramilitary violence, when the trend had been steadily returning towards pre-ceasefire incidence — a trend only modestly and temporarily affected by the Agreement (see Figure 4.2).[73]

Figure 4.2: 'Security-Related Incidents' as Logged by the Police

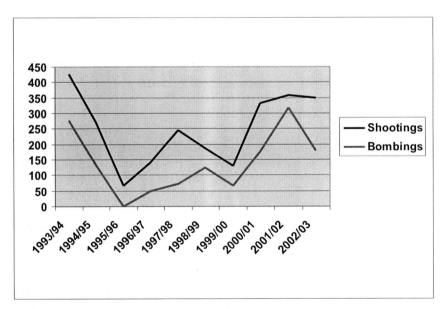

Remarkably similarly, the latest data from the Northern Ireland Life and Times Survey (NILTS) showed the first upturn for years in confidence about community relations, which had been heading downwards to pre-ceasefire levels — again despite a limited post-agreement boost (see Figures 4.3 & 4.4).[74]

The precise political significance of this is hard to assess. The 2002 NILTS data were collected shortly *after* the devolved institutions had been

[72] We are indebted to Dominic Bryan, who observed the parade, for this 'sash count'.

[73] Police Service of Northern Ireland, *Report of the Chief Constable 2002–2003*, (Belfast: PSNI, 2003).

[74] We are indebted to Lizanne Dowds for this graphic information.

suspended, so can hardly be interpreted as a positive comment on the modest achievements of the latter in this area. Yet, taken with the poor mobilisation for Protestant communal parades this summer and the equally weak response by Catholics to the call by SF to join its 'Democracy Denied' protests against the postponement of the Assembly election, as well as interim results from University of Ulster (UU) polling research showing significant electoral apathy, a pattern perhaps emerges.

Figure 4.3: % Believing that Relations Between Protestants and Catholics Are Better Now Than 5 Years Ago (by religion)

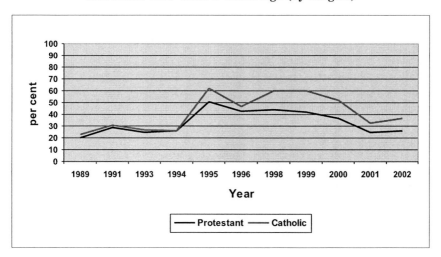

Figure 4.4:% Believing that Relations Between Protestants and Catholics Will be Better in 5 Years Time (by religion)

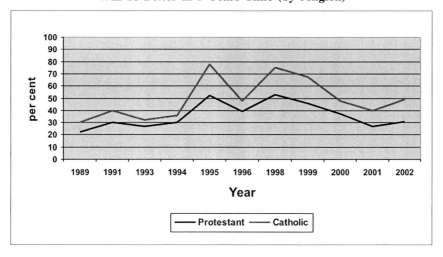

It is of a population suffering from *Politikverdrossenheit* — a weariness with what passes for politics in Northern Ireland, following the earlier weariness with the so-called 'war'. As one of the authors of the UU research, Pete Shirlow, put it, 'Quite a lot of those who said they had voted [in the 1998 referendum] said they thought this would all be over by now . . .'[75] And just as 'war-weariness' had brought paramilitaries to cease their offensive campaigns, it might just be that the protracted efforts by Messrs Trimble and Adams to restore devolution, albeit unsuccessful, reflected a similar awareness of popular impatience with the impacted character of politics to date.

MAKING A DIFFERENCE?

While devolution could have bedded down by attenuating Northern Ireland's deep communal divisions, a more modest ambition would have been to create an instrumental attachment through evidence of practical benefits in conventional policy domains, such as health or the economy, as compared with the experience of direct rule. And there was some evidence of success in that regard.

Data from the Life and Times Survey showed overall a positive disposition towards the devolution experience (Figures 4.5 & 4.6). Only 11 per cent of respondents in 2002 said that the Assembly and Executive had made 'a bad job' of running Northern Ireland. But the warmth was rather lukewarm: 51 per cent said the Assembly had achieved little (and 18 per cent nothing). And among the key swing Protestant constituency it was decidedly tepid: 78 per cent believed devolution had made little or no difference.

Figure 4.5: Overall, Do You Think That the Northern Ireland Assembly Achieved a Lot, a Little, or Nothing At All?

	Catholic	Protestant	All
	%	%	%
A lot	36	17	26
A little	50	53	51
Nothing at all	10	25	18
Don't know	5	5	6

This had the key effect of reducing the pressure on unionist politicians to accept renewed devolution in the absence of dramatic moves by republicans.

[75] 'Voters to shun elections', *Belfast Telegraph*, 15 October 2003.

Towards the end of the survey period, one adviser to the First Minister quipped: 'What's the difference between direct rule and devolution? Direct rule is popular!' And a very senior former civil servant, operating post-retirement in the private sector, confided how he found it remarkable that none of his new colleagues outside government ever volunteered any interest in what happened at Stormont.

Figure 4.6: And How Good a Job Do You Think the Assembly and Executive Did in the Ordinary Day to Day Running of Northern Ireland?

	Catholic	Protestant	All
	%	%	%
A good job	56	29	41
Neither a good nor a bad job	33	50	42
A bad job	6	15	11
Don't know	6	6	7

Devolution in Northern Ireland was not associated with the embarrassment as in Scotland and Wales of the escalating cost of new parliament and Assembly buildings. Parliament Buildings at Stormont, relic of ancien-régime unionist supremacism, was finally put to good, if interrupted, use. But the 'over-government' associated with the politically driven inefficiencies of the Belfast Agreement, allied to the general amateurism of Northern Ireland's political class, led to deep disaffection over the 'value for money' devolution offered. That disaffection was crystallised by the revelation in our August 2002 monitoring report of the way, as we predicted, the Office of the First Minister and Deputy First Minister had grown 'like Topsy', as a proxy centre for the d'Hondt-derived government of departmental fiefdoms.[76]

Yet there was still a sense, which a renewed devolution could build upon, that a government at Stormont, warts and all, is more accessible to the citizen than direct rule. The last pre-suspension Life and Times Survey (2001) found that what might be called this democratic attachment to devolution was also significant.[77] Overall, 40 per cent of respondents said the Assembly

[76] See *Devolution and Northern Ireland Monitoring Report August 2002* (London: The Constitution Unit). The report is available at http://www.ucl.ac.uk/constitution-unit/monrep/ni/ni_august_2002.pdf.

[77] McGinty, R., *A Breathing Space for Devolution: Public Attitudes to Constitutional Issues in a Divided Northern Ireland* (Swindon: ESRC, 2003), p. 6.

was 'giving people more say' in how Northern Ireland was governed, while only 8 per cent said 'less say'. The same caveats nevertheless apply as above. Forty-four per cent said the Assembly was 'making no difference' in this regard and this rose to 50 per cent among Protestants.

The key devolution vehicle for 'making a difference' — in substantive and governance terms — to the sceptical and alienated citizenry of Northern Ireland was the Programme for Government. In our first contribution to this series, we identified it as having the potential capacity, 'in more benign circumstances', to act as the 'glue' holding the fissiparous, four-party coalition together.[78] The qualification was important: the virtuous circle of co-operation and collective responsibility never overcame the centrifugal logic of government by d'Hondt.

Nevertheless, the first two PfGs did get one very important thing right.[79] They ensured that policy was considered in a citizen-centred, 'joined-up' way, with the programme being organised around overall governmental priorities, rather than departmental services. These priorities, established de novo by the devolved Executive, marked a break from direct rule, whereas a more conventional approach might have succumbed to the inertia dictated by embedded departmental stances.[80] Indeed, the initial work on the programme in 1998 by advisers to the First and Deputy First Ministers designate had consisted in canvassing permanent secretaries for their views on the main issues to be addressed — rather than, more logically, the queries flowing in the opposite direction.[81]

PfGI, followed by PfGII, identified the following set of devolved priorities:[82]

- growing as a community,
- working for a healthier people,
- investing in education and skills,
- securing a competitive economy, and
- developing north/south, east/west and international relations.

It was under this banner that Ministers, as they mantra-like began to do, could claim that devolution would be 'making a difference', the title of the first two programmes.

---

[78] Wilford and Wilson, 2000, p. 107.

[79] Northern Ireland Executive, *Making a Difference: Programme for Government 2001–2004* (Belfast: Office of the First Minister and Deputy First Minister, 2001); Northern Ireland Executive, *Making a Difference: Programme for Government 2002–2005* (Belfast: Office of the First Minister and Deputy First Minister, 2002).

[80] One of the authors was involved in the preparatory discussions.

[81] Wilford, R., and Wilson, R., 'Northern Ireland: endgame', in Trench, A., (ed.) *The State of the Nations: The Second Year of Devolution in the United Kingdom* (Exeter: Imprint Academic, 2001), p. 107.

[82] Wilford and Wilson, 2001, p. 96.

Over time, however, this innovative approach experienced slippage; with the absence of a clear political steer from the ruling parties, a more technocratic style crept in. In PfGI, unlike in Scotland and Wales, the architecture of Public Service Agreements (PSAs) was adopted wholesale, with no understanding of its originating political context in London. Moreover, in PfGII, a Blairite language of 'delivery' and 'reform' of taken-for-granted *services* — as against a focus on new public *policies* — was increasingly in evidence. The wood was being lost in the trees.

Suspension added a further twist. Direct-rule Ministers, while anxious to be seen to be grasping *inherited* nettles — such as on community relations and acute hospitals — were highly reluctant to send out any signal that could be interpreted as implying direct rule was here to stay. They were thus determined to stay within the policy mandates bequeathed to them.

So even though PfGIII had been drafted pre-suspension — and had, notably, dropped the *Making a Difference* title in favour of a *Reinvestment and Reform* strapline — what followed in December 2002 was a rather slimmer document from the direct rulers, even though it was compiled by the same officials in the Economic Policy Unit of OFMDFM who had been responsible for the programme. [83] While Wales was establishing 'clear red water' from Westminster, the former Welsh Secretary, Mr Murphy, was promising in his foreword no larger ambition than 'the delivery of high quality public services to all the people of Northern Ireland' while the return of devolution was awaited.

With that horizon repeatedly receding in 2003, the same process was begun again, with an ersatz draft programme published in October.[84] Again, the Northern Ireland Secretary indicated that the 'core of this document has a focus on improving service delivery'. The goal was still 'the restoration of devolution as soon as agreement can be reached with local politicians', yet a speech at the launch by the junior NIO Minister Ian Pearson could have been written in No 10, with its 'focus' on 'reform and modernisation'.[85] While the document, like its predecessor, did reflect the input of progressive officials, in commitments on tackling sectarianism and poverty, a sense of marking time remained.

[83] Northern Ireland Executive, *Draft Programme for Government, September 2002* (Belfast: Office of the First Minister and Deputy First Minister, 2002); Economic Policy Unit, *Building on Progress: Priorities and Plans for 2003–2006* (Belfast: Office of the First Minister and Deputy First Minister, 2002).

[84] Economic Policy Unit, *Northern Ireland Draft Priorities and Budget 2004–2007* (Belfast: Office of the First Minister and Deputy First Minister, 2003).

[85] Available at http://www.pfgbudgetni.gov.uk/speech.pdf.

CONCLUSION

The fortunes of the parties at the 26 November election will structure the outcomes of the scheduled review of the Agreement and the inter-party negotiations designed to restore devolution that will resume in its wake. Elsewhere, we have proposed a number of structural and procedural reforms to the 1998 template that are pertinent to the review and that are designed to provide a bridge across the communal divide.[86] As to the prospect of the return of devolution, the immediate prognosis seems bleak, even given that preponderant majorities of unionist (and nationalist) electors would welcome its restoration if the outstanding matter of IRA decommissioning is resolved in a transparent and timetabled way.

Tangible policy benefits have flowed from the stuttering outworking of devolution, some of which have been indicated earlier. Less obvious, perhaps, are the formal and informal means adopted to assist the Assembly, especially its committees, to scrutinise the Executive in a joined-up way, albeit that there is still scope for improvement in this regard. Evidence of joined-up government is less apparent, though the PfGs and, more particularly, the innovative 'Executive Programme Funds' (EPFs) intended to promote cross-cutting policies, demonstrated the preparedness of Ministers, especially within OFMDFM, to sow the seeds of inter-party co-operation.[87]

One area of common concern among the parties has been irritation with the Barnett formula, and its inability to provide sufficient resources to tackle Northern Ireland's 'infrastructure deficit'. Such irritation has not, however, promoted unity on the means to raise additional public finance. While SF, the SDLP and the Alliance Party each favour the devolution of tax-varying powers, this option is not shared by the UUP or the DUP.

In May 2002, alongside the Prime Minister and the Chancellor, the First and Deputy First Ministers unveiled in Belfast a new 'Reinvestment and Reform Initiative' (RRI), designed in part to lever in private finance to promote economic growth and to tackle the reform of public services.[88] In the short run, that is until March 2004, the RRI will benefit from a £125 million on loan from the Treasury, repayable from regional rate income, supplemented by £75 million from the Executive's own resources, including

---

[86] Wilford and Wilson, 2003b.

[87] The EPFs were introduced in the first draft PfG as a means of focusing resources on a number of its priorities and to encourage co-operation between departments to deliver those priorities in effective ways. Five cross-cutting priorities were identified: social inclusion /community regeneration; service modernisation; new directions; infrastructure /capital renewal; and the children fund. These were new cross-cutting programme areas that encapsulated the objective of improving their relevant public services. Between 2001-02 and 2003-04 departmental expenditure limits (DEL) for the five EPFs was planned to grow from £16 million to £200 million from total planned DEL of, respectively £5.734 billion and £6.36 billion. See www.ofmdfmni.gov.uk/publications/pfg/annexa.htm.

[88] See *NIO press release*, 2 May 2002.

resources available from end-year flexibility and departmental underspends. In the longer run, a new loan facility is to come into effect from 2004, enabling the Executive to lever in low-cost borrowing designed to accelerate infrastructure investment. The management and financing of this investment was to be administered by a new Strategic Investment Board, under the control of OFMDFM and fully accountable to the Executive and subject to the scrutiny of the Assembly and its committees.

Represented by the Chancellor as 'an economic settlement' for Northern Ireland, the RRI has not been short of critics, who are concerned about the financial implications for householders and ratepayers. Concurrent with the announcement, Executive reviews were underway about the reform of the rating system and the introduction of water charges, the latter falling outside the Barnett formula. In the event, because of suspension it has fallen to the NIO to implement the reforms — to the great relief, it has to be said, of at least some of the formerly devolved Ministers.

This, in a sense, brings us full circle. Devolution was delayed for more than 18 months because of the impasse over decommissioning: it is now suspended, and is likely to remain so, not because decommissioning has not occurred but because of its lack of transparency and its seeming open-endedness. When General de Chastelain was asked on 21 October 2003 when the decommissioning process would end, he answered: 'It takes as long as it takes' — a somewhat ill-chosen, if realistic, phrase, that sits uneasily alongside the IRA's and SF's stated commitment, in Mr Adams' words, to 'the full and final closure to the conflict'.[89] The path to closure, while meandering and obstacle-strewn, cannot be endless.

Thus, for the time being, direct rule remains in place and is being pursued actively rather than passively. Twenty-one orders in council have been made post-suspension, work on the review of public administration continues and draft budget proposals for 2004–05 have been published by the relevant NIO Minister. The prospect that those (amended) proposals will be implemented by a devolved Minister seems unlikely. But, whatever the outcomes of the election and the ensuing negotiations, it will be to devolution allied to egalitarian political accommodation that London, Dublin and, hopefully, the region's political actors, will be constrained to return.

---

[89] *SF press release*, 21 October 2003.

APPENDIX: NI ASSEMBLY ELECTION RESULTS
26 November 2003

With the final results declared late on the afternoon of 28 November, the distribution of seats in the (virtual) Assembly saw the realisation of David Trimble's 'nightmare scenario': the DUP and Sinn Féin emerged as the two largest parties, with the UUP and SDLP relegated to third and fourth places, respectively. The consequences of this set of results are for the most part imponderable — save, that is, for the continuation of direct rule in the foreseeable future.

Figure 4.7: NI Assembly Election Results

	1998			2003		
Party	First Preference Votes			First Preference Votes		
	N	(%)	Seats	N	(%)	Seats
DUP	145917	18.1	10	177944	25,7	30
UUP	172225	21.3	28	156931	22.7	27
SDLP	177963	22	24	117547	16.98	18
SF	142858	17.7	18	162758	23.5	24
Alliance	52636	6.5	6	25372	3.68	6
UKU	36541	45.5	5	5700	0.82	1
PUP	20634	2.6	2	8032	1.16	1
Ind*				6158	0.88	1
NIWC	13019	1.6	2	5785	0.83	0
Others	47452	5.8	3**	25801	3.7	0
Total	824391		108	692028		108
Turnout		69.5			63.1	

** Dr Kieran Deeny (West Tyrone). Dr Deeny ran on a single issue: the retention of acute hospital services in Omagh, Co. Tyrone. He topped the poll in the constituency, attracting first preference votes from both unionist and nationalist electors.

** Three Independent Anti-Agreement Unionists.

When the final results were known, the UK and Irish Governments issued a joint statement, agreed at the British-Irish Council meeting held in Cardiff on 28 November. Surveying what the Taoiseach prior to the election had forecast would be 'a mess', Bertie Ahern and Tony Blair restated their shared view that the 1998 Agreement 'remains the only viable political framework that is capable of securing the support of both communities in Northern Ireland' and that '[I]ts fundamentals are not open to renegotiation'.[90]

Therein lies the problem. The DUP's view is that the Agreement is, in the words of Ian Paisley Jr, 'dead in the water' whereas the other three major parties — or, in the case of the UUP, its current leadership — believe it to be the template for stable and secure government. Now that the DUP — for only the second time in its existence[91] — has emerged as the larger of the two main parties, the onus is on it to act responsibly in seeking to achieve what its election literature defined as 'a fair deal' for both unionists and nationalists.[92] Formally, the two governments are committed to a review of the operation of the Agreement's Strand One institutions, namely the Executive and the Assembly. The DUP, however, is seeking to renegotiate all three Strands, that is including the north-south and east-west dimensions of the devolved architecture.

Beyond its objective of securing 'stable, accountable, effective and efficient devolution', the DUP's ideas about an alternative to the 1998 template are difficult to fathom with any certainty. Initial exploratory meetings convened by Paul Murphy were held in the immediate aftermath of the election but as yet there is little to suggest that there is any clear direction or momentum towards the restoration of devolution. The DUP's position remains that it will not negotiate directly with Sinn Féin — the stance taken by the UUP prior to 1996, as Gerry Adams has pointed out.[93]

For its part, Sinn Féin's electoral success has not only increased its lead over its nationalist rival, the SDLP, but anchored mainstream republicanism to the bedrock of the political process. The outcome is a vindication of the Adams/McGuinness strategy and one they will not allow to be jeopardised in the face of local government elections in the Republic of Ireland in the summer of 2004 and simultaneous elections to the European Parliament on both sides of the border.

The SDLP has been left reeling by the results. In 1998, and for the first time, it emerged as the largest party in Northern Ireland: now it has slipped to

[90] Press Release, Northern Ireland Office, 28 November 2003.

[91] The DUP did emerge, narrowly, as the leading unionist party at the 1981 local government elections.

[92] See 'The DUP Vision for Devolution' available at http://www.dup2win.com/articles.asp?Article_ID=216

[93] BBC News Online, 29 November 2003.

fourth place, losing six Assembly seats in the process and ending up with the same number as Sinn Féin won at the first Assembly election. Deprived of some of its leading figures as candidates — including John Hume, Seamus Mallon, Brid Rodgers and Eddie McGrady — it now faces the prospect of serious electoral decline. The success of John Hume in encouraging republicanism to commit more fully to the political process has, it seems, come at a cost: that of the SDLP becoming the perennially junior nationalist party.

As for the UUP, the outcome is a decidedly mixed blessing. Overhauled by the DUP, and relegated to third place in terms of its share of the vote, David Trimble's position as party leader is now under threat. Even before the final results were declared, his potential nemesis, Jeffrey Donaldson, stated on local television and in subsequent interviews, that should the party fall behind the DUP in terms of seats won, then Mr Trimble's leadership was 'no longer tenable'. Having secured a massive personal vote in his own constituency, Lagan Valley, and being joined by four other UUP MLAs-in-waiting whose attitude towards the Agreement and the Joint Declaration is a hostile one, Mr Donaldson seems poised to challenge for the leadership.

Mr Trimble, for his part, seems to relish the prospect of a battle for the top spot. He can point to an increase in the UUP's share of the vote, compared to 1998, and to have actually emerged with a gain of one seat compared to the number of MLAs the party commanded in the Assembly at the time of suspension in October 2002.[94] Moreover, the UUP did not lose a seat to the DUP at the election. The latter's gains came almost exclusively at the expense of the anti-Agreement unionist minnows who had been elected in 1998, only one of whom — Robert McCartney UKUP — retained a seat. Mr Trimble's position is by no means wholly secure, but he has given every indication of his preparedness to take on his internal critics and opponents and, indeed, the DUP, which he regards as having been elected on a false prospectus. There is, in David Trimble's view, no viable alternative to the Agreement, provided that it is implemented fully which, of course, means the republican movement concluding the necessary 'acts of completion'.

While the electoral dust settles, the preparations for the review of the Agreement are underway and are likely to begin in January 2004. In the interim, direct rule continues into its second year.

---

[94] Peter Weir (North Down) had defected to the DUP during the life of the Assembly and Pauline Armitage (Londonderry East) had been suspended from the UUP and ran as a UKUP candidate at the election. At the time of suspension in October 2002, the UUP had 26 MLAs.

BIBLIOGRAPHY

Primary and Official Documents

The Agreement: Agreement Reached in the Multi-party Negotiations (Belfast and London: Northern Ireland Office, 1999).

Report from the First Minister (Designate) and Deputy First Minister (Designate), report NNIA 7 (Belfast: New Northern Ireland Assembly, 1999).

Acute Hospitals Review Group, *Report, June 2001* (Belfast: DHSSPS, 2001).

Community Relations Unit, *A Shared Future: A Consultation Paper on Improving Community Relations in Northern Ireland* (Belfast: Office of the First Minister and Deputy First Minister, 2003).

Department of Health and Social Services, *Putting it Right: The Case for Change in Northern Ireland's Health Service* (Belfast: DHSS, 1998).

Department of Health, Social Services and Public Safety, *Developing Better Services: Modernising Hospitals and Reforming Structures* (Belfast: DHSSPS, 2002).

Department of Health, Social Services and Public Safety, *Investing for Health* (Belfast: DHSSPS, 2002).

Economic Policy Unit, *Building on Progress: Priorities and Plans for 2003-2006* (Belfast: Office of the First Minister and Deputy First Minister, 2002).

Economic Policy Unit, *Northern Ireland Draft Priorities and Budget 2004-2007* (Belfast: OFMDFM, 2003).

Northern Ireland Executive, *Draft Programme for Government, September 2002* (Belfast: OFMDFM, 2002).

Northern Ireland Executive, *Making a Difference: Programme for Government 2002-2005* (Belfast: OFMDFM, 2002).

Northern Ireland Executive, *Making a Difference: Programme for Government 2001-2004* (Belfast: OFMDFM, 2001).

Northern Ireland Human Rights Commission, *Making a Bill of Rights for Northern Ireland: A Consultation by the Northern Ireland Human Rights Commission* (Belfast: NIHRC, 2001).

Police Service of Northern Ireland, *Report of the Chief Constable 2002–2003* (Belfast: PSNI, 2003).

Secondary Sources

Boyle, K., and Hadden, T., *Northern Ireland: The Choice* (London: Penguin Books, 1994).

Elliott, S., 'The Northern Ireland Forum / Entry to Negotiations election 1996', *Irish Political Studies*, 12 (1997).

Greer, S., 'Policy divergence: Will it change something in Grennock?', in Hazell, R., (ed.) *The State of the Nations 2003: The Third Year of Devolution in the United Kingdom* (Exeter: Imprint Academic, 2003).

Hillyard, P., Kelly, G., McLaughlin, E., Patsios, D., and Tomlinson, M., *Bare Necessities: Poverty and Social Exclusion in Northern Ireland — key findings* (Belfast: Democratic Dialogue, 2003).

Hough, D., and Jeffrey, C., 'Elections in Multi-Level Systems: Lessons for the UK from Abroad', in Hazell, R., (ed.) *The State of the Nations 2003: The Third Year of Devolution in the United Kingdom* (Exeter: Imprint Academic, 2003).

McGinty, R., *A Breathing Space for Devolution: Public Attitudes to Constitutional Issues in a Divided Northern Ireland* (Swindon: ESRC, 2003).

O'Leary, C., Elliott, S., and Wilford, R., *The Northern Ireland Assembly 1982-1986: A Constitutional Experiment* (London: Hurst, 1988).

Pollak, A., (ed) *A Citizens' Inquiry: The Opsahl Report on Northern Ireland* (Dublin: Lilliput Press, 1993).

Whyte, J., H., *Interpreting Northern Ireland* (Oxford: Clarendon Press, 1990).

Wilford, R., and Elliott, S., 'Small Earthquake in Chile: The First Northern Ireland Affairs Select Committee', *Irish Political Studies*, 14: 23-42, (1999).

Wilford, R., and Elliott, S., 'The Northern Ireland Affairs Select Committee', *Irish Political Studies*, 10: 216-224, (1995).

Wilford, R., and Wilson, R., 'A "bare knuckle ride": Northern Ireland', in Hazell, R., (ed.) *The State and the Nations: The First Year of Devolution in the United Kingdom* (Exeter: Imprint Academic, 2000).

Wilford, R., and Wilson, R., *A Democratic Design? The Political Style of the Northern Ireland Assembly* (London: The Constitution Unit, 2001).

Wilford, R., and Wilson, R., *Devolution and Northern Ireland Monitoring Report August 2002* (London: The Constitution Unit). All monitoring reports are available at http://www.ucl.ac.uk/constitution-unit/leverh/monitoring.htm.

Wilford, R., and Wilson, R., *Devolution and Northern Ireland Monitoring Report November 2002* (London: The Constitution Unit).

Wilford, R., and Wilson, R., 'Northern Ireland: valedictory?', in Hazell, R., (ed.) *The State of the Nations 2003: The Third Year of Devolution in the United Kingdom* (Exeter: Imprint Academic, 2003a).

Wilford, R., and Wilson, R., *Northern Ireland: A Route to Stability* (Swindon: ESRC, 2003b).

Wilson, R., (ed.) *Agreeing to Disagree? A Guide to the Northern Ireland Assembly* (Belfast: The Stationery Office, 2001).

Wilson, R., and Wilford, R., 'Northern Ireland: endgame', in Trench, A., (ed.) *The State of the Nations: The Second Year of Devolution in the United Kingdom* (Exeter: Imprint Academic, 2001).

Wolff, S., 'Conclusion: the peace process in Northern Ireland since 1998', in Neuheiser, J., and Wolff, S., *Peace at Last? The Impact of the Good Friday Agreement on Northern Ireland* (New York and Oxford: Berghahn Books, 2002).

5

English Regions
The Quiet Regional Revolution?

John Tomaney and Peter Hetherington[1]

It is an axiom of writing on the constitutional changes that have occurred over the four years since 1999 that they largely bypassed England. The question of England's position in the new devolved United Kingdom remained unanswered in late 2003. However, it would wrong to conclude from this that devolution has not affected England. The UK Government's answer to the English Question has become more clearly focused on regionalisation, with alternatives apparently slipping off the agenda. This quiet regionalisation has begun to be embedded in England — and even accepted by some who were its opponents — and this may prove to be a lasting legacy. This chapter begins by examining the impact of the institutional developments that have occurred since 1999, focusing primarily on the triumvirate of organisations that now lie at the heart of the governance of the English regions: Regional Development Agencies (RDAs), voluntary Regional Assemblies and Government Offices (GOs) of the regions. The chapter then examines the forces that are promoting (and hindering) English regionalism. The administrative regionalisation, however, has been driven less by the search for constitutional symmetry, than by a desire to tackle to persistent regional inequality and pursue innovative forms of regional policy in England.

The chapter concludes by assessing the outlook for regionalism in England, with the prospect of referendums in three northern regions in 2004. In 2002 and 2003, the regional agenda in England took an important step forward with the enactment of the Regional Assemblies (Preparations) Act and the completion of the UK Government's 'soundings' exercise, which led the deputy prime minister to announce that three regions would hold referendums in October 2004 on the establishment of elected regional assemblies.[2] For John Prescott, in particular, an affirmative vote in one or more northern regions would be a vindication of his long-held vision of a devolved England.

---

[1] The authors would like to thank Emma Pinkey of the English Regions Monitoring Team.

[2] Office of the Deputy Prime Minister, *Your Region, Your Say* (London: The Stationery Office, 2003). Available at http://www.odpm.gov.uk/stellent/groups/odpm_regions/documents/pdf/odpm_regions_pdf_023485.pdf.

In 1999 it was by no means certain that regionalisation would be the order of the day in England five years later. Although the Government had instituted the Regional Development Agencies Act, regionalism competed for political space with two potentially large ideas. One touted alternative to regionalisation that had some support in government was the idea of directly-elected local mayors for large English cities to provide political leadership for their attendant city regions. Implicit in this argument was that idea that executive mayors could move out from beyond the world of party politics.[3] While this agenda received influential support from some elements of government by 2003 only eleven elected mayoralties had been created in England and none in the large cities. Moreover, a minority of the mayors came from beyond the usual party channels. All in all this amounted to rather less than the revolution in local government that its proponents had hoped for. London, of course, saw the successful introduction of an executive mayor during the same period. The effect of this development in the English regions was twofold: on the hand the incumbent mayor, Ken Livingstone, raised the question of London's 'fair share' of resources, in ways which probably fuelled the debate about regionalism in some parts of England, while on the other the powers and functions of the mayor became a model for the powers of elected regional assemblies in England.[4]

On the other side of the coin, despite a brief flirtation by the Conservatives under William Hague with the idea, the debate about an English parliament as an appropriate response to Scottish devolution failed to ignite. In part, this may have been because senior Tory local government figures quickly found themselves entrenched in the emerging apparatus of regional governance which developed after 1999, but also because the cause of an English parliament failed to find a resonance among the Party's own members and media supporters.

Regional campaigners, notably in the three northern regions of England, could take some satisfaction from the extent to which their agenda had advanced relative to its competitors. The work of the Constitutional Conventions, notably in the North East, represented part of the pressure that was exerted on the UK Government in order to further advance the regional agenda.[5] The Conventions served three purposes. First, they kept the issue of regional governance in the eye of the regional media. Second, they sought to address the practical issues surrounding elected assemblies, which ensured that political regionalisation did not disappear as a public policy issue. Finally, especially in regions like the North East, they took the discussion of

---

[3] See for example Stoker, G., 'Is regional government the answer to the English Question?', in Chen, S., and Wright, T., (eds.) *The English Question* (London: The Fabian Society, 2000).

[4] See also chapter 6.

[5] Tomaney, J., 'Democratically elected regional government in England: the work of the North East Constitutional Convention', *Regional Studies*, 34 (4), pp. 383–388, (2000).

regional assemblies outside the Labour Party, where it had previously resided. This latter activity was not always popular with Labour politicians, but connected the issues of regionalism with wider civic concerns.

Regional campaigners were also influential in ensuring the issue maintained a profile in Westminster and Whitehall. Two bodies played a critical role. First, the Campaign for the English Regions (CfER), representing the various campaign bodies across the English regions, continued to press for the UK Government to address the devolution issue. It played a critical role in supporting the efforts of parliamentarians who supported the case for regional assemblies. Alongside this the Regional Policy Forum (RPF), established with support from the private sector and other bodies and closely linked to John Prescott and the Office of the Deputy Prime Minister (ODPM), played a quiet but influential role in linking the debate about regional assemblies to the debate about regional policy, which was becoming of increasing interest to the Treasury. As well as contributing to the debate about regional assemblies, the Regional Policy Forum helped to make the case for bolstering the role of existing regional institutions in England. To the extent that, both CfER and the RPF had largely achieved their objectives by 2003 — insofar as they had secured referendums on regional assemblies in three northern regions and existing regional institutions had been strengthened — they could be said to have punched above their weight.

INSTITUTIONAL DEVELOPMENTS SINCE 1999

Prior to 1997 the regions of England had been governed in a highly fragmented way. In the period after the Second World War, all governments had acted through a growing number of regional organisations in fields such as economic development, planning and health. In part this reflected the practical requirements of governing a large unitary state. In part state-sponsored regionalism after the 1960s was also driven by the search for a solution to the economic problems of the regions, especially the ailing northern regions. During the 1960s the Wilson Labour governments both massively expanded expenditure on regional policy and created Regional Economic Planning Councils, which in some regions began to develop strategies for land-use and economic development. One of the first acts of the Thatcher government in 1979 was to abolish the Regional Economic Planning Councils and radically reduce expenditure on regional policy. Ironically in this context, perhaps, it was the Major government, which in 1994 initiated the reconstruction of regional institutions, by creating ten Government Offices in England, which drew together existing central government functions in order to better integrate their activities.

Since 1997, the architecture of English regionalism has been bolstered significantly. The English regions are now governed by a triumvirate of organisations with overlapping responsibilities, but with slightly different roles.[6] The elements of this triumvirate have either been created or substantially strengthened since 1999. The most high profile of these bodies are Regional Development Agencies. The creation of RDAs was an outcome of the proposals made by the Regional Policy Commission established by John Prescott when Labour was in opposition. For Prescott RDAs were intended to be part of a larger effort to boost the institutional capacity of the English regions in order to tackle persistent regional inequalities. The inspiration for RDAs was the Scottish Development Agency (renamed Scottish Enterprise) and the Welsh Development Agency, created in the 1970s in response to devolutionary pressures but which were seen as pioneering a more integrated approach to tackling regional problems. In Prescott's vision, RDAs were conceived as powerful organisations, responsible for a swathe of government expenditure in the regions and which would become accountable to elected regional assemblies.

The birth of RDAs proved difficult. On the one hand their creation was decoupled from that of elected regional assemblies. Instead, private sector support for their role was won by ensuring that boards of RDAs, which were appointed by the Secretary of State, would be 'business led'. On the other hand, the range of functions allocated to RDAs was less than that anticipated by the Regional Policy Commission. RDAs drew together some functions from central government, including Government Offices (GOs), regional investment promotion bodies, English Partnerships and the Rural Development Commission. Much of the budgets of RDAs, moreover, was already allocated to government programmes, which RDAs delivered on behalf of UK Government departments. This latter arrangement partly reflected the reluctance of some Whitehall departments to hand over powers and functions to RDAs. As such RDAs began their lives as rather slight creatures. Their powers looked modest when measured against the scale of the task of tackling regional inequalities and they looked set for a marginal role in the government system. Early critics of RDAs stressed the degree to which they simply added to the quango state that Labour had criticised in opposition, represented an amalgamation of existing bodies rather than a real devolution of power and resources and lacked direct accountability to the regions they served.

Despite their difficult birth, the strength and status of RDAs slowly grew after 1999. Their Regional Economic Strategies emerged as important policy instruments in the regions, influencing the activities of local

---

[6] For a more detailed discussion see Tomaney, J., and Mawson, J., (eds.) *England: the state of the regions* (Bristol: Policy Press, 2002).

authorities and other agencies in the regions. This growth reflected their incorporation into the UK Government's larger agenda — driven by the concerns of the Treasury — of raising UK productivity. A shift in sponsorship of RDAs from the then Department of Environment, Transport and the Regions (DETR) to the Department of Trade and Industry (DTI) was emblematic of the new view of RDAs as key instruments of economic policy. In particular, the growing interest of the Treasury in regional policy boosted the profile RDAs considerably, with RDA chairs gaining direct access to the Chancellor — and to his highly influential Chief Economic Advisor, Ed Balls — to push the credentials of their organisations. RDAs were increasingly seen important mechanisms for delivering improvements in the Treasury's priority areas of skills, investment, innovation, enterprise and competition.

After 2001, the resources available to RDAs were increased. Accompanying this increase in resources was the creation of a 'single pot' — an arrangement that gives RDAs a greater financial flexibility — albeit within the context of targets agreed with central government. Moreover, on an experimental basis, RDAs gained new responsibilities to integrate transport and training policy with their regional economic strategies. Within the regions themselves, RDAs therefore emerged as pre-eminent actors in the field of economic development policy, with a key role in orchestrating the range of actors, including local authorities, which have a stake in economic development. The regional agenda became embedded and widely accepted relatively quickly in England, notably in regions that did not have traditions of regional working. It was too early in 2003 to judge the real impact of RDAs on the social and material conditions in each region: the task facing RDAs in the lagging regions was of enormous magnitude if their target to close the economic gap with the south was to be met.[7] Moreover, although the relative weight of expenditure, and hence the political profile of RDAs, tended to be higher in the north, the overall expenditure of RDAs remained modest at 1 per cent of total government expenditure in the regions and low compared to the level of expenditure on regional policy in 1960s and 1970s.

Regional Assemblies were constituted as voluntary groupings of local authority representatives and 'stakeholders' (business, trade unions, voluntary organisations and some statutory bodies). The Regional Development Agencies Act 1999 gave the Secretary of State the authority to designate an assembly in each region, ostensibly for the purpose of scrutinising the work of the relevant RDA and representing the interests of the region to the UK Government. RDAs were given a statutory duty to consult Regional Assemblies in the preparation of the regional economic strategies. Regional

[7] See for example Dobbie, B., 'Towards regional government', in Tomaney, J., and Pike, A., (eds.) *Towards Regional Government in England* (Seaford: Regional Studies Association, 2002).

Assemblies were the weakest element of the triumvirate. They had little statutory basis for their actions.

Yet Regional Assemblies remained important because they gave a large range of organisations a new stake in regional governance. The Act specified that a minimum of 30 per cent of members should come from outside the local government sector. The precise size and structure of each Assembly varied between regions, giving each organisation a different working culture. By virtue of their local authority representation, the Assemblies were clearly political structures and the pattern of political representation in each region also affected their working practices.

Assemblies, however, like RDAs saw incremental growth in the functions and responsibilities. In 2001, the Chancellor of the Exchequer and the deputy prime minister jointly announced that Assemblies would have access to a fund of £15 million over five yeas in order to support their scrutiny activities. Notably, the Regional Assemblies (Preparations) Act made existing Assemblies the regional planning bodies, with responsibility for producing regional spatial strategies, including regional transport and waste strategies.

Assemblies have began to assert themselves, despite their low profile in the eyes of the public. An early example came in the perhaps unlikely shape of the East of England Regional Assembly, which in 2001 rejected the draft regional economic strategy of the East of England Development Agency, largely on the grounds that it was too focused on the needs of the hi-tech Cambridge region and paid insufficient attention to the broader social and environmental consequences of its proposed growth targets. The South East England Regional Assembly proved itself to be assertive in criticism of the land-use and waste strategy plans of the Mayor of London. In the latter case, despite articulating the regional interest, there was scant evidence that the Mayor took much notice. As the voice of the regions, voluntary Assemblies lacked the legitimacy and authority of their elected counterparts and frequently struggled to articulate a perspective that moved beyond the lowest common denominator of amalgamated local concerns.

The final element of the triumvirate of regional governance was the Government Offices. As noted previously, GOs were formed initially by the last Conservative government in 1994. They brought together the hitherto separate regional offices of the Departments of Environment, Transport, Trade and Industry and Education and Employment in an effort to overcome fragmentation, which was seen as leading to waste, duplication and confusion. The creation of GOs by a party that in 2003 was implacably opposed to regionalisation was testament to the desire of successive governments in the period after the Second World War to achieve more integrated government action in the regions. From the outset, Regional Directors of GOs were simultaneously supposed to represent the UK Government in the regions and represent regional concerns to Government.

Following the arrival in power of Labour in 1997, like the other members of the triumvirate, GOs have seen their stock rise. The augmentation of the role of GOs was preceded by an influential study by the UK Government's Performance and Innovation Unit (PIU), *Reaching Out: the role of central government at the local and regional level*, published in 2001.[8] The report drew attention to the fragmentation of action on the part of government in the regions and the degree to which this affected policy outcomes. It saw GOs as having a potentially important role in 'joining up' government activity in the regions, but also saw the need for regional concerns to be better represented in Whitehall's deliberations.

The outcome of the report was the gradual expansion of departmental representation within GOs, so that by 2003 some nine departments were represented, although the degree of regionalisation on the part of some departments such as the Home Office was relatively modest. By 2003 GOs were responsible for administering a range of central government programmes including the Neighbourhood Renewal Fund (for the Home Office), Regional Selective Assistance up to a threshold (for the DTI) and the Housing Investment Programme (for ODPM) and the Local Capital Transport Settlement (for the Department of Transport). Consequently, GOs found themselves interacting directly and regularly with a large number of organisations, including local government, voluntary organisations and business. As such GOs saw their role as a repository of administrative author-ity in the regions increased. Chapter 2 of the UK Government's White Paper *Your Region Your Choice*, set out new tasks for GOs, including making inputs into Spending Reviews and undertaking policy development tasks.[9]

Despite their growing range of activities, GOs fell short of being inte-grated territorial department along the lines of the Scottish Office or Welsh Office prior to devolution of the Scottish Executive or Welsh Assembly Government post-devolution. This is not simply a function of their much smaller budgets and more restricted range of activities, but also of the fact that integration was a formal type, with staff in GOs remaining employees of their parent department with consequent implications for career strategies. Moreover, Regional Directors did not have access to a 'single pot' of the type available to RDAs. Most of their funds were already allocated to depart-mental programmes. On the other hand, there appeared to be a new tendency for Regional Directors to be appointed from outside the civil service, often

---

[8] Performance and Innovation Unit, *Reaching Out: the role of central government at the local and regional level* (London: The Stationery Office, 2001). The report is available at http://www.number-10 .gov.uk/su/reaching/regions/default.htm

[9] Cabinet Office and Department for Transport, Local Government and the Regions, *Your Region, Your Choice: Revitalising the English Regions*, Cm 5511, (London: The Stationery Office, 2002).

from a local authority background. Regional Directors were also granted a modest degree of financial and organisational flexibility in their administrative responsibilities, although not in relation to their programmes. Despite these developments GOs have some way to go before they evolve into organisations that are more explicitly regional in character rather than being outposts of the civil service.

A second outcome of the PIU report was the creation of the Regional Coordination Unit (RCU) located (in 2003) in the Office of the Deputy Prime Minister. The RCU was a concrete expression of the desire to ensure that regional concerns are more effectively taken account of in Whitehall. Its function was to manage GOs in an integrated way — previously the GO Director reported to separate departments — and to ensure the success of cross-cutting programmes. The RCU was given a particular role managing Area Based Initiatives (initiatives with a cross-cutting character and a territorial focus) which became a major theme of the UK Government's approach to tackling localised deprivation.

A consequence of the quiet regionalisation of England was the more explicit financial treatment of the English regions. The Spending Review 2002 was the first to contain a separate chapter on the English Regions. As well as outlining the UK Government's financial commitments to bodies such as RDAs, the Spending Review introduced a new Public Service Agreement (PSA) which committed to reducing disparities in regional growth rates. The Spending Review announced that the Government was committed to a fair allocation of public spending to encourage equality across the regions.

Devolution to Scotland and Wales was accompanied by growing claims of financial injustice — attributed to the effects of the Barnett Formula — on the part of the northern regions, notably the North East, after 1999.[10] Although the Labour government showed no appetite for responding to these claims, it did sponsor research aimed identifying the flow of domestic and European expenditure into the English regions. The research demonstrated the poor understanding within government about the territorial impact of its expenditure, but generally gave support to arguments that current systems underpinned claims about injustice.[11]

A new architecture of regional governance became embedded in England in the period since 1999. Its growth, which built on earlier developments by the previous Conservative administration, was striking. At the same time, this growth should be kept in proportion. The new triumvirate remains a small element of the total amount of government activity in the regions and it

[10] Jones, P., 'Barnett plus needs: the regional spending challenge in Britain' in Tomaney, J., and Mawson, J., (eds.) *England: the state of the nations* (Bristol: Policy Press, 2002).

[11] MacLean, I., *Identifying the flow of domestic and European expenditure into the English Regions*, Report to the Office of the Deputy Prime Minister September 2003, (Oxford: Nuffield College, 2003). Available at http://www.nuff.ox.ac.uk/projects/odpm/.

remains heavily circumscribed by central government stipulations. The forces shaping English regionalism are several and complex and analysed below.

Running in parallel to the growth of administrative regionalism was the development of the debate on elected regional assemblies. The debate progressed slowly during Labour's first term, but gathered pace as the 2001 election approached, with both John Prescott and Gordon Brown making speeches in support of regionalism. Following the election, the UK Government announced that it would publish a White Paper outlining the potential shape of English regional assemblies. After a protracted preparation, the White Paper *Your Region, Your Choice* appeared in May 2002. The production of the White Paper was the subject of intense debate within Whitehall and within the Cabinet. Like the Regional Development Agencies before them, the final shape of the proposed elected assemblies offered much to pattern of compromises that John Prescott, as architect of the policy, was able to achieve with Cabinet colleagues. This meant that core functions of the proposed assemblies focused on spatial planning, economic development and housing investment, funded by a single block grant from central government, with some precepting powers. The proposed structure owed a lot to the Greater London Authority model. With the emphasis on their responsibilities for strategic tasks, the White Paper proposed only small assemblies of 25–35 members, elected by proportional representation. A compromise central to its appearance, insisted upon by the Prime Minister, was that moves to a regional assemblies should be accompanied by a move to unitary local government. Underlying this compromise were two related concerns: a fear on the part of 10 Downing Street about accusations of additional bureaucracy, and the *sotto voce* concern about the quality of local politicians in the regions most likely to support assemblies in a referendum. Despite their difficult gestation, in 2003 the prospect of elected assemblies moved closer when legislation was placed before Parliament to allow referendums to take place in those regions that wanted them.

Figure 5.1: Chronology of Events 2002–2003

2002	
13 November	Queen's Speech: announcement of legislation 'to provide for the holding of referendums on the issue of regional governance in England'.
14 November	Introduction of the Regional Assemblies (Preparations) Bill to Parliament.
2 December	Announcement that UK Government would take 'soundings' in regions to test support for a referendum.

2003	
8 May	Regional Assemblies (Preparations) Act becomes law. The Government had accepted amendments on extending the minimum period following a no vote in a referendum before a further referendum can be held from 5 to 7 years and giving voters in 2–tier local authority areas a choice on the form of unitary local government in their area if an elected regional assembly was introduced.
6 June	A District Auditor in North East England judged that publicity issued by NEA could be seen to be contravening Part II of the Local Government Act 1986 and DoE Circular 20/88 — Code of Recommended Practice on Local Authority Publicity, by supporting an elected assembly.
June 16	Deputy Prime Minister announced that referendums on regional assemblies are to be held in three regions, the North East, Yorkshire and the North West.
June 16	Boundary Committee for England begins review of structure of local government in the three nominated regions in order to make two recommendations for unitary local authorities in each area currently governed by a county council.
July 31	Boundary Committee for England concludes initial consultation.

REGIONALISM IN 2003

The English regional agenda made a number of major steps forward in 2002 and 2003. Quietly and unobtrusively, the Regional Assemblies (Preparations) Bill became law on 8 May 2003. With the UK Government occupied with contentious issues of war and European integration, very little attention was paid to a piece of legislation that proposed to reshape government in England. The legislation's passage through the House of Lords saw the original Bill changed in a significant way. This was the result of an amendment, agreed as a compromise between the Government and the Liberal Democrats, designed to give voters in areas currently governed by two-tier local authorities a choice over the type of single-tier local government they would have in the event that voters chose a regional assembly in a referendum. Without this compromise, it is clear that Ministers believed the Bill would not have completed its passage. Additionally, the UK Government announced that it would endeavour to produce a draft Bill for Parliament's consideration prior to the proposed referendums. The Liberal Democrats saw in this the possibility of strengthening the powers of the proposed assemblies. However, there seemed little appetite on the Government side for revisiting the delicate compromise that produced the White Paper in 2002.

On 16 June the Deputy Prime Minister announced that referendums on regional assemblies would be held in three regions: the North East, Yorkshire and the Humber, and the North West, anticipated for October 2004. The announcement followed the results of a 'soundings exercise', which tested the degree of support for the holding of a referendum in each region of England.[12] David Davies, then the Conservative spokesperson on the regions, predicted defeat for the proposition and that the Government would be 'deeply embarrassed'. The national media gave the announcement scant attention but, where it did, it greeted the proposals with almost universal hostility.

In the week following the announcement, campaigners in the North East of England announced the launch of a 'Yes' campaign — 'Yes4thenortheast' — based in Durham, with initial funding from private subscriptions, trade unions and reform trusts.[13] In Yorkshire and the North West the 'No' campaigns announced themselves, with the No campaign in the North West chaired by the former Conservative Minister Sir David Trippier, but vice-chairs in the form of Labour MPs George Howarth and Graham Stringer.

The North West was also characterised throughout 2003 by a bitter dispute between the North West Regional Assembly (NWRA) and Lancashire County Council, which centred on Lancashire's claim that NWRA had exceeded its authority by actively campaigning for regional government. Lancashire County Council announced its opposition to the Government's linking of local government reform to elected regional assemblies. The dispute involved the exchange of press releases and contrasting legal opinion. Among the three northern regions in 2003, the North West seemed to contain the most potential for the regional assembly issue to provoke recrimination, with both Labour and the Liberal Democrats containing divisions and little consensus about local government reform. It was in the North West, therefore that first indications were given of the potential for the local government reform cause internecine warfare on the regional front.

In this context, as the prospect of a referendum drew closer, in June, it is ironic that it was following a complaint from a No campaigner in the North East, that the District Auditor gave his opinion that the existing North East Assembly had exceeded its authority by campaigning for an elected Assembly. The effect of the opinion in the North East was to see a reduction of the

---

[12] Office of the Deputy Prime Minister, 2003.

[13] One of the authors (Tomaney) is chairman of 'Yes4thenortheast'.

public profile of the leaders of the non-elected North East Assembly in the debate about regional assemblies.

The soundings exercise presented the range of evidence that had been gathered on the state of public opinion in the regions. An analysis of the results by Birmingham University suggested that affirmative votes were likely in the three northern regions, but with turnouts of less than 30 per cent. But opinion research also indicated low levels of public understanding and large groups of 'don't knows' among those canvassed.[14]

Figure 5.2: Support for Regional Assemblies[15]

Region	Yes	No	Don't Know/ Wouldn't Vote
North East	51	19	32
North West	50	21	29
Yorkshire and the Humber	49	18	34
West Midlands	43	21	35
East Midlands	43	16	41
South West	41	22	37
South East	40	25	35
East of England	36	25	39
Total	44	21	35

At the same time as announcing the prospect of referendums, Mr Prescott announced that the Boundary Committee for England would begin reviewing the structure of local government in the three nominated regions in order to make two recommendations for unitary local authorities in each area currently governed by a county council. Voters in areas currently governed by county councils (but not elsewhere) would then choose which option they prefer when they vote in the referendum. The Boundary Committee's initial consultation process was officially concluded on 31 July. The Committee's draft recommendations were due by the end of November 2003 (see Figure 5.3).

[14] Jeffrey, C., *The English Regions Debate: What do the English Want?*, ESRC Devolution Briefing No. 3, (Swindon: ESRC, 2003).
[15] Source: County Councils Network, reported in Jeffery, 2003.

Figure 5.3: Timetable of the Boundary Committee for England 2003–04

Stage One:	
(17 June–31 July)	Start review and study submission of proposals from councils and other interested parties. Starts opinion polling. 31 July marks last day for councils to submit completed financial returns to committee.
Stage Two:	
(9 September–1 December)	Committee considers proposals, determines draft recommendations report and (2 December) publishes report and invites representations.
Stage Three:	
(3 December–23 February)	After publishing draft report, committee asks for views of local councils and the public. Undertakes further opinion polling to determine views on various options.
Stage Four:	
(24 February–25 May)	Committee considers responses, reaches conclusions, and submits final report to the Deputy Prime Minister, John Prescott.

The Boundary Committee officially began work on 17 June with a 12–week public consultation involved commissioning extensive opinion polling from MORI (both quantitative and qualitative 'focus groups') in the county areas and interviews with council leaders and chief executives. It also involved a study of the financial position of councils, an assessment of their corporate structures and capacity for good governance and — crucially — an examination of the results of the Audit Commission's comprehensive performance assessment (CPA) inspections.

THE POLITICS OF REGIONALISM

Since 1997 England has seen significant changes in the structures of regional governance — incremental, yet significant nonetheless — but also a shift in the political mindset across parties. Even some formerly hostile and sceptical Conservatives in local authorities had begun to accept that a future Tory government would find it difficult to unpick some of the new structures, particularly RDAs. This acceptance points to the degree to which regionalism has become embedded within England. But a clear division has emerged between Conservatives — along with sections of the business lobby — and Labour and the Liberal Democrats over what the Deputy Prime Minister presented as the central plank of the UK Government's regional agenda: English devolution embodied in elected assemblies, starting with the three northern regions.

While John Prescott remained the driving force of regionalism in England, other ministers remained more cautious. Nevertheless the prospect of three regional referendums in October 2004 transformed regionalism from an administrative to a more directly political project. The model of regional government on offer was criticised, notably by the Liberal Democrats, as lacking some key powers. But it reflected the deal that Mr Prescott had reached with other ministers and their departments. The imperfections of the model of regional government outlined in the White Paper mean that it could either lead to profound changes in the government of England, potentially a building-block for wider constitutional reform, or become a damp squib with new assemblies punching below their weight and hemmed in by a sceptical Whitehall, always assuming devolution crosses the first hurdle in the three referendums.

Whatever the limits of the UK Government's proposals, the prospect of a potentially radical reshaping of government in England continued to elicit little publicity. The London-based press tended to pay the issue scant attention, although when it did, some were extremely hostile in their coverage. Papers such as the *Daily Mail* and the *Daily Telegraph* chose to link the regionalisation of England to the alleged ambitions of the European Union. Pro-regional assembly campaigners and the Government itself faced the difficulty of overcoming a combination of antipathy and disinterest on the part of the London media in events in the English periphery. While in regions like the North East, the main newspapers were sympathetic, the *Yorkshire Post* ('Yorkshire's National Newspaper') for instance, remained implacable in its opposition to a regional assembly. Elsewhere, local papers gave the issue sporadic coverage, coming alive when the prospect of local government reform came to fore. All of this contributed to the lack of information bemoaned by respondents to opinion pollsters, a lacuna which led the Government to announce its intention of launching an information campaign to explain its proposals to the 11 million voters in the three northern regions.

In addition to sections of the media, the forces ranged against the regional agenda included some local government leaders, particularly Conservatives, for whom the new structures represented an expansion of the 'quango state', ultimately answerable to Whitehall and therefore centralist in nature rather than decentralising. In the North West some Labour county council leaders largely shared the view of the Tory counterparts. Along with some Labour MPs, they looked likely to campaign actively against assemblies. From the outset there were tensions and contradictions in New Labour's approach to the regions, which appeared to combine both administrative devolution and centralisation at one and the same time. Part of the problem was that RDAs, and the anticipated powers for elected regional assemblies, represented the uneven gains achieved by Mr Prescott in inter-departmental discussions with other senior ministers in the late 1990s.

As a result of those discussions, the RDAs were born amid discord and uncertainty within government. Although their subsequent transfer to the Department of Trade and Industry after the 2001 general election with a 'single pot' of funding, rather than a variety of funding streams, formalised and entrenched their position in Whitehall. Significantly, in several regions, notably Yorkshire and the Humber and the North West, the RDAs could claim to have made a difference by partnering local councils in innovative urban renewal programmes, laying the foundations for new enterprises and championing the causes of their regions — campaigning particularly about poor rail and transport links which, they argued, were damaging job creation prospects. In this respect, they were punching above their weight.

John Prescott's regional agenda seemed stalled following the creation of RDAs and the voluntary regional assemblies in Labour's first term. The Prime Minister appeared to remain decidedly sceptical about the idea of elected assemblies altogether. Other ministers, notably Jack Straw, whose intervention as a shadow minister in 1996 considerably watered down Labour's devolution commitment to the English regions, were equally lukewarm, if not hostile. But towards the end of Labour's first term, the political ground began shifting. The Chancellor, Gordon Brown — Labour's regional spokesman in a much earlier political life — took the debate onto a more philosophical plane. He connected the debate about regional economic development to broader constitutional questions, with remarks which seemed to align himself with the arguments in favour of regional government. Prudent constitutionally as well as fiscally, he has always been careful to speak of 'decentralisation' rather than 'devolution', but he emerged as a powerful supporter of the Prescott agenda.

Although for some regional assemblies were the answer to a constitutional question — the English Question — for others the case for regional assemblies grew less from a reaction to Scottish self-government and the perceived injustice of the Barnett Formula and its impact on regions like the North East. Rather it was a response to the need to find new ways to tackle regional inequalities. The Prime Minister initially dismissed talk of a north-south divide as an over-simplification. But when several cabinet colleagues, notably Stephen Byers, raised the question of a 'winners circle' emerging in the south — with the clear implication that several other regions were the losers — the tone began to change. RDAs were increasingly seen in a new light — indeed, they were seen as a key instrument to raise the economic performance of poorly performing regions as part of the Treasury's drive to improve the overall productivity of the UK. In the days before the 2001 UK general election, Gordon Brown extolled the virtues of his alliance with Prescott, and on the stump linked his new approach to a regional economic strategy that gave new resources and new responsibilities to the RDAs with the need for local and regional accountability.

The position of the Prime Minister remained more ambiguous. In a speech to the National Assembly for Wales on 30 October 2001, Blair acknowledged the emerging debate in the English regions, placing Welsh devolution in the context of moving Britain away from a centralised state to a more democratic and decentralised one.[16] He has rarely returned to the theme since, apart from contributing a preface to the White Paper *Your Region, Your Choice* in May 2002 where he noted a manifesto commitment 'to provide for directly elected regional assemblies *in those regions that want them*'.[17] Number 10 aides faced the conundrum of the extent to which the Prime Minister might involve himself directly in any campaign for elected assembly, especially in the North East in which his own constituency is located, although at the Labour party conference in Bournemouth in 2003 Mr Blair met directly with assembly campaigners for the first time.

Despite its apparent growth in importance, the regional agenda also appeared to lie at the margins of the Government's concerns. The UK Government's ambiguity was linked to its understanding of the economic geography of the UK. The dominant view in the UK Government could be summed up thus: underpinning growth in the south of England, and particularly in the east around the greater-Cambridge bio-technology and IT cluster, is crucial to the Treasury's vision of a modern economy; this is one area where Britain is a world leader. It is growing fast. Incomers need lots of new houses and ODPM is the nearest thing there is in the UK to a European-style planning ministry and it has produced plans for large-scale housing expansion in the south east.

The basis of the alliance struck between Chancellor and Deputy Prime Minister appeared to be that in return for Mr Prescott approving a string of new townships in four new growth areas of the south and east (principally greater Cambridge-Stansted-Harlow; the 40-mile Thames Gateway corridor; greater Milton Keynes) in his sustainable communities plan for England Mr Brown was happy to push support devolution plans for the north as a counterweight to growth in the south.

John Prescott's sojourn at the Cabinet Office immediately after the 2001 election distanced him from direct contact with regional matters and

[16] Tony Blair, Speech to the Welsh Assembly, 30 October 2001. Available at http://www.number10.gov.uk/output/Page1636.asp.
[17] Cabinet Office / DTLR, 2002, preface.

possibly slowed the appearance of the English regions White Paper. His return to a substantive portfolio within the Office of the Deputy Prime Minister following the demise of Stephen Byers put him in effect in charge of a department of local government and the regions. The significance of this comeback probably cannot be under-estimated in terms of consolidating the regional agenda within Whitehall. Together with his minister of state, Nick Raynsford (with whom he has good working relationship) Mr Prescott found himself once again with overall control of the local and regional governance agenda in England. Mr Raynsford piloted the Greater London Authority Act through Parliament. With a reputation for attention to detail, Mr Raynsford was the key player in driving through the Regional Assemblies (Preparations) Act — forever known as the RA(P) Act — which paved the way for regional referendums.

Given the low-key character of much of the debate on the English regions, John Prescott's announcement that the three northern regions had been chosen for referendums with the passage of the RA(P) Act seems all the more remarkable. Mr Prescott told MPs on 16 June 2003 that if people in any, or all of the regions, vote for regional assemblies in (almost certainly) October 2004, the first assemblies could be up and running early in the next parliament. That, he added, would be another significant step on the road to regional government for England, an opportunity for those regions wanting change to determine their own future.

But the regional agenda posed difficulties for Labour. Senior Government figures feared the impact of a disputatious reform of local government, leading to splits in the party, especially in the North West. On the other hand, the process of local government reform began in a relatively quiet and consensual way elsewhere. The prospect of referendums held out the danger that they could be a test of the Government's popularity in the aftermath of difficult local and European elections. The regional agenda faced the danger of being caught in wider political malaise comprising growing disenchantment with politics in general and Labour in particular. The challenge for the Yes campaigns was both to raise awareness of the issue and to convincingly present the case for stronger northern voice and the chance to make more decisions in the regions as the logical and widely supported choice.

CONCLUSION

The UK Government's regional agenda followed twin tracks after 1999. On the one hand administrative regionalism grew and strengthened. There is growing evidence that this administrative regionalism had become more embedded with England. It was a degree of regionalism that went further than that of the 1960s and 1970s in terms of its scope, although levels of expenditure on regional policy remained lower. Moreover, it was more firmly linked into the activities of central government and had become a key delivery mechanism for Government policy on economic regeneration, spatial planning and housing. Another Labour Government held out the prospect of administrative regionalism becoming further entrenched and extended. Senior Tories in local government, especially, appeared accepting of the advantages of institutions such as RDA and the value they added to regional economic planning; such that by 2003 it was becoming increasingly unlikely that a future Conservative government would find it easy in political and administrative terms to unpick the new structures.

By contrast, what might be termed political regionalism — the strategy of making the burgeoning regional bureaucracies accountable to electors in the regions — still appeared more fragile, notwithstanding the apparent eclipse of other ideas such as elected mayors, which had appeared to present alternatives. Its flag-bearer remained John Prescott, with some important new supporters such as Ian McCartney, the Labour Party chairman and senior political figures such as Peter Mandelson and Ed Balls. But 10 Downing Street and the Prime Minister, in particular, remained ambivalent about the agenda. For sceptics in the Government, the political costs of the venture outweighed the potential gains. Some Ministers remained firmly hostile to the project on what could be described as ideological grounds not dissimilar to the Conservatives: to wit, regionalism is not part of the English political tradition.

Those making the case for regional assemblies faced some difficult challenges by the end of 2003. As the Fraser Inquiry raked over the question of the costs of the Holyrood Parliament, devolution was no longer simply the inspiring prospect it looked in 1999, but more of an imperfect reality. Pro-assembly campaigners could point to the difference that devolution had made in Scotland, Wales and London. But they faced the difficulty of engaging a national (English) media which was more widely read in the northern regions than the regional press and which remained either indifferent or hostile to the regional agenda. English regionalism was on the cusp at the close of 2003. It faced one of two prospects either remaining as administrative convenience of Whitehall or becoming a new political force within the UK. The people of the three northern regions were due to pass judgment on the outcome in October 2004.

BIBLIOGRAPHY

Primary and Official Documents

Cabinet Office / DTLR, *Your Region, Your Choice: Revitalising the English Regions*, Cm 5511, (London: The Stationery Office).

Performance and Innovation Unit, *Reaching Out: the role of central government at the local and regional level* (London: The Stationery Office, 2001). The report is available at http://www.number-10.gov.uk/su/reaching/regions/default.htm

Office of the Deputy Prime Minister, *Your Region, Your Say* (London: The Stationery Office, 2003). Available at http://www.odpm.gov.uk/stellent/groups/odpm_regions/documents/pdf/odpm_regions_pdf_023485.pdf.

Secondary Sources

Stoker, G., 'Is regional government the answer to the English Question?', in Chen, S., and Wright, T., (eds.) *The English Question* (London: The Fabian Society, 2000).

Dobbie, B., 'Towards regional government', in Tomaney, J., and Pike, A., (eds.) *Towards Regional Government in England* (Seaford: Regional Studies Association, 2002).

Jeffrey, C., *The English Regions Debate: What do the English Want?*, ESRC Devolution Briefing No. 3, (Swindon: ESRC, 2003).

Jones, P., 'Barnett plus needs: the regional spending challenge in Britain' in Tomaney, J., and Mawson, J., (eds.) *England: the state of the nations* (Bristol: Policy Press, 2002).

MacLean, I., *Identifying the flow of domestic and European expenditure into the English Regions*, Report to the Office of the Deputy Prime Minister September 2003, (Oxford: Nuffield College, 2003). Available at http://www.nuff.ox.ac.uk/projects/odpm/.

Tomaney, J., 'Democratically elected regional government in England: the work of the North East Constitutional Convention', in *Regional Studies*, 34 (4), pp. 383–388, (2000).

Tomaney, J., and Mawson, J., (eds.) *England: the state of the regions* (Bristol: Policy Press, 2002).

6

The Governance of London
Strategic Government and Policy Divergence

Mark Sandford

Attempts to create new institutional machinery for London face a conflict between the desire to achieve effectiveness by giving greater powers to one body or individual and a need to trade off the many, powerful borough and local interests throughout the metropolitan area. History and the current politics of London suggest that this conflict will never be easily resolved.[1]

I think we've f***ed it up.[2]

The new devolved governments of Scotland, Wales and Northern Ireland are powerful bodies. Two of them have legislative powers over the majority of domestic political and policy issues; the third, Wales, has secondary legislative and full executive power over only a slightly smaller range of domestic issues. Other chapters of this book demonstrate the extent to which devolution has created new policy communities in Belfast, Edinburgh and Cardiff, and the degree to which it has permitted considerable policy divergence in the three devolved territories.

The GLA was purposely created as a unique experiment in British politics: an executive city mayor was to act as a co-ordinating 'voice for London', bringing together government agencies and the voluntary and private sector in a form of light-touch policy advocacy that has become known as 'strategic government'. This chapter explores institutional questions about the Greater London Authority (GLA), which have been conspicuous by their absence over the last three years (perhaps drowned out by personality politics, the congestion charge and the battle for control of London Underground). It asks how far the GLA resembles the hopes and expectations of its creators, and seeks to assess how far the GLA can steer a distinctive policy course for London on the issues for which it is responsible. It argues that the story so far of the devolved administration in London suggests that the foundation stones of policy divergence are real executive power (including non-interference by central government) over a broad range of policy, and a generous block grant budget, with full freedom for the

---

[1] Travers, T., and Jones, G.W., *The New Government of London* (York: Joseph Rowntree Foundation, 1991), p. 102.

[2] Senior GLA officer on devolution in London, personal communication to the author, 2003.

devolved governments to spend as they see fit. It explores the possibilities for policy divergence in London in the absence of the foundations mentioned above. The chapter draws conclusions about the efficacy of strategic government — what it can and cannot be expected to do — and briefly considers the implications of the GLA for the proposals for elected regional assemblies elsewhere in England (discussed in chapter 5).

BEFORE THE GLA: THE EXPECTATIONS

The creation of a Greater London Authority required a leap of faith.[3]

The GLA is a very different form of devolution from that in Scotland, Wales and Northern Ireland. The most significant differences are the limited amount of executive power transferred to it, the devolution of responsibility without power, in the form of obligations to write 'strategies' but no proper functions, and the manifold peculiarities of the structures of the GLA.

The executive powers of the GLA are embodied in four separate 'functional bodies':

- Transport for London (TfL);
- London Development Agency (LDA) [covering economic development];
- Metropolitan Police Authority (MPA);
- London Fire and Emergency Planning Authority (LFEPA).

Each of these functional bodies has a management board, with board members who are appointed by the Mayor, except for a minority of independent members and magistrates on the MPA. Each receives the majority of its funding from central government grant. The Mayor cannot move funding from these grants between these bodies, although he can add to them through his limited revenue-raising powers (discussed in more detail below).[4] Hence, the Mayor's control of these bodies operates at one remove; he must approve the economic development and transport strategies, for instance, but day-to-day management is in the hands of the boards and their senior staff.

As a result of hiving off most powers and money into 'functional bodies', the 'core' GLA is a very small organisation. It was initially expected to have no more than 250 staff, although this has subsequently risen to some 600. These staff are responsible for writing strategies, servicing the Assembly, planning, and policy advice to the Mayor. Oddly, the Assembly (rather than the Mayor) has the power to appoint most of the staff of the GLA, meaning that relationships have had to be built between them and the Mayor's office.[5]

---

[3] Pimlott, B., and Rao, N., *Governing London* (Oxford: Oxford University Press, 2002), p. 65.

[4] See also sections 100–103 of the Greater London Authority Act 1999.

[5] See Travers, T., 'Decentralisation London-style: the GLA and London Governance', *Regional Studies*, 36 (7), pp. 784–785, (2002).

Much of the extra staff capacity relates to culture, environment and health. These are routinely identified in the media as GLA powers, but in reality they are virtual powers. No functional bodies or GLA budgets exist for them, and central government continues to deliver policies for London in these fields through centrally-appointed executive agencies. As Travers remarks, 'the powers of the mayor are largely those of . . . patronage, through his or her ability to appoint to the functional bodies; persuasion, using limited control over resources and position at the centre of what is a continuing system of network and multi-level governance; and publicity through exploiting the mayor's legitimacy, accountability and democratic claim to "speak for London"'.[6]

Besides functional limitations, the Greater London Authority Act 1999 imposes far-reaching limits on the flexibility of the Authority. Section 41 (5) provides that Mayoral strategies must be 'consistent with national policy'. This appears to rule out any policy divergence from the start. And the Mayor may not duplicate policies of any other body — although the Mayor is given a power of general competence, stringent limits are set on this by section 31 (3), which debars him from using that power to spend money on housing, education, social services or health services, or functions of any London borough or other public body.

Meanwhile, the constitutional oddities of the GLA are sufficient to be more than arcane concerns; they confuse relationships, particularly account-ability, between the bodies of London government. The Mayor appoints most members of the boards of all of the functional bodies, but on two (MPA and LFEPA) he must appoint a majority of London Assembly members, and may appoint Assembly members to the LDA board. Those Assembly members must also be appointed according to the Assembly's political proportionality. This implies that the London Assembly has a share in execu-tive control of these organisations, but its purpose is also to scrutinise the actions of the Mayor. Hence, many Assembly members could be both scruti-nisers and scrutinised.[7]

Apart from these appointments, structural links between the Mayor and Assembly are extremely weak. There are no mechanisms through which the Assembly can ensure its voice is taken into account, and thus no reliable means for it to influence policy. The effect of this has been to drive policy-making away from the elected institution and into a range of more informal networks, involving the Mayor, stakeholders, public and private institutions, and local government. Added to the need to create and maintain networks to make strategic government effective, there is an incentive to

[6] Travers, T., *The Politics of London: Governing an Ungovernable City* (Basingstoke: Palgrave Macmillan, 2004), p. 68.

[7] For more in-depth analysis of the constitutional problems of the GLA see Travers, 2002 and Greer, S., and Sandford, M., *Fixing London* (London: The Constitution Unit, 2003).

give these networks priority over more normal democratic arrangements. Hence, the character of London governance is strongly influenced by the weaknesses of the GLA.

Figure 6.1: Chronology of Events 1999–2003

Date	Event
1999	
1 October	Conservative Party selects Jeffrey Archer as Mayoral candidate
20 November	Jeffrey Archer resigns as Mayoral candidate
2000	
17 January	Steven Norris selected as new Conservative Party candidate
19 February	Frank Dobson selected as Labour Party candidate
6 March	Ken Livingstone announces independent candidacy
4 May	Ken Livingstone elected as Mayor of London
10 October	Robert Kiley appointed Transport Commissioner by Ken Livingstone
2001	
4 May	Robert Kiley appointed chair of London Transport
6 June	UK General Election
17 July	Robert Kiley sacked as chair of London Transport
30 July	Mayor and Transport Commissioner lose first court case against UK Government over PPP for London Underground
2002	
21 June	Launch of London Plan (Sustainable Development Strategy)
26 July	Mayor and Transport Commissioner withdraw second court case opposing Underground PPP against Government
6 November	Nicky Gavron selected as Labour Mayoral candidate for 2004
30 December	First contracts signed for London Underground PPP

Date	Event
2003	
18 January	Trevor Phillips, first chair of London Assembly, resigns to become head of the Commission for Racial Equality
5 February	Mayor agrees terms of transfer of London Underground with UK Government
17 February	Congestion charging introduced
15 May	Government agrees to back a London bid for the 2012 Olympics

EXPLANATIONS OF THE GLA'S WEAKNESS

Partly these extreme limits on GLA power reflect 'the degree to which the GLA model is recognisably a local government one'.[8] Pimlott and Rao stress that the structure of the GLA — a separate directly-elected Mayor and Assembly — derived from the same source of thinking as the proposals for local authority mayors, an idea which emerged around 1996 with the strong support of Tony Blair. It was expected that London would be the first of several major UK cities to vote for a directly-elected mayor. As the GLA was a local authority — albeit a large, unique and experimental one — it could not but inherit the tight statutory framework to which local government has become accustomed.

But the GLA was also an experiment and innovation from the beginning — as Tomaney states, 'it probably also reflects an alleged shift . . . in the nature and art of government. In this perspective, government is about the exercise of influence in networks, rather than the exercise of authority in organisations'.[9] Government is replaced by 'governance'. The Green Paper claims to want to build on 'the willingness of the private and voluntary sectors to play a part in the formulation and delivery of policy at a strategic level', a focus which according to Pimlott and Rao 'was arguably a logical extension of the post-abolition thinking'.[10]

Implicitly, a very strong guiding factor in Labour policy-making was the desire to 'work with the grain of London', to avoid charges of extra bureau-

---

[8] Tomaney, J., 'The Governance of London', in Hazell, R., (ed.) *The State and the Nations: The First Year of Devolution in the United Kingdom* (Exeter: Imprint Academic, 2000), p. 248.

[9] Tomaney, 2000, pp. 242–3.

[10] See Department of the Environment, Transport and the Regions, *New Leadership for London* (London: The Stationery Office, 1998), p. 2; Pimlott and Rao, 2002, p. 59.

cracy or of 'GLC mark II'.[11] Between 1986 and 2000, the private and voluntary sectors made considerable efforts to develop cross-London co-ordination of policy and are generally considered to have had a positive, though necessarily limited, influence. The main added value of the existence of a London-wide authority was perceived (by both Labour and most commentators) to be land-use and transport planning and co-ordination of existing policy, rather than creating a new government with a wide range of new or transferred functions. There was very little support for a stronger form of devolution approaching the Scottish or Welsh models. The following paragraph from the Green Paper is a fair representation of the debate:

> Well-judged co-ordination of action, in line with agreed strategies, will pay dividends for London . . . We do not consider that the mayor needs powers over and above these [appointments and executive functions] to secure compliance with his or her strategic objectives — the mandate from the electorate will give the mayor considerable authority and we see him or her working with the assembly and with a wide range of organisations to create a consensus.[12]

This paragraph explains both the paucity of executive power and the provision for the Mayor to exercise influence through writing strategies. The GLA Act provides that eight statutory strategies must be written by the Mayor, and the current Mayor has chosen to produce six additional ones (see Figure 6.2). The existence of such a range of strategies, on issues for which the Mayor has no executive responsibility or budget, is the essence of the concept of 'strategic government'. The strategies were a means to a public-private consensus, which would produce policies which run 'with the grain of London'. The Mayor would broker the negotiations and seal the result with democratic legitimacy. However, apart from economic development and transport, written jointly with the relevant functional body, the Mayor has neither carrots nor sticks to enforce these strategies.

---

[11] Department of the Environment, Transport and the Regions, *A Mayor and Assembly for London* (London: The Stationery Office, 1999), p. 8. The Greater London Council (GLC) covered the same geographical area as the GLA. It existed from 1964 to 1986, when it was abolished by the Conservative government following increasingly vocal political opposition. The last leader of the GLC was Ken Livingstone, who became the first Mayor in 2000.

[12] DETR, 1998, p. 6.

Figure 6.2: Mayoral strategies

Statutory	Non-statutory
Air Quality	Children
Ambient Noise	Childcare
Culture	Drugs and alcohol
Economic Development (with LDA)	Energy
Transport (with TfL)	Rough Sleepers
Spatial Development	Domestic violence
Biodiversity	
Waste Management	

What results were expected from such an experimental, hybrid body? The small literature at the time indicates that a strategic, co-ordination role, with a diffusion of political power between Mayor and Assembly and the political parties within the Assembly (through proportional representation) was seen as the way of building upon the relative stability of London governance since 1986. The White Paper, *A Mayor and Assembly for London*, mentions international promotion of London, cultural and sporting events, and achievement of consensual progress as Government aspirations for the GLA. In reality, the GLA has been dominated by the big policy fields under its wing: transport in particular, and also policing. Its 'strategic' impact has been less clear, with some positive and some negative signs. It has also developed its role in a number of new policy areas which do not appear to have been foreseen by its creators. In a number of ways it is taking tentative steps away from the local government model within which it was conceived. But it has not been able to establish a new kind of politics, nor has the Mayor influenced central policy in London to the degree that some commentators suggested that he would by dint of his visibility and electoral mandate.

What, then, has been achieved? The following sections divide the activities of the GLA into four parts: executive power; strategies; 'foster policies'; and the role of the multiplicity of actors, including the London Assembly, in the governance of London.[13]

---

[13] As the executive power of the GLA is in the hands of the Mayor, in the following section I refer to the Mayor, not the GLA, taking actions and developing policies. The London Assembly (*not* the Greater London Assembly, as it is often called) has a peripheral role in the majority of issues discussed here, which itself is an issue that will be examined later.

EXECUTIVE POWER: TRANSPORT FOR LONDONERS

The prioritisation of transport and policing by the Mayor does not merely result from the fact that transport and policing have long been the two leading issues in London-wide politics. As with most of the Mayor's activity, these priorities have structural roots. The Metropolitan Police Authority (MPA) and Transport for London (TfL) are the two largest of the four GLA functional bodies, by both staffing and budget. They are the most politically salient issues for almost all inhabitants of London. Transport benefits in particular from the Mayor being able to appoint himself chair of TfL — thus bringing himself closer to the action — and from central government's unwillingness to take a substantial lead in addressing the never-ending conundrum of transport policy.

The Mayor has exercised his power to appoint himself chair of TfL, and is generally considered to be in control of the board. Changes introduced since 2000 include compulsory registration of minicabs, CCTV on London buses, a range of new bus routes and ticketing options (many of which permit cheap travel through buying in advance), the replacement of old buses with new vehicles, and the introduction of compulsory pre-purchase of tickets before boarding buses in central London. TfL's control of trunk roads has enabled the introduction of many extra bus lanes, and two-person police teams have begun to travel on London buses in response to public concerns about security. These two policies are textbook examples of the kind of cross-cutting working that can be achieved by sub-national government. It is not surprising that the Mayor 'has seen the transport strategy as key to his personal agenda'.[14]

The changes to the bus service demonstrate the results that can be achieved from the presence of a number of factors. These include financial flexibility at the margins (new buses, new tickets and bus lanes are relatively cheap), a devolved political authority willing to encourage and act on new thinking, and substantial impact on the service through a range of small but strategically-thought-out adjustments. The introduction of the congestion charge was an integral part of this policy; this was one of the few issues on which genuine policy divergence could take place in London. But this very fact emphasises the crucial point about policy divergence. In London, it has taken place in transport, where the Mayor has real executive power, not in the areas where the GLA has diffuse responsibility without clear functions. And the changes have been made through executive decisions, not through strategy, partnership and negotiation. The Mayor has been quoted as saying of transport:

[14] Rydin, Y., Thornley, A., Scanlon, K., and West, K., *The Greater London Authority — A Clash of Organisational Cultures* (LSE London Discussion Paper 6, March 2002), p. 17.

That's the only area where I've got real power, in everything else it's marginal. . . . Nothing else is in that league. In the transport sphere, so long as Government continues to give me the money and to co-operate with congestion charging, I've got the ability to turn it round.[15]

The contrast with the London Underground could not be greater. Financial flexibility will not be large enough to build new lines or rebuild many stations due to the high costs. Until a deal between the Mayor and central government in February 2003, there has been no devolved political authority, requiring managers to follow central guidelines, and there has also been no possibility to integrate policy for the tube into London transport policy.

Policing also has high political salience in London. However, the creation of the Metropolitan Police Authority as a 'tripartite' authority, together with far higher UK Government interest in crime issues, has tended to limit the Mayor's ability to impose changes. The Metropolitan Police enjoy operational independence. Most notable was the complete absence of any role for the Mayor in the aftermath of 11 September 2001; London policing was clearly still regarded as a national issue. The Home Secretary was quoted as saying to the Metropolitan Police, 'We will give you the freedom to do the job, but if you don't do it, I'll have to intervene. Because in the end, the people of London, as with the rest of the country, will turn to me as home secretary and say what did you do about it?'[16] This exemplifies the conundrum in which the GLA finds itself in almost all policy areas.

The gradual change of policy in London in transport and policing resembles what takes place in Scotland, Wales and Northern Ireland — an accumulation of marginal changes which will lead to considerable differentiation over time. This is less easy to analyse in London, because TfL, for instance, has no equivalent in any other UK region (unless and until elected assemblies are established in other English regions). The congestion charge, the first of its kind in the world, reflects the uniqueness of London in this respect. But it is clear that the presence of the GLA has led to policy divergences which otherwise would not have taken place — albeit from a very limited range of options.

FOSTER POLICIES: ISSUES WITHOUT INSTITUTIONAL HOMES

A more unexpected, and interesting, development in London government is the Mayor's interest in 'foster policies'. The GLA has increasingly moved into policy issues which either do not have an institutional home, or which are only just becoming regarded as part of 'public policy' at all. This issue

---

[15] Quoted in West, K., Scanlon, K., Thornley, A., and Rydin, Y., *The Greater London Authority — Problems of Strategy Co-ordination* (LSE London Discussion Paper 7, March 2002), p. 10.

[16] 'Blunkett issues ultimatum to Met', *The Guardian*, 14 February 2002.

does not appear to have been anticipated either by commentators or by UK Government.[17] The policy fields into which the Mayor has moved can be divided into three kinds:

- relatively visible 'quick wins';
- agreements led by the Mayor between private organisations;
- long-term investment policies.

Quick Wins

'Quick win' policies are easy and cheap to carry out. They are relatively high-profile, satisfy at least a portion of the electorate, and are largely self-contained. A prime example of this is the 'partnerships register' instituted by the Mayor in 2001. This allows the registration of same-sex (and different-sex) partnerships. The register has no legal or statutory applicability. Around 300 partnerships have so far been registered, and the policy has been hailed as a breakthrough for same-sex relationships. This policy is self-contained and will not cause or lead to a great number of other changes.

It may be that the interest in quick wins is a part of the Mayor's personal political style, and that this would not have been such a noticeable factor had a different candidate been elected Mayor. But a government which is so limited in powers inevitably faces the temptation to make use of quick win policies. This chimes with the evaluation of the Mayor's prioritisation process by Rydin et al.:

> There is a fairly simple dynamic at work here and that is the pursuit of re-election in 2004 . . . Translating this political agenda into a policy agenda results in a very clear focus on a limited number of projects that are deemed salient with the electorate and where the results of the Mayoral system can be demonstrated.[18]

Private Agreements

Private agreements are characterised by the Mayor establishing separate companies or partnerships to carry out particular tasks, or negotiating joint promotions. Being outside the statutory framework of the GLA Act, added flexibility is available to these bodies or events.

The promotion with the highest profile was 'Totally London', which took place throughout summer 2003. A wide range of cinemas, theatres, hotels, and tourist attractions such as London Zoo, offered special deals and reduced prices on particular days throughout the summer. The campaign was funded

---

[17] It could be argued that foster policies are an extension of the requirements that the Mayor pursue sustainable development in the United Kingdom and have regard to the health of Londoners (statutory requirements in section 30 of the GLA Act), but the foster policies that have been introduced extend far beyond those cross-cutting concerns, and merit discussion as a class of policy in their own right.

[18] Rydin, Y., Thornley, A., Scanlon, K., and West, K., 2002, p. 10.

by the LDA and London Tourist Board, and was accompanied by special fare deals on public transport. People were encouraged, by a Mayoral publicity campaign, to visit central London on those days and take advantage of the offers — which resulted in a rise in takings both for many of the groups taking part and for central London retail and other businesses. This kind of brokerage has affinities to the concept of the 'voice for London'.

London Waste Action was set up as a 'public private partnership' between the GLA and Association of London Government (ALG). It obtained £21.3 million of funding from the Government's Waste Minimisation and Recycling Fund, which became the London Recycling Fund. A further £23 million was levered in from other sources. Funds from this are being distributed to local projects to encourage household recycling as highlighted in the Mayor's Waste Strategy.

Another instance of joint working between the GLA and ALG is 'LondonConnects'. This is a not-for-profit agency designed to promote the use of information technology in and by government set up in late 2000 with support, both financial and in-kind, from individual boroughs, the GLA, the Corporation of London, the NHS, and LFEPA. The agency was also able to obtain £900,000 of funding from central government. It has set up a number of projects relating to public sector ICT requirements in London such as data sharing and data protection applications and transport smart cards. It also runs seminars for public sector staff. This is an example of the use of innovative structures to deliver public policy goals, as the status of LondonConnects as an independent agency allows it more financial flexibility than is available to the GLA. An alternative model is offered by the London Hydrogen Partnership, which is run by a steering group, with representatives from various power or fossil fuel-related companies plus TfL, the Department for Trade and Industry, the LDA, and the ALG. The Chair is a Mayoral policy advisor. The Partnership will produce a strategy for developing hydrogen power — with implicit support from the private sector, which may bring resources to support action later.

Long-Term Investments

Long-term investment policies include both strategies and the work of the policy commissions (see below). They are gap-filling policies, joining up a variety of activities that are already taking place and making suggestions to improve their delivery. Although such strategies may have a negligible initial impact on policy divergence, it is possible for them to set in train different ways of *thinking* about problems of policy which may, in several years' time, find their way into the mainstream. Equally, this type of policy will pay few political dividends to its instigators and will rarely become known to the general public.

The Rough Sleepers' Strategy demonstrates the way in which strategic government rests at one remove from executive action.[19] The Strategy commits the GLA to 'improve the delivery of statutory services by working in partnership with providers to develop a Rough Sleepers' Charter that commits providers to best practice linked to specific outcomes'. The language used indicates the GLA's inability to provide services itself (homelessness is a borough responsibility and hence covered by the prohibition on service duplication under section 30 of the GLA Act), obliging it to create partnerships of existing services. The Strategy also aims to improve access to information about services for rough sleepers, and to 'increas[e] the supply of move-on accommodation and the effectiveness of meaningful occupation programmes'. A series of 'regular outreach Mayoral surgeries' is also proposed, to link rough sleepers with services. The GLA will 'facilitate bids to funding bodies . . . to deliver a network of inclusion centres'.

The proposals in the Children and Young People's Strategy[20] also run up against the weakness of the Mayor's position. The foreword states that 'The strategy also contains a number of proposals for consideration by key partners across London'. This language indicates the inability of the Mayor to enforce strategic policy — neither carrots nor sticks are available to him. The Childcare Strategy suffers from similar drawbacks. Much of the introduction is concerned with the low take-up of the Working Families Tax Credit, a national policy which the Mayor wishes to see improved, while suggesting that 'employers can support staff through flexible and family-friendly employment policies'.[21] In October 2003 the Mayor announced a scheme to offer cheap transport to people claiming Working Families Tax Credit.[22] This is an innovative use of the financial incentives available to the Mayor, but it also demonstrates once again that the policy tools which are most easily available and used in London are those for which he holds executive power.

The Domestic Violence Strategy, while making the case admirably for its own existence, contains recommendations such as 'all systems and agencies should give out clear and consistent messages, information and referral to women, children and abusers'.[23] Few of its recommendations can be argued with, but they may lack precision for the (no doubt overworked) organisations putting them into practice.

---

[19] The Mayor of London, *From Street to Stability: The Mayor's Rough Sleepers Strategy* (GLA, London, 2001), p.vii.

[20] The Mayor of London, *Towards a Child-Friendly London* (GLA, London, 2003), p. i.

[21] The Mayor of London, *The London Childcare Strategy: Towards affordable good quality childcare for al* (GLA, London, 2003), p.38.

[22] Muir, H., 'Plan for 30% fare cut to encourage Londoners to work', *Guardian*, 16 October 2003.

[23] The Mayor of London, *1 in 4: the London Domestic Violence Strategy* (GLA, London, 2001), p. 28.

These are all small, incremental actions, which are not the responsibility of any one of the state, private or voluntary organisations involved in the provision of services. They are distinct from the statutory strategies, which deal with more mainstream policy agendas, in that they relate to cross-cutting issues which currently have no institutional home. Effective co-ordination may help to assert the GLA's right to lead on these issues.

'Foster' Policies as a Distinct Form of Governance

Foster policies derive both from the limits on the GLA's role and from its status as a London-wide authority. They bring together private-sector interests and expertise with representatives from the GLA's functional bodies to work on policy issues which will deliver benefits only in the medium to long term. Here again the structure of the GLA is key. Being a strategic authority, it has a greater incentive to focus on policies which have no other institutional home. Such incremental policies assume disproportionate significance in a strategic authority which runs few services and cannot aspire to run more. Local authorities, by contrast, are more likely to view strategic, long-term, cross-cutting issues as optional extras, to be focused on in good funding years; most of the time they are obliged by electoral pressures and regulation to focus simply on maintaining services.

These policy issues are united by two things. First, they are institutionally homeless. No other level of government leads on any of these issues, and hence the GLA is able to move into the vacuum. Second, they are also cross-cutting issues. To some extent, promises within them can be delivered within other, existing programmes. For instance, there are links between rough sleeping and affordable housing, and the Mayor proposes to use Section 106 agreements to increase affordable childcare.[24] Indeed, there is a tendency to 'double-count' these policies in promotional material; another form of quick win. For instance, roadside vehicle emissions testing, instituted by TfL, appears both as a transport policy and as an achievement in the Air Quality strategy. This may be an inevitable characteristic of cross-cutting policies.

It appears clear, however, that foster policies are an integral part of 'strategic government'. A number of factors provide incentives for the GLA to develop them. First, they can be done cheaply. For developing issues such as renewable energy, bringing people together and exploring possibilities for joint working is a correct approach. Building wind farms in the Thames Estuary would be a disproportionate response at present.[25] Second, at least in

[24] Section 106 agreements permit local authorities to conclude agreements with planning applicants for any purpose: these would be the means by which builders can be obliged to provide a set percentage of affordable housing, for instance.

[25] The lack of capital budget is a contributing factor to GLA behaviour: the initiatives described are relatively cheap. It may also be easier to obtain support in kind, or even small pots of funding for

some cases (such as the partnerships register) their profile outweighs their cost. Third, there is no risk of duplicating the work of other levels of government, avoiding disputes. Fourth, in the longer term the GLA is asserting its right to lead on the policy areas in question, and establishing them as regional as opposed to local concerns — a kind of speculative investment. If those subjects do become mainstream public policy in the next two decades, the GLA may be able to claim extra resources for them from central government, and will be adding to the list of reasons why it is needed.

THE STRATEGIES: LOW-KEY AND LOW RESULTS

The GLA Act provides for exhaustive statutory consultation procedures on the Mayor's statutory strategies. The strategies are intended to set out the direction of policy in Greater London for 15–20 years, for public, private and voluntary bodies. The Mayor has little or no budget with which to enact the strategies and no legal sanctions with which to enforce them.

The concept of a government which would successfully harness public and private bodies to its cause by writing strategies was essentially untested before the existence of the GLA. The problems with such a constitutional set-up are fairly obvious. Other organisations would have no incentive to follow a Mayoral strategy unless it benefited them directly; the Mayor has no sticks or carrots with which to create incentives; and central government agencies answer to central government and would follow its priorities in the event of any divergence between central and Mayoral aims. The strangeness of this model of strategic government is compounded by the fact that many of the strategies have not been completed until the second or third year of the Mayor's first term. It is not clear what happens if the current Mayor loses his position in 2004; will the newcomer then spend half their term of office revising the strategies to reflect his or her own manifesto?

The impact of these limits is clearly visible in the strategy documents. They are enormous documents, most being between 250 and 450 pages.[26] They contain substantial descriptions of research and of current developments and programmes, many of which have nothing to do with the Mayor. They generally contain 'suggestions' or 'recommendations', or policies which 'promote', 'encourage' and 'support' existing programmes or generalised future aspirations. Where proposals for actual action are made, they are almost all related to executive Mayoral powers (mostly transport) or to the Mayor's authority to refuse 'strategic' planning applications. Proposals

exploratory or pilot work, from partner organisations, when the GLA's approach is one of partnership and relative poverty instead of a hero-project mentality.

[26] Regional Chambers, which are also tasked with producing 'strategies', are increasingly producing 20-page 'framework documents' in place of exhaustive tomes.

from the strategies include setting up working groups, ensuring the GLA follows the strategy's recommendations, and better data collection. The Air Quality Strategy's recommendations are devoted almost entirely to re-presentation of transport policies, pointing out (correctly) that the Mayor has no powers over such factors as aviation and industry. The Biodiversity Strategy supports a number of progressive policies without promising action. The Ambient Noise Strategy focuses 'on reducing noise through better management of transport systems, better town planning and better design of buildings' — all relating to Mayoral executive powers. This focus suggests that strategic government, in order to be effective, is inevitably attracted back to 'in-house' executive powers to make its strategies count.

West et al suggest that, through the first two years of the GLA, joining-up of strategies has taken place purely through monthly meetings of strategy officers where an update on each strategy was provided.[27] It was an officer initiative, which drew relatively little interest from the Mayor's office. They suggest that a clash of cultures between the Mayor's office and those parts of the GLA bureaucracy that predate the GLA itself has prevented the strategies from being anything more than footnotes in Mayoral policy.

THE ACTORS: COMMISSIONS, CABINETS, AND ASSEMBLY MEMBERS

> [The aim was] that the Assembly would and should have a substantial and positive input into the decision-making process rather than remain a mere forum for harassing and embarrassing the Mayor.[28]

The various actors in the creation of the GLA wrestled largely unsuccessfully with the question of how to give all executive power to the Mayor and ensure that the London Assembly remained a valid voice. The Assembly's one real power is to reject the Mayor's budget, but this is a 'nuclear option' which in practice is irrelevant to the day-to-day debate over policy options. Assembly members, *as assembly members*, have been largely overlooked, and this is perhaps unsurprising in a governance system which places so much emphasis on partnership, joint working and consensus. Travers notes that, especially in the early days of the GLA, 'the role of the mayor's gate-keepers, his close advisers, is considerably enhanced . . . Who you know and who has access has become more important'.[29] A system of governance that relies on networking and cutting deals can easily crowd out substantive input from elected politicians. The five Mayoral Commissions and the Mayor's advisory cabinet demonstrate this — only a minority of the cabinet, and only

[27] West, K., Scanlon, K., Thornley, A., and Rydin, Y., *The Greater London Authority — Problems of Strategy Co-ordination* (LSE London Discussion Paper 7, March 2002), p. 12–13.
[28] Pimlott and Rao, 2002, p. 66.
[29] Travers, 2004, p. 110.

a tiny proportion of each policy commission, were drawn from the Assembly.

Five Mayoral Commissions have been set up to enquire into particular issues: Crime and Community Safety, Housing, Health, Equalities, and Environment. They are very large bodies, with between 18 and 43 members. In three cases members of both the Assembly and the Mayoral cabinet sat on the commission: in only one case (Elizabeth Howlett on the Health Commission) did an Assembly member sit who was not also a Cabinet member. The GLA, the Government Office for London (GOL), borough, and functional body staff were frequently represented, but the majority of each commission (with the exception of Equalities) came from outside the GLA 'family', from a variety of private and voluntary organisations with interests in the subject under discussion. It was intended that the commissions would feed into a Mayoral Prospectus to be published in late 2000, but this never materialised.

The Mayor's Advisory Cabinet was set up shortly after his election. It contains 20 members: minutes indicate that the average attendance is around half of the members, and on one occasion was only five (including the Mayor himself). It contains four Labour Assembly members (including the chairs of MPA and LFEPA), two Labour MPs, two Liberal Democrat Assembly members, one Labour councillor, the chair of the London Development Agency, and a range of other appointments representing race, disability, planning, health, unions, and gay and lesbian issues.

Members consider reports (sometimes from members but often from officers) and officers advise on technical issues. The members, many of whom are appointed for their expertise, often make points relating to their specific field of expertise or knowledge; in this respect the Cabinet may be able to act as a forum for joining up London issues. The items presented to the Cabinet appear to be those across the Mayor's interests which are high-profile or central to his policy commitments, and range from transport issues such as 'bendy buses' to environmental strategies. Minutes as well as procedures strongly resemble those of an old-style local government Policy and Resources committee in many respects. There does not appear to be any formal link mechanism with Assembly committees, despite the presence of six Assembly members on the Cabinet, once again showing the weakness of the GLA's constitutional structures.

As the Mayor has created a superstructure of policy committees distinct from the Assembly, what role can the Assembly play within the Greater London Authority? The Assembly suffers from two problems: one political, one constitutional. The political problem is the existence of an independent Mayor, who has no party links with any Assembly members. In most legislatures, government backbenchers can gain a modicum of influence through party links with the executive but there is no means for this to happen in the

GLA. This is aggravated by the fact that the Assembly has no sanctions over the Mayor apart from rejecting his budget. Specific policy disagreements can therefore be overridden by the Mayor.

Constitutionally, the Assembly is not helped by the requirement in the GLA Act that the Mayor appoint large numbers of Assembly members to the boards of the GLA functional bodies. Apart from the contradiction of members of a scrutinising Assembly sitting on the boards of organisations that it is meant to scrutinise, this means that individual Assembly members have several jobs, and very likely have more influence outside the Assembly than within it. The Assembly comes to resemble a reserve army of public appointees, with the scrutiny and policy development roles second best:

> Leading Assembly figures found themselves bound to a mayor who did not, in practice, have much interest in what they had to say about his business . . . There was no statutory requirement for the executive parts of the Authority to incorporate opposing views, merely to provide for their expression and reception.[30]

The Assembly's constitutional weakness is unfortunate, as it has begun to produce some interesting reports as part of its 'scrutiny' role. It scrutinises each of the Mayor's statutory strategies, some of the other non-obligatory strategies, and the annual budget. It has also produced a number of scrutiny reports on 'matters of concern to Londoners', which are not under the Mayor's control — examples are a scrutiny of football stadiums, the future of Mail Rail, infant immunisation, asylum seekers, flooding, 24-hour opening of licensed premises, and London Weighting of public-sector pay.

Though valid in themselves, the problem with all of these issues is that the recommendations are frequently directed either at central government, which has no incentive to listen, or they urge the Mayor to lobby or call for improvements from central government. In this respect the GLA represents a London-wide elected interest group. It may lobby on a national policy, and may be one of many voices which contributes to a rethink by central government, but this is a very attenuated form of democratic politics. Travers suggests that:

> While the Assembly must perform scrutiny and policy oversight functions, they are not under pressure to deliver budgets, executive control or policies. This lack of pressure to control the authority removes the need for a managed political leadership . . . Generally there appear[s] to be a reluctance to pursue the detail of Mayoral policy implementation. Question time sessions with the Mayor produced short, combative sessions . . . rather than deep probing of particular mayoral policy.[31]

---

[30] Pimlott and Rao, 2002, pp. 164–174.
[31] Travers, 2002, p. 787.

FINANCE

The structure of the GLA influences the priorities of the Mayor in another very important way: the raising of revenue. The Mayor has three sources of funding alongside Government grant: a precept on the London boroughs, the congestion charge (road pricing), and a workplace parking levy. The precept on the boroughs incorporates precepts for the Metropolitan Police and the former London Transport, which prior to the GLA were set by those organisations themselves and passed on to the boroughs. In each of the GLA's first three years the precept has increased sharply.[32] In the face of complaints from boroughs about the costs of GLA bureaucracy, the Mayor has claimed that the extra money raised has been used to raise the number of police officers in London by 2,000 (and to fund a rise in the London Weighting element of Police pay), and to replace the ageing fleet of London buses.

The rising precept demonstrates the severe limitations on a government which has no capital budget and cannot vire funds between budget heads. Without extra money, obtained from his small range of own taxes, the Mayor would have been unable to fund the capital costs of new buses, the freeze in bus and tube fares, the range of new forms of ticketing, or installing CCTV on buses. And the GLA's finances will be seriously affected by the drop in the estimated revenue from the congestion charge — halved from £130 million to £65 million per annum. Indeed, there has been recent strong criticism from Assembly members that the Mayor's budgetary predictions will lead to a deficit of £600 million by 2008. The Mayor has attempted to negotiate extra funding from central government, but so far without success.

RELATIONS WITH THE UK GOVERNMENT

> Far from being constrained in his core area of responsibility, the Mayor is more likely to be an important influence even on policies such as health and education, where he has very limited formal powers.[33]

In the run-up to the election of the Mayor and Assembly, many commentators asserted that the Mayor would be able to overcome many of the limitations on his power through electoral mandate and negotiation. The clash which would demonstrate the degree to which the *Economist's* view above was correct was expected to take place over the public-private partnership on London Underground. Pimlott and Rao suggested that 'all those involved in London government were playing a waiting game, as they worked out the

[32] This is partly because the precept is subject to the 'gearing' effect: a small rise in Mayoral revenue equates to a proportionately larger rise in the precept. The precept forms about 15–20% of the GLA's income.

[33] *The Economist*, 11 December 1999, p. 34.

true significance of hitherto untested negotiations'.[34] In the event, any expectation of American-style intergovernmental disputes ran up against the immovable object of parliamentary sovereignty.

The Mayor took the Government to court over the proposals for a public-private partnership (PPP) on the London Underground in 2001–02. The Government proposed to let three thirty-year contracts for the running of Tube services, whilst leaving the maintenance and ownership of the network with Transport for London. The three contracts were each to consist of three to four Underground lines each, to be signed by the Government before control of the Underground was handed over to Transport for London, and hence to the Mayor. All of these provisions were set out in considerable detail in sections 210–239 of the GLA Act.

When Ken Livingstone stood for the Mayoralty, he made it plain that he would oppose this arrangement with every means at his disposal. His argument in taking the Government to court was that 'privatisation' of the London Underground would prevent him from carrying out various of his statutory duties relating to the health of Londoners. The thirty-year contracts would be signed by the Government and would not be subject to variation by the Mayor. In this sense, he attempted to use one part of the GLA Act, effectively the GLA's 'constitution', against another, arguing that the provisions for PPP should be waived. The judgment of the court was that it was for the Government, and not the Mayor, 'to have the last word'.

This episode demonstrated that a UK sub-national government, whose power is tightly constrained by the Act of Parliament setting it up, cannot face down the central government in a legal battle. The idea that Livingstone could use politics, via his large electoral mandate, his 'influence', or his position as the 'voice for London', to override the fundamental power and legal relations of the UK state was shown to be without foundation. In the constitutional context of the UK, when faced with a UK Government committed to a policy sub-national governments can only negotiate marginal victories because of the vicissitudes of politics and timing. Indeed, in the 2003 deal which led to the transfer of control over the Underground to the GLA, the Mayor was able to negotiate an extra £200 million of transport funding in return for dropping all threats of future legal action.[35]

Relationships with central government have not always been so adversarial. London's proposed bid for the Olympic Games in 2012 came about through lobbying of government by the Mayor and the GLA, and its passage was helped by the Mayor's promise of considerable funds provided by the precept (yet another instance of executive power making the

[34] Pimlott and Rao, 2002, p. 172.

[35] It may be that Livingstone's tactic was to demonstrate to the electorate that he had done his utmost to oppose the PPP, having opposed it in his election manifesto, so that he should shift the blame for any failures attributable to the PPP — rather than being concerned to win the court battle itself.

difference). However, central government support for the bid was still vital: had the Government opposed or stood neutral, the GLA is unlikely to have been able to handle such an event itself. The bid is a good example of the use of the 'voice for London', a concept which was much promoted in the run-up to the first elections, and it provides an example of the role of partnership working and lobbying in achieving results in London's new dispensation.

THE LESSONS OF STRATEGIC GOVERNMENT

The Greater London Authority has taken on a subtly different position from what its creators expected. The policy initiatives it has taken, its approach to strategic government, and its use of revenue-raising powers to ramp up expenditure on policies such as transport, do not add up to the gradual development by consensus that was anticipated in 1998–1999. The directions in which it has moved reflect shifts in the debate about governance since the early years of the Blair government — most notably, away from an all-pervading faith in inclusiveness and consensus as the source of policy progress, and away from local authority elected mayors as a 'big idea'. Ultimately, Ken Livingstone has not been able to use 'strategic government' to break the golden rule — that 'he who has the gold makes the rules'. The fact that the role of the Greater London Authority has begun to seep out of the straitjacket which was designed for it can be seen as a response to the problems of running a strategic government. However, this should come as no surprise, because there are striking similarities between this analysis of the GLA and the directions taken by the previous attempt at strategic London government, the GLC.

For instance, the GLC set up the Greater London Enterprise Board (GLEB) in the early 1980s, with the aim of supporting business enterprise which could not find support from conventional lending institutions. There are affinities between GLEB and the concept of regional development agencies. At GLEB, 'projects meeting the particular employment needs of women, ethnic minorities and people with disabilities [were] given special consideration'.[36] This is an early example of cross-cutting working: economic development policy, ostensibly unrelated to equalities issues, was used to promote equalities.

There were also pressures on the GLC to diversify from its statutory role, and to take on roles in a manner similar to those described here as 'foster policies'. For instance, it organised over 800 events at the South Bank and elsewhere. It developed early bottle banks and recycling programmes. It made grants to community arts organisations, of sums which are small beer by public spending standards but which can transform the work of such

---

[36] Wheen, F., *The Battle for London* (London: Pluto Press, 1985), pp. 79–80.

groups. It established a centre for rough sleepers in Waterloo in 1983, and bought hotels to re-use as hostels for the homeless.

The GLA has found itself driven to tackle many of the same issues in many of the same ways. Ken Livingstone, as Mayor, has presided over a Rough Sleepers' Strategy; has made small grants to arts organisations; has helped obtain funding for a borough recycling scheme; and has organised a number of large outdoor events in the centre of London. In part the similarities with the early 1980s may reflect the fact that the same person is in charge, and that London faces many of the same issues now as it did in 1986. But it also shows that the nature of today's strategic government has strong affinities with yesterday's. Both GLA and GLC found themselves inhibited in their intended role; both used unexpected and innovative policies to add value London-wide.

These similarities suggest that the essential task of strategic government under each authority was the same. Both the GLC and GLA are tasked with co-ordinating other actors, but both have largely eschewed the task of 'pure' co-ordination in favour of drawing in partners to participate in a variety of small-scale schemes, in policy areas which are either non-traditional or do not have an institutional home. As Hebbert says, 'the logic of circumstances tended to deflect it [the GLC] from an intended strategic . . . role within the metropolitan region, on to a miscellaneous set of activities under its own control'.[37] It is likely that any Mayor who wanted to innovate and move outside the core tasks of the GLA would have to do so in some of the ways described in this chapter.

But the similarities should not be overstated. The GLC had three vital advantages that the GLA lacks. First, it had a substantial block budget over which it had executive control. Second, the lines of responsibility between it and the boroughs were not as clearly drawn as in the GLA Act, permitting it to take on a wider range of roles. Third, the GLC inherited a vast range of residuary responsibilities and municipal properties from its predecessors, the London and Middlesex County Councils.[38] This property facilitated such policies as holding events and providing cheap accommodation without needing to liase with (or pay) outside bodies.

THE LONDON REGION?

From the vantage point of 2003, the GLA can be better understood as a regional government than as an experimental local government. Both the GLA itself, and the ALG, refer to it as 'England's first regional government',

---

[37] Hebbert, M., *London: more by fortune than design* (Chichester: John Wiley, 1998), p. 114.

[38] All of the property referred to was either sold off or passed to the boroughs by the London Residuary Body following the abolition of the GLC in 1986.

and the template for elected assemblies in other regions of England set out in the Government's White Paper *Your Region, Your Choice*, in 2002, clearly owes much in terms of functions, structure, and process, to the GLA.[39] Regional government in England, both of the informal, partnership style already in existence in the Regional Chambers and the style planned for elected assemblies, is characterised by a focus on inclusiveness, civic engagement, effective scrutiny, and strategic planning: all of these are familiar experimental forms of governance from the GLA.

The clearest lesson for regional governments elsewhere in England must be that they cannot be expected to have a significant impact on policies for which they have no powers or budget. They will be judged on what they can do, and their politicians and administrative machines will, accordingly, concentrate on the issues where they can make changes and insert themselves into public awareness. Gaining legitimacy will be an enormous challenge for elected regional assemblies. Even if they are established following a popular referendum vote, they will have to overcome considerable indifference, hostility and dismissal of their usefulness from the general public, elites and media. They cannot afford to trade purely on the marginal impacts of foster policies. However valid and progressive any of the impacts of foster policies may be, they will never be enough in themselves to justify an extra tier of government.

Likewise, the issues with which regional assemblies are tasked need to be politically salient. Transport is the ideal politically-salient issue for the GLA, because concern about it unites the electorate of London. It is hard to see a similar issue in the White Paper on regional government which could catch the 'regional imagination'. Most policy responsibilities proposed for the regional assemblies are 'back-room' policies which will be hard to sell to electorates, and there must be a risk that regional assemblies will opt instead for quick wins and starting political arguments — with the Barnett Formula likely to be the most appealing subject of the latter.

It is hard to see a solution to this conundrum which does not involve giving substantial extra powers and/or money to the proposed elected assemblies. Strategies and foster policies demonstrate the thinness of the GLA's policy capacity. The GLA has no capital budget and only as much 'soft money' as it can raise through the precept on the boroughs (congestion charge revenue must be spent on transport). It is likely, therefore, that the effect of initiatives such as the domestic violence strategy and rough

---

[39] This similarity is often missed, or dismissed, because of the existence in the 'GLA model' of a single-person executive in the form of the Mayor. However, it is beyond doubt that there are strong similarities between the role of the GLA and the role of elected assemblies in other regions — even if this was not intended by the creators of any of these institutions. See Cabinet Office and Department of Transport, Local Government and the Regions, *Your Region, Your Choice: Revitalising the English Regions*, Cm 5511, (London: The Stationery Office, 2002).

sleepers' strategy is to give the impression that the Mayor is acting when, with the best will in the world, he cannot. It may be that, for a government whose only tool is strategy, all problems appear to be solvable by the use of the 'voice for London'.

BIBLIOGRAPHY

Primary and Official Documents

Cabinet Office and Department for Transport, Local Government and the Regions, *Your Region, Your Choice: Revitalising the English Regions*, Cm 5511, (London: The Stationery Office, 2002).

Department of the Environment, Transport and the Regions, *New Leadership for London* (London: The Stationery Office, 1998).

Department of the Environment, Transport and the Regions, *A Mayor and Assembly for London* (London: The Stationery Office, 1999).

The Mayor of London, *1 in 4: the London Domestic Violence Strategy* (London: GLA, 2001).

The Mayor of London, *From Street to Stability: The Mayor's Rough Sleepers Strategy* (London: GLA, 2001).

The Mayor of London, *Towards a Child-Friendly London* (London: GLA, 2003).

The Mayor of London, *The London Childcare Strategy: Towards affordable good quality childcare for all* (London: GLA, 2003).

Secondary Sources

Greer, S., and Sandford, M., *Fixing London* (London: The Constitution Unit, 2003).

Hebbert, M., *London: more by fortune than design* (Chichester: John Wiley, 1998).

Pimlott, B., and Rao, N., *Governing London* (Oxford: Oxford University Press, 2002).

Rydin, Y., Thornley, A., Scanlon, K., and West, K., *The Greater London Authority — A Clash of Organisational Cultures* (LSE London Discussion Paper 6, March 2002).

Tomaney, J., 'The Governance of London', in (ed.) Hazell, R., *The State and the Nations: The First Year of Devolution in the United Kingdom* (Exeter: Imprint Academic, 2000).

Travers, T., 'Decentralisation London-style: the GLA and London Governance', *Regional Studies*, 36 (7), pp. 784–785, (2002).

Travers, T., *The Politics of London: Governing an Ungovernable City* (Basingstoke: Palgrave Macmillan, 2004).

Travers, T., and Jones, G. W., *The New Government of London* (York: Joseph Rowntree Foundation, 1991).

West, K., Scanlon, K., Thornley, A., and Rydin, Y., *The Greater London Authority — Problems of Strategy Co-ordination* (LSE London Discussion Paper 7, March 2002).

Wheen, F., *The Battle for London* (London: Pluto Press, 1985).

Part II

The State

7

The More Things Change,
The More They Stay the Same
Intergovernmental Relations Four Years On

Alan Trench

When the proposals for devolution were being put in place in 1997–9, public interest centred on what devolution would mean for Scotland, Wales or Northern Ireland. Concern about the UK-wide dimensions of devolution was largely limited to the future of the Union. Much less attention was given to less dramatic issues affecting the UK as a whole: what sort of arrangements there would be for intergovernmental relations (IGR), how finance would be allocated across the UK, how the civil service would function after devolution, and how the UK Government would organise itself in response. These were important questions with major long-term implications, but they were addressed largely in private, with public and media attention looking instead at what devolution would mean for the territories where it was on offer. As a result the arrangements for intergovernmental relations were made away from the public gaze, and although given the form of agreements between governments they were not in fact open for negotiation. So, by and large, they have remained, with interest concentrated in the academic community and practitioners. Only in 2003, with the House of Lords Constitution Committee's report on *Devolution: Inter-institutional relations in the United Kingdom*, was there a sustained and formal examination of these issues.[1]

Asking 'has devolution made a difference?' about intergovernmental relations is difficult. The subject did not, after all, exist in the UK before devolution.[2] This chapter seeks to look at the impact of devolution by asking two questions. First, how do intergovernmental relations affect the ability of the devolved institutions to exercise their powers? Do they enable them to exercise the autonomy that devolution is said to have conferred on the devolved institutions, or do they act as a brake or restraint, a back-door channel by which the UK Government has taken back with one hand what it gave with

---

[1] House of Lords Select Committee on the Constitution, *Devolution: Inter-institutional Relations in the United Kingdom*, Session 2002–03, Second Report, HL Paper 28, (London: The Stationery Office, 2003a). The author served as specialist adviser to the Committee for the inquiry.

[2] Except, of course, for the study of relations between central and local government; but the clear constitutional subordination of local government meant that these were qualitatively different to the sort of intergovernmental relations introduced by devolution.

the other? Second, how has devolution affected the organisation and work-ing of the UK state at the centre? Has it led to a restructuring of the state, so that Whitehall (and Westminster) are able to respond fully to the challenges devolution poses? Or has the state simply treated devolution as another Brit-ish oddity to be incorporated into the existing structures with the minimal change necessary? This chapter will address these issues, looking first at the nature of constitutional change that devolution constituted for the United Kingdom at the centre, followed by the financial arrangements for devolution, the mechanisms by which intergovernmental relations are managed across the UK and organised in Whitehall, relations between the devolved adminis-trations and the European Union, and the extent to which elected Parliaments or Assemblies play a role in IGR, either directly or by scrutinising it.

Figure 7.1: Chronology of Events September 2002–October 2003

2002	
26 September	Richard Commission on powers and electoral arrangements of National Assembly for Wales starts taking evidence.
27 September	Meeting of JMC (Europe)
22 October	Plenary meeting of Joint Ministerial Committee at 10 Downing Street
27 October	Meeting of JMC (Europe)
18 December	Helen Liddell announces size of Scottish Parliament to remain at 129 MSPs, following consultation exercise.
2003	
15 January	House of Lords Select Committee on the Constitution publishes its report on *Devolution: Inter-institutional relations in the United Kingdom.*
30 January	Meeting of JMC (Europe)
12 March	Publication of UK Government response to House of Lords Select Committee report on *Devolution: Inter-institutional relations in the United Kingdom.*
27 March	Publication of House of Commons Welsh Affairs Committee report on *The Primary Legislative Process as It Affects Wales.*
1 May	Elections to Scottish Parliament and National Assembly for Wales.

12 June	UK Government reshuffle announced: Wales and Scotland Offices become part of new Department of Constitutional Affairs, post of Secretary of State for Scotland given to Alistair Darling (also Transport Secretary) and post of Secretary of State for Wales retained by Peter Hain who also became Leader of the House of Commons.
20 June	House of Lords debate on Select Committee on the Constitution's report on *Devolution: Inter-institutional relations in the United Kingdom.*
17 July	Publication of UK Government response to House of Commons Welsh Affairs Committee report on *The Primary Legislative Process as It Affects Wales.*
6 October	Meeting of JMC (Europe)
31 October	Meeting of JMC (Officials)

THE NEW DEVOLVED CONSTITUTION OF THE UNITED KINGDOM

Perhaps the first question that needs to be considered is the nature of the change that devolution constituted. It is easy to exaggerate the scope of that change, and miss its real significance as a result. The UK has long organised some functions territorially. The Scottish and Welsh Offices each have fairly long pedigrees of providing territorially-distinct administrations. Those administrations were part of a single UK Government, however, headed by a Secretary of State accountable to Parliament at Westminster and forming part of a UK-wide Cabinet. They had bilateral relationships with other UK Government departments, whether central departments like the Treasury or the Cabinet Office, or line departments responsible for particular functions such as health or education. Devolution built on those arrangements so that administration in the territories involved became accountable to bodies elected within that territory, and ceased to be accountable to Westminster. That local accountability was accompanied (in Scotland and spasmodically in Northern Ireland) by legislative capacity. However, this only related to certain areas of government, and key functions including the macro-economy, foreign affairs, defence, immigration and citizenship remained as matters for action only at UK level. Parliament at Westminster remains sovereign and devolution does not create any legal constraints on what Parliament may do — rather, the restraints on how Parliament may legislate are political in nature.[3] From this executive-centred focus (and intergovernmental relations is about

---

[3] That is not so for most executive functions, which are transferred outright to the devolved administration involved, not shared.

how governments relate to each other, not territories), the key changes are the emergence of local (in Scotland and Wales, national) democracy, and accountability to a democratic body based in that territory. That in turn could result in the governments having a different composition to the UK Government in London, although it has not so far done so. It did not dramatically transform the responsibilities of the government involved, or its nature in other respects, though the changes open the door to other developments in the future.

One characteristic of devolution is the limits on what the devolved institutions may do. While devolution created new elected devolved bodies with a wide range of responsibilities, the UK remains emphatically a Parliamentary state. Westminster retains the legal right to legislate on all matters throughout the UK — expressly stated in the Scotland and Northern Ireland Acts 1998 — although the UK Government has clearly stated in the Sewel convention its intention not to use that power.[4] But that is only a statement of the executive's intentions, is not yet a binding constitutional convention, and it has not been expressly adopted by Parliament either. As conventions can change, and Parliament can do things that the executive may not expect, the convention cannot be regarded as an absolute limit on Parliament's action. (It has also never properly applied to Northern Ireland, even when the Northern Ireland Assembly has been functioning, partly because the Assembly never established a procedure for dealing with requests for consent under the convention.) Perhaps contrary to expectations that devolution would mean an end to Westminster's role in legislating for Scotland, the Sewel Convention has been widely used, with forty-two motions passed (none rejected, though several were opposed) during the first Scottish Parliament, and four between June and October 2003.[5] The number of statutes touching on various aspects of the functions of the National Assembly for Wales is also considerable — 18 in the sessions 1999–2000 and 2000–01, for example. Westminster's power is not a constitutional principle but an everyday reality of government in all parts of the United Kingdom.

Moreover, the UK Government has retained control of a wide range of functions necessary for the running of the UK state. These include such matters of 'high politics' as the constitution, taxation, the economy and

---

[4] Scotland Act 1998, s. 28 (7); Northern Ireland Act 1998, s. 5 (6). In its authoritative form, the convention provides 'The United Kingdom Parliament retains authority to legislate on any issue, whether devolved or not. It is ultimately for Parliament to decide what use to make of that power. However, the UK Government will proceed in accordance with the convention that the UK Parliament would not normally legislate with regard to devolved matters except with the agreement of the devolved legislature. The devolved administrations will be responsible for seeking such agreement as may be required for this purpose on an approach from the UK Government.' *Memorandum of Understanding and supplementary agreements between the United Kingdom Government, Scottish Ministers, the Cabinet of the National Assembly for Wales and the Northern Ireland Executive Committee*, Cm 5240, (London: The Stationery Office, 2001) (henceforth 'Memorandum of Understanding'), para. 13.

[5] Information supplied by Public Information Service of the Scottish Parliament. The resolutions related to 39 Westminster bills, as one needed two Sewel motions and another three.

currency, defence, the conduct of foreign affairs, social security or immigration, asylum and nationality. They also include a number of other matters: much of the demand side of the economy (including competition law, energy, the regulation of financial services and employment law), areas where the emergence of different rules would cause serious practical and legal problems (such as company law or the licensing of medicines), or politically sensitive issues (the control of abortion).

This has several key implications. First, it means that a number of important matters are beyond the control of the devolved institutions. While they can express a view about such matters, they have no control over them, as was vividly illustrated in Scotland with the row about conditions at the Dungavel centre for asylum-seekers in 2003 — asylum matters being reserved, all the relevant decisions had been taken by the Home Office. If the devolved institutions want to influence what happens regarding these matters, the only way they can do so is by persuading the UK Government. They therefore have to act as institutional lobbyists. Second, the scope of the matters retained at UK level means that governments will need to deal with each other for many policy initiatives of the devolved administrations — either because the UK Government has parallel responsibilities as 'government for England', or because of the interaction of devolved functions and those retained at UK level. An example of the latter is the interaction of social security (eligibility for attendance allowance) with the Scottish Executive's policy of paying for long-term care for the elderly.[6] Intergovernmental relations are therefore a key element of the structure of devolution in the UK, even if the framework within which they operate was something of an afterthought to devolution.

A third structural aspect of devolution makes intergovernmental relations integral to the UK's system of devolution. That relates to the internal constitutions of the devolved institutions. Except for a small number of minor matters, it is beyond the power of the devolved bodies to alter their structure or internal arrangements (such as legislative-executive relations) – that is reserved to the UK Parliament. The ingenuity with which the devolved institutions have usually approached these constraints (as with the National Assembly for Wales) were of no avail when confronted with an express restriction, as for example when Sir David Steel's ill-health meant he needed to be absent for medical treatment, but a third deputy presiding officer could not be appointed as the Scotland Act limited the number to two and this was beyond the Parliament's power to amend.[7] While devolution may be, in Ron

---

[6] See Simeon, R., 'Free Personal Care: Policy Divergence and Social Citizenship', in Hazell, R., (ed.) *The State of the Nations 2003: The Third Year of Devolution in the United Kingdom* (Exeter: Imprint Academic, 2003), p. 219.

[7] Scotland Act 1998, Schedule 4, para. 4, and sections 29 and 53. The number of deputy presiding officers is fixed by section 19.

Davies's hackneyed phrase, 'a process rather than an event', its development is a process for which reference needs to be constantly made to Westminster. Thus in 2002 and 2003 we have seen the Secretary of State for Scotland take more than twelve months to determine whether the size of the Scottish Parliament should remain at 129 or be reduced in line with the reduction of the number of Scottish Westminster MPs, as provided for in the Scotland Act 1998 — a minor matter in a UK context, but important in Scotland.[8] In Wales the issue is much more significant and concerns the powers of the National Assembly and its electoral arrangements, presently being considered by the Richard Commission.[9] The Secretary of State for Wales has started to set out his stall for dealing with the Commission's report, suggesting that the main criterion for him to endorse change should be whether changes would improve the delivery of public services in Wales.[10] That is a questionable criterion to use, and if its effect were to block change for which there was general demand in Wales it would be likely to have serious political consequences.

The sense that the devolved administrations are not masters in their own houses is reinforced by the position of the Home Civil Service (so far as Scotland and Wales are concerned; once again, Northern Ireland is different). The position of the civil service and its operation as a single civil service are preserved.[11] That is tempered in practice by the amendment made to the Civil Service Code providing that officials owe their loyalty to the administration in which they serve, not a single UK Government, and by the grant of very considerable autonomy to individual departments (including both Whitehall departments and the devolved administrations) for matters including grading structures, staffing and pay levels. The Home Civil Service therefore starts to resemble a brand and a set of safeguards for integrity, impartiality and independence, under the aegis of the UK Civil Service

---

[8] See The Scotland Office, *The Size of the Scottish Parliament: A Consultation*, (London: The Stationery Office, 2001); Scotland Office Press Release, 'Liddell announces decision on MSP numbers', 18 December 2002.

[9] Commission on the Assembly's Powers and Electoral Arrangements *The Powers of the National Assembly for Wales - issues and questions for consultation* (November 2002) and *The Electoral Arrangements of the National Assembly for Wales - issues and questions for consultation* (March 2003); available at: http://www.richardcommission.gov.uk/content/consultation/index.htm

[10] See for example his evidence to the Richard Commission, available at http://www.richard commission.gov.uk/content/evidence/oral/sosw/index-e.htm. For a critique, see Trench, A., 'After the Richard Commission: How will Hain decide what to do?' *Agenda*, November 2003 (Cardiff: Institute of Welsh Affairs).

[11] Scotland Act 1998, s. 51 and Schedule 5, para. 8; Government of Wales Act 1998, s. 34. For Northern Ireland, the separate Northern Ireland Civil Service is protected from political interference by making the functions and procedures of the Civil Service Commissioners for Northern Ireland a reserved matter: Northern Ireland Act 1998, Schedule 3, para. 16. The Northern Ireland Assembly can therefore only legislate on the matter with the consent of the Secretary of State.

Commissioners.[12] But accountability within the Civil Service still ends in Whitehall, with the Cabinet Secretary in his capacity as Head of the Home Civil Service, and the UK Prime Minister as Minister for the Civil Service. The fact that the Permanent Secretary of a devolved administration is not accountable to the First Minister for any staffing decisions he or she takes has a more immediate effect; that has caused some rows behind the scenes, notably involving Muir Russell and Jack McConnell in Scotland.[13] That this rather odd arrangement has not led to worse problems is fortuitous and unlikely to continue, even if there are few pressures to compel change at present.[14]

The asymmetric nature of devolution reinforces the central role of intergovernmental relations. The asymmetry arises in three ways: first, the fact that devolution is largely limited to Scotland, Wales and Northern Ireland, with a prospect of it extending to England but little actual transfer of functions so far; second, that the arrangements for devolution to each territory are different, creating a different set of constitutional issues for them; and third; the significant differences that exist in the functions exercised by each devolved administration and its Parliament or Assembly. This means that each devolved territory has concerns with the UK Government that will largely be unique, not shared with the other devolved territories. It follows that each territory has little reason to develop its relations with institutions from the other devolved territories, because their concerns are for the most part specific to that territory, and there is little scope to form a common front with the other devolved institutions.

These structural features mean that, from the outset, intergovernmental relations in the UK were likely to be dominated by the UK Government — by its role as gatekeeper for both many matters of policy and for constitutional change, by sheer size, and by its role as government of England in making policy for the largest part of the UK. They mean that the expectations of the changes devolution would bring about need to be treated with caution. It was a major change, but it was also easy to exaggerate its scope. That in turn raised the question of whether the UK Government's dominance would impinge on the autonomy of the devolved administrations.

---

[12] Notwithstanding the revelations of attempts at political interference revealed during summer 2003 by evidence to the Hutton Inquiry into the death of Dr David Kelly. Lord Hutton's report had not been published at the time of writing.

[13] Discussed in Trench, A., 'Intergovernmental Relations: Officialdom Still in Control', in Hazell, R., (ed.) *The State of the Nations 2003: The Third Year of Devolution in the United Kingdom* (Exeter: Imprint Academic, 2003a), p. 155.

[14] The Lords Constitution Committee was satisfied by the present arrangements: see House of Lords Select Committee on the Constitution, 2003a, chapter 5.

FOLLOWING THE MONEY:
THE FINANCIAL ASPECTS OF DEVOLUTION

While devolution brought about considerable legal and constitutional changes, it scarcely affected the financial structure of the UK. This is both one of the paradoxes of devolution — that upheaval in one area was accompanied by negligible change in its counterpart — and the most important single area in which the framework of devolution remains half-completed.

The centrepiece of the financial arrangements for devolution is the Barnett formula — widely referred to, if less often understood.[15] The formula is often regarded as fearsomely complex, although in truth it is simple in itself but has unintended and increasingly dysfunctional consequences, which are complex. The key elements of the formula are well-known (and were explained by David Bell and Alex Christie in *The State of the Nations 2001*).[16] Its key features are set out in Figure 7.2.

Figure 7.2: Key Fatures of the Barnett Formula

- It is simply the formula by which HM Treasury calculates how much money should be allocated to the devolved administrations (strictly, to the Scottish Parliament, National Assembly for Wales and Northern Ireland Assembly). That money is then paid from the Consolidated Fund to the relevant Secretary of State, as authorised by the annual Appropriation Act, and the Secretary of State transfers the money to the devolved institutions after deducting the costs of running his or her Office.

- The formula allocates increases in the funding of the devolved administrations (or in principle reductions) in proportion to increases on comparable services provided by the UK Government in England.

- The increases are calculated on the basis of the population of the territory of the devolved administration in relation to that of England. Scotland, with a little under 10 per cent of England's population, receives just under £1 more for every extra £10 spent in England.

- The baseline on which those increases are calculated is a historic one; for each year, the baseline is the total of the year before's starting point, plus increases made during the year, and so on back to 1978-9 (when the formula was introduced in its current form).

---

[15] This is set out in HM Treasury, *Funding the Scottish Parliament, National Assembly for Wales and Northern Ireland Assembly: a Statement of Funding Policy*, 3rd edition, (London: The Stationery Office, 2002).

[16] Bell, D., and Christie, A., 'Finance – The Barnett Formula: Nobody's Child' in Trench, A., (ed.) *The State of the Nations 2001: The Second Year of Devolution in the United Kingdom* (Exeter: Imprint Academic, 2001).

- The funding so calculated is paid in the form of a block grant. Once it is in the hands of the devolved administration, that administration can spend the funding as it wishes. The fact that an increase in grant has been caused by an increase in health spending in England does not create any formal obligation to spend the money on health (although it may create political pressures to do so).
- There remain a number of ways that the Barnett formula can be by-passed, notably for claims made by a devolved administration on the UK Reserve (which the Treasury maintains. Such claims are wholly matters for the Treasury to decide, using its discretion).[17]

The Barnett formula takes no account of need in allocating funding. Moreover, it will act as a brake on spending increases for all the devolved administrations, especially for Scotland and (to a lesser degree) Northern Ireland, which start with markedly higher levels of per capita public spending than in England. As Bell and Christie showed, that convergence occurs for mathematical reasons as spending increases. It also means that the devolved administrations have no control over increases in their budgets from year to year (or even within a year), which is driven by increases in funding for services in England. That is not to say that the formula does not have strong points. In particular, it provides for a degree of consistency and reliability in funding (as the details of how much spending will be available are forecast through the Comprehensive Spending Review process and become available as part of the UK Government's Budget Statement). It also gives very considerable freedom to the devolved administrations, as the block grant gives them the discretion to decide how to allocate their funds. Compared with Whitehall departments, which have always had to negotiate their funding with the Treasury and are now subject to public service agreements to determine their policies and their success in achieving them, as well as their goals more generally, the devolved administrations have a great deal of room for manoeuvre.

Before devolution, it helped that the formula was acknowledged to be a somewhat rough-and-ready way of making that allocation, and could be set aside if there were a good reason. That happened with a nurses' pay award in 1983 (which the Scottish Office considered it could not otherwise fund), and at least one subsequent Secretary of State for Scotland has emphasised the value of arrangements outside the formula to benefit Scotland.[18] It has also helped that the amounts of spending under the control of the devolved administrations are small by Treasury standards — they account for 8.8 per

[17] See generally House of Lords Select Committee on the Constitution, 2003a, chapter 3, and on formula by-pass Heald, D., 'Territorial Public Expenditure in the United Kingdom', *Public Administration*, 72, (1994), pp. 147-75, at pp. 168-170.

[18] See Heald, 1994; Lang, I., *Blue Remembered Years: a political memoir* (London: Politicos, 2002), pp. 193–4.

cent of the total amount of spending by the UK Government.[19] The formula is highly appropriate for distributing funding within a single government but makes much less sense in the context of devolution, when calls for funding to be allocated according to transparent, comprehensible criteria justifiable by some external standard (such as need) are made loudly and become harder to resist.

The alterations made to the pre-devolution arrangements were very limited. First, the formula itself was published and therefore became more transparent — but also harder to depart from. The Treasury has become wary of setting precedents that may increase its spending commitments to the devolved administrations, or have ramifications for other spending departments. There have been some negotiations about what items attract a consequential payment if spending in England increases, but even these are limited.[20]

Finance has therefore become more sensitive an issue but, by and large, less negotiable. Second, when extra funding has been allocated, it has been outside the formula. This may have been in a clear and transparent manner (such as the payment of some expenses arising from the 2001 outbreak of Foot and mouth disease), or in a manner that was harder to understand. A notable example is the additional funds made available to the National Assembly as a consequence of North and West Wales and the Valleys being granted Objective 1 status by the European Commission — a decision explicable only because the Treasury controversially changed its mind.[21] No other part of the UK receives or has received such privileged treatment for Objective 1 funds, with the exception of the 'PEACE II' cross-border programme to support the Northern Ireland peace process.

Third, the devolved administrations have approached the Comprehensive Spending Review rounds as an opportunity to negotiate such extra funding. The 2002 round produced comparatively little benefit for the devolved administrations, however. (Wales obtained nothing extra, Northern Ireland a

---

[19] According to the estimates for 2003–04 set out in the 2002 Comprehensive Spending Review, total UK spending will be £418.4 billion, and the spending by the Scottish Parliament, National Assembly and Northern Ireland Assembly total £36.8 billion. This includes spending on such UK functions as defence and social security. See HM Treasury, *2002 Spending Review: New Public Spending Plans 2003–2006*, Cm 5570, (London: The Stationery Office, 2002), Tables 1.1 and 22.1.

[20] The 2001 Comprehensive Spending Review saw transport in London being shifted from counting as a 'UK service' to an 'England service', meaning extra spending will trigger a consequential payment to the devolved administrations.

[21] House of Commons Welsh Affairs Select Committee, *Objective 1 European Funding in Wales*, Session 2001–02, Second Report, HC 520, (London: The Stationery Office, 2002) Minutes of Evidence, 21 January 2002, QQ. 62. 63, 65 and 70. The failure to provide extra funding had occasioned the downfall of Alun Michael as First Secretary of the National Assembly; see Osmond, J., 'A Constitutional Convention by Other Means: the First Year of the National Assembly for Wales' in Hazell, R., (ed) *The State and the Nations: The First Year of Devolution in the United Kingdom* (Exeter: Imprint Academic, 2000).

power to borrow under the Reinvestment and Reform Programme.) That may explain increased doubts about the formula that have been expressed by the devolved administrations since then.

These have been very modest changes, however. The freedom of the administrations in allocating funding is considerable and means that their autonomy in making policy is hampered to only a limited degree by the arrangements. However, the lack of fiscal accountability for the devolved administrations affects their relations with their legislatures and the publics that elect them, and so their autonomy in a broader sense. So far, this has not led to serious consequences, but the structure of the relationship is fundamentally unequal. Moreover, the adjustments made to the pre-devolution arrangements have been minimal. The system as a whole not only closely resembles that preceding devolution but is highly appropriate for distributing money among departments of a single government. It provides certainty and a crude measure of fairness, but is very unlike the arrangements one might expect certainty for allocating finance between different governments which may have fundamentally different policies or ideologies.

The main development that has occurred since devolution has been the increasingly serious debate about public funding, concerning not just the devolved territories but also spending across the regions of England.[22] The Treasury has taken the lead in encouraging, even funding, much of this work, and it is clear that Treasury officials are not merely being polite when they say that they follow academic discussions on the topic with interest.[23] This is clearly a debate that is going somewhere, even if the destination or arrival time are presently unknown.

THE ARRANGEMENTS FOR INTERGOVERNMENTAL RELATIONS

IGR Across the UK

Much of the literature on intergovernmental relations in the UK emphasises the degree to which it is un-institutionalised.[24] The formal institutional arrangements are limited and not widely used in practice. The Memorandum

[22] See Maclean, I., and Macmillan, A., 'The Distribution of Public Expenditure across the UK Regions', *Fiscal Studies*, 24, no. 1, pp. 45–71, (2003); Maclean, I., et al *Identifying the flow of domestic and European expenditures into the English Regions*, Final Report, September 2003, available at http://www.nuff.ox.ac.uk/projects/odpm/ ; Maclean, I., and Macmillan, A., *New localism, new finance* (London: New Local Government Network, 2003); Heald, D., *Funding the Northern Ireland Assembly: Assessing the Options* (Belfast: Northern Ireland Economic Council, 2003).

[23] It is also notable that these officials diligently attend academic seminars on devolution finance.

[24] See for example House of Lords, 2003a, especially chapter 1; Trench, 2003a; Trench, A., 'Intergovernmental Relations: Whitehall Still Rules UK', in Trench, A., (ed.) *The State of the Nations 2001: The Second Year of Devolution in the United Kingdom* (Exeter: Imprint Academic, 2001); Hazell, R., 'Intergovernmental Relations: Whitehall Rules OK?', in Hazell, R., (ed.) *The State and the Nations: The First Year of Devolution in the United Kingdom* (Exeter: Imprint Academic, 2000).

of Understanding and specific departmental concordats are largely procedural not substantive in nature, avowedly have no legal status, and are
seldom used or referred to by officials. Updating them has usually occurred
when UK Government departments' functions change, not because of a
change in the relationship between the governments involved. Meetings of
the Joint Ministerial Committee (JMC), whether in plenary or functional
forms, occur relatively infrequently. The plenary JMC meets more or less
annually, as required by the Memorandum of Understanding (though the
2003 meeting was arranged only to take place in mid-December, nearly 14
months after the previous one). Transparency is also a problem, but so far as
one can tell its meetings are ceremonial, even ritualistic in character — the
communiqués regularly talk of 'sharing experiences' and 'best practice'.
The meetings do not serve as a forum for the airing of differences let alone
(as was originally intended) the resolution of disputes. No such dispute
appears ever to have been brought to the JMC, even when political tensions
have run high. The closest this came was with the funding of long-term care
for the elderly in Scotland, and the fact that the Scottish Executive's policy
would save the UK Treasury about £21 million by removing the entitlement
to attendance allowance from elderly people in Scotland. The Department of
Work & Pensions declined to transfer the funding it saved as a result to the
Executive, and while the Executive was unhappy it chose not to take the
point any further.

On the legal side, there has been a marked aversion to any sort of litigation
between governments. The only cases challenging the powers of the
devolved institutions to go to the courts have been brought by third parties,
involved human rights issues, and mostly have been based on issues of Scots
criminal law or procedure.[25] The courts have resisted attempts (notably in the
Mills case, discussed in *The State of the Nations 2003*) to fill gaps in the
devolution legislation or how it relates to other statutes, in that case, the
Human Rights Act 1998.[26]

A large part of the explanation of why there have been so few disputes is
the high level of political consensus there has been between the UK Government and devolved administrations. Labour has formed not only the Government in London since before 1999, but also that in Cardiff Bay in 1999–2000
and since the 2003 elections. It has dominated the coalitions in Scotland
since 1999, and in Wales between 2000 and 2003. Even in Northern Ireland

---

[25] There have been two cases challenging legislation of the Scottish Parliament on human rights
ground. The challenge to the Mental Health (Public Safety and Appeals) (Scotland) Act 1999 was
dismissed in *Anderson, Reid and Doherty v. Scottish Ministers and Advocate General for Scotland.*
Two challenges to the Protection of Wild Mammals (Scotland) Act 2002, in the cases of *Jeremy Whaley
and Brian Friend v. the Lord Advocate* and a judicial review application brought by *Trevor Adams and
others* were dismissed by the Outer House of the Court of Session on 20 June 2003 and 31 July 2003
respectively.

[26] Trench, 2003a, pp. 162–3.

there is no political competition between Labour and the major parties in the Assembly. That both creates the context for highly consensual IGR, and enables it to rely heavily on informal mechanisms. The Welsh First Minister and the Secretary of State meet every week, although for Scotland such meetings in person are less frequent. There are also often bilateral meetings of UK Ministers and their devolved counterparts, and frequent contact by telephone or e-mail as well as in person on the part of officials. Most of that involves those concerned with particular policy areas — agriculture ministers speaking to agriculture ministers, and so forth — rather than the officials at the centre of each government dealing with each other. In any event, those officials are few in number (especially in the devolved administrations), and sometimes combine those responsibilities with other matters as well.

This sort of contact is ad hoc, driven by current policy issues or pending legislation, and relatively unstructured. It assumes a consensus of approach even though those involved serve different administrations — a point most clearly highlighted by Helen Liddell who explained that such informality worked because when she spoke to the Scottish First Minister they knew they were 'among friends'.[27] It is seen by many of those involved as reflecting the success of devolution, because more formal arrangements are not needed. But it comes at a price. It is clear that in some cases devolved administrations have been consulted very late in the day about UK Government initiatives, usually by oversight or because final decisions in Whitehall are taken very late in the day, allowing no time for consulting the devolved administrations. This appears to have happened recently with the White Paper on higher education in England, published in January 2003.[28] Some officials in Whitehall appear unaware of what devolution means in terms of the policy responsibilities they may have, or the implications of asymmetry — they assume that consultation with one devolved administration means all devolution questions have been covered, for example. It raises the key question of what will happen when serious political differences emerge, whether within parties or between them, to which the attitude of UK Government appears complacent, as the House of Lords Constitution Committee found.

In this area, relatively little has changed — certainly, less than was expected before devolution.[29] What has developed is a pattern that is part-way between the sort of form that intergovernmental relations

[27] House of Lords Select Committee on the Constitution, *Devolution: Inter-institutional Relations in the United Kingdom Evidence complete to 10 July 2002*, Session 2001–02, HL Paper 147, (The Stationery Office, 2002), Evidence of Mrs Liddell, 10 April 2002, Q. 157.

[28] Department for Education and Skills, *The future of higher education*, Cm 5735, (London: The Stationery Office, 2003).

[29] See for example Cornes, R., 'Intergovernmental Relations in a Devolved United Kingdom: Making Devolution Work', in Hazell, R., (ed.) *Constitutional Futures: A history of the next ten years* (Oxford: Oxford University Press, 1999), chapter 9; Bogdanor, V., *Devolution in the United Kingdom* (Oxford: Oxford University Press, 1999), chapter 7; Burrows, N., *Devolution* (London: Sweet & Maxwell, 2000), chapter 5.

commonly take in federal systems, where round-table meetings between ministers from state or province and the federal government take place regularly, both to deal with particular policy sectors and (at the level of premier or prime minister) to deal with high-level political and constitutional issues. That may be complemented by bilateral and informal contacts, but the use of a more institutionalised framework is central to the 'grammar' of intergovernmental relations.

In other respects, what happens in the United Kingdom resembles the way UK Government departments deal with each other. In this sense devolution can be seen as building directly on the system of departmental interaction that operated before devolution. As departments of a single UK Government, responsible to a UK Government Minister who was part of the UK Cabinet and bound by the doctrine of collective responsibility, the Scottish and Welsh Office and Northern Ireland departments enjoyed considerable autonomy (tempered in the case of Northern Ireland by Ministers who had no political base in the province and who had more pressing political concerns).[30] Run by ministers who were part of a single government, even if they had serious disagreements with one another, and by officials who were all part of the same civil service although loyal to different ministers (Northern Ireland again being an exception), a particular way of dealing with one another developed. The Memorandum of Understanding and concordats sought to preserve this so far as possible, by putting in writing the key aspects of those understandings that needed to be preserved in the absence of collective responsibility and a common political direction. Thus the Memorandum of Understanding makes great play of the 'four Cs'; communication, consultation, co-operation and confidentiality. [31] In practice, interaction between the four governments resembles very largely the pattern of interaction that previously took place within a single if fragmented government — which can, of course, involve fierce disputes about policy between departments.[32]

The role of the Joint Ministerial Committee as the highest forum for intergovernmental relations is curious. Its intended functions as set out in the Memorandum of Understanding are

---

[30] See Mitchell, J., *Governing Scotland* (Basingstoke: Palgrave Macmillan, 2003); Deacon, R. M., *The Governance of Wales: the Welsh Office and the policy process 1964–1999* (Cardiff: Welsh Academic Press, 2002); Rose, R., *Ministers and Ministries* (Oxford: Oxford University Press, 1987).

[31] Memorandum of Understanding, paras 4–12. The best discussion of the arrangements put in place by these remains Rawlings, R., 'Concordats of the Constitution', *Law Quarterly Review* , 116, pp. 257–286, (2000), but Rawlings does not discuss this point.

[32] See Daintith, T., and Page, A., *The Executive in the Constitution: structure, autonomy, and internal control* (Oxford: Oxford University Press, 1999).

a) to consider non-devolved matters impinging on devolution responsibilities and devolved matters impinging on non-devolved
responsibilities;

b) where agreed, to consider devolved matters if discussion of their
respective treatment across the UK is beneficial;

c) to keep arrangements for liaison between the UK Government and
the devolved administrations under review

d) to consider disputes between administrations.[33]

The first is the customary role of a forum for intergovernmental discussion
along the lines of federal-state or federal-provincial meetings in classic
federal systems, where the functions of the two levels or orders of government need to take account of policies of the other. To a degree the fourth is
similarly a usual function of such systems. But the JMC, in both 'plenary'
and 'functional' forms, has only been of limited use for such matters, and
even that has depended considerably on the nature of the subject-matter
involved. The nature of plenary JMC meetings has already been discussed.
With the functional forms, much depends on the nature of the issue involved
and the interest shown by the UK Government and its key ministers. For
example, there have been frequent meetings of the JMC (Europe), particularly in the run-up to the Giscard Convention on the Future of Europe and
during the early stages of the Convention's work, apparently to discuss the
emergent agenda for the Convention and the UK's policy toward it.
However, that has been supplemented by meetings of a group of more junior
ministers, MINECOR, which met six times in 2002 and four times between
January and November 2003. The EU has created a similar need for regular
discussions of agriculture matters, particularly while the restructuring of the
Common Agriculture Policy has been on the agenda of the Council of Ministers, and there have been frequent meetings of agriculture ministers for that
purpose. (Attendance has been the rural affairs ministers from Scotland and
Wales, the agriculture minister from either the Northern Ireland Executive or
the Northern Ireland Office, the Minister of State from MAFF or DEFRA, to
speak for England, and the UK Secretary of State in the chair.) But these
have taken place outside the JMC framework altogether, partly because they
are informal and working meetings but also because the devolved ministers
were concerned that the formality of a JMC would risk an open confrontation
with the UK Government that would not help them regarding the immediate
issue but would sour future relations.[34] This trend is continuing: the finance
ministers from the UK Government, Northern Ireland Office and Scottish
and Welsh devolved administrations met (twice) outside the JMC

---

[33] Memorandum of Understanding, para. 23 (slightly abridged).
[34] Interviews with devolved administration officials and politicians.

framework in 2003, the meetings being convened by Paul Boateng as Chief Secretary to the Treasury.[35]

At the same time, the specific formats of the JMC to deal with the Knowledge Economy, Poverty and Health have worked less effectively. That dealing with the Knowledge Economy came to an end when Tony Blair's interest moved on, and (curiously) it appears to have played little role if any in the development of the knowledge economy as an economic development policy in Scotland, Wales or Northern Ireland. Something similar has happened with the JMC (Health), which met four times in 2000 but not since — it stopped meeting when the UK Prime Minister's concerns changed.[36] The JMC (Poverty) met several times in 1999–2000 and then became moribund until September 2002, when it was revived and an ambitious work programme and series of further meetings for 2003 outlined. Its revival suggested that Gordon Brown had become concerned about the Treasury's lack of influence on devolved functions and that he wished to use the JMC as a means to shape devolved policy, perhaps in a way similar to that of public service agreements with Whitehall departments. However, none of the planned further meetings has taken place — supposedly because of diary pressures, perhaps also because of the Chancellor's other political and personal concerns, but perhaps also because its priority has declined after the Treasury concluded that the JMC would not in fact help it advance its agenda.[37] Yet the devolved administrations appear to be keen on the Chancellor's initiative of establishing a new functional form of the JMC, for economic matters, expected to meet for the first time early in 2004.

The JMC's functions have also been paralleled by those of the British-Irish Council (BIC), established under Strand 3 of the Belfast Agreement. The BIC, called the 'council of the Isles' by some when it was established, brings together the UK and Irish Governments with the devolved administrations from Scotland, Wales and Northern Ireland, and the governments of Guernsey, Jersey and the Isle of Man. Its membership ranges greatly in terms of status, legal powers, population and wealth. Again, its meetings have had a ceremonial air about them. However, there have been two surprises with the BIC. The first is that, after a slow start, in a number of policy areas it has undertaken functional work which has been found useful by many of those involved. These have included policy about

---

[35] The Chancellor is responsible for macro-economic management and the raising of revenue by taxation, the Chief Secretary for the allocation of spending among UK Government departments. The lack of separate tax-raising powers means that the devolved finance ministers are similarly only for allocating funding, not raising it, so their analogue in the UK Government is the Chief Secretary.
A Treasury Press Statement confirmed the first meeting, on 10 March 2003, but none was issued for the second.
[36] I am indebted to my colleague Scott Greer for information on this point.
[37] UK Government officials involved have simply not known why the further meetings did not happen other than diary congestion.

drugs, the knowledge economy, and sharing experiences about minority languages. The BIC has, of course, no formal standing in relation to these areas, but the fact of its existence means it has taken on a role which was probably not contemplated when it was established. The second surprise has been the continuation of BIC's existence and work while devolution to Northern Ireland has been suspended, since October 2002, accomplished through a further agreement between the UK and the Republic of Ireland.[38]

Because of the political setting in which it operates, the JMC has not been called on to deal with many of its formal functions. It has taken on rather different ones, which start from those allocated to it by the Memorandum of Understanding but move a considerable way beyond that. Many of those derive from the interests of the principal political figures in the UK Government, and when those interests move on arrangements to use the JMC framework are abandoned. But more often the framework is simply unused, leaving intergovernmental business to be conducted in a similar sort of obscurity to meetings between UK Government Ministers or departments. The preference for informal and often bilateral meetings and arrangements, combined with the way the JMC framework responds to the priorities of politicians at the centre of government, strongly resembles the way the UK Government acted internally before devolution. It also reinforces the relative dominance of the UK Government in relation to the devolved administrations. It therefore suggests both that IGR could hamper the ability of the devolved institutions to exercise their powers (even though it has not done so to date), and that the response of the UK state has been to accommodate devolution with minimal change.

Organising Whitehall For Devolution

The UK Government's arrangements for dealing with devolution have evolved slowly but markedly since 1999. The question is whether the UK Government has done more than the minimum to accommodate devolution within the ministerial and civil service structures of Whitehall. While the parts of central government responsible for dealing with the devolved administrations have been reshaped, there has been little attempt to create the 'strong centre' forecast by Hazell and Morris in the run-up to devolution.[39] Many of the changes appear to have been driven by short-term considerations and what ministers suit which portfolios at a particular time, rather than a more structured or coherent approach to the structure of government. Given that the lead for such matters lies firmly with the Prime Minister and that Tony Blair is famously uninterested in machinery of government issues, this is not surprising, but it has had significant consequences.

[38] See chapter 4.
[39] Hazell, R., and Morris, R., 'Machinery of Government: Whitehall' in Hazell, 1999.

The first change was to constitute four key offices. Three were concerned with specific territories; the renamed Scotland and Wales Offices carved out of the former Scottish and Welsh Offices, and the reshaped Northern Ireland Office. Each was headed by a Secretary of State, a senior figure from (in the case of Scotland and Wales) the nation in question, supported by a Parliamentary Under-Secretary of State. The Scotland and Wales Offices have some programme responsibilities, including for devolved Parliament or Assembly elections, while the Northern Ireland Office retained responsibility for the peace process overall, and also for the excepted functions of crime and criminal justice, security and policing. Their main focus is instead the relationship between that territory, including its devolved administration, and the UK Government. The roles of the offices and the ministers in them were set out most clearly in the Devolution Guidance Notes issued by the Cabinet Office, discussed in chapters about intergovernmental relations in previous volumes of *The State of the Nations*.[40] These offices were to play a number of roles:

- to be the guardian of the devolution settlement relating to that territory. In practice this means being the UK Government's in-house experts on the devolution settlement affecting that territory — important given the distinctive character of each set of arrangements
- to advise the Secretary of State on reserved or non-transferred matters affecting that territory, deriving from the fact that each Secretary of State retains a small number of functions and acts as transmission-belt for the block grant to the devolved administration, and sits on large numbers of Cabinet committees (somewhere between 15 and 25, depending on the number of committees in being), including practically all those dealing with domestic affairs.
- to support the Secretary of State in his or her representative role, of speaking for the UK Government on matters relating to that territory and of speaking for the territory on matters on which it had dealings with the UK Government.

The last role, in particular, was always likely to give rise to confusion — who should speak for a territory, the head of its elected government or a UK politician chosen by the Prime Minister? And while each might claim a mandate to speak for the territory, what about speaking for its devolved administration? Paul Murphy, when Secretary of State for Wales, was keen to emphasise that he presented the views of the devolved administration within the

---

[40] See in particular Hazell, R., 'Intergovernmental Relations: Whitehall Rules OK?' in Hazell, R., (ed.) *The State and the Nations: The First Year of Devolution in the United Kingdom* (Exeter: Imprint Academic, 2000).

UK Government, but did not represent it.[41] That is an important distinction, but one which fails to deal with the problem of what happens when the views are imperfectly presented, or when the devolved administration may not have a view because the UK Government has not felt able to involve the devolved administrations in its internal deliberations.

A further problem has been that the real work of a Secretary of State for a devolved territory not only takes place behind the scenes but also requires relatively little time. There will be occasional crises to deal with, and more routine political liaison, but nothing like enough to need the full-time attentions of a senior minister. There are, after all, no programme responsibilities. The Tories, having spotted this, suggested at the 2001 UK general election that the posts become part-time.[42] Helen Liddell was clearly well aware of it too, starting initiatives such as the international network 'Friends of Scotland' to raise the Office's profile, but she became a particular target of the press when her diary was published showing her taking French lessons during working hours. When Paul Murphy was moved to Northern Ireland in October 2002 and Peter Hain became Secretary of State for Wales, Hain retained his responsibilities as the UK Government's representative on the Convention for the Future of Europe and so in reality was a part-time Secretary of State. In June 2003 and with the work of the Convention almost finished, Hain also became Leader of the House of Commons, following the resignation of Robin Cook (and a short interregnum). At the same time, Alistair Darling became Secretary of State for Scotland, in combination with the Transport job. The UK Government has therefore clearly accepted that these are part-time jobs — but believes that the nations still need their own spokesman in Cabinet, even if an increasing amount of the work will actually be done by the junior Minister in each Office.[43]

That approach is significantly at odds with the view expressed by many observers of devolution. one of the key recommendations of the Lords

[41] House of Lords Select Committee on the Constitution, 2002, Evidence of Mr Murphy, 10 April 2002, Q. 175.

[42] See The Conservative Party, *Time for common sense in Wales* (London: The Conservative Party, 2001), p.34; The Conservative Party, *Time for common sense in Scotland* (London: The Conservative Party, 2001), p.45. The claim did not appear in the UK manifesto.

[43] On the implications for devolution of the 2003 reshuffle, see Hazell, R., 'Merger: What Merger? Scotland, Wales, and the new Department for Constitutional Affairs', *Public Law*, Winter 2003, pp. 650–655. Both Alistair Darling and Peter Hain gave evidence to the relevant territorial select committee about the restructuring of their offices: Scottish Affairs Committee, *Minutes of Evidence for Tuesday 17 June 2003: Rt Hon Alistair Darling MP, Secretary of State for Scotland, Mrs Anne McGuire MP, Parliamentary Under-Secretary of State, Department for Constitutional Affairs and Mr David Crawley, Head of the Scotland Office*, Session 2002–03, HC 815, (London: The Stationery Office, 2003); Welsh Affairs Select Committee, *Minutes of Evidence for 25 June 2003: Rt Hon Peter Hain MP, Secretary of State for Wales, Mrs Alison Jackson, Head of Wales Office and Mr John Kilner, Head of Finance, Wales Office*, Session 2002–03, HC 883, (London: The Stationery Office, 2003). Both are available from the Committees' pages at http://www.parliament.uk/parliamentary_committees/ parliamentary_committees15.cfm.

Constitution Committee, was that there should be a single 'devolution department', headed by a Cabinet Minister and supported, if necessary, by more junior ministers responsible for a particular territory.[44] That would enable the UK Government to take an overview of devolution and its policy toward the devolved territories and their institutions, rather than leaving matters to be dealt with ad hoc. However, the UK Government had little time for such recommendations, noting that there were no plans to change the allocation of Ministerial portfolios (or administrative responsibilities relating to devolution), although both were kept under review.[45]

The restructuring of Ministerial jobs has been paralleled by what has happened on the official level. The Scotland and Wales Offices were headed, not by Permanent Secretaries, but by officials at Grade 2 or 3 (the former Deputy or Under-Secretary levels). They were comparatively small in terms of staff, the Wales Office much more so than the Scotland Office given the relative populations of Wales and Scotland and their responsibilities, particularly primary legislation for Wales.[46] Part of the reason for that was the way the Scotland Office had grown under John Reid, who wished the Office to have its own capacity to develop policy for Scotland. The difference in size between the two had become such an anomaly that by 2002 the Wales Office was reviewing its staffing and looking to increase its size.

With the June 2003 reshuffle both Offices were incorporated into the new Department for Constitutional Affairs (DCA). But each retained its distinctive identity, neither formed part of the Department's Constitution Directorate (which was concerned with such matters as human rights, freedom of information and the abolition of the office of Lord Chancellor), and each was said only to form part of the Department for 'pay and rations' purposes.[47] Each continued to work to the territorial Secretary of State. The Wales Office has resisted further integration into DCA, and has continued to grow, while the Scotland Office has shrunk.[48] It is therefore not clear what control DCA and the Secretary of State for Constitutional Affairs have even over 'pay and rations' for the territorial Offices.

[44] House of Lords Select Committee on the Constitution, 2003a, especially chapter 2 and recommendation 6.

[45] House of Lords Select Committee on the Constitution, *The Government's Response to the Second Report of the Select Committee on the Constitution, Session 2002–03 (HL Paper 28) Devolution: Inter-institutional Relations in the United Kingdom*, Cm 5780, (London: The Stationery Office, 2003).

[46] House of Lords Select Committee on Constitution 2003a, para. 67.

[47] Scottish Affairs Committee, *Minutes of Evidence for Tuesday 17 June 2003,* especially Q. 1 and Q. 6; Welsh Affairs Select Committee, *Minutes of Evidence for 25 June 2003*: QQ. 25–34.

[48] Interview with UK Government official, August 2003. On 9 September 2003 Alistair Darling confirmed further reductions in the size of the Scotland Office, involving the Office reducing its headcount from 96 to 65 and closing its Glasgow offices: HC Deb, 9 September 2003, col 23. It had already shed 'Friends of Scotland', and transferred the legal staff working for the Solicitor to the Advocate-General to other parts of DCA.

The other UK Government office concerned with devolution is the smallest but perhaps the most important. That is the team of officials forming the core of central advisers on devolution. It is small, with only about half a dozen people, and has had an itinerant life since it was first formed after the 1997 UK election to work on devolution policy within the Cabinet Office's Constitution Secretariat. It moved into the Office of the Deputy Prime Minister within the Cabinet Office in 2001 after the Constitution Secretariat was wound up, remained in ODPM when that became a free-standing department in 2002, and then was transferred to DCA in June 2003. Its roles include advising on the Government's devolution policy and acting as the UK part of the secretariat for JMC meetings.[49] While DCA has the potential to accommodate the sort of overarching 'department of devolution' recommended by the Lords Constitution Committee, the maintenance of the organisational division between the Wales and Scotland Offices (and their physical separation) and the former ODPM team make that harder to happen. A move of the key former ODPM staff to other duties within DCA in November 2003 will aggravate that, with a great deal of accumulated expertise being lost.

The other part of the story is what has happened in line departments. Many of these had established their own 'devolution' or constitutional sections in the run-up to devolution, to advise their own staff about devolution matters without involving the territorial offices or the Cabinet Office. However, these have been wound down in many line departments as devolution has become established, so that by 2003 the only one surviving is that in the Home Office.[50] The official justification for such changes is that such sections are no longer needed now that devolution has 'bedded in' and devolution knowledge 'mainstreamed' across all officials. In fact there are grounds to doubt just how widespread, or how deep, such knowledge is among policy officials. (Interviewing suggests it is more firmly grounded among UK Government lawyers, however. That may be helped by the fact that departments maintain designated and active legal 'devolution contacts' when the network of devolution contacts on the policy side has fallen away.) The problem is compounded by the way in which most Whitehall departments cover both devolved and non-devolved functions, it is often hard for officials to keep track of exactly what the department's responsibilities are in territorial terms. There is no such thing as an 'English' or even 'English and Welsh' department, as even departments like Health or Education have retained a number of UK-wide functions, often relating to international

[49] The Secretariat for JMC meetings is provided by the UK Government and devolved administrations jointly. See Memorandum of Understanding, Agreement on the Joint Ministerial Committee, section A2.

[50] The Foreign and Commonwealth Office and Ministry of Defence also have such offices, but do not have functions that are devolved.

matters. The closest was the Lord Chancellor's Department before the 2002 reshuffle, although this combined responsibilities for the court service and civil law in England and Wales with responsibility for a number of UK-wide functions, such as international legal matters or the Tribunal Service.

The overall outcome is that the centre of UK Government has made only the smallest adjustments necessary to accommodate devolution, and it has taken some considerable time to make those adjustments. There has been no attempt to reshape either particular parts of government, or the centre as a whole, to suit the new constitutional landscape. The changes that have been made have generally been occasioned by short-term factors, and followed rather than led the institutional logic inherent in devolution. But the pattern remains confused and confusing, with little consistency of approach but rather a great deal of fragmentation, with particular departments deciding their own ways of operating. None of this is likely to surprise a seasoned observer of the British state.

TALKING TO BRUSSELS:
UK INTERGOVERNMENTAL RELATIONS AND THE EU

The increasing influence of the European Union means that Brussels has very considerable importance for the devolved administrations. While the claim that 80 per cent of the Scottish Executive's business is governed by EU matters may be an exaggeration, London is by no means the only centre of power that matters to the devolved administration.[51] The EU is significant on several levels: for substantive policy debates affecting the devolved administrations directly (whether regarding pending legislation, broader initiatives such as reform of the CAP or the Structural Funds); for more immediate issues concerning them (in particular funding through the Structural Funds); and for high-level debates such as the European Constitution which will have a longer-term effect. Moreover, experience from other EU member states is that sub-national governments, bound by EU policy but not involved in the Union's institutions, can lose control over their functions to a startling degree. This has been most notable (and the cause of greatest concern) in Germany, but has affected Belgium and Spain too.[52]

There are a number of channels for the devolved administrations to seek to exercise their influence. One that has proved to be of little value is the Committee of the Regions, which is hamstrung by its very diverse membership and weak institutional position. More important are direct contacts with the institutions, particularly the Commission, and seeking to influence the

[51] For the claim by the Scottish Executive, see Memorandum by the Scottish Executive, para. 19; House of Lords Select Committee on the Constitution, 2002, p. 110.

[52] For a recent survey, see Kottman, J., 'Europe and the Regions: sub-national entity representation at Community level', *European Law Review*, vol. 26, pp. 159–176, (2001).

UK Government's stance.[53] For direct contacts the key mechanisms are the offices each administration maintains in Brussels, to lobby, to network and to gather information. One trend since devolution (apparent for both Scotland and Wales) has been to seek to separate the 'official' office, representing the devolved government, from an office providing facilities to several public-sector bodies from that territory. The most vivid example concerned Wales, where the Welsh Assembly Government sought to withdraw from the Wales European Centre to establish its own office, only to realise the cost implications of running that and finding a compromise of hiring premises which it sublet to other interests — one front door with two door-plates and some internal partitions. The value of such offices depends in part, however, on the fact that they count as part of the UK Government's 'family', and receive the information collected and distributed by the UK's Permanent Representation (UKREP) as well as what their own contacts supply. The UKREP information includes much that is otherwise confidential or extremely hard to obtain (Council of Ministers agendas and papers, for example), and makes a very considerable difference to the effectiveness with which the office can represent the relevant interests.

The most important source of influence remains the UK Government. Here the influence the devolved administrations can exercise is hard to measure, as all the relevant contacts take place in private and confidentiality is a touchstone of what goes on. Devolved administration ministers can attend Council of Ministers meetings, but only at the invitation of the UK Government. When they do so, they speak for the UK, not just their part of it, and must therefore express the agreed UK position. That position is formulated in private and its confidentiality must be protected.[54] Ministers from the devolved administrations have taken advantage of their power to speak for the UK on a number of occasions, but while often trumpeted as an achievement by the ministers involved (or their press officers) that is an unreliable indicator of their administration's influence. (If anything, it indicates that a meeting or issue is not particularly important for the UK Government. Otherwise it would arrange for one of its own Ministers to lead.) The problem is the nature of the compromises needed to secure influence — not only to formulate the single UK line, but then to secure agreement of enough other member states to carry the day. Again, the pattern of interaction resembles the sort of inter-departmental negotiation that took place before devolution.

It is worth briefly comparing the position of the UK's devolved administrations with what happens in other member states. In the two formal federations, Belgium and Germany, there are elaborate mechanisms to identify

---

[53] See House of Lords Select Committee on the Constitution, 2003a, chapter 6.

[54] See Memorandum of Understanding, Supplementary Agreement B, *Concordat on Co-ordination of European Union Policy Issues*.

who will attend Council meetings on behalf of the state, depending on whether the subject-matter under discussion is the responsibility of the federal or community/regional/*Land* government. By contrast, in Spain (and other regionalised states), the central government maintains a monopoly of access to Council meetings and may, or may not, consult the regional governments as it formulates its position. The UK appears to stand some-where between these two yardsticks, with the devolved administrations apparently able to exercise a good deal of influence, but doing so in private and in such a way that it is impossible to measure what degree of influence they in fact have. These arrangements are also poorly protected formally — they could be departed from in a particular case, or changed altogether, and the devolved administrations would be able to do little in response. To that extent, their autonomy is contingent on neither the EU institutions or the UK Government acting in a way that interferes with their functions.

PEERING THROUGH THE MICROSCOPE:
THE SCRUTINY OF INTERGOVERNMENTAL RELATIONS

As the name suggests, intergovernmental relations are precisely that: rela-tions between governments. However, one would expect it to be an interest of considerable interest to legislatures, so that they can meaningfully hold the executive to account.[55] However, that does not appear to be the case. Interest from elected members in the Scottish Parliament, National Assem-bly for Wales or Northern Ireland Assembly appears distinctly limited. While a good number of back-bench questions ask about contacts with the Secretary of State, that often presages either an attempt to raise a matter retained at UK level or an attempt to contrast policy in that territory with the UK Government's policy for England. Serious questioning about relations with the UK Government is rare. Similarly, committee inquiries have seldom dealt with issues of intergovernmental relations.[56]

It is curious that Westminster has proved a partial exception to this. While questions to ministers have little more to commend them than those in the devolved assemblies, committee inquiries have proved notable exceptions. Two inquiries in particular stand out: that of the Lords Constitution Commit-tee which reported in January 2003, discussed above, and that of the Commons Welsh Affairs Committee into *The Primary Legislative Process as It Affects Wales*, which was published in March 2003.[57] (There is a marked

---

[55] A separate issue is how elected parliaments and assemblies relate to each other. The best coverage is this is Winetrobe, B., 'Inter-Parliamentary Relations in a Devolved UK: an Initial Overview', in House of Lords Select Committee on the Constitution Session, 2003a, pp. 56–69.

[56] See House of Lords Select Committee on the Constitution, 2003a, chapter 4, especially pp. 34–5.

[57] House of Commons Welsh Affairs Committee, *The Primary Legislative Process as it affects Wales*, Session 2002–03, Fourth Report, HC 79, (London: The Stationery Office, 2003).

contrast between the Commons Welsh Affairs and Scottish Affairs Committees, with the former conducting a number of serious inquiries into aspects of Wales-UK relations and the latter largely avoiding them, trying to find its subject-matter in the few areas of domestic interest in Scotland that are reserved to the UK level.) It is encouraging that at least some Westminster Parliamentarians have taken devolution and its implications seriously, and think that it needs periodic and sustained investigation.

While intergovernmental relations are unlikely ever to prove an exciting area for backbench scrutiny, the subject's importance means that attention needs to be paid to it. The alternative — which has happened in many federal states — is that it simply disappears off the radar-screen and enjoys a neglect that is seldom benign. The Lords Constitution Committee recommended that there be a review of intergovernmental relations once during each Parliament (every five years or so), to be carried out by a joint committee of both Houses.[58] That may ensure that legislators keep their eye on this particular ball.

CONCLUSION: DIFFERENCES AFTER DEVOLUTION

At the start of this chapter, two questions were raised: how intergovernmental mechanisms affect the ability of the devolved institutions to exercise their powers, and how devolution has affected the organisation and working of the UK state at the centre.

So far as the organisation of the state is concerned, devolution has led to minimal changes. The adjustments made have been the smallest possible, both in degree and in extent. The constitutional changes have preserved the key aspects of the UK's constitution consistent with establishing devolved bodies. Westminster remains sovereign in theory and active in practice. The UK Government starts from a position of institutional strength, and that is reinforced by the informality of relations. The formal structure is itself modest, and is frequently by-passed in favour of informal or unofficial ways of doing things. The finances of the devolved administrations operate within much the same framework as before devolution, as does the civil service. Whitehall's own organisation pays little attention to devolution, with few officials dealing with devolution matters and doing so in a manner that prevents them taking an overview of its constitutional implications. The UK Government also controls many of the channels of access to the European Union. In this sense, devolution has changed very little.

What is striking is that this has had relatively little impact on the autonomy of the devolved administrations in practice. They have still been able to use the powers allocated to them freely, and have very often been helped by the UK Government rather than impeded by it. Even where the UK

---

[58] House of Lords Select Committee on the Constitution, 2003a, para. 117.

Government has objected to a devolved administration's policy (as with long-term care for the elderly in Scotland), the UK Government did not seek to obstruct the devolved policy and only acted on its objection when a reserved matter was affected. This is largely due to the favourable political climate that has accompanied devolution's early years — in the sense that Labour politicians share a view of the world, and want to help each other out, but also in the sense that all involved have a common interest in making devolution appear to be a success. They have therefore actively sought to ensure that the devolved administrations are able to do what they wish. There has also, for similar reasons, been a desire to avoid intergovernmental disputes (whether legal or political in nature), as these are regarded as sign of failure. That devolution needs to be made to appear a success, rather than simply accepted as part of the new constitutional landscape, says a good deal about how new Labour views it — as a policy, not a fact, and as subject to challenge because it is a compromise between old-fashioned Unionism as unsuccessfully practised by Conservative governments of the 1980s and 1990s, independence as espoused by the SNP or Plaid Cymru, and a federal UK as advocated by the Liberal Democrats.

The inherent problem of intergovernmental relations is what will happen when that favourable political climate disappears, as sooner or later it will. Will the sort of informality that has developed in the first few years prove a durable basis for governments to deal with each other? Or will they have to abandon the loose conventions and ways of working that presently apply, and find more formal ways of working and sorting out the rather hazy lines between the responsibilities of each government? That is a big question for the future, and its ultimate solution may mean that devolution has to be reshaped.

BIBLIOGRAPHY

Primary and Official Documents

Department for Education and Skills, *The future of higher education*, Cm 5735, (London: The Stationery Office, 2003).

HM Treasury, *Funding the Scottish Parliament, National Assembly for Wales and Northern Ireland Assembly: a Statement of Funding Policy*, 3rd edition, (London: The Stationery Office, 2002).

HM Treasury, *2002 Spending Review: New Public Spending Plans 2003–2006*, Cm 5570, (London: The Stationery Office, 2002).

House of Lords Select Committee on the Constitution, *Devolution: Inter-institutional Relations in the United Kingdom Evidence complete to 10 July 2002*, Session 2001–02, HL Paper 147, (London: The Stationery Office, 2002).

House of Lords Select Committee on the Constitution, *Devolution: Inter-institutional Relations in the United Kingdom*, Session 2002–03, Second Report, HL Paper 28, (London: The Stationery Office, 2003a).

House of Lords Select Committee on the Constitution, *The Government's Response to the Second Report of the Select Committee on the Constitution, Session 2002–03 (HL Paper 28) Devolution: Inter-institutional Relations in the United Kingdom*, Cm 5780, (London: The Stationery Office, 2003b).

Memorandum of Understanding and supplementary agreements between the United Kingdom Government, Scottish Ministers, the Cabinet of the National Assembly for Wales and the Northern Ireland Executive Committee, Cm 5240, (London: The Stationery Office, 2001).

The Conservative Party, *Time for common sense in Wales* (London: The Conservative Party, 2001).

The Conservative Party, *Time for common sense in Scotland* (London: The Conservative Party, 2001).

The Scotland Office, *The Size of the Scottish Parliament: A Consultation* (London: The Stationery Office, December 2001).

House of Commons Scottish Affairs Select Committee, *Minutes of Evidence for Tuesday 17 June 2003: Rt Hon Alistair Darling MP, Secretary of State for Scotland, Mrs Anne McGuire MP, Parliamentary Under-Secretary of State, Department for Constitutional Affairs and Mr David Crawley, Head of the Scotland Office*, Session 2002–03, HC 815, (London: The Stationery Office, 2003).

House of Commons Welsh Affairs Select Committee, *The Primary Legislative Process as it affects Wales*, Session 2002–03, Fourth Report, HC 79, (London: The Stationery Office, 2003).

House of Commons Welsh Affairs Select Committee, *Minutes of Evidence for 25 June 2003: Rt Hon Peter Hain MP, Secretary of State for Wales, Mrs Alison Jackson, Head of Wales Office and Mr John Kilner, Head of Finance, Wales Office*, Session 2002–03, HC 883, (London: The Stationery Office, 2003).

Secondary Materials

Bell, D., and Christie, A., 'Finance — The Barnett Formula: Nobody's Child' in A. Trench (ed.) *The State of the Nations 2001: The Second Year of Devolution in the United Kingdom* (Exeter: Imprint Academic, 2001).

Bogdanor, V., *Devolution in the United Kingdom* (Oxford: Oxford University Press, 1999).

Burrows, N., *Devolution* (London: Sweet & Maxwell, 2000).

Cornes, R., 'Intergovernmental Relations in a Devolved United Kingdom: Making Devolution Work' in Hazell, R., (ed.) *Constitutional Futures: A history of the next ten years* (Oxford; Oxford University Press, 1999).

Daintith, T., and Page, A., *The Executive in the Constitution: structure, autonomy, and internal control* (Oxford: Oxford University Press, 1999).

Deacon, R.M., *The Governance of Wales: the Welsh Office and the policy process 1964–1999* (Cardiff: Welsh Academic Press, 2002).

Hadfield, B., 'The United Kingdom as a Territorial State' in Bogdanor, V., (ed.) *The British Constitution in the Twentieth Century* (Oxford: Oxford University Press for British Academy, 2003).

Hazell, R., (ed.) *The State and the Nations: The First Year of Devolution in the United Kingdom* (Exeter: Imprint Academic, 2000).

Hazell, R., (ed.) *The State of the Nations 2003: The Third Year of Devolution in the United Kingdom* (Exeter: Imprint Academic, 2003).

Hazell, R., 'Merger, What Merger? Scotland, Wales and the Department for Constitutional Affairs', *Public Law*, Winter 2003, pp. 650–655, (2003).

Hazell, R., and Morris, R., 'Machinery of Government: Whitehall' in Hazell, R., (ed.) *Constitutional Futures: A history of the next ten years* (Oxford; Oxford University Press, 1999).

Heald, D., 'Territorial Public Expenditure in the United Kingdom', *Public Administration,* 72, pp. 147–75, (1994).

Heald, D., *Funding the Northern Ireland Assembly: Assembly: Assessing the Options* (Belfast: Northern Ireland Economic Council, 2003).

Kottman, J., 'Europe and the Regions: sub-national entity representation at Community level', *European Law Review*, vol. 26, pp. 159–176, (2001).

Lang, I., *Blue Remembered Years: a political memoir* (London: Politicos, 2002), pp. 193–4.

McLean, I., and McMillan, A., 'The Distribution of Public Expenditure across the UK Regions', *Fiscal Studies*, vol. 24, no. 1, pp. 45–71, (2003).

Maclean, I., et al *Identifying the flow of domestic and European expenditures into the English Regions*, Final Report for Office of the Deputy Prime Minster, (September 2003).

Maclean, I., and MacMillan, A., *New localism, new finance* (London: New Local Government Network, 2003).

Mitchell, J., *Governing Scotland* (Basingstoke: Palgrave Macmillan, 2003).

Rawlings, R., 'Concordats of the Constitution', *Law Quarterly Review*, vol. 116, pp. 257–286, (2000).

Rhodes, R.A.W., Carmichael, P., McMillan, J., and Massey, A., *Decentralizing the Civil Service: from unitary state to differentiated polity in the United Kingdom* (Buckingham: Open University Press, 2003).

Rose, R., *Ministers and Ministries* (Oxford: Oxford University Press, 1987).

Simeon, R., 'Free Personal Care: Policy Divergence and Social Citizenship', in R. Hazell (ed.) *The State of the Nations 2003: The Third Year of Devolution in the United Kingdom* (Exeter: Imprint Academic, 2003).

Trench, A., 'Intergovernmental Relations: Whitehall Still Rules UK', in Trench, A., (ed.) *The State of the Nations 2001: The Second Year of Devolution in the United Kingdom* (Exeter: Imprint Academic, 2001).

Trench, A., 'Intergovernmental Relations: Officialdom Still in Control', in Hazell, R., (ed.) *The State of the Nations 2003: The Third Year of Devolution in the United Kingdom* (Exeter: Imprint Academic, 2003).

Trench, A., (ed.) *The State of the Nations 2001: The Second Year of Devolution in the United Kingdom* (Exeter: Imprint Academic, 2001).

Winetrobe, B., 'Inter-Parliamentary Relations in a Devolved UK: an Initial Overview', in House of Lords Select Committee on the Constitution, *Devolution: Inter-institutional Relations in the United Kingdom*, Session 2002–03, Second Report, HL Paper 28, (London; The Stationery Office, 2003).

8

The Impact of Devolution on Westminster
If Not Now, When?

Guy Lodge, Meg Russell and Oonagh Gay

After one full term of the Scottish Parliament and National Assembly for Wales, the impact of devolution on Westminster remains minimal. Despite initial interest in reform, what enthusiasm there was for Parliamentary changes seems largely to have drained away, leaving Westminster looking much the same as it did before devolution.[1]

This is all the more surprising given some of the key events that occurred in 2003, which appeared to provide an opportunity for reform. The second elections to the devolved institutions, which were generally seen as proof that the devolution settlement was 'bedding down', brought a consequent reshuffle of UK Ministers that could have allowed Westminster arrangements to be rationalised. Additionally, two of the anticipated triggers for a row on the West Lothian Question — an 'English' vote carried by non-English MPs and a Scottish Minister running a largely English department — occurred. However, though these events were noted, they generated little public reaction. Finally, reform to include elected members in the upper house, long awaited and long proposed to create a link between devolution and the Westminster Parliament, was effectively abandoned by the UK Government. In the end 2003 proved a very interesting year for what failed to happen, but not for any reform that actually went ahead.

This chapter reviews these developments during 2003 which nearly, but not quite, saw devolution finally recognised at Westminster. These are considered within the context of the last four years, to examine the overall effect of devolution. We start with a discussion of the machinery of government changes in Whitehall and their impact on territorial forums in the House of Commons. We then consider the events around the 'English question'. We review the results of the 2003 elections to the Scottish Parliament and the National Assembly for Wales, considering how local relationships between members (perhaps the area of greatest overall impact so far) have changed since 1999. Finally, we consider developments with respect to

---

[1] For a fuller discussion of some of the proposals floated as the devolved bodies were established, see Russell, M., and Hazell, R., 'Devolution and Westminster: Tentative Steps towards a More Federal Parliament', in Hazell, R. (ed.) *The State and the Nations: The First Year of Devolution in the United Kingdom* (Exeter: Imprint Academic, 2000).

House of Lords reform, and the shrinking prospect that the devolution settlement will come to be recognised through arrangements in the upper house.

THE EFFECTS OF THE 2003 RESHUFFLE: NEARLY BUT NOT QUITE?

At the end of 2003 the formal arrangements for dealing with territorial matters at Westminster remained largely as they were before the devolved institutions were created in 1999.[2] Every four weeks the Secretaries of State for Scotland and Wales answered oral questions in the House of Commons for 30 minutes each, as well as written questions.[3] Select Committees continued to shadow the work of both departments, despite the reduction in its volume in the Scottish case in particular. Grand Committees, including all Scottish and Welsh MPs as members, continued to meet.

At the outset of devolution there had been a flurry of interest in these matters, with two Parliamentary committees (the Procedure Committee and the Scottish Affairs Select Committee in the House of Commons) and one outside commission making recommendations on changes to Westminster arrangements to accommodate devolution.[4] However, the proposals from inside Westminster were modest, and the UK Government's response even more so. Even the Procedure Committee's proposal for the suspension of the Scottish and Welsh Grand Committees (which were in part created as an alternative to devolution) was not acted upon.[5] Further changes, to the select committees or question times, were unlikely without corresponding machinery of government changes, as structures at Westminster conventionally mirror those in Whitehall departments. In the absence of such changes, Westminster remained largely as it was.

In 2003, following the second Scottish and Welsh elections, there were expectations that the Whitehall arrangements would be reformed. For some weeks before the June 2003 reshuffle it was rumoured at Westminster that the posts of Secretary of State for Scotland and Secretary of State for Wales were to be abolished or merged, as had been recommended by various

---

[2] In this chapter we focus on arrangements with respect to Scotland and Wales. Many of the same issues also apply to Northern Ireland when devolution is operational, but are largely omitted here due to the suspension of the Northern Ireland Assembly through much of the period.

[3] Scottish questions were reduced in length from 40 to 30 minutes in 1999, following a recommendation of the Procedure Committee. Welsh questions were not cut at that time, but reduced at a subsequent routine reorganisation of departmental question times.

[4] Procedure Committee, *Procedural Consequences of Devolution: Second Interim Report*, HC 376, (London: The Stationery Office, 1999); Scottish Affairs Select Committee, *The Operation of Multi-Layer Democracy*, Session 1997–98, Second Report, HC 460–I, (London: The Stationery Office, 1998); Report of the Commission to Strengthen Parliament, *Strengthening Parliament*, Conservative Party, July 2000.

[5] For background to the Grand Committees see Seaward, P., and Silk, P., 'The House of Commons', in Bogdanor, V., (ed.) *The British Constitution in the Twentieth Century* (Oxford: Oxford University Press, 2003).

bodies. The Constitution Unit had proposed a merger of the Secretaries of State in 2001, and this is understood to have been proposed by the Cabinet Office to the incoming administration.[6] In February 2003 the House of Lords Select Committee on the Constitution proposed that such a merger be followed by creation of a single Cabinet post responsible for intergovernmental relations.[7] Changes of this kind would have led naturally to changes in the territorial representative arrangements at Westminster, naturally implying a single select committee and question time dealing with the affairs of that department. This might also have led to the dismantling of the separate Grand Committees.

In the end the reshuffle failed to deliver significant territorial reform despite initially appearing to do so.[8] A new Department for Constitutional Affairs (DCA) was created, under Lord Falconer, with the Scotland and Wales Offices 'located within' it (see chapter 7).[9] However, the two Secretaries of State found that their posts were not abolished or merged but instead combined with other Cabinet positions. Thus Peter Hain remained Welsh Secretary, but was also given the job of Leader of the House, while the Transport Secretary Alistair Darling became the new Scottish Secretary.

These more modest arrangements approximated to those proposed by the Conservative Party at the 2001 UK general election.[10] However, instead of using the reshuffle as an opportunity to call for consequent reforms at Westminster, the Conservative Party choose to oppose the Government's reforms. The Liberal Democrats and Scottish National Party (SNP), despite having supported the abolition of the post of Scottish Secretary, were also silent about proposed changes to Westminster procedures.

Subsequent debate focused on the need for Westminster arrangements to remain unchanged.[11] The Parliamentary statement by the Prime Minister on

---

[6] Hazell, R., *Three into One Won't Go: the future of the Territorial Secretaries of State* (London: The Constitution Unit, 2001).

[7] House of Lords Constitution Committee, *Devolution: Inter-Institutional Relations in the United Kingdom*, Session 2002–03, Second Report, HL Paper 28 (London: The Stationery Office, 2003).

[8] Initial reports on the reshuffle suggested that the Scotland and Wales Offices, along with the positions of Secretary of State for Wales and Scotland had been abolished. This did not turn out to be the case. The reshuffle was, by all accounts, poorly communicated.

[9] See http://www.number-10.gov.uk/output/Page3894.asp for the Downing Street press release. For a fuller description of these changes see Hazell, R., 'Merger: what merger? Scotland, Wales and the Department for Constitutional Affairs', *Public Law*, Winter 2003, pp. 650–655, (2003); and Lodge, G., *Devolution and the Centre Monitoring Report August 2003*(London: The Constitution Unit), available at http://www.ucl.ac.uk/constitution-unit/monrep/centre/centre_august_2003.pdf.

[10] The Conservative Party, *Time for common sense in Wales* (London: The Conservative Party, 2001), p. 34; The Conservative Party, *Time for common sense in Scotland* (London: The Conservative Party, 2001), p. 45.

[11] Indeed rather than fewer committees dealing with territorial matters there is now potentially one more. The Lord Chancellor's Department committee in the House of Commons, which had been set up only in January 2003, was renamed the Constitutional Affairs Committee after the establishment of the

the reforms confirmed that oral and written questions would continue to be answered by both Secretaries of State.[12] Questioned by the Scottish Affairs Committee about its own role, Alistair Darling stated that 'Select Committees are a matter for the House and the convention is that there is a Select Committee more or less mirroring each Government Department. I would be surprised, therefore, if there was not a Scottish Select Committee. However, at the end of the day it is [a matter] for the House . . . not for the Government'.[13]

So why, four years on, do these forums for debate of Scottish and Welsh business remain largely untouched, despite the creation of the devolved institutions? Why is Westminster so reluctant to adapt and respond to the devolution settlement? There seem to be three reasons for this inertia.

First, there are some strong defenders of the current arrangements, while few are motivated to press for reform. In a survey in 2002, 96 per cent of Scottish MPs responding favoured the retention of the Scottish Affairs Select Committee and 63 per cent favoured retention of the Scottish Grand Committee. Similarly, 89 per cent of Welsh MPs that expressed an opinion wanted to preserve their Select Committee and 80 per cent their Grand Committee.[14] And while 61 per cent of English Conservative MPs and 41 per cent of English Labour MPs supported abolition of the Scottish Grand Committee when asked, they have no particular incentive for seeking to remove these forums from their Scottish and Welsh colleagues.[15]

A second problem exists because although formally Westminster retains control of its own procedures, in practice it will be guided by developments in Whitehall. The potential for reform to the territorial departments raises more politically difficult issues than most machinery of government changes. Scottish and Welsh MPs are an important interest group at Westminster and a potentially important link, through their parties and their constituents, between the institutions. This suggests a need to co-ordinate changes in the two branches of government and reach agreement on the way forward. Yet this would be difficult in practice given the sensitivity of reshuffle arrangements, and the lack of a corporate voice (other than the Leader of the House, on this occasion one of the subjects of the reshuffle) to speak for Westminster.

The third and most important factor is the complexity of the question. Following devolution, what arrangements would be most appropriate to

new department. It is the only departmental committee to be chaired by a Liberal Democrat, Alan Beith MP, and its members all represent English constituencies.

[12] HC Deb, 18 June 2003, col. 358.

[13] Scottish Affairs Select Committee, Oral Evidence, HC 815, 17 June 2003.

[14] Survey for the Leverhulme-funded Devolution and Westminster project, The Constitution Unit. For Scotland n=27 and for Wales n=21.

[15] The views of the English MPs with respect to the other three committees were virtually identical.

represent territorial interests at Westminster? While the likely fallout of an isolated decision taken in Whitehall would be pressure for abolition of committees or questions, this seems unlikely to be the solution — the asymmetry of the devolution settlement demands something more imaginative. Although the Scottish Secretary may now have relatively little to report, the need for accountability of the Welsh Secretary, with his complex relationships with the institutions in Wales, is clearly greater. While the Scottish Affairs Select Committee struggles to find a role (apart from providing a handy diversion for Scottish MPs), the role of the Welsh Affairs Select Committee has developed in useful directions, such as working with Assembly Members in scrutinising draft Wales-only bills. In 2003 the Lords Constitution Committee proposed that this legislative scrutiny role be further extended.[16] In 2003 Peter Hain acknowledged that the Welsh Affairs Committee may now be 'even more important than it was'.[17] In its 1998 inquiry the Scottish Affairs Committee suggested a similar new role for itself scrutinising legislation on reserved matters as it applied to Scotland.[18] This has failed to develop, but the possibilities for such work should be growing, due to the UK Government's recent commitments to publish more bills in draft for scrutiny by select committees.[19]

If the existing territorial committees develop in these ways, the obvious inequity may not be their existence, but the lack of similar arrangements for the English. In April 2000 Parliament decided to reconvene the Standing Committee on Regional Affairs as a specific England-only forum.[20] However, it has not been a success and its England-wide remit would not make it the appropriate forum for such work.[21] However, a new set of English regional select committees, which could work in concert with bodies out in the regions, including elected assemblies as and when they are established, might be more appropriate vehicles. Establishment of such committees is known to have some support among senior Ministers. Arrangements like these could help neutralise tensions about the existing Scottish and Welsh committees, while helping improve legislative scrutiny and accommodating existing asymmetries.

---

[16] House of Lords Select Committee on the Constitution, 2003, p. 37.

[17] Welsh Affairs Select Committee, Oral Evidence, HC 883, 25 June 2003.

[18] Scottish Affairs Select Committee, 1998.

[19] See the report approved by the House in October 2002: Modernisation Committee, *Modernisation of the House of Commons: A Reform Programme*, Second Report, HC 1168–I, (London: The Stationery Office, 2002).

[20] The Standing Committee on Regional Affairs was formed in 1975 and continued to meet up until 1978. For more on the decision to revive the Committee see HC Deb, 11 April 2000, col. 289.

[21] For more on the Standing Committee on Regional Affairs see Masterman, R., and Hazell, R., 'Devolution and Westminster', in Trench, A., (ed.) *The State of the Nations 2001: The Second Year of Devolution in the United Kingdom* (Exeter: Imprint Academic, 2001).

The Procedure Committee's inquiry in 1999 attempted to look at what Westminster reforms would be appropriate in response to devolution. They, and the Modernisation Committee, remain the most appropriate forums for such deliberation. The 1999 report was too early in the devolution settlement to be sure how things would develop, and so was cautious. However, it concluded that the committee intended to carry out 'a full review of the procedural consequences of devolution in due course'.[22] This inquiry now appears overdue. It would be in Westminster's interests for this issue to be revisited before any future machinery of government changes, in order that it can make considered recommendations for its own future, rather than being forced to respond to an agenda determined in Whitehall.

THE WEST LOTHIAN QUESTION: GLIMMERS OF INTEREST AT LAST?

At the outset of devolution the Westminster-related issue that probably caused greatest interest was the 'West Lothian Question'. First aired by Tam Dalyell, MP for that constituency during the devolution debates of the 1970s, it asks how it can be justified for Scottish MPs to make decisions on English matters, when English MPs can no longer do the same on Scottish matters.[23] The question has rumbled on in the four years since devolution was established, and although there have been occasional calls to address the anomaly, these have as yet failed to capture the English public's imagination.[24] In 2003 the situation anticipated by the question finally materialised, as the UK Government relied on Scottish and Welsh votes to legislate for a policy that would only apply in England. Yet the issue still showed little sign of stimulating interest among the public.

The first major argument of 2003 related to the Whitehall arrangements following the June reshuffle, as the new Health Secretary, John Reid, represented a Scottish seat.[25] Health is one of the most extensively devolved policy areas, making the Department for Health largely 'English-only'. The Conservatives wasted no time in reminding the Government of the words of fellow Scot, Robin Cook, when he was Shadow Health Secretary in 1992 that, 'Once we have a Scottish Parliament handling health affairs in Scotland it would not be possible for me to continue as Minister of Health,

---

[22] Procedure Committee, *The Procedural Consequences of Devolution*, Session 1998–99, Fourth Report, HC 185, (London: The Stationery Office, 1999).

[23] The Question also applies to Northern Ireland (when devolution is operational) and to a lesser extent, MPs from Wales.

[24] For discussion see chapters in previous volumes of this series, and Hazell, R., *An Unstable Union: Devolution and the English Question* (London: The Constitution Unit, 2000).

[25] The need to fill this post followed the surprise resignation from the cabinet of previous Health Secretary Alan Milburn, and thus may have resulted in a change of plan. Reid was moved from his position as Leader of the House of Commons, which he had held for only two months. He was replaced by Peter Hain (see above).

administering health in England'.[26] Conservative leader Iain Duncan Smith described the appointment as a 'democratic monstrosity'.[27] The appointment sparked controversy in the press, across the political spectrum. The *Daily Express* suggested that this move was 'highly vulnerable to an outbreak of Middle England outrage'.[28] Any such outrage quickly seemed to pass, though not without comment by English Labour MPs.[29] *The Independent*, normally dismissive of the question, also argued that the move could damage the Government.[30]

However, Tony Blair remained unmoved. Under questioning his Official Spokesperson stated that the Prime Minister 'didn't think members of the public up and down the country were particularly concerned about what part of the United Kingdom John Reid came from. What they were concerned about was whether he had the necessary abilities to do the job and the Prime Minister believed that he did'.[31] Questioned at the time by Iain Duncan Smith, the Prime Minister pointed out that the Conservatives' Shadow Secretary of State for Scotland represented a London constituency, while similarly the party's Shadow Welsh Secretary, Nigel Evans, represents Ribble Valley in Lancashire.[32] These appointments, necessitated by their lack of seats in Scotland and Wales, helped take the sting out of the Conservatives' attack.

What made Reid's appointment more interesting was that one of his first tasks was piloting the UK Government's Health and Social Care (Community Health and Standards) Bill through the Commons. Enshrined in this Bill were the extremely sensitive measures designed to create foundation hospitals — provisions that did not apply to Scotland or Wales, and the principle of which had been explicitly rejected by both the Scottish Parliament and National Assembly for Wales.[33] John Reid therefore quickly found himself responsible for introducing a controversial policy that would apply to English constituencies but not to constituencies in Scotland or Wales, including his own.

[26] Quoted in Bogdanor, V., *Devolution in the United Kingdom* (Oxford: Oxford University Press, 1999), pp. 227–228.

[27] Quoted in *The Independent*, 14 June 2003.

[28] *Daily Express*, 14 June 2003.

[29] Andrew Mackinlay (Thurrock) stated that 'I am not happy that the health ministry, which is almost totally an English ministry, is headed up by a member of parliament representing a Scottish constituency' — see HC Deb, 17 June 2003, col. 224.

[30] 'This "hazy" reshuffle has underlined the weakness of the Prime Minister', *The Independent*, 14 June 2003.

[31] Prime Minister's Official Spokesman, Government Press Briefing, 13 June 2003. See http://www.number-10.gov.uk/output/Page3916.asp.

[32] HC Deb, 18 Jun 2003, col. 363. In government their last two Welsh Secretaries were John Redwood (Wokingham) and William Hague (Richmond).

[33] This prompted Tam Dalyell to describe the situation as 'the West Lothian Question with a vengeance'. BBC Online, 'Labour vote reignites row', 9 July 2003.

The difference between this and previous (minor) controversies over the West Lothian Question since 1999 was the split within Labour's own ranks. While Labour continues to enjoy a comfortable majority within England (currently 322 seats to other parties' 207) it will generally be highly unlikely to depend on Scottish and Welsh votes to get its legislation through. But in the face of a backbench rebellion, this may cease to be the case. On the health bill this point was picked up by the Labour rebels themselves. Former Health Secretary Frank Dobson MP, a leading rebel, made the inappropriateness of Scottish votes on the issue central in his campaign.[34]

The key vote was on an amendment tabled by Labour MP and chairman of the Health Select Committee, David Hinchcliffe, which would have deleted the foundation trust proposals from the bill. Hinchcliffe, called on Scottish and Welsh MPs to take the 'honourable route of abstaining'.[35] The full results of the vote, broken down by party and nation, are shown in Figure 8.1. The rebellion, with 60 Labour members voting against the whip and a further 66 absent, cut the Government's majority to only 35. As Dobson had predicted, the result was indeed sufficiently close that Scottish and Welsh votes made a critical difference. Among English MPs there was a majority of one in favour of the hostile amendment. The UK Government won the vote with the support of 42 Labour MPs representing Scottish constituencies and 25 representing Welsh constituencies (with only three and four respectively voting against). The outcome thus further outraged the Labour rebels. Alice Mahon said that, after supporting devolution, she now felt 'betrayed', and insisted that something had to be done to resolve the West Lothian anomaly.[36] On the morning after the vote the press took the view that if such a situation repeated itself in the future it could potentially fuel resentment within England, although it did concede that it was not an easy issue to resolve.[37]

[34] See for example his article on the day of the vote Dobson, F., 'This is not a cure for the NHS', *The Guardian*, 8 July 2003.

[35] Quoted in 'Foundations rocked in Labour rebellion', *The Herald*, 9 July 2003.

[36] 'Fury over 'lobby-fodder' Scot MPs', *The Scotsman*, 9 July 2003.

[37] For contrasting views see 'At ease with the anomaly', *The Guardian*, 9 July 2003; 'Scotland's MPs have shown the limits of out newly devolved democracy', *The Independent*, 10 July 2003; 'Weak Foundations', *The Daily Telegraph*, 9 July 2003.

Figure 8.1: Foundation Hospital Vote Broken Down By Party and Nation[38]

Nation	Party	FOR Government	AGAINST Government
England	Conservatives	0	132
	Labour	217	53
	Lib Dem	0	32
	Other	0	1
	Total	*217*	*218*
Scotland	Conservative	0	0
	Labour	42	3
	Lib Dem	0	9
	SNP	0	5
	Total	*42*	*17*
Wales	Labour	25	4
	Lib Dem	0	1
	Plaid Cymru	0	4
	Total	*25*	*9*
N. Ireland	UUP	2	2
	DUP	0	5
	Total	*2*	*7*
Total	Conservative	0	111
	Labour	284	60
	Lib Dem	0	42
	SNP	0	5
	Plaid Cymru	0	4
	NI parties	2	7
	Other	0	2
	Total	*286*	*251*

[38] Source: HC Deb, 8 July 2003.

It seems clear, however, that debates on such matters at Westminster are not driven primarily by constitutional purism. The behaviour of all groups in this vote illustrates both the difficulty of defining which MPs are 'justified' in voting on what matters before Parliament, and the tendencies on all sides to pursue the politically expedient route. After consideration, the Liberal Democrats have concluded — like the UK Government — that all MPs are entitled to vote on all matters before the UK Parliament. Nine of their ten Scottish members, alongside one of their two Welsh members, lined up with English members in an attempt to defeat the Government. Perhaps more surprising was the full participation in the vote of the SNP and Plaid Cymru groups, which both also joined the opposition forces. The SNP has a policy of not participating in votes on non-Scottish matters (a policy they adhered to on the Second Reading of the Bill).[39] But on this occasion they argued in debate that Scottish members were entitled to participate, as funding decisions with respect to the English health service would have a knock-on effect under the Barnett formula. Scottish and Welsh MPs also argue that many of their constituents — particularly those living near the border — make use of English services, and also that policy decisions in England are likely to influence future Scottish and Welsh debates.[40]

The group that has most consistently raised the issue of the West Lothian Question is the Conservative Party. Their leader from 1997–2001, William Hague, made much of the importance of 'English votes on English laws', and a commitment to enforce this principle featured in the party's 2001 manifesto.[41] Since 2001 the party has one MP representing a Scottish seat (Peter Duncan) and he has taken an abstentionist position on non-Scottish business, so did not participate in the health debate. Speaking after the vote the Conservative shadow Secretary of State for Scotland, Jacqui Lait, reiterated the party's commitment to ban Scottish MPs voting on English-only legislation.[42] The Conservatives thus appear to take a more principled position on such matters than the other parties. However, their respect for such boundaries is selective. The 2002–3 session saw the second Wales-only bill since devolution, the Health (Wales) Bill. Although this passed its second and third readings without a vote, the House divided on two Conservative-sponsored amendments at report stage on 9 January.[43] Yet the party has had no MPs in Wales since before the 1997 UK election.

One of the difficulties about resolving the West Lothian anomaly is that, even excluding the arguments about cross-border interests, it is not

---

[39] See HC Deb, 7 May 2003.

[40] Leverhulme / ESRC funded interviews with Scottish and Welsh MPs, 2002–3.

[41] See Russell and Hazell 2000; Masterman and Hazell 2001.

[42] 'Scots MPs save Blair from defeat', *The Herald*, 9 July 2003.

[43] Similarly the Conservatives had voted against the second reading of the Children's Commissioner for Wales Bill on 16 January 2001.

technically straightforward to determine which votes relate to matters of direct relevance to which members. The Health and Social Care (Community Health and Standards) Bill offers a perfect example. The technical 'extent' of the bill applies to England and Wales (though Part 1 of the bill covering foundation hospitals was said not to apply to Wales).[44] However, it had also been subject to a 'Sewel motion' in the Scottish Parliament, whereby Westminster legislation for a devolved matter is approved.[45] So some of its provisions applied also to Scotland. This single case thus helps to illustrate the complexities that would face Scottish and Welsh MPs if they were to decide how to cast their votes on a case-by-case basis. The territorial extent clause in each bill may often be a poor guide to the actual application of legislation. England and Wales is one legal jurisdiction so bills in practice only affecting England (such as the Regional Assemblies (Preparations) Bill) or Wales (such as the Health (Wales) Bill) in the 2002–3 session were classified as affecting both England and Wales. This matter is further complicated by the unexpectedly large number of bills subject to Sewel motions — 11 in the 2002–3 session. Though the Welsh Affairs Committee, in its 2003 report on the *Primary Legislative Process as it affects Wales*, suggested that bills affecting Wales should have a separate part setting out the law as it affects Wales, the parliamentary draftsmen are resistant to such proposals due to the complete entanglement of the two bodies of law.[46] Even if the technical complexities of such matters could be worked out, this would create a system far too complex to be applied at the political level.

A detailed analysis of voting in the first three Parliamentary sessions since devolution shows the extent to which this constitutional nicety is not an issue in practice. There is little discernible difference in behaviour between Scottish MPs voting on UK Government bills that do and do not apply to Scotland. Figure 8.2 summarises the turnout of Scottish MPs on Government bills affecting Scotland (including bills subject to Sewel motions) and affecting only other parts of the UK (i.e. bills classified as covering only England and Wales, Wales or Northern Ireland).[47] Comparative data for the 2002–3 session is not yet available. This shows that overall Scots vote less than their English counterparts, which is probably mainly due to leniency by the whips towards those with constituencies in far-flung places. In all three sessions, Scots appear marginally more likely to have voted in legislation covering Scotland compared to legislation not covering Scotland. However, there are

[44] HL Bill 94, Health and Social Care (Community Health and Standards) Bill, *Explanatory Notes*, 9 July 2003.

[45] The Sewel motion related to Part 3, concerning recovery of NHS costs where a third party pays compensation to the person receiving treatment.

[46] Welsh Affairs Select Committee, *The Primary Legislative Process as it affects Wales*, Session 2002–03, Fourth Report, HC 79, (London: The Stationery Office, 2003).

[47] This analysis is based on the stated 'territorial extent' of the entire bill and so is necessarily crude.

many possible reasons for this, including the particular nature and timing of the small number of 'non Scottish' bills. In the 1999 session English MPs were also more likely to vote on legislation covering Scotland — indeed showing a far larger difference in behaviour than Scottish MPs. The pattern in the later sessions is more what might be expected if MPs took territorial extent into account when deciding whether to cast their votes, but the differences between groups are relatively small. Comparing these to the turnout among Scottish MPs for the foundation hospitals vote, at 82 per cent, suggests that the political controversy surrounding a bill — and consequent activity levels by the whips — remains a far greater influence on turnout than is its territorial extent.

Figure 8.2: Turnout of Scottish and English MPs on Scottish and Non-Scottish Legislation 1999–2002

	Legislation covering Scotland	Legislation not covering Scotland
1999–2000		
Scottish MPs	52.6%	48.6%
English MPs	66.6%	54.4%
2000–2001		
Scottish MPs	48.6%	46.6%
English MPs	62.3%	71.3%
2001–2002		
Scottish MPs	70.1%	61.2%
English MPs	68.9%	70.6%

The political obstacles to responding to the West Lothian question are, if anything, even greater than the technical obstacles. The logical conclusion of forbidding Scottish and Welsh MPs from voting on English matters could be a UK Government with a small Commons majority that was unable to legislate for the largest part of the UK. In the absence of a separate government for England this would create intractable constitutional deadlock. Hence the UK Government's refusal to countenance a system at Westminster that creates 'two classes of members'.[48]

It is the Conservatives who feel that they could benefit from an institutionalised response to the West Lothian question, as they envisage a future

[48] See most recently Tony Blair when he was questioned on the matter by the Liaison Committee on the day of the foundation hospital vote: House of Commons Liaison Committee, Oral Evidence by the Prime Minister, HC 344–ii, 8 July 2003, Q281.

Labour Government with a narrow majority that is dependent on the votes of Scottish and Welsh MPs. A survey of MPs conducted in 2002 found that 79 per cent of Conservative members believed that Scottish and Northern Irish MPs should be excluded from legislation affecting only England and Wales, while only 13 per cent of Labour members agreed.[49] But despite their protestations, an arrangement that denied the UK the ability to speak with one voice at UK general elections would also run counter to the traditional unionist instincts of many Conservatives.

Letting the issue lie (as Iain Duncan Smith did) may have been a rational response to the fact that outside Westminster the West Lothian Question still fails to excite much interest among the English. Even the arguments surrounding the territorial propriety of the vote on foundation hospitals soon died away. Such discussions were notable by their absence in the vote on foxhunting in June 2003 — another devolved issue that has previously provoked controversy.[50] Labour rebellions aside, the question is unlikely to make much impact until support for Labour in England declines significantly and the arithmetic at Westminster is very different.

IMPACT OF THE 2003 ELECTIONS AND BOUNDARY CHANGES

One of the areas where the impact of devolution on Westminster was less anticipated but has most been felt is in the local work of Scottish and Welsh MPs. These members have had to negotiate new relationships at a local level with MSPs and AMs. Given the importance of constituency work to most members of the House of Commons, the arrival of new elected members within their patch has been a significant event.

Evidence from MPs shows that local relationships are most likely to be tense where the individuals elected to represent the constituency in the two institutions come from opposing parties.[51] After the 1999 devolved elections this applied to five constituencies in Scotland and seven in Wales. Following the May 2003 elections the number in Scotland rose to eleven and in Wales fell to four. Figure 8.3 shows all those constituencies where the political control at Westminster now differs from that in the devolved institution, including changes in control at the 2001 general election and 2003 devolved elections. As can be seen, the divergence in Scotland largely resulted from

---

[49] Leverhulme / ESRC funded survey. For the Conservatives n=54, for Labour n=99.

[50] See Russell and Hazell, 2000, p.209. The issue of Scottish members voting in the fox hunting debate in June generated no interest in the English media, where it might have been expected, though it did attract quite a lot of comment in the Scottish press — see for example 'Scotland's MPs should not have voted', *The Scotsman*, 2 July 2003; and 'Backlash from the shires foxed by English apathy', *The Sunday Times*, 6 July 2003.

[51] Leverhulme / ESRC funded surveys and interviews with MPs in 2000 and 2002.

Labour losing seats to other parties in 2003 that they held at Westminster.[52] In Wales the opposite applied: a convergence resulted from Labour winning four constituencies (Conwy, Islwyn, Llanelli and Rhondda) from Plaid Cymru that were held by Labour MPs.[53]

Figure 8.3: Constituencies Where MPs Face AMs or MSPs from Opposing Parties

Constituency	MP	MSP/AM	Change 1999–2003
Scotland			
Aberdeen North	Malcolm Savidge (Lab)	Brian Adam (SNP)	SNP gain 2003
Aberdeen South	Anne Begg (Lab)	Nicol Stephen (LD)	None
Ayr	Sandra Osborne (Lab)	John Scott (Con)	None
Dundee East	Iain Luke (Lab)	Shona Robison (SNP)	SNP gain 2003
Edinburgh South	Nigel Griffiths (Lab)	Mike Pringle (LD)	LD gain 2003
Edinburgh Pentlands	Lynda Clark QC (Lab)	David McLetchie (Con)	Con gain 2003
Falkirk West	Eric Joyce (Lab)	Denis Canavan (Ind.)	None
Galloway & Upper Nithsdale	Peter Duncan (Con)	Alasdair Morgan (SNP)	Con gain 2001
Inverness E., Nairn & Lochaber	David Stewart (Lab)	Fergus Ewing (SNP)	None

[52] In addition in 2001 the Conservatives won one seat from the SNP, bringing mixed control to Galloway and Upper Nithsdale. Labour gained one seat which had been held by expelled Labour MP Tommy Graham. His West Renfrewshire constituency was already held by Labour in the Scottish Parliament.

[53] In addition Labour lost one seat (Camarthen East) at the 2001 general election to Plaid Cymru where the AM already represented Plaid Cymru. It gained Ynys Môn from Plaid Cymru, resulting in a split of control. Another such split was formally caused by the defection of ex MP John Marek from the Labour Party prior to the 2003 election.

Constituency	MP	MSP/AM	Change 1999–2003
Scotland (cont.)			
Ochil	Martin O'Neill (Lab)	George Reid (SNP)	SNP gain 2003
Strathkelvin & Bearsden	John Lyons (Lab)	Jean Turner (Ind)	Ind. gain 2003
Wales			
Cardiff Central	Jon Owen Jones (Lab)	Jenny Randerson (LD)	None
Monmouth	Huw Edwards (Lab)	David Davies (Con)	None
Wrexham	Ian Lucas (Lab)	John Marek (Ind.)	Ind. gain 2003
Ynys Môn	Albert Owen (Lab)	Ieuan Wyn Jones (PC)	Lab gain 2001

The 2003 results suggest that tensions are due to become more strained at local level in Scotland, as a result of voting habits at the two levels of government diverging. Greater resentment is felt towards the regional list AMs and MSPs from opposing parties, whom all Welsh and Scottish MPs face. In 2002, 74 per cent of Scottish Labour MPs said these relationships were always or sometimes competitive.[54] Such tensions have fed into the stalled debate on electoral reform for the House of Commons, with Scottish and Welsh MPs (not all of them previously hostile to PR) issuing warnings about the dangers of additional member systems such as that proposed by the Jenkins commission.[55] Partly as a result of such concerns, Labour's 2001 UK election manifesto committed them to a review of the operation of the systems in Scotland and Wales before any proposals are made for Westminster — a promise that remains unrealised. In 2003 similar arguments also spilled over into the debate about reform of the House of Lords.

In the future, tensions in Scotland look to rise further still. Local relationships will once again need to be renegotiated as the UK Government has announced that it does not intend to enforce the previously planned reductions in the number of Scottish Parliament constituencies to match the reduc-

---

[54] Leverhulme / ESRC funded survey. For Scottish Labour n=23.
[55] *Report of the Independent Commission on the Voting System*, Cm–4090–I, October 1998.

tions due in the House of Commons.[56] The Scotland Act 1998 links the number of constituency MSPs to the number of Scottish MPs at Westminster, and the Boundary Commission of Scotland had recommended that this number should reduce from 72 to 59 to bring constituencies into line with the size of those in England. Rather than enforce this reduction on the Scottish Parliament — where members had expressed concern about the ability to carry out committee and other work if the number of MSPs reduced — the UK Government announced in 2003 that it intends to amend the Act. This is, however, a controversial decision, as it will end co-terminosity between constituencies in the two institutions, at a time when relations are already tense. Many Scottish MPs are concerned about local party organisation and MP–MSP relations, as some Westminster constituencies will coincide with as many as three or four Scottish Parliament constituencies.[57] Following the Government's announcement the Scottish Affairs Committee consequently opened an inquiry into the issue of co-terminosity. The reduction in Scottish MPs is expected to take place before the next UK general election, depending on its date.

THE IMPACT OF DEVOLUTION ON HOUSE OF LORDS REFORM

While progress in adapting to devolution in the House of Commons has been slow, there are also possibilities for reflecting the new settlement in a reformed House of Lords, and these have been under discussion since 1999. This would bring Westminster into line with most other bicameral parliaments, where second chambers are increasingly used to reflect the territorial structure of the state.[58] However, while such proposals have gained support since 1999, in 2003 they were kicked decisively into the long grass. Ironically, arguments about the impact of devolution in local representation may have played a part in their demise.

The first body to propose that devolution should be reflected in a reformed upper house was the Royal Commission on the Reform of the House of Lords, which started its work shortly before the devolved bodies came into existence. The Commission recommended a chamber in which between 12 per cent and 35 per cent of members were elected under a proportional list system, using the nations and regions as large multi-member constituencies. Among the appointed members who would make up the remainder of the house there would also be a requirement to achieve territorial balance. In addition the commission recommended that the reformed chamber establish

---

[56] HC Deb, 18 December 2002, col. 859–861.

[57] Leverhulme / ESRC funded interviews with Scottish MPs, 2002–3.

[58] See Russell, M., *Reforming the House of Lords: Lessons from Overseas* (Oxford: Oxford University Press, 2000).

a Devolution Committee, to keep under review the relations both between the devolved institutions, and between them and the centre.[59]

Since then, the issue of representation of the nations and regions has featured in most official proposals for upper house reform (although the idea of the Devolution Committee was not generally taken up). Labour's 2001 manifesto included an acceptance of the Royal Commission's main principles, and a commitment to implement them 'in the most effective way possible'.[60] The White Paper issued in November 2001 proposed a 20 per cent elected upper house, where the elected members would represent the nations and regions, and the appointments commission would 'have regard to the importance of ensuring fair overall representation of both the nations and regions of the UK'.[61] However, the poor reception given to these proposals (largely focusing on the relatively low proportion of elected members) effectively led to them being withdrawn. A report by the Public Administration Select Committee during the consultation period proposed a 60 per cent elected house, using regional boundaries.[62] In May 2002 the UK Government announced that a new Joint Committee of both Houses of Parliament would be established, and asked to prepare options on the composition of a reformed upper house, to be put to both chambers in free votes.[63]

The first report of the Joint Committee, setting out the options for debate, was published in December 2002.[64] This took as its starting point five principles for the composition of the reformed upper house, one of which was 'representativeness'.[65] The committee emphasised the importance of territorial balance, noting that the present house 'has a disproportionate number of members from the south-east and too few from the English regions'.[66] The Joint Committee proposed seven options, ranging from a fully elected to a fully appointed house. There were seven such options in total, including 20 per cent, 40 per cent, 50 per cent, 60 per cent and 80 per cent elected. No preference was expressed for any particular option and the committee did not specify what electoral system should be used. The two chambers were thus to be asked to consider the principle of the balance between elected and

---

[59] Royal Commission on the Reform of the House of Lords, *A House for the Future*, Cm 4534, (London: The Stationery Office, 2000).

[60] Labour Party, *Ambitions for Britain*, 2001, p.35.

[61] Lord Chancellor's Department, *The House of Lords: Completing the Reform*, Cm 5291, (London: The Stationery Office, 2001), para. 66.

[62] Public Administration Select Committee, *The Second Chamber: Continuing the Reform*, Session 2001–02, Fifth Report , HC 494–I, (London: The Stationery Office, 2002).

[63] For an account of these developments see Norton, P., 'Reforming the House of Lords: Falling between the Stages', *Representation* (forthcoming), 2004.

[64] Joint Committee on House of Lords Reform, *First Report*, HC 171, (London: The Stationery Office, 2002).

[65] The other principles were legitimacy, no domination by any one party, independence and expertise.

[66] Joint Committee on House of Lords Reform, 2002, para. 33.

appointed members, with the committee returning to draw up the detailed proposals later.

After debates in each House the votes on the seven options were staged on 4 February 2003. Debate focused on the issues surrounding the choice of elected/appointed balance, including accountability, legitimacy, expertise, independence and public engagement. However, while an elected element had been presented as a means of ensuring representation of all nations and regions of the newly devolved UK, the experience of devolution was also used by those arguing against an elected element.

In an earlier adjournment debate Scottish backbencher Eric Joyce MP had argued that 'Some list Members of the Scottish Parliament have taken on roles as shadow constituency MSPs in ways that people did not foresee when the Scotland Act 1998 was passed. I suspect that some of the same practices would operate in a Lords or a senate . . . I believe that many practices would be imported'.[67] These sentiments were echoed in the debates over the Joint Committee's report. Scottish Labour MP George Foulkes argued that 'List MSPs . . . cherry-pick the high-profile issues; they challenge the position of constituency MSPs, and indeed MPs, and build up a profile and a platform to stand against constituency MSPs in their constituencies. Elected members of the upper House . . . would do the same'.[68]

In the Commons the outcome of the votes was inconclusive, with none of the seven options gaining a majority.[69] The most popular option was an 80 per cent elected house, defeated by just 283 to 286. The least popular option was an all appointed house, defeated by 247 to 325. However, in the House of Lords the all appointed option was the only one to pass — by 335 to 110.

It seems likely that the emphasis put on dangers of competition between elected upper house members and MPs was sufficient to affect the outcome of the extremely close Commons vote on an 80 per cent elected house. The complaints of Scottish members such as Joyce and Foulkes may have created nervousness among some of their English colleagues. It is notable that only 20 per cent of Scottish Labour MPs supported this option. However, the hostility to elections did not appear to extend to Wales, where 55 per cent of Labour MPs voting (compared to 46 per cent of English Labour MPs) supported 80 per cent elected. And some of the most vocal members of the pro-election camp (such as Robin Cook and Chris Bryant) represented constituencies in Scotland and Wales.

In the aftermath of the votes the way ahead was unclear. There were some suggestions that having rejected both appointment and direct election, the

[67] HC Deb, 17 June 2002, col. 127.

[68] HC Deb, 21 January 2003, col. 213.

[69] For a detailed analysis see McLean, I., Spirling, A., and Russell, M., 'None of the above: The UK House of Commons votes on reforming the House of Lords', *Political Quarterly*, vol. 74 (3), pp. 298–310, (2003).

Commons might accept the compromise of an indirectly-elected house, which had been proposed by some members in debate.[70] A short report issued by the Joint Committee following the votes suggested that 'members of a reformed House could be indirectly elected by [English regional assemblies] together with the Scottish Parliament and the Welsh Assembly'.[71] However, this option had already been rejected by both the Royal Commission and the UK Government as impractical and had drawn little enthusiasm from the devolved institutions themselves.[72] Though tempting, there was also no basis in logic for assuming that a new option would prove any more acceptable to the Commons than the seven it had already rejected.

In September the UK Government indicated in a new White Paper that its preferred option was to drop the notion of elections to the upper house for the foreseeable future.[73] Instead it proposed to introduce a bill to remove the remaining hereditary peers from the chamber (along with the Law Lords, who would disappear as a result of the new Supreme Court), and put the appointments commission on a statutory basis. Thus four years on, the prospect of representatives chosen directly by the nations and regions for the new upper house appeared finally to have been snuffed out. The White Paper included no suggestion that there would be a regional element to the appointments process — there would be just one UK-wide appointments commission. A minor concession to territorial concerns was that the commission would be charged with maintaining balance among the prescribed 20 per cent of members who would represent no political party. However, the matter of whether a similar requirement should apply to the party nominees that made up the other 80 per cent was left open. Given that recent figures show 41 per cent of peers (compared to 23 per cent of MPs) come from London and the South East, the chamber will remain unbalanced and unable to take up any meaningful territorial role unless this responsibility on the parties is taken seriously.[74]

---

[70] See for example David Clelland MP, HC Deb, 21 January 2003, col. 251.

[71] Joint Committee on House of Lords Reform, *Second Report*, HC 668, (London: The Stationery Office, 2003), para. 35.

[72] The responses to the consultation were summarised in Lord Chancellor's Department, *The House of Lords, Completing the Reform: Analysis of Consultation Responses* (London: The Stationery Office, 2002).

[73] Department for Constitutional Affairs, *Constitutional Reform: Next Steps for the House of Lords*, CP14/03, 2003.

[74] Figures provided by Andrew Holden, Campaign for the English Regions.

CONCLUSION

In a survey conducted in 2000 86 per cent of MPs said that they thought devolution would have a significant impact on Westminster in the future.[75] Four years into devolution, little change has been seen. In many ways 2003 was the year in which expectations of change should have been realised but, despite a number of potential triggers, and greater debate than in any year since 1999, no major change came to pass.

The reshuffle after the 2003 elections to the devolved institutions offered an opportunity to reshape Whitehall arrangements in a way that would have had a consequence for the territorial structures at Westminster. In the event the changes proved minor, and no consequential amendment was necessary. However, this episode illustrated how the structures at Westminster are dependent on machinery of government changes over which Parliament has no control. Now that devolution has bedded down the time seems right for bodies at Westminster to themselves propose what arrangements would best serve the needs of an asymmetrically devolved UK.

The 'West Lothian Question' remained a complaint with no answer, and took on new dimensions in 2003. This had previously been seen as a Conservative question, whose realisation would come when Labour was dependent on a far smaller Commons majority than it enjoyed in either 1997 or 2001. The new spirit of rebellion in the Parliamentary Labour Party (PLP) however saw the question reach centre stage in 2003 and cause tensions between English and Scottish Labour MPs. It may return again over further Labour controversies such as university top-up fees, and will gain further attention if Labour's majority is formally diminished after a UK general election. However, there remains no adequate answer to the question short of government for England, as the technical and political obstacles to its accommodation at Westminster remain too great. At least while England remains a predominantly Labour-voting country, pressures from outside on this issue look likely to remain muted.

Perhaps the biggest change that devolution has brought is to the local roles of Scottish and Welsh MPs, as a result of the arrival in their 'patch' of constituency and list members from the new institutions. The tensions caused by these relationships have already fed through into Labour's debate on electoral reform, and in 2003 may have had an impact on House of Lords reform. The rejection by the House of Commons of a largely-elected chamber (as well as all other options) has shut down the immediate prospect of formal recognition of devolution through the reformed upper house. Local tensions in Scotland also present a challenge to the UK Government in

---

[75] Leverhulme-funded survey, The Constitution Unit.

implementing an outstanding part of the Scotland Act to reduce the number of Scottish MPs.

All of these developments seem to demonstrate one thing. The constitutional theorists may have had ideas about how Westminster should adapt neatly to accommodate the new devolution settlement, but in practice politics has got in the way. Westminster remains a party-dominated Parliament, and the influence of party politics can be seen as a major factor in why Westminster has not been more responsive. In traditional British style the arrangements remain counterintuitive and messy, and are likely to be subject to debate and piecemeal reform over many years to come.

Figure 8.4: Chronology of Events 2002–2003

2002	
11 December	Joint Committee on House of Lords Reform publish their *First Report*.
18 December	Helen Liddell, then Scottish Secretary, announces the Government's decision not to reduce the number of MSPs. This move means that the Scotland Act will have to be amended.
2003	
9 January	Vote on the Health (Wales) Bill.
15 January	House of Lords Constitution Committee publish *Devolution: Inter-institutional Relations in the United Kingdom*.
4 February	Both Houses vote on options on Lords reform.
17 March	Leader of the House of Commons Robin Cook resigns from the Government over the Iraq war.
24 March	The Welsh Affairs Select Committee publish *The Primary Legislative Process as it affects Wales*.
4 April	John Reid appointed Leader of the House of Commons.
1 May	Elections to the Scottish Parliament and the National Assembly for Wales.
9 May	Joint Committee on House of Lords Reform publish their *Second Report*.
12 June	UK Government reshuffle. The post of Secretaries of State for Wales and Scotland are merged with other Cabinet posts, and the Department for Constitutional Affairs is established in Whitehall. John Reid becomes Secretary of State for Health.

17 June	Alistair Darling gives evidence to the Scottish Affairs Select Committee on the reshuffle.
18 June	Prime Minister's statement to the House on *The Machinery of Government Changes.*
25 June	Peter Hain gives evidence to the Welsh Affairs Select Committee on the reshuffle.
8 July	An amendment opposing the UK Government's plans for foundation hospitals is defeated in the Commons.
9 July	Vote on the Hunting Bill in the House of Commons.
10 July	The Welsh Affairs Select Committee publish their response to the Government's *Draft Public Audit (Wales) Bill.*
17 September	The Scottish Affairs Select Committee launch their inquiry *Coincidence of Parliamentary Constituency Boundaries in Scotland and the Consequences of Change.*
18 September	The Department for Constitutional Affairs publish *Constitutional Reform: Next Steps for the House of Lords* White Paper.

BIBLIOGRAPHY

Official Documents

Department for Constitutional Affairs, *Constitutional Reform: Next Steps for the House of Lords*, CP14/03, (London: The Stationery Office, 2003).

House of Lords Constitution Committee, *Devolution: Inter-Institutional Relations in the United Kingdom*, Session 2002–03, Second Report, HL Paper 28, (London: The Stationery Office, 2003).

HL Bill 94, Health and Social Care (Community Health and Standards) Bill, *Explanatory Notes*, 9 July 2003.

Joint Committee on House of Lords Reform, *First Report*, HC 171, (London: The Stationery Office, 2002).

Joint Committee on House of Lords Reform, *Second Report*, HC 668 (London: The Stationery Office, 2003).

Labour Party, *Ambitions for Britain*, 2001.

Liaison Committee, Oral Evidence by the Prime Minister, HC 344–ii, 8 July 2003.

Lord Chancellor's Department, *The House of Lords: Completing the Reform*, Cm 5291 (London: The Stationery Office, 2001).

Lord Chancellor's Department, *The House of Lords, Completing the Reform: Analysis of Consultation Responses* (London: The Stationery Office, 2002).

Modernisation Committee, *Select Committees*, First Report, HC 224–I (London: The Stationery Office, 2002).

Modernisation Committee, *Modernisation of the House of Commons: A Reform Programme*, Second Report, HC 1168–I (London: The Stationery Office, 2002).

Procedure Committee, *The Procedural Consequences of Devolution*, Session 1998–99, Fourth Report, HC 185 (London: The Stationery Office, 1999).

Procedure Committee, *Procedural Consequences of Devolution: Second Interim Report*, HC 376 (London: The Stationery Office, 1999).

Public Administration Select Committee, *The Second Chamber: Continuing the Reform*, Session 2001–02, Fifth Report , HC 494–I (London: The Stationery Office, 2002).

Report of the Independent Commission on the Voting System, Cm–4090–I, October 1998.

Royal Commission on the Reform of the House of Lords, *A House for the Future*, Cm 4534 (London: The Stationery Office, 2000).

Scottish Affairs Select Committee, *The Operation of Multi-Layer Democracy*, Session 1997–98, Second Report, HC 460–I (London: The Stationery Office,1998).

Scottish Affairs Select Committee, Oral Evidence, HC 815, 17 June 2003.

The Conservative Party, *time for common sense in Wales* (London: The Conservative Party, 2001).

The Conservative Party, *time for common sense in Scotland* (London: The Conservative Party, 2001).

Welsh Affairs Select Committee, *The Primary Legislative Process as it affects Wales*, Session 2002–03, Fourth Report, HC 79 (London: The Stationery Office, 2003).

Welsh Affairs Select Committee, Oral Evidence, HC 883, 25 June 2003.

Secondary Sources

Bogdanor, V., *Devolution in the United Kingdom* (Oxford: Oxford University Press, 1999).

Hazell, R., *Three into One Won't Go: the future of the Territorial Secretaries of State* (London: The Constitution Unit, 2001).

Hazell, R., *An Unstable Union: Devolution and the English Question* (London: The Constitution Unit, 2000).

Hazell, R., 'Merger: what merger? Scotland, Wales and the Department for Constitutional Affairs', *Public Law*, Winter 2003, pp. 650–655, (2003).

Lodge, G., *Devolution and the Centre: Monitoring Report August 2003* (London: The Constitution Unit).

Masterman, R., and Hazell, R., 'Devolution and Westminster', in Trench, A., (ed.) *The State of the Nations 2001: The Second Year of Devolution in the United Kingdom* (Exeter: Imprint Academic, 2001).

McLean, I., Spirling, A., and Russell, M., 'None of the above: The UK House of Commons votes on reforming the House of Lords', *Political Quarterly*, vol. 74 (3), pp. 298–310, (2003).

Norton, P., 'Reforming the House of Lords: Falling between the Stages', *Representation* (forthcoming), 2004.

Report of the Commission to Strengthen Parliament, *Strengthening Parliament*, Conservative Party, July 2000.

Russell, M., *Reforming the House of Lords: Lessons from Overseas* (Oxford: Oxford University Press, 2000).

Russell, M., and Hazell, R., 'Devolution and Westminster: Tentative Steps towards a More Federal Parliament', in Hazell, R., (ed.) *The State and the Nations: The First Year of Devolution in the United Kingdom* (Exeter: Imprint Academic, 2000).

Seaward P., and Silk, P., 'The House of Commons', in V., Bogdanor, (ed.) *The British Constitution in the Twentieth Century* (Oxford: Oxford University Press, 2003).

9

Restoring Confidence and Legitimacy?
Devolution and Public Opinion

John Curtice

INTRODUCTION

For many of its advocates the creation of devolved institutions in Scotland and Wales had two key objectives. First it was hoped the establishment of new institutions that were physically more proximate to their populations and which operated in a more open and participatory style would help to reverse an apparent decline in both trust and confidence in the political system and in willingness to vote. Second it was anticipated that by demonstrating that the United Kingdom could accommodate the distinctive identities and policy preferences of people in Scotland and Wales, devolution would help eliminate demands for independence for those two countries without causing undue acrimony in England. In short, devolution would both enhance the legitimacy of the Union in the two countries and also help ensure that people had confidence in the manner of its working.[1]

On 1 May 2003 the people of Scotland and Wales had their first opportunity to express a judgement on what they thought of devolution in practice. And the votes that they cast suggested that in one respect at least devolution had had some success in delivering its objectives. In Scotland support for the Scottish National Party (SNP), was five points lower than it had been four years previously on the first vote and six points down on the second. Meanwhile in Wales Plaid Cymru (PC) suffered an even bigger reverse, losing seven points in the constituency contests and no less than eleven points in the regional list vote. Devolution seemed to be helping put the nationalist genie back in the bottle.

But so far as devolution's other key objective is concerned, the election suggested that failure was in the air. In Scotland just under half the registered electorate voted while in Wales less than two in five did so. In Wales this represented an eight point drop on the 1999 figure and in Scotland a nine point fall. Rather than helping reverse the apparent decline in voters'

---

[1] Dewar, D., (1998) 'The Scottish Parliament', *Scottish Affairs*: Special Issue on Understanding Political Change, pp. 4–12.

engagement with the political system, devolution appeared to have made its own distinctive contribution to the trend towards disengagement.

But inferring voters' attitudes and motivations from election results is always a hazardous operation. People may have failed to vote for the nationalists for reasons that have nothing to do with their attitudes towards independence. They might, for instance, have disliked the nationalists' leaders, wanted to reward the incumbent coalition administrations for having done a good job, or disapproved of nationalist policies other than independence. Equally, voters may not have stayed at home because of their views about devolution. They may have felt there was not much to choose between the parties, been uninspired by the party leaders, or reckoned that the outcome of the election was a foregone conclusion. In short while the results of the devolved elections certainly raise some important questions about how the public has reacted to devolution so far, we should not rely on those results alone to ascertain the answers.

Instead, to find out what the public really thinks of devolution we need to look at the evidence collected by representative sample surveys that asked their respondents their views about how devolution has worked and their preferences as to how their country should be governed in future. This is the task that this chapter undertakes.[2] In so doing we look not only at how attitudes have developed in Scotland and Wales over the first four years of devolution, but also at the contours of public opinion in England. After all, devolution would do little to help strengthen the Union if its establishment in Scotland and Wales resulted in a backlash from the United Kingdom's largest part. In any event devolution is not simply passing England by. In 2000 Greater London acquired its own elected assembly and in 1999 the UK Government established both regional development agencies and unelected regional chambers or assemblies in each of the eight provincial English regions. In addition the UK Government has now indicated its intention to hold referendums on creating elected regional assemblies in the three northernmost regions of England in the autumn of 2004.[3] In short what England thinks about devolution is important to its success in delivering its objectives too.

In setting about this task we are fortunate in having access to a set of co-ordinated attempts to measure public attitudes towards devolution throughout Great Britain in recent years. Between them the Scottish Social Attitudes (SSA) survey, the Welsh Life and Times survey (WLTS), and in England the British Social Attitudes (BSA) survey have not only regularly charted public opinion towards devolution in their respective corners of the United Kingdom, but they have done so by asking many of the same or

---

[2] Note that because of the extended period of suspension of the devolved institutions together with the postponement of the Assembly election from May to November 2003, this chapter does not look at what has happened in Northern Ireland.

[3] See chapter 5.

similar questions both over time and across all three countries. This material provides us with a unique ability to compare public opinion now with what it was four years ago and to compare trends in one part of the United Kingdom with those in another part.[4] Where appropriate we also supplement the information available from these surveys with evidence from other relevant surveys.

This inquiry falls into two halves. First it looks at the degree to which devolution has helped to restore trust and confidence in the political system or whether it might even have contributed to public disenchantment and falling turnout by failing to meet public expectations. Second, it looks at public attitudes towards the constitutional structure of the United Kingdom and whether devolution appears to have strengthened or weakened public support for the Union.

CONNECTING WITH THE PUBLIC?

Hopes that devolution would help to restore public confidence and interest in the political system rested on two important assumptions. The first was that the institutions would be thought to matter. As the European Parliament has learnt to its cost, political institutions that are deemed to be an irrelevance are unlikely to attract the public's interest or attention let alone its active participation.[5] The second assumption was that the way in which the devolved institutions worked would persuade people that they were being better governed. Neither assumption has so far been realised in practice.

One indication of the perceived relative importance of the devolved institutions is shown in Figure 9.1. In Wales just over a fifth now believe that the National Assembly has most influence over how Wales is run. Meanwhile even though the formal powers of the Scottish Parliament are greater than those of the National Assembly for Wales, in Scotland the equivalent figure is, at one in six, even lower. In both cases these perceptions are at variance with the expectations that many people had at the time of the first devolved

---

[4] For earlier discussions of this material see Bromley, C., Curtice, J., Hinds, K., and Park, A., (eds.) *Devolution — Scottish Answers to Scottish Questions?* (Edinburgh: Edinburgh University Press, 2003); Curtice, J., 'Devolution, The Union and Public Opinion', in House of Lords Select Committee on the Constitution, *Devolution: Inter-institutional Relations in the United Kingdom*, Session 2002–03, HL Paper 28, (London: Stationery Office, 2002); Curtice, J., and Seyd, B., 'Is devolution strengthening or weakening the UK?', in Park, A. , Curtice, J., Thomson, K., Jarvis, L., and Bromley, C., (eds.) *British Social Attitudes: the 18th report. Public policy, Social ties* (London: Sage, 2001); Curtice, J., 'Devolution Meets the Voters: The Prospects for 2003', in Hazell, R., (ed.) *The State of the Nations 2003: The Third Year of Devolution in the United Kingdom* (Exeter: Imprint Academic, 2003); Heath, A., Rothon, C., and Jarvis, L., 'English to the core', in Park, A., Curtice, J., Thomson, K., Jarvis, L., and Bromley, C., (eds.) *British Social Attitudes: the 19th report* (London: Sage, 2002); Wyn Jones, R., and Scully, R., 'A Settling Will? Wales and Devolution, Five Years On' in *British Elections and Parties Review*, 13, pp. 86–106, (2003). Note that data for England for 2003 were not yet available at the time of writing.

[5] Reif, K., and Schmitt, H., 'Nine Second Order Elections', in Reif, K., (ed.) *The European Elections: Campaign and Results of the 1979/81 First Direct Elections to the European Parliament* (Aldershot: Gower, 1980).

elections in 1999. At that time, as many people in Scotland thought that the Scottish Parliament would have most influence over the way that Scotland was run as thought that the UK Government would. And while expectations were not so high in Wales it was still the case that three in ten expected the National Assembly to have most influence.

Figure 9.1: The Perceived Importance of Institutions[6]

% saying has most influence (1999 will have) over how Scotland/Wales/England is run				
Scotland	1999	2000	2001	2003
	%	%	%	%
Scottish Parliament	41	13	15	17
UK Government	39	66	66	64
Local Councils	8	10	9	7
European Union	4	4	7	5
Wales	1999	2000	2001	2003
	%	%	%	%
Welsh Assembly	30	n/a	16	21
UK Government	44	n/a	61	54
Local Councils	12	n/a	15	14
European Union	7	n/a	3	4
England	1999	2000	2001	2002
	%	%	%	%
Regional chambers or Assemblies	n/a	n/a	2	2
UK Government	n/a	n/a	75	71
Local Councils	n/a	n/a	8	7
European Union	n/a	n/a	11	14

[6] Sources: Scottish Social Attitudes Survey; Welsh Assembly Election Study 1999; Welsh Life and Times Surveys 2001, 2003; British Social Attitudes Survey. n/a: not available.

This mismatch between expectations and perceived reality appears to have set in fairly early on in the life of the new institutions. After just a year of its operation only one in eight were of the view that the Scottish Parliament had most influence over how Scotland was run. Equally, by 2001 the proportion thinking that the National Assembly had most influence over how Wales was run was little more than half the proportion who had expected it to be the most powerful. Of course, one possibility is that it was bound to take time before the importance of the devolved institutions became apparent to the public. But so far at least the trend in public perceptions over the second half of the first period of devolved government provides only slight evidence that the devolved institutions are beginning to make more of an impression upon the publics they seek to serve.

Perhaps unsurprisingly in view of their limited powers, hardly anyone in England thinks that their regional chamber or assembly has most influence over how England is run. But the assemblies have little visibility either. In both 2001 and 2002 no less than 61 per cent of people in England said that they had heard nothing at all about the work of their regional chamber or assembly. Apart from London where only 23 per cent (in both years) said that they had heard nothing at all about the work of the Greater London Authority, the only regional chamber that appears to have made much impression on the public is that in the North East where by 2002 only 40 per cent said they had heard nothing at all. For the most part English regional devolution has so far at least barely registered its presence with the general public.

Maybe this is to set devolution rather too hard a test. Perhaps it was always unrealistic to believe that the institutions would come to be seen as more powerful than Westminster. Even if they are regarded as less important than Westminster they might still be thought to be important in their own right. One possible indication of whether or not this is indeed the case is the degree of importance that the public attaches to the outcome of devolved elections. If the outcome of devolved elections is thought to make as much difference as does the result of a UK general election then arguably the devolved institutions will have secured as much importance in the public's mind as they could ever be expected to achieve. As Figure 9.2 shows, in Scotland at least that position did indeed pertain, not only after the 1999 devolved elections but also on the occasion of the last UK general election. But now six per cent fewer people think that the outcome of a Scottish Parliament election matters a 'great deal' or 'quite a lot' than say the same of a Westminster election. Meanwhile in Wales, National Assembly elections have never been regarded as important as House of Commons elections.

**Figure 9.2: How Much Difference Who Wins an Election
is Thought to Make[7]**

	Scotland					
	Scottish Parliament Elections			House of Commons Elections		
	1999	2001	2003	1999	2001	2003
	%	%	%	%	%	%
Great Deal	28	15	17	27	16	20
Quite a Lot	28	28	24	28	29	27
Some	19	22	20	18	19	19
Not Very Much	18	25	28	22	25	24
None at all	5	8	9	4	8	7
	Wales					
	National Assembly Elections			House of Commons Elections		
	1999	2001	2003	1999	2001	2003
	%	%	%	%	%	%
Great Deal	24	13	16	29	20	23
Quite a Lot	22	22	25	28	27	28
Some	19	20	19	16	17	15
Not Very Much	22	30	25	20	26	23
None at all	9	11	11	7	8	9

One problem bedevilling devolution therefore is that the institutions are
often not thought to be particularly important. Meanwhile there are question
marks too in the public's mind about the degree to which they have improved
the way they are governed. As Figure 9.3 shows the institutions in Scotland
and Wales have certainly not matched up to the public's initial high expectations. At the time of the 1997 referendum at least seven in ten people in Scotland reckoned that having a Scottish Parliament would give them more say
in how they were governed, give Scotland a stronger voice in the UK, and

[7] Sources: Scottish Attitudes Survey; Welsh Assembly Election Study 1999; Welsh Life and Times
Surveys 2001, 2003.

increase education standards in Scotland. After four years' experience of devolution less than half think that any of these things is actually happening. Indeed so far as education standards are concerned, less than one in four think they are being increased. In Wales expectations were never so high with only around half thinking at the time of the 1997 referendum that having an Assembly would deliver any of the three objectives. Even so, well under half now think that ordinary people are acquiring more say in how they are governed or that education standards are increasing. And while a little over half think that devolution is giving Wales a stronger voice, that figure is still below the 62 per cent who took that view at the time of the first devolved election.

Figure 9.3: Expectations and Evaluations of the Devolved Institutions in Scotland and Wales[8,9]

Scotland						
	1997 Referendum	1999	2000	2001	2002	2003
	%	%	%	%	%	%
Perceived impact on Scotland's voice in the UK						
Stronger	70	70	52	52	39	49
No Difference	17	20	40	40	52	41
Weaker	9	7	6	6	7	7
Perceived impact on giving ordinary people a say in how Scotland is governed						
More	79	64	44	38	31	39
No Difference	17	32	51	56	62	54
Less	2	2	3	4	4	4
Perceived impact on education						
Increase standards	71	56	43	27	25	23
No Difference	19	36	49	59	58	59
Reduce standards	3	3	3	5	6	7

continued overleaf

[8] The introduction to the question in each year was as follows: 1997, 1999: 'As a result of having a Scottish Parliament / National Assembly will . . .'; 2000: 'Is having a Scottish Parliament going to give . . .'; 2001–2003: 'Do you think having a Scottish Parliament / National Assembly is giving . . .'.

[9] Sources: Scottish and Welsh Referendum Studies 1997; Scottish Social Attitudes Survey 1999–2003; Welsh Assembly Election Study 1999; Welsh Life and Times Survey 2001 & 2003.

Wales				
	1997 Referendum	1999	2001	2003
	%	%	%	%
Perceived impact on Wales's voice in the UK				
Stronger	50	62	49	52
No Difference	33	32	45	42
Weaker	12	5	3	4
Perceived impact on giving ordinary people a say in how Wales is governed				
More	54	56	34	38
No Difference	36	39	60	54
Less	4	3	3	6
Perceived impact on education in Wales				
Increase standards	50	42	22	27
No difference	37	48	64	53
Reduce	5	3	3	6

Still, few think the new institutions are making things worse. The proportion taking that view in respect of any of the items in Figure 9.3 fails to come even close to one in ten. There is some sign too that the decline in the proportion thinking that the institutions are improving the way they are governed may have been arrested. Even so, these figures still suggest that for most people most of the time devolution in Scotland and Wales is simply not thought to be making much of a difference.

Much the same can be said of the current unelected regional assemblies in England. Only a quarter expect them to give ordinary people more say in how they are governed, while only just a fifth reckon they will contribute to one of the key objectives of the UK Government's plans, improving the region's economy. While the already elected Greater London Authority receives somewhat more positive evaluations, even here a majority do not think the institution is going to make any difference. And on the question of giving ordinary people say at least, there has been a measurable decline in expectations in London since the first election for the capital's new institutions in May 2000.[10]

So given this evidence we should then perhaps not be surprised that the advent of devolution has apparently failed to help restore confidence in the way that people are governed. To demonstrate this we can look at some measures of political efficacy, that is the degree to which people believe that the political system is able and willing to respond when demands and pressure for change are put upon it.[11] In Figure 9.5 (overleaf) we show recent trends in the answers to three key questions designed to measure this sense of efficacy. As agreement with each of our items implies criticism of the degree to which the political system is efficacious, the higher the figures in Figure 9.5, the lower the level of efficacy.

Figure 9.4: Expectations of English Regional Assemblies[12]

	All England		London		
	2001	2002	2000	2001	2002
	%	%	%	%	%
Perceived impact on giving ordinary people more say					
More say	32	25	45	38	35
No difference	55	59	45	51	51
Less say	2	3	6	2	3
Perceived impact on region's economy					
Better	29	21	n/a	34	24
No difference	55	60	n/a	50	54
Worse	3	4	n/a	3	7

[10] Curtice, J., Seyd, B., and Thomson, K., 'Devolution to the Centre: Lessons from London's First Mayoral Elections', (Paper presented at the Annual Conference of the Political Studies Association, Manchester, 2001).

[11] Marsh, A., *Protest and Political Consciousness* (Beverley Hills, Sage, 1977).

[12] Sources: London Mayoral Election Study 2000; British Social Attitudes survey 2001, 2002. n/a: not available.

Figure 9.5: Recent Trends in Political Efficacy[13, 14]

% agree	1997 general election	1999	2000	2001	2002	2003
Scotland						
MPs lose touch	n/a	66	72	72	71	71
Parties only interested in votes	64	65	73	73	73	73
Doesn't matter who in power	42	55	75	n/a	75	n/a
Wales						
MPs lose touch	n/a	68	n/a	76	n/a	77
Parties only interested in votes	n/a	67	n/a	77	n/a	77
Doesn't matter who in power	n/a	59	n/a	n/a	n/a	n/a
England						
MPs lose touch	n/a	n/a	76	71	73	
Parties only interested in votes	62	n/a	75	75	75	
Doesn't matter who in power	44	n/a	71	62	69	

People clearly took a fairly cynical view of the British political system in general even before devolution occurred. For example, in 1997 nearly two thirds of people in both England and Scotland agreed that parties are only interested in votes and not in people's opinions, while over two in five thought that it does not matter which party is in power even though Labour

[13] The detailed wording of the three questions is as follows: 'Generally speaking those we elect as MPs lose touch with people pretty quickly.'; 'Parties are only interested in people's votes, not in their opinions.'; 'It doesn't really matter which party is in power, in the end things go on much the same.'

[14] Sources: British Election Study 1997; Scottish Election Study 1997; Scottish Social Attitudes Survey 1999–2003; Welsh Assembly Election Study 1999, Welsh Life and Times surveys 2001, 2003; British Social Attitudes Survey 2000–2002. n/a: not available.

had just won power from the Conservatives.[15] But even so, voters in Scotland and Wales appear to be even more critical of the political system after experiencing four years of devolution. For example, in Scotland nearly three quarters now think that parties are only interested in votes. In Wales there has been a ten point increase in those taking that view since 1999. Meanwhile all the other items in Figure 9.5 tell much the same story. Between them the measures we have suggest that political efficacy took a tumble during the first year or so of devolution and has failed to recover thereafter.

On the other hand it does not appear that there is anything exceptional about this trend in Scotland or Wales. The story in England is much the same. For example, the proportion of people in England thinking that parties were only interested in votes climbed from 62 per cent in 1997 to 75 per cent by 2002. There has then been a decline in political efficacy across Britain as a whole. That this happened irrespective of the degree of devolution enjoyed in different parts of Britain suggests that devolution itself may not be particularly responsible for the decline. But equally it is also clear that devolution has been unable to fulfil its advocates' hopes that it would help restore trust and confidence in the political system.

RESTORING FAITH IN THE UNION?

If devolution has failed to help restore trust and confidence in the political system, has it been more successful in increasing support for the maintenance of the Union? Has it improved people's perceptions of the way in which the United Kingdom operates such that demands for independence have begun to melt away, as demonstrated by the sharp decline in nationalist support in both Scotland and Wales in the 2003 elections? And has this been achieved without giving rise to a backlash in England?

Figure 9.6 looks at the first step in this argument by examining what impact the creation of the Scottish Parliament and the National Assembly have had on perceptions of the way that Britain as a whole is governed. It shows that it has consistently been the case in both Scotland and in Wales that more people believe that the creation of their devolved institution has improved the way that Britain is governed than feel it has made matters worse, with a particularly favourable balance of opinion in Scotland. But it

---

[15] For a more extended discussion of trends in political efficacy see, Bromley, C., and Curtice, J., 'Where have all the voters gone?' in Park, A., Curtice, J., Thomson, K., Jarvis, L., and Bromley, C., (eds.) *British Social Attitudes: the 19th report* (London: Sage, 2002); Bromley, C., and Curtice, J., 'Are Voters Cynics Anyway?' (Paper presented at the conference on 'Can Vote, Won't Vote', Goldsmiths College, London, 2003); Bromley and Curtice, 2003; Bromley, C., Curtice, J., and Seyd, B., 'Political engagement, trust and constitutional reform', in Park, A., Curtice, J., Thomson, K., Jarvis, L., and Bromley, C., (eds.) *British Social Attitudes: the 18th report. Public policy, Social ties* (London: Sage, 2001); Curtice, J., 'Devolution and Democracy: New Trust or Old Cynicism?', in Curtice, J., McCrone, D., Park, A., and Paterson, L., (eds.) *New Scotland, New Society? Are social and political ties fragmenting* (Edinburgh: Polygon, 2001).

has also consistently been true that over half believe that the creation of their devolved institution has not made much difference.

Figure 9.6: Perceived Impact of Devolution on How Britain is Governed[16]

	2000 %	2001 %	2002 %	2003 %
Scotland				
Improved	35	35	30	30
Made no difference	54	54	54	56
Made worse	10	8	10	9
Wales				
Improved	n/a	22	n/a	24
Made no difference	n/a	59	n/a	62
Made worse	n/a	11	n/a	8
England				
Improved	18	18	19	
Made no difference	54	54	54	
Made worse	13	13	10	

Equally there is little sign of any backlash in England. Here the figure shows what impact the creation of the Scottish Parliament is thought to have had. The proportion of people who think that creating the Scottish Parliament has improved the way Britain as a whole is governed has always been between five and nine points higher than the proportion who think matters have been made worse. Meanwhile, the dominant perception in England, as in both Scotland and Wales, has simply been that devolution has not made any difference. That of course is all that that we need to support the claim that devolution has not produced a backlash.

The limited impact that devolution has had on people's perceptions of the way Britain as a whole is governed is underlined by the results in Figure 9.7. It shows how people in Scotland and England reacted when asked how well

[16] Source: Scottish Social Attitudes Survey; Welsh Left and Times Survey; British Social Attitudes Survey. Figures for Scotland and England are for perceptions of the impact of creating a Scottish Parliament. Figures for Wales are for creating a National Assembly. n/a: not available.

they think the present system of governing Britain works, a question that was first asked in survey work undertaken for the Kilbrandon Commission in 1973.[17] Even though in both countries more people thought that devolution had improved the way Britain as a whole is governed than thought it had made it worse, more people now think that the system of government could be improved than was the case either at the time of the 1997 UK general election or when the devolution institutions were first created in 1999. In Scotland 62 per cent now think that the system of governing Britain could be improved 'a lot' or that it 'needs a great deal' of improvement, compared with just 47 per cent who took that view in 1997. In England there was an increase in the proportion adopting that view from 41 per cent to 69 per cent between 1997 and 2002. So whatever benefit devolution is thought to have brought to the way that Britain is governed, it has evidently been too small to withstand the impact of other adverse forces that have apparently served to produce an adverse trend in how well people think Britain as a whole has been governed.

Figure 9.7: Trends in Attitudes Towards How Well Britain is Being Governed

% saying present system of governing Britain:	1997 G.E.	1999	2000	2001	2002	2003
Scotland						
Could not be improved	3	1	1	2	2	1
Could be improved in small ways	45	43	31	38	34	35
Could be improved a lot	39	45	50	46	45	47
Needs a great deal of improvement	8	9	16	13	17	15
England						
Could not be improved	5	3	2	2	2	
Could be improved in small ways	50	47	34	42	36	
Could be improved a lot	32	37	46	43	41	
Needs a great deal of improvement	9	11	15	12	18	

[17] Royal Commission on the Constitution, *Memorandum of Dissent*, (London: The Stationery Office, 1973). G.E.: General Election.

It would seem that while devolution may not have done any damage to people's perceptions of how well the United Kingdom works, it may not have done much good either, and certainly not enough to give much reason to believe that support for independence should have declined. Figure 9.8 suggests that no such decline has occurred in either Scotland or Wales. In Scotland, at 26 per cent, the proportion who favour independence is exactly the same now as it was at the time of the 1997 general election. Meanwhile the one in eight who support devolution in Wales is more or less exactly the same as the proportion who took that view at the time of the 1997 referendum.

So it seems that the decline in nationalist support in Scotland and Wales in 2003 was not an indication of any decline in the level of support for independence. In both countries support for independence has remained more or less unchanged. This should not surprise us; it has long been clear that there are plenty of people in Scotland who back independence but not the SNP, and vice-versa.[18] Equally, it has also been clear that the surge in nationalist support in Wales in 1999 had little to do with attitudes towards independence.[19]

Figure 9.8: Trends in Constitutional Preference in Scotland and Wales[20]

	1997 G.E.	1997 Refer- endum	1999	2000	2001	2002	2003
	%	%	%	%	%	%	%
Scotland							
Independence either in or outside the EU	26	37	28	30	27	30	26
Stay in UK, with parliament with taxation powers	42	32	50	47	54	44	48
Stay in UK, with parliament with no taxation powers	9	9	9	8	6	8	7
Stay in UK, with no parliament	17	17	10	12	9	12	13
							cont.

[18] Brown, A., McCrone, D., and Paterson, L., *Politics and Society in Scotland*, 2nd. edn. (Basingstoke: Macmillan, 1998); McCrone, D., *Understanding Scotland: the Sociology of a Nation*, 2nd. edn. (London: Routledge, 2001); Rosie, M., and Bond, R., 'Identity Matters: The Political and Social Significance of Feeling Scottish', in Bromley, C., Curtice, J., Hinds, K., and Park, A., (eds.) *Devolution – Scottish Answers to Scottish Questions?* (Edinburgh: Edinburgh University Press, 2003).

[19] Trystan, D., Wyn Jones, R., and Scully, R., 'Explaining the Quiet Earthquake: Voting Behaviour in the First Election to the National Assembly for Wales', *Electoral Studies*, 22, pp. 635–50.

[20] Source: British Election Study 1997; Scottish and Welsh Referendum Studies 1997; Scottish Social Attitudes Survey 1999–2003; Welsh Assembly Election Study 1999; Welsh Life and Times Survey 2001, 2003. G.E.: General Election.

	1997 Referendum %	1999 %	2001 %	2003 %
Wales				
Independence either in or outside the EU	13	9	12	12
Stay in UK with parliament with tax and law-making powers	18	35	37	20
Stay in UK with assembly without tax and law-making powers	25	35	25	41
Stay in UK with no parliament or Assembly	37	18	23	11

There are some other important messages in Figure 9.8 too. Whatever disappointment there might have been with devolution in practice does not seem to have eroded support for devolution in principle. In Scotland around half say that having a devolved Parliament that has some taxation powers is their preferred option, just as they did in 1999. Only around one in eight wish to be rid of the Parliament entirely. And according to a YouGov poll conducted just before the 2003 election, 70 per cent of those with a clear view on the subject say they would vote in favour of establishing a Scottish Parliament if another referendum were to be held now, only a little lower than the 74 per cent who actually voted in favour in 1997.[21] In Wales support for devolution has increased since the very narrow vote in favour recorded in the 1997 referendum, such that around three in five now support some form of devolution while only just over one in ten wish to revert to the status quo ante.[22] It appears that for the majority of people of Scotland and Wales some form of devolution is now part of the integral fabric of the country's position within the United Kingdom.

But has this also become true of people in England who as a result of seeing what has happened in Scotland and Wales now wish to enjoy the

[21] For details of YouGov's polls see www.yougov.com.

[22] Readers may have noted that there does however appear to have been a decline over the last two years in the level of support for a more powerful National Assembly than currently exists in Wales. However, thus decline is not replicated in a survey conducted by NOP for the Electoral Commission immediately after the election which found 37 per cent in favour of a parliament with law-making powers, only a little down on readings of 44 per cent and 38 per cent that the same organisation recorded in surveys it undertook immediately before and after the 2001 UK general election See Glendinning, R., Sood, A., Llwyd Evans, G., and Scully, R., *National Assembly for Wales 2003: Opinion Research* (London: NOP Research, 2003). Available at www.electoralcommission.gov.uk.

fruits of devolution? It is far from clear that they do. In Figure 9.9 shows the results that have been obtained by the British Social Attitudes survey in recent years when people in England have been asked to chose between three different options for their country, that is creating an English Parliament much like that which Scotland already has, establishing assemblies in each of the regions of England that enjoy a measure of administrative devolution similar to that exercised by the National Assembly for Wales, and keeping things as they are at present. The results suggest there is little enthusiasm for devolution. Well over half say that England should continue to be run from Westminster, while the remainder are more or less evenly divided between preferring an English Parliament or preferring regional assemblies, albeit perhaps with a modest move of opinion in favour of the latter.

Figure 9.9: Constitutional Preferences for England[23]

	1999 %	2000 %	2001 %	2002 %
England be governed as it is now, with laws made by the UK Parliament	62	54	57	56
Each region of England to have its own assembly that runs services like health	15	18	23	20
England as whole to have its own new parliament with law-making powers	18	19	16	17

This apparent reluctance of people in England to wish to ape the political institutions of their Celtic neighbours is still apparent when the issue of whether England deserves to have what Scotland and Wales have already is put more directly. In 2002 just 27 per cent agreed that, 'Now Scotland has its own parliament and Wales its own assembly, every region of England should have its own assembly too', while 37 per cent disagreed. Meanwhile no less than 23 per cent neither agreed nor disagreed and a further 12 per cent felt they unable to say whether they agreed or disagreed. It appears that rather than being widely opposed, English regional devolution is greeted with indifference if indeed it evokes any reaction at all.

This indifference may help to account for the apparent discrepancy between these results and those of two other recent surveys. In March 2002 Opinion Research Business conducted a survey for the BBC which found 63

[23] Source: British Social Attitudes Survey

per cent in favour of the creation of a regional assembly for their region and only 22 per cent opposed. However, among the 63 per cent were no less than 44 per cent who said they were 'somewhat in favour' rather than 'strongly in favour'. Moreover, the option of being nether in favour nor against was not explicitly offered to respondents by the survey. It is likely that in these circumstances many of those who are indifferent to devolution said they were' somewhat in favour'. Meanwhile a poll conducted by ICM Research for the County Council Network in January 2003 found that 41 per cent of those living outside London would vote in favour of having a regional government in a referendum while only 21 per cent say they would vote against. But the lack of enthusiasm for English regional devolution is revealed by the 35 per cent who say they would not vote or do not know how they would vote.[24] And of course being in favour of regional devolution for one's own region does not necessarily mean being in favour of regional devolution all round. Nor does it necessarily mean that regional devolution is regarded as a response to what has happened in Scotland and Wales.

So it appears that the creation of devolved institutions has neither undermined nor underpinned public support for the Union. Most people think it has made no difference to how well Britain as a whole is governed. Support for independence in Scotland and Wales remains at much the same level as it was before devolution. Meanwhile there is little sign that England either disapproves of the impact of devolution on the government of Britain or believes that it needs to have its share of devolution as well.

CONCLUSION

The fall in turnout in the 2003 devolved elections was a much better guide to the public's reaction to devolution than the fall in support for the nationalist parties. The latter was not indicative of any decline in support for independence for Scotland and Wales. The former was an indication that devolution has not helped to reconnect the public with the way they are governed. Not that devolution itself has apparently helped to undermine public confidence in their political system or its support for the Union despite its failure to live up to expectations. It simply has not made much difference one way or the other. And if the reaction in Scotland and Wales has been so muted, little wonder that the reaction in England appears to have been quiet too.

Of course many of the potential tensions in the current devolution settlement did not manifest themselves in its first four years. Labour has not been reliant on its Scottish MPs to form a majority at Westminster. The political colour of the administrations in Scotland and Wales has been similar to that

---

[24] For further details of the ORB and ICM polls see Jeffrey, C., *The English Regions Debate: What do the English Want?*, ESRC Devolution Briefing No. 3, (Swindon: ESRC, 2003).

in London, and all institutions in the United Kingdom have been enjoying growth in public expenditure. Perhaps it is only when circumstances are less benign that devolution will engage hearts and change minds. But for the moment at least, for many people devolution has simply become part of the furniture of the British state — always in the background but rarely the subject of much interest or attention.

ACKNOWLEDGEMENT

The collection of the data reported in this chapter was funded either by three bodies. These are the Leverhulme Trust under grants made as part of its *Nations & Regions* research programme at UCL and the University of Edinburgh, the Economic & Social Research Council under grants funded as part of its Research Programme on *Devolution and Constitutional Change*, its Research Programme on *Democracy and Participation*, its funding of the Centre for Research into Elections and Social Trends and its Research Grants scheme, and finally the Office of the Deputy Prime Minister. The chapter has benefited from many conversations with colleagues who form part of the collaborative ventures that were funded by these grants.

BIBLIOGRAPHY

Primary and Official Sources

House of Lords Select Committee on the Constitution, *Devolution: Inter-Institutional Relations in the United Kingdom*, Session 2002–03, Second Report, HL Paper 28, (London: The Stationery Office, 2003).
Royal Commission on the Constitution, *Memorandum of Dissent* (London: The Stationery Office, 1973).

Secondary Sources

Bromley, C., and Curtice, J., 'Where have all the voters gone?', in Park A., Curtice, J., Thomson, K., Jarvis, L., and Bromley, C., (eds.) *British Social Attitudes: the 19th report* (London: Sage, 2002).
Bromley, C. and Curtice, J., 'Are Voters Cynics Anyway?', (Paper presented at the conference on 'Can Vote, Won't Vote', Goldsmiths College, London, 2003).
Bromley, C., and Curtice, J., 'The Lost Voters of Scotland', in *British Elections and Parties Review,* 13: 65–85, (2003).
Bromley, C., Curtice, J., Hinds, K., and Park, A., (eds.) *Devolution — Scottish Answers to Scottish Questions?* (Edinburgh: Edinburgh University Press, 2003).
Bromley, C., Curtice, J., and Seyd, B., 'Political engagement, trust and constitutional reform', in Park, A., Curtice, J., Thomson, K., Jarvis, L., and Bromley, C., (eds.)

British Social Attitudes: the 18ᵗʰ report. Public policy, Social ties, (London: Sage, 2001).

Brown, A., McCrone, D., and Paterson, L., *Politics and Society in Scotland,* 2ⁿᵈ edn. (Basingstoke: Macmillan, 1998).

Curtice, J., 'Devolution and Democracy: New Trust or Old Cynicism?', in Curtice, J., McCrone, D., Park, A., and Paterson, L., (eds.) *New Scotland, New Society? Are social and political ties fragmenting?* (Edinburgh: Polygon, 2001).

Curtice, J., 'Devolution, The Union and Public Opinion', in House of Lords Select Committee on the Constitution, *Devolution: Inter-institutional Relations in the United Kingdom,* Session 2002–03, HL Paper 28, (London: Stationery Office, 2002).

Curtice, J., 'Devolution Meets the Voters: The Prospects for 2003', in Hazell, R., (ed.) *The State of the Nations 2003* (Exeter: Imprint Academic, 2003).

Curtice, J., and Heath, A., 'Is the English lion about to roar? National identity after devolution', in Jowell, R., Curtice, J., Park, A., Thomson, K., Jarvis, L., Bromley, C., and Stratford, N., (eds.) *British Social Attitudes: the 17ᵗʰ Report: Focusing on Diversity* (London: Sage, 2000).

Curtice, J., and Seyd, B., 'Is devolution strengthening or weakening the UK?', in Park, A., Curtice, J., Thomson, K., Jarvis, L., and Bromley, C., (eds.) *British Social Attitudes: the 18ᵗʰ report. Public policy, Social ties,* (London: Sage, 2001).

Curtice, J., Seyd, B., and Thomson, K., 'Devolution to the Centre: Lessons from London's First Mayoral Elections', (Paper presented at the Annual Conference of the Political Studies Association, Manchester, 2001).

Dewar, D., 'The Scottish Parliament', *Scottish Affairs: Special Issue on Understanding Political Change,* 4–12, (1998).

Glendinning, R., Sood, A., Llwyd Evans, G., and Scully, R., *National Assembly for Wales 2003: Opinion Research* (London: NOP Research, 2003). Available at www.electoralcommission.gov.uk.

Heath, A., Rothon, C., and Jarvis, L., 'English to the core', in Park, A., Curtice, J., Thomson, K., Jarvis, L., and Bromley, C., (eds.) *British Social Attitudes: the 19ᵗʰ report* (London: Sage, 2002).

ICM Research, *Scottish Elections Research 2003* (London: ICM Research, 2003). Available at www.electoralcommission.org.uk.

Jeffrey, C., *The English Regions Debate: What do the English Want?*, ESRC Devolution Briefing No. 3, (Swindon: ESRC, 2003).

McCrone, D., *Understanding Scotland: the Sociology of a Nation,* 2ⁿᵈ edn., (London: Routledge, 2001).

Marsh, A., *Protest and Political Consciousness* (Beverley Hills, Sage, 1977).

Paterson, L., Brown, A., Curtice, J., Hinds, K., McCrone, D., Park, A., Sproston, K., & Surridge, P., *New Scotland, New Politics?* (Edinburgh: Polygon, 2001).

Reif, K., and Schmitt, H., 'Nine Second Order Elections', in Reif, K., (ed.) *The European Elections: Campaign and Results of the 1979/81 First Direct Elections to the European Parliament* (Aldershot: Gower, 1980).

Rosie, M., and Bond, R., 'Identity Matters: The Political and Social Significance of Feeling Scottish', in Bromley, C., Curtice, J., Hinds, K., and Park, A., (eds.)

Devolution — Scottish Answers to Scottish Questions? (Edinburgh: Edinburgh University Press, 2003).

Scully, R., Wyn Jones, R., and Trystan, D., 'Turnout, Participation and Legitimacy in Post-Devolution Wales', *British Journal of Political Science* (forthcoming).

Trystan, D., Wyn Jones, R., and Scully, R., 'Explaining the Quiet Earthquake: Voting Behaviour in the First Election to the National Assembly for Wales', *Electoral Studies*, 22: 635–50.

Wyn Jones, R., and Scully, R., 'A Settling Will? Wales and Devolution, Five Years On', *British Elections and Parties Review*, 13: 86–106, (2003).

Wyn Jones, R., and Scully, R., 'Coming Home to Labour? The 2003 Welsh Assembly Election', *Regional and Federal Studies*, 13: 125–32.

Part III

Public Policy:
The Emergence of Divergence

10

The Making of Social Justice Policy in Scotland
Devolution and Social Exclusion

Helen Fawcett[1]

INTRODUCTION: DEVELOPMENT OF THE WELFARE STATE UNDER DEVOLVED AUTHORITY

> The ability to take distinctive action on social policy has been one of the main justifications for a Scottish Assembly or Parliament. From one angle, the thought of the legislature and government as a powerhouse for a distinctively Scottish attempt to improve social conditions (especially bad physical conditions) has been a motivating force for devolution.[2]

As Parry suggests, what is now known as social justice policy played an important role in the debates around devolution. After the second election to the Scottish Parliament in May 2003 we have the chance to assess how the first Holyrood administration addressed this issue. As one might expect, social justice policy-making has played a role in establishing the credibility of the new constitutional settlement. The Executive has been very active in devising a set of proposals that demonstrate that this issue is being taken seriously. Indeed, social justice policy-making, and its relationship to the issue of social exclusion and inclusion, raised some interesting challenges for the new constitutional arrangements. The powers relevant to social exclusion are divided between the two levels of government. As a result, effective policy-making depends on co-ordination and interdependence. This chapter assesses whether the division of powers has, in practice, obstructed rational policy making and impeded effective solutions to a range of social problems, or whether the two authorities in Westminster and Holyrood have found a way to co-ordinate their strategies in a highly complex area of policy-making. On the whole, we can view the history of the last four years as a success story for devolution, in that both authorities have been able to move towards their objectives without hindering or coming into conflict

[1] The author wishes to acknowledge the support of the Economic and Social Research Council (Grant No. L219 25 2010). In addition, she is very grateful to Ms Fiona Wager for her assistance.
[2] Parry, R., 'The Scottish Parliament and Social Policy', *Scottish Affairs*, 20, p. 34, (1997).

with the other. However, this has been the result of the Labour party's electoral dominance in both jurisdictions, which has facilitated the development of workable solutions.

The powers devolved to the Scottish Parliament mean that legislators do not have power over all areas of social welfare policy. The Scottish Parliament has legislative competence in the areas of health, personal social services, education, training, local government and housing. However, it has no power to legislate (or the Executive to act) in the fields of social security or employment policy, which are classified as reserved areas of business.[3] As a result, the Scottish Executive cannot pursue its own anti-poverty policy because it has no control over income maintenance. The examination of the social inclusion strategy in Scotland is important because it relies on shared competencies, effective policy co-ordination and interdependency. In order to produce workable, coherent strategies there has to be to co-operation and consultation between the two jurisdictions. The formal procedures to facilitate this process are already set out in the Memorandum of Understanding and the specific concordat between the former Department for Social Security and the Scottish Executive.[4]

One of the major questions that has been posed in connection with the devolution settlement is whether it would lead to policy divergence. At first sight, the weakness of the Scottish Executive's control over policy areas relating to social welfare would suggest that the implementation of the New Labour's welfare reform programme would be unproblematic. The Labour party controls both the legislature and the executive in Westminster and dominates them in Holyrood. Consequently, the 'government' in Scotland does not oppose the UK Government's plans. However, the story becomes more complex because there is also pressure on the Executive to demonstrate that devolution rather than independence can deliver tangible policy results for the Scottish nation. Hence there is a need to be distinctive; to demonstrate that there are policies designed for Scottish conditions. Labour's electoral fortunes in Scotland add to this pressure. The party faces an electoral challenge from a party of the left — the Scottish Nationalist Party (SNP) — whereas in the rest of the UK, Labour is the main party of the left. In addition, it is in coalition with the Liberal Democrats. Thus, the strength of party competition in Scotland offsets New Labour's dominance in the rest of the UK to a certain extent.

The Blair administration has been committed to a programme of radical welfare reform and has its own perspective on social exclusion. From the

---

[3] Scotland Act 1998, Schedule 5, Part II, Heads F and H.

[4] *Memorandum of Understanding and supplementary agreements between the United Kingdom Government, Scottish Ministers, the Cabinet of the National Assembly for Wales and the Northern Ireland Executive Committee*, Cm 5240, (London: The Stationery Office, 2001); *Concordat between the Department of Social Security and the Scottish Executive*, Cm 4444, 6 December 1999.

time of the Borrie Commission in the early 1990s, which was instituted under the then leader John Smith, the Labour party had discussed the need to adapt traditional Labour values and policies towards the welfare state.[5] Under Tony Blair, this trend went a great deal further. The party leader argued that there was a need to modernise and reform the British welfare state and pursued one of the most comprehensive reviews of policy since the Second World War. The reform programme was premised on the need to restrict public spending, to end welfare dependency, and to provide individuals with the appropriate education and training to equip them for the labour market. The new policy objectives were heavily influenced by President Clinton's welfare reform programme in the USA. This strand of policy ran parallel to a commitment to 'joined-up' government — the belief in cross departmental and multi-agency responses to complex problems. However, at the same time, the new administration was committed to a programme of devolution. As a result, there is a certain tension between the trend towards greater administrative centralisation and the trend towards devolving powers. The issue of social exclusion, which is at the heart of Labour's welfare reform agenda, appears to cut across both these trends. In addition, how public opinion in Scotland would respond to the New Labour agenda has been something of an unknown quantity.

In fact the overall story of the last four years is one of a strong level of continuity between England and Scotland. A variety of factors have contributed this — some of which might be anticipated, while others are more unexpected. The formal division of powers has played a key role with all income maintenance policies effecting Scotland being generated from Westminster. As a result, New Labour's flagship policies such as the New Deal for the Unemployed and the Working Families Tax Credit (WFTC) are devised and decided in Westminster. The Scottish Executive has adopted these measures into its long-term aims and objectives. Thereafter, the Executive has focused on the areas where it has competence to act under the settlement. It has been particularly active in the areas of housing and area-based regeneration and has used these two areas as a way of constructing a strategy to tackle social exclusion that is based on the policy areas it controls — re-focusing its efforts on the notion of helping communities. Obviously, Labour control of both authorities has been the key to facilitating this. However, the story is a little more complex because Labour in Scotland built on existing policy legacies and inheritance, which were highly influential in determining their strategy.

---

[5] Commission on Social Justice, *Social Justice: Strategies for National Renewal* (London: Vantage, 1994).

THE POLICY CONTEXT: THE CONCEPT OF SOCIAL EXCLUSION

The nature of social exclusion itself is important to this discussion because of the complexities involved in its interpretation. Although it is often confused with the notion of poverty it actually refers to numerous components of social disadvantage: unemployment, low pay, lack of access to health and education, as well as spatial disadvantage.[6] In addition it refers to solidaristic notions of social integration, citizenship and community.[7] Thus policies geared towards creating social inclusion — a concept which is less well specified — are likely to be both extensive and expensive, which in turn implies that policy-makers will be forced to be selective in their response. However, the breadth of the concept and the array of possible strategies allow policy-makers to 'cherry-pick' the aspects of the concept and the policies that best suit their domestic situation, priorities, and political outlook. In some respects, this has helped the development of the Scottish approach by enabling politicians to focus on areas under their control and produce a convincing strategy.

New Labour's use of the term 'social exclusion' departed form the existing European understanding of the term. Its interpretation drew on ideas of the underclass and welfare state dependency influenced by American authors such as Charles Murray and Lawrence Mead.[8] Crucially, the UK Government asserted that increasing the income of welfare claimants was not the route out of poverty. They rejected the academic consensus that held that social exclusion was best tackled by increasing income. Instead they emphasised the behavioural causes of poverty — in particular lack of preparation for work (employability). However, many of the concepts associated with social exclusion were not unfamiliar in the British social policy debate. The work of Peter Townsend in the late 1960s focused on understanding poverty as relative deprivation. He argued that individuals lacking in a range of material resources can be said to be excluded from participation in normal social life. Thereafter, the concepts of multiple disadvantage and transmitted inter-generational deprivation were used in both the academic literature and in policy circles throughout the 1970s and 1980s. Given the division of powers under the devolution settlement a huge body of legislation relevant to tackling social exclusion was to be generated from Westminster. Control over social security policy and hence income maintenance resides with two

---

[6] See Hantrias, L., *Social Policy in the European Union* (London: Macmillan, 1995); Levitas, R., *The Inclusive Society? Social Exclusion and New Labour* (London: Macmillan, 1998).

[7] Room, G., (ed.) *Beyond the Threshold: the Measurement and Analysis of Social Exclusion* (London: Polity Press, 1995), p. 5.

[8] See Fawcett, H., 'New Labour, New Welfare: The 'Modernisation' of the British Welfare State under the Blair Administration', paper presented to the American Political Science Association Annual Meeting, Atlanta, September 1999; and Levitas, 1998.

major Westminster Departments — the Treasury and the Department of Work and Pensions (formerly the Department of Social Security). The cornerstone of the Labour UK Government's strategy was represented by the New Deal for the Unemployed, and the WFTC with a focus on encouraging the individual into work and assisting the low-paid. However, if work was seen as the main route out of poverty and disadvantage, the UK Government also advocated tackling a range of social issues, which were seen as obstacles to work. In short, the UK Government directed its attention towards 'the most excluded', and this was defined both in terms of the exclusion of the individual and disadvantaged or deprived areas.

In 1997 the Social Exclusion Unit (SEU) was established and located in the Cabinet Office (it re-located to the Office of the Deputy Prime Minister in 2002). The Unit's remit was defined by the Prime Minister:

> I established the Social Exclusion Unit in December 1997. Its remit is to help improve Government action to reduce social exclusion by producing 'joined up solutions to joined up problems'. Most of its work is on specific projects, chosen by me following consultation with other Ministers and suggestions from interested groups.[9]

The Social Exclusion Unit defines social exclusion as:

> a shorthand term for what can happen when people or areas suffer from a combination of linked problems such as unemployment, poor skills, low incomes, poor housing, high crime environments, bad health and family breakdown[10].

The focus of the SEU's work has been on deprived areas and groups deemed to be at the highest risk of social exclusion. Thus the first projects and reports reflected the Prime Minister's interest in particular problems that were regarded as requiring immediate action:

Truancy and School Exclusion (May 1998)

Rough Sleeping (July 1998)

Bringing Britain Together: A National Strategy for Neighbourhood Renewal (September 1998; published as Cm 4045)

Teenage Pregnancy (June 1999)

Bridging the Gap: New Opportunities for 16–18 year olds not in education employment or training (July 1999)

Young Runaways (March 2001)

Transport and Social Exclusion (May 2002)

Reducing Offending by Ex-Prisoners (July 2002)[11]

---

[9] Cabinet Office, *Review of the Social Exclusion Unit*, December 1999, p. 11. See http://www. cabinet-office.gov.uk/seu.

[10] http://www.cabinet-office.gov.uk/seu

[11] All the Social Exclusion Unit's reports are available from http://www.socialexclusionunit. gov.uk/published.htm

One controversial feature of the Unit has been the definition of its remit in terms of the absence of a direct involvement with economic exclusion. The SEU adopted a project-led approach based on an agenda that was determined at the beginning of their work. Their objectives can be characterised as finding ways to reintegrate the most excluded. One justification of this approach is that these groups are consistently over-represented in measures of poverty and deprivation. In addition, it is felt important to focus on these groups to build an element of prevention into policy-making, the incentive being that a failure to tackle exclusion is expensive.

Bringing Britain Together: A National Strategy for Neighbourhood Renewal placed emphasis on new funding programmes to support neighbourhood regeneration and placed an emphasis on finding policy solutions to the most difficult problems faced by these neighbourhoods.[12] For this strand of policy making 18 Policy Action Teams (PATS) worked to fast-track policy-making alongside 10 Whitehall Departments. The Policy Action Teams examined issues such as financial exclusion, neighbourhood wardens, unpopular housing, and anti-social behaviour. Together with the New Deal for Communities, and action to address the problem of housing reform and homelessness, this area / community-based approach was echoed in Scotland.

However, the Unit's remit is restricted to England and Wales. Scottish interests were represented on a cross-departmental Ministerial Network. As a result a Minister from Scotland was to be in attendance and would have some knowledge of policy debates and developments taking place in England. However, the importance the SEU has had across Whitehall points to a perceived weakness in the devolution settlement, and perhaps one of the most interesting and important of questions to emerge. It is obvious that some of the most important stages of policy development in terms of problem-framing, issue-definition and agenda-setting take place in London. The question is how far is Scotland included in those debates and how far is it able to shape the agenda. Is it possible that Scotland loses something because of the devolution settlement, because Westminster policy-makers now focus on their own remit and as a result Scotland has perhaps become rather isolated from mainstream UK policy-making?

The co-ordination process between Scotland and the UK Government has been largely informal. However, the Joint Ministerial Committee (JMC) on Poverty resumed its meetings in September 2002.[13] The agenda for that meeting reflected the importance the UK Government placed on its poverty

[12] Cabinet Office, *Bringing Britain Together: A National Strategy for Neighbourhood Renewal*, Cm 4045, (London: The Stationery Office, 1998).

[13] Joint Ministerial Committee on Poverty (2002) JMC(P) Communiqué on 18/9/2002. See www.devolution.opdm.gov.uk/jmc.

initiatives, and focused on issues relating to poverty, unemployment and childcare. In particular, the JMC discussed further action to meet the UK Government's targets on child poverty. The JMC's communiqué underlined the need to establish common indicators to measure the progress made towards reaching the UK Government's targets. Finally, there was some discussion of how the two administrations could exchange information and learn lessons regarding support for pre-school children in deprived areas. The importance of the JMC would appear to be a mechanism for reviewing how well each jurisdiction is making progress towards meeting its targets and milestones, and what remedial action needs to be taken if progress is unsatisfactory.

THE SOCIAL INCLUSION NETWORK SCOTLAND: A NEW STRUCTURE OF GOVERNANCE

In 1998, Donald Dewar set up a Social Exclusion Unit within the Scottish Office staffed by civil servants, charged with developing a strategy for Scotland. This was followed by a process of lobbying by a range of interested organisations for a more 'inclusive' type of organisation which represented the views of those working in the field. This led to the creation of a new structure of governance in the run-up to devolution: the Scottish Social Inclusion Network. The SEU in London is staffed by civil servants and individuals on secondment. By contrast, the Social Inclusion Network in Scotland was a committee structure, of whom half were civil servants and the rest were representatives from local authorities and NGOs with experience and expertise relevant to this area of policy development. In this sense, the creation of the Network was the product of historical opportunity. In the run-up to devolution there was much discussion of the 'new politics' of Scotland, to be more 'inclusive' of Scottish society than the old. Hence, the arguments put forward for the Social Inclusion Network suited the rhetoric of the time. However, this was the first sign of a divergence from the Westminster model of policy-making.

Another rationale for the creation of the Network was resource inter-dependency. The old Scottish Office had no experience or traditions in this area of policy-making outside of area-based regeneration. The Social Inclusion Network's membership consisted of representatives from well-established pressure groups and NGOs with interests in poverty, housing, area regeneration, health, crime, education and social work. It was immediately apparent that in the context of the new institutional structure both civil servants and Ministers required advice and expertise. The creation of a Network allowed Ministers and civil servants easy access to the major players in this policy area. Equally, although this may not have been explicit at the time, it provided a sounding board with which Ministers could monitor opinion. Assessing the popularity and the perceived feasibility of policies is better done in an informal and relatively private arena (although web-based minutes of discussions were available) than in the full glare of publicity. The existence of the Network served as a source of legitimacy for government policy. Executive officials could claim that a policy has been discussed and approved by the Network, showing that they have fulfilled perceived obligations to consult, and to expose their work to the scrutiny of experts. This proved a controversial area from time to time because some Network members felt unhappy about requests to 'rubber stamp' policies they had not been involved in developing and did not necessarily agree with.

From the point of view of the members of the Network, they also gained political resources by their participation. Most of the non-civil servants on the committee appreciated the importance of access to decision-makers. This was most marked in those representing smaller organisations with little access to government by other means. Obviously, larger organisations with a higher level of integration in the political process (whether before or after devolution) such as Scottish Homes or Scottish Enterprise already had significant access, although the level of consultation of these issues might have varied. The question of access should be viewed in tandem with the relationship these organisations had with previous Conservative administration. Both in terms of the administrative arrangements prior to devolution, and the dominance of the Conservative party at UK level, many of these organisations were effectively excluded from influencing political decision-making. However, in the run-up to devolution, the success of the lobbying process led to them being included in the process of policy development.

The Network was not an elected body, and the process by which a group or individual was nominated onto the Network was highly informal. In addition, there has been continuing confusion about its precise remit and terms of reference. At first its role was said to be 'to co-ordinate Government responses to the problems of social exclusion within Scotland'.[14] However, the remit of the committee became a problem. By March 2000, the Social Inclusion Network was said to be advisory to Ministers on matters of social justice.[15] The lack of clarity can work in two ways. It is clear that most members of the Network who were there in the early days believed that they were charged with the significant role in developing policy. In the run-up to devolution, supported by the emphasis on a more inclusive Scotland, the work of the Network was perceived by some to be part of this new politics. This side-stepped any debate about its status and the role it played in relation

---

[14] Scottish Office, *Social Exclusion in Scotland: a consultation paper*, JI6477 2/98, (London: The Stationery Office, 1998).
[15] Minutes of the Scottish Social Inclusion Network, SSIN, (9) 2, March 2000.

to the Scottish Parliament and Scottish MPs at Westminster. However, the lack of clarity in its remit also created disappointment; as time went on it became very unclear what role the Network was to play in policy-making.

THE SCOTTISH SOCIAL JUSTICE POLICY

The Scottish Executive through its Social Inclusion Division and the Social Inclusion Network developed a Social Inclusion Strategy.[16] Action teams were established to examine key areas of inclusion policy, action at local level, and programme evaluation.[17] *Social Justice: A Scotland where every-one matters* set out ten targets and twenty-nine milestones for delivering social justice in Scotland. These targets referred to both Scottish and UK-wide policies and were to be audited on an annual basis. The focus was on children, young people, families, older people and communities. In the process of policy development, the Network insisted on the use of a different terminology in Scotland (inclusion rather than exclusion), and this immediately highlighted an unintended consequence of devolved authority: the ability to change the emphasis of government policy in important ways. The use of different language is important in a variety of ways. It represented a rejection of many of the ideas associated with social exclusion prior to the 1997 UK general election: most notably the focus on the behavioural causes of poverty. Network members were conscious of the dangers of 'pathologising' certain groups such as the homeless, the unemployed or lone parents. However, *Social Justice: A Scotland Where Everyone Matters* complemented and was strongly influenced by Alistair Darling's *Opportunity for All: Tackling Poverty and Social Exclusion.*[18] Although there might have been some pressure on the Executive to be distinctive, there was a far greater pressure to conform, and co-ordinate policy so that it almost mirrored that of New Labour at Westminster.

ATTITUDES TO SOCIAL EXCLUSION: DID DEVOLUTION MAKE A DIFFERENCE?

Although the Scottish Executive followed the UK Government's social exclusion policy very closely, it is possible to identify a number of ways in

[16] Scottish Executive, *Social Justice: A Scotland Where Everyone Matters* (Edinburgh: The Stationery Office, 1999a).

[17] Report of the Strategy Action team, *All Together: Local Action to Tackle Poverty* (Edinburgh: The Stationery Office, 1999a); Report of the Strategy Action team, *Excluded Young People* (Edinburgh: The Stationery Office, 1999b); Report of the Strategy Action team, *Inclusive Communities* (Edinburgh: The Stationery Office, 1999c); Report of the Strategy Action team, *Making It Happen* (Edinburgh: The Stationery Office, 1999d).

[18] Scottish Executive, 1999a; Department for Social Security, *Opportunity for All: Tackling Poverty and Social Exclusion,* Cm 4445, (London: The Stationery Office, 1999).

which devolution made a difference. From the outset it must be clearly stated that the most marked differences lie in the area of attitudes and values, and that is not necessarily translated into policy proposals. The existence of the Scottish Social Inclusion Network and its role in constructing the early policy statements is significant here. From the time of the return of the first consultation documents, there was a focus on the economic causes of exclusion and income adequacy. It has become clear that poverty and social exclusion became a more urgent priority for Westminster as time went on. However, in Scotland it was clear the Network was not going to allow poverty to be marginalised as an issue. This was linked to a consistent rejection of some of the 'negative' language associated with the social exclusion debate and the focus on group problems and behaviour. In this sense, the Network made a strong impression on early development of the Social Justice strategy by introducing the language of inclusion. The attempt to use the language and values of inclusion is obviously limited when it comes to policy development. However, it can be used as a way of framing problems and a means of gaining leverage when policies are evaluated. For example, it is significant that the Social Inclusion Network identified the role of the exclusion of social groups. As a result, gender, race, disability and sexuality play a part in the social inclusion agenda in Scotland. By contrast, in England there is a sharp divide between the social exclusion agenda and this type of inclusion.

After the first elections to the Scottish Parliament, the influence of the Network declined. (It was eventually abolished soon after the May 2003 election by Margaret Curran, the new Minister for Communities.) With the election of the Parliament and the establishment of a Parliamentary Committee on Social Justice, the role of the Network was marginalised. Equally, as the Executive gained confidence and experience and consolidated its approach to social justice, the role of the Network diminished. However, although the Executive funds a great deal of research and evaluation studies, in many ways Scotland lacks an expert body comparable to the SEU in London. Some argue that Scotland has been weak in policy development and innovation as a result, because by being out of the debate at the crucial framing and agenda-setting stage, Scotland loses out. In addition, the way that policy-makers in Scotland comment on reserved areas that are relevant to Scotland but decided at Westminster will continue to be vital.

The history of the Network's role in the policy-making process did highlight one issue which is likely to remain on the political agenda in the future. Many of the non-civil service members of the Network felt frustrated at their inability to discuss reserved matters of business on the committee. From their point of view, developing coherent strategies for social justice relates to the reserved areas of business. Hence, the Scottish view of Westminster policy proposals and their applicability in Scotland was crucial. In an area such as social exclusion it is very important to know how Scotland will influence trans-national policy. Civil servants, in general, approach the matter from a rather different perspective. There seems to be a degree of tension around reserved matters because the main issue seems to be the fear of encroaching into non-devolved policy areas and re-writing the constitutional settlement by stealth. However, although the formal position is clear, it is safe to predict that the issue of Scottish influence over policies which affect it but which are reserved to Westminster is likely to re-emerge.

POLICY LEGACIES AND AREA-BASED REGENERATION

Since devolution Scotland has pursued a set of policies which have been broadly congruent with those of England and Wales. At the beginning of the devolution process there was much discussion of the potential for conflict or the possibility of policy divergence. As was seen in the case of the Sutherland Report on Long Term Care for the Elderly, or the Cubie proposals on student fees, Scotland has sometimes diverged where it has had the powers to act, causing tension with London.[19] In the case of social exclusion/inclusion strategy conflict has rarely arisen and there is little sign of policy divergence. Clearly, as discussed above, the powers of the Scottish Parliament and the Executive determine whether or not Scotland has the capacity to develop a viable social inclusion strategy of its own. Is it possible to have an effective strategy, or does policy-making without competence for social security mean 'doing the do-able' rather than developing coherent policy responses?

In England and Wales, the UK Government accorded a high priority to the issue of area-based regeneration, with the New Deal for Communities and its strategy for neighbourhood renewal. In Scotland this approach has also been at the heart of the social inclusion strategy. However, in this particular case it did not represent a slavish adherence to New Labour's strategy as decided in London. Rather, it was a continuation and enhancement of a policy of area-based regeneration which had operated in Scotland under both Labour and Conservative administrations for nearly thirty years. As a result, policy-makers in Scotland had a great deal of experience in this area and already had the institutional structures to support implementation. By contrast, many of the areas associated with social exclusion / inclusion had not been under their control in the past, and the Executive needed to develop capacity in these areas over time.

[19] Independent Committee of Inquiry into Student Finance, (The Cubie Report), *Student Finance: Fairness for Scotland* (Edinburgh, 1999). Royal Commission on Long Term Care (1999) *With Respect to Old Age: Report of the Royal Commission on Long Term Care*, Cm 4192–1, (London: Stationery Office, 1999).

The direction of policy in Scotland has been strongly influenced by pre-existing institutional legacies. It may have been easier to build on pre-existing expertise and experience rather than to attempt innovation in uncharted areas. Thus the new Executive was attracted to areas where there is a stronger capacity to develop, support and implement policy. For example, in introducing the Social Inclusion Partnerships in 1999, the Executive explicitly draws on the structure of multi-agency regeneration partnerships instituted in 1996. Prior to this, the Scottish Office was experienced in operating the Urban Programme (1969), and New Life for Urban Scotland (1988) which created four regeneration partnerships and was extended under the Programme for Partnership in 1996 which created Priority Partnership Areas and Regeneration Programmes.[20] In this sense the creation of 48 Social Inclusion Partnerships in 1999 is a continuation of the partnership structure and area-based approach to deprivation and builds on existing sources of knowledge. This was not a new technique for dealing with social exclusion but a re-labelling of existing structures. There was some incremental change, by allowing a number of experimental thematic Social Inclusion Partnerships dealing with issues such as young people leaving care, but for the most part the Social Inclusion Partnerships built on past policy. They used their funding to pump-prime local projects and to lever support from larger organisations (or 'bending the mainstream' as it is known). The most notable difference with past policy was the emphasis on partnership working with other agencies, NGOs and local government.

Since November 2001 we have seen major administrative change. Responsibility for regeneration has shifted from the Scottish Executive to the newly-created Communities Scotland. Originally Scottish Homes, this powerful and influential agency was responsible for the physical regeneration and housing initiatives. Now regeneration has been incorporated into the brief and as a result Communities Scotland acquired responsibility for funding, and evaluating the Social Inclusion Partnerships.

In 2003 Communities Scotland published its corporate plan for 2003-6, announcing a five-point approach to housing and regeneration. It intends to support Social Inclusion Partnerships to promote regeneration. The community planning process is to be used to tackle crime, anti-social behaviour and poverty. Communities Scotland will also support social economy organisations to tackle poverty and disadvantage. Thereafter, the focus will be on the traditional concerns of housing. The aim is to provide good, affordable housing that will contribute to the regeneration of disadvantaged areas, support rural development, increase the overall supply of housing, and aid those with special housing needs. The agency will fund local authorities to support

[20] Scottish Executive, *The Monitoring Framework for Social Inclusion Partnerships* (Edinburgh: The Stationery Office, 1999b).

private sector housing improvements, and will also fund the Central Heating Programme and Warm Deal to help tackle fuel poverty. In addition, Communities Scotland will fund local authorities to provide private sector housing improvements.

In order to deliver good quality housing, Communities Scotland allocated £313.5 million on their Housing development programme and support for the private sector. Their Regeneration budget for 2003–4 was £93 million of which the vast majority was allocated towards funding Social Inclusion Partnerships. Social Inclusion Partnerships were allocated £68.7 million. Other regeneration programmes received £16.3 million; Wider Role support for housing associations was £8 million; and other regeneration programmes £16.3 million. Thus the total spent on regeneration was £93m. However, in order to tackle poverty and to help vulnerable people another £51.5 million was located in the budget. £35.2 million was allocated to Homelessness programmes, £7.2 million to Mortgage to Rent schemes, and £9 million on a Central Heating Programme (for registered social landlords).[21]

In June 2001, the Scottish Executive produced its community regeneration statement, *Better Communities in Scotland: Closing the Gap*.[22] This document represented a consolidation and a rationalisation of the Executive' approach to social inclusion. The overall objective of the strategy is to decrease inequalities between communities by narrowing the gap between the disadvantaged and everyone else. Using the area-based approach to understanding poverty and disadvantage, the Executive argues that there have been marked variations in the rate of improvement throughout Scotland. Its aim was to build communities: 'Where people feel safe in their homes and their neighbourhood; where people have a sense of belonging and trust; where people want to live; where people have the opportunity to learn, work and play; and where people can grow up, work, bring up children and retire'.[23]

The argument is that these communities will offer a better quality of life with more jobs, higher incomes, better qualifications and skills, improved standards of health and less risk of crime.

The administrative solution to these problems is the introduction of Community planning:

> Community Planning is the way in which councils and other national and local organisations agree local priorities with the community and then work together to provide the services that are needed at local level. We have recently introduced the Local Government in Scotland Bill. Under this Bill all local authorities must

[21] Scottish Executive, *Summary Corporate Plan 2003–6, Communities Scotland* (Edinburgh: The Stationery Office, 2003).

[22] Scottish Executive, *Better Communities in Scotland: Closing the Gap* (Edinburgh: The Stationery Office, 2001). See also http://www.scotland.gov.uk.

[23] Scottish Executive, 2001, p. 1.

put arrangements in place for community planning in their area and identify other important organisations — for example health boards, police boards and Scottish Enterprise — which must be involved in the process.

We believe that community planning offers a new opportunity to improve how community regeneration is delivered in Scotland by joining up national and local priorities and by tackling problems of deprived neighbourhoods, not alone, but as part of the wider community plan.[24]

As a result the Community Regeneration statement sets out two priorities for action. First, the Executive wishes to make five priority services — health, education, transport, justice and employment (as well as housing, social work and child care) work as effectively as possible in deprived areas. The second priority is to build social capital aiming to ensure that individuals and communities have the skills, confidence, networks and resources to take advantage of the opportunities available to them.

The statement argues that there needs to be fundamental change in the way that regeneration work is undertaken in Scotland. The aim is to integrate regeneration within community planning. It is claimed that this will enable policy-makers to 'join up' national, regional and local priorities and overcome problems of fragmentation and lack of cohesion which reduced the impact of previous regeneration initiatives. As a result, the institutions already involved in regeneration work, the Social Inclusion Partnerships will be integrated into the community planning process. Communities Scotland has been given the responsibility of developing a framework for transferring them to Community Planning Partnerships. By the same token, the Executive budget for 2003–6 was presented as 'closing the opportunities gap', and emphasised that achieving social justice in Scotland was the responsibility of mainstream services providers and not just those concerned with regeneration directly. This level of administrative re-organisation is combined with target setting. In order to evaluate the success of community regeneration, the Executive produced a set of indicators that it would use to measure the Executive's contribution to closing the opportunity gap between deprived communities and the rest of Scotland.[25]

CONCLUSION

The academic literature relating to federalism suggests that federal authorities can act as veto points in welfare reform, and that the progress of reform

[24] Scottish Executive, 2001, p. 3.

[25] These indicators relate to children achieving basic educational qualifications: death from coronary heart disease; mothers smoking during pregnancy; levels of house breaking; road accidents involving children; access to a local bus service; homes with poor energy efficiency; unemployment rates; 16–19 year olds who are not in education, training or employment; children in workless households.

efforts should be easier in unitary states. Devolution is a far weaker constitutional and administrative arrangement, but has it created difficulties in formulating and implementing policy? At the outset of this discussion it was asked whether devolution has obstructed New Labour's programme of welfare reform. The answer to the question is an unequivocal 'no': in relation to the example of social exclusion / inclusion policy, the Scottish proposals are not in conflict with those set out by Westminster. The other areas — student fees and long term care for the elderly — demonstrate greater variation due to the existence of devolved powers and (in the case of student fees) the configuration of party competition — the Liberal Democrats being in coalition with Labour. For the most part, Labour leaders in both Scotland and England have devised a workable strategy, based on a close co-operation between the two sets of politicians. Scotland has integrated Westminster-based initiatives into their overall plan for social justice, and has adopted a system of long-term targets to demonstrate results over time. In addition, they have used the powers available to them to develop a strategy in which they attack the problems of deprived areas, using the tools at their disposal to reduce poverty and social exclusion. This is also consistent with the Westminster approach which focuses on the New Deal for Communities and neighbourhood renewal. The adoption of this approach owed much to the legacies of past policy. In this sense, although there has been administrative reform, we see a great deal of continuity with past Scottish policy in which area-based regeneration dominated.

The close match between policy development in Scotland and the rest of the UK indicate that the formal and informal procedures for policy co-ordination are working effectively. But the lack of tension in welfare state policies is largely due to the fact that Labour is in control in both jurisdictions (although in coalition in Scotland) — the situation might be different if Labour's dominance in Scotland were reduced. Developments in Scotland have been determined by party control and the structure of the devolved powers. However, if Labour comes under electoral pressure in Scotland in the future we can expect that this area of policy will become much more unstable.

BIBLIOGRAPHY

Official Sources

Cabinet Office / Social Exclusion Unit, *Bringing Britain Together: A National Strategy for Neighbourhood Renewal*, Cm 4045, (London: The Stationery Office, 1998).

Cabinet Office, *Review of the Social Exclusion Unit*, (London: The Stationery Office, 1999).

Cabinet Office / Social Exclusion Unit, *National Strategy for Neighbourhood Renewal: A framework for consultation* (London: The Stationery Office, 2000).

Concordat between the Department of Social Security and the Scottish Executive, 6 December 1999

Devolution and Concordats, House of Commons Research Paper 99/84

Department for Social Security, *Opportunity for All: Tackling Poverty and Social Exclusion*, Cm 4445, (London: The Stationery Office, 1999).

Memorandum of Understanding and Supplementary Agreements Between the UK Government, the Scottish Ministers, the Cabinet of the National Assembly for Wales and the Northern Ireland Executive Cm 5240 (London: The Stationery Office, 2001); first published 1999 as Cm 4444.

Independent Committee of Inquiry into Student Finance, (The Cubie Report), *Student Finance: Fairness for Scotland* (Edinburgh, 1999).

Report of the Strategy Action team, *All Together: Local Action to Tackle poverty* (Edinburgh: The Stationery Office, 1999a).

Report of the Strategy Action team, *Excluded Young People* (Edinburgh: The Stationery Office, 1999b).

Report of the Strategy Action team, *Inclusive Communities* (Edinburgh: The Stationery Office, 1999c).

Report of the Strategy Action team, *Making It Happen* (Edinburgh: The Stationery Office, 1999d).

Royal Commission on Long Term Care (1999*) With Respect to Old Age: Report of the Royal Commission on Long Term Care*, Cm 4192–1, (London: Stationery Office, 1999).

Scottish Office, *Scotland's Parliament*, Cm 3658, (Edinburgh: Stationery Office, 1997).

Scottish Office, *Social Exclusion in Scotland: a consultation paper*, JI6477 2/98, (London: The Stationery Office, 1998).

Scottish Executive, *Social Justice: A Scotland where everyone matters* (Edinburgh: The Stationery Office, 1999a).

Scottish Executive, *The Monitoring Framework for Social Inclusion Partnership* (Edinburgh: The Stationery Office, 1999b).

Scottish Executive, *Social Inclusion: Opening the Door to a Better Scotland* (Edinburgh: The Stationery Office, 1999c).

Scottish Executive, *Making it work Together: a Programme for Government* (Edinburgh: The Stationery Office, 1999d).

Scottish Executive, *Better Communities in Scotland : Closing the Gap* (Edinburgh: The Stationery Office, 2001).

Scottish Executive, *Summary Corporate Plan 2003–6, Communities Scotland* (Edinburgh: The Stationery Office, 2003).

Secondary Sources

Castles, F.G., 'Decentralisation and Post-war Political Economy', *European Journal of Political Research*, 36 (1), (1999).

Commission on Social Justice, *Social Justice: Strategies for National Renewal* (London: Vantage, 1994).

Cornes, R., in Hazell, R., (ed.) *Constitutional Futures: A History of the Next Ten Years* (Oxford: Oxford University Press, 1999).

Dolowitz, D., and Marsh, D., 'Who Learns from Who: A Review of Policy Transfer Literature', *Political Studies*, 44, pp. 343–57, (1997).

Elcock, H., and Keating, M., *Remaking the Union: Devolution and British Politics in the 1990s* (London: Frank Cass, 1998).

European Anti-Poverty Network, *Social Inclusion: A Priority Task for the New Structural Funds*, 1998.

Fairley, J., 'Labour's New Deal in Scotland', *Scottish Affairs*, no. 25, pp. 90–109, (1998).

Fawcett, H., 'Social Exclusion Social Citizenship and De-Commodification: An Evaluation of the Adequacy of Support for the Unemployed in the European Union', *West European Politics*, 20 (03), pp. 1–30, (1997).

Fawcett, H., 'New Labour, New Welfare: The 'Modernisation' of the British Welfare State under the Blair Administration', paper presented to the American Political Science Association Annual Meeting, Atlanta, September 1999.

Fawcett, H., 'Social Exclusion/Inclusion in Scotland and the UK: devolution and the welfare state', paper presented to Research Committee 27: Structure and Organisation of Government (International Political Science Association), University of Oklahoma, March 29-April 1st 2001.

Hantrais, L., *Social Policy in the European Union* (London: Macmillan, 1995).

Hassan, G, and Warhurst, C., (eds.) *A Moderniser's Guide to Scotland: A Different Future,* (Glasgow: The Big Issue in Scotland and The Centre for Scottish Public Policy Publications, 1999).

Hassan, G., and Warhurst, C., (eds.) *The New Scottish Politics. The first year of the Scottish Parliament and beyond.* (London: Stationery Office, 2000).

Hills, J., Le Grand J., Piachaud, D., *Understanding Social Exclusion* (Oxford: Oxford University Press, 2002).

Jordan, B., *A Theory of Poverty and Social Exclusion* (London: Polity Press, 1996).

Keating, M., 'What's Wrong with Asymmetrical Government?', in Elcock, H., and Keating, M., (eds.) *Remaking the Union: Devolution in British Politics in the 1990s* (London: Frank Cass, 1998).

Levitas, R., *The Inclusive Society? Social Exclusion and New Labour* (London: Macmillan, 1998).

Maxwell, S., 'Social Policy and the Scottish Parliament: A Response to Richard Parry', *Scottish Affairs*, 21, pp. 54–59, (1997).

Parry, R., 'The Scottish Parliament and Social Policy', *Scottish Affairs*, 20, pp. 34–46, (1997).

Paterson, L., 'Scottish Autonomy and the Future of the Welfare State', *Scottish Affairs*, 19, pp. 55–73, (1997).

Pierson, P., *Dismantling the Welfare State? Reagan and Thatcher and the Politics of Welfare State Retrenchment*, Cambridge: Cambridge University Press, 1994).

Political Quarterly Special Issue*: Focus on Scotland, Welfare Reform: has devolution made a difference?*, 74 (4), (2003).

Room, G., (ed.) *Beyond the Threshold: the Measurement and Analysis of Social Exclusion* (London: Polity Press, 1995).

Ross, F., 'Cutting Public Expenditures in Advanced Industrial Democracies: the Importance of Avoiding Blame', *Governance*, 10 (2), pp. 175–200, (1997).

Steinmo, S., Thelan, K., and Longstreth, F., (eds.) *Structuring Politics: Historical Institutionalism in Comparative Analysis* (Cambridge: Cambridge University Press, 1992).

Toynbee, P., and Walker, D., *Did Things Get Better? An Audit of Labour's Successes and Failure.*(London : Penguin, 2001).

Turok, I., and Hopkins, N., *Picking winners or Passing the Buck? Competition and Area selection in Scotland's New Urban Policy*, (Glasgow: Centre for Housing Research and Urban Studies, Glasgow University, 1997).

Webster, D., 'Scottish Social Inclusion Policy: A Critical Assessment', in *Scottish Affairs*, 30, Winter, pp. 28–50, (2000).

11

Conclusion:
The Unfinished Business of Devolution

Robert Hazell

Devolution feels like a coiled spring which has yet to realise its full potential. Each year the settlement continues to evolve, but the bigger changes always seem to lie out of reach. This chapter begins with a brief commentary on the evolutionary developments in 2003, but the major focus is on the unfinished business of devolution. Northern Ireland is clearly unfinished business, but as chapter 4 shows, any solution lies with the political leaders in Northern Ireland, and is not in the gift of the UK Government. This chapter focuses on the other big devolution policy issues which still await resolution. The big items of unfinished business are the unsatisfactory nature of the devolution settlement in Wales; the absence of any significant measure of devolution in England; and the minimalist response to devolution in central government, in terms of adapting the machinery of Westminster and Whitehall. The case for change may be strong, but the forces of inertia may yet prove stronger. The chapter concludes with an assessment of the likelihood of further change, and the consequences for the devolution settlement if no further change comes about.

FINE-TUNING THE DEVOLUTION SETTLEMENT

2003 saw further marginal adjustments to the devolution settlement, fine tuning rather than major change. At the conclusion of its review of the statutory reduction in the size of the Scottish Parliament the UK Government announced that it would introduce legislation to enable the Scottish Parliament to remain at its present size of 129 members. In the June 2003 reshuffle which led to the creation of the new Department for Constitutional Affairs, the Scotland Office and Wales Office ceased to be separate departments of state, and were merged into the new department. In the proposals for a new Supreme Court, issued a month later, the Government proposed transferring the jurisdiction of the Privy Council to hear devolution cases to the new Supreme Court.[1]

---

[1] Department for Constitutional Affairs, *Constitutional Reform: A New Supreme Court for the United Kingdom*, consultation paper CP 11/03, (London: The Stationery Office, 2003).

None of these adjustments constitutes a major change. The first — maintaining the Scottish Parliament at its present size — constitutes no change, although legislation is required to preserve the *status quo*. The second, merging the Scotland and Wales Offices into the new Department for Constitutional Affairs, involves little change of substance, since they retain their own part-time Secretaries of State, and full autonomy. The third, transferring the devolution jurisdiction of the Privy Council, is hypothetical at this stage, since no dispute about the division of powers has yet been tested in the courts.

But the larger picture is still unfolding, and will continue to unfold for many years to come. Devolution has released powerful political forces, which are still working their way through the system. The incomplete nature of the settlement in Wales and in the English regions are the major items of unfinished business.

WHITHER WALES?

The key question in Wales is whether the National Assembly should be granted powers of primary legislation, putting it on a par with the Scottish Parliament and the Northern Ireland Assembly. In the past year a succession of official inquiries have highlighted the frustrations and complexities which result from the Assembly being so dependent on Westminster for all its primary legislation. The House of Lords Select Committee on the Constitution was strongly critical of the present arrangements, in a major report issued in January 2003; the Commons Welsh Affairs Select Committee added its own voice three months later, with a long list of suggestions for improvement; and the Richard Commission has spent 18 months addressing the question in its inquiry into the adequacy of the powers of the National Assembly.[2]

Welsh Dependency on Westminster for Primary Legislation
There are three fundamental difficulties which have come out in the evidence to these three inquiries:

- The Westminster legislative programme is chronically congested, so that it is always hard to find space for Wales
- The UK Government will inevitably be driven by English priorities
- Legislation is frequently drafted or amended at the last moment, leaving little time for Wales to be properly consulted.

---

[2] House of Lords Select Committee on the Constitution, *Devolution: Inter-Institutional Relations in the UK*, Session 2002–03, Second Report, HL Paper 28 (London: The Stationery Office, 2003), paras 119–124; House of Commons Welsh Affairs Select Committee, *The Primary Legislative Process as it affects Wales*, Session 2002–03, Fourth Report, HC 79 (London: The Stationery Office, 2003).

Competition each year to get into the legislative programme is extremely fierce, with typically only around a quarter of departmental bids managing to gain legislative slots. Into this fierce competition have to be inserted the bids for primary legislation that come up from the National Assembly. Judged simply in terms of Wales-only bills, the success rate of the Welsh Assembly Government has not been high. For the 2002–03 session the Assembly put forward eight bids. None became a Wales-only bill but most found a place in England and Wales bills where the UK Government could find a convenient legislative vehicle and one became a draft bill, the Public Audit (Wales) Bill, which should go before Parliament in the 2003–04 session. This does not make for clarity in finding and understanding the law relating to Wales. Nor does it make for confidence or certainty that a legislative vehicle can always be found. In the words of the Lords Constitution Committee, 'Wales figures in such arrangements largely as an afterthought appended to a process driven by the UK Government's concerns rather than those of Wales in general or the National Assembly'.[3]

Whitehall consultation with the Assembly has improved since the early days of devolution, but there is no disguising the weakness of the Assembly's position. What issues gain legislative slots depends on the political priorities in England. Assembly officials depend on Whitehall departments to keep them informed about forthcoming legislative proposals, and are entirely dependent on departments keeping them in the loop thereafter. Nor is it always possible for the Assembly to negotiate a different policy solution for Wales; in at least one case that was not permitted by the Whitehall department.

These fundamental weaknesses — the chronic legislative logjam, Whitehall's overriding priorities, and the rush in which Westminster legislation is prepared — lead in turn to a number of undesirable consequences. Legislation for Wales is often fragmented and incomplete, because the Assembly needs to grab every legislative opportunity it can. As a consequence, primary legislation for Wales is hard to find and to understand, because some of it is in patchwork instalments in different statutes. And because the timetables of Westminster and the Assembly do not always coincide, legislation for Wales can fall between the two legislatures and be poorly scrutinised.

Most legislation for Wales is contained in combined England and Wales bills, but in practice Parliamentary scrutiny at Westminster focuses overwhelmingly on the English arrangements. This is perfectly understandable given that England represents 85 per cent of the UK population, and Wales just 5 per cent. Welsh MPs rarely get more than one or two places on a Standing Committee. This means that even when whole parts of England and

---

[3] House of Lords Select Committee on the Constitution Committee, 2003, para 123.

Wales bills are dedicated to separate Welsh provisions, Westminster scrutiny tends to be seriously inadequate.

Scotland Gets the Best of Both Worlds, Wales Risks Getting the Worst

It is hard not to conclude that Wales gets short shrift under the present arrangements; and to contrast the very different position in Scotland. In its first four years the Scottish Parliament passed over 60 Acts. Most of the legislation passed by the Scottish Parliament has been in subject areas that would be of interest to Wales (i.e. they are devolved to Wales in terms of executive power, but not yet in terms of legislative power). In addition the Scottish Parliament has consented to Westminster legislating on matters devolved to Scotland almost as often as it has legislated for itself, signifying that consent with 42 'Sewel resolutions' in the first four years.[4]

It was not originally expected that Westminster would legislate quite so often on matters devolved to Scotland, and some in Scotland have criticised their Parliament for neglecting its legislative duty. But to the more distant observer it seems the Scots may have got the best of both worlds. They legislate for themselves on the whole range of social and domestic policy matters which would be of interest to Wales — health, education, social services, environment, transport, housing. And when it suits them they let Westminster legislate. While in the first four years of devolution the Scottish Parliament passed 62 Acts, in the same period Wales managed to squeeze just two Wales-only statutes out of Westminster. Even in the most benign of political circumstances, with a sympathetic administration in London, the record in terms of primary legislation for Wales is not impressive. Without political goodwill it could be non-existent. Welsh interests will always be marginal in Whitehall and Westminster's priorities, and under the present settlement Wales risks getting the worst of both worlds.

The Richard Commission Present Their Report

This is the case for change presented to the Richard Commission, now expected to publish their report in early 2004. They report back in a different political context from the one in which they originated. The Commission was first proposed as part of the coalition agreement between Labour and the Liberal Democrats in October 2000. It was appointed in July 2002 by the Labour / Liberal Democrat coalition headed by Rhodri Morgan as First Minister, with terms of reference reflecting the conflicting expectations of the coalition partners. The Liberal Democrats have never been in doubt of the need for a larger assembly with primary legislative powers. The Welsh Labour Party is still full of doubters, reflected in their evidence to the Commission.

[4] See chapter 7.

Following the Assembly elections of May 2003 the political context is very different. In place of the coalition there is single-party Labour government, which has jettisoned any pretence at accommodating the wishes of the opposition parties. Rhodri Morgan has made no secret of his own belief that the National Assembly needs primary legislative powers, and confirmed his view in oral evidence to the Lords Constitution Committee.[5] When he first commissioned the report, it is likely that his strategy went roughly as follows. The Richard Commission would recommend powers of primary legislation in their report. The UK Labour party would include a commitment to implement the proposals of the Richard Commission in their next election manifesto. Labour would win the next general election, expected in 2005, and would introduce a new Wales Act to increase the powers of the National Assembly early in their third term; possibly as early as 2006.

It is by no means a foregone conclusion that the Richard Commission will recommend powers of primary legislation. They may not all be persuaded, or they may decide to trim their recommendations to fit the new political context of single-party Labour government in Wales. But it is likely that the Commission will recommend at least some increase in the Assembly's legislative powers, perhaps on a phased or gradual basis. It would follow the weight of much of the expert evidence they have received, including evidence of a dramatic shift in Welsh public opinion. Support for a Welsh Parliament doubled between 1997 and 2001, from 20 to 40 per cent, so that after only two years of devolution it had become the most favoured constitutional option amongst the people of Wales.[6]

If Richard Says Yes To Legislative Powers, Will London Still Say No?

Formally the government in London has no cognisance of the Richard Commission, which was not its creature. As Secretary of State for Wales Peter Hain will be the crucial gatekeeper. In his public statements he has shown little sympathy for further change. In oral evidence to the Commission at Westminster he argued that it would be disruptive to introduce radical or substantive reforms while the current system was still bedding down.[7] He was against further constitutional reform for its own sake, and insisted that any reforms would have to demonstrate the practical improvements they

---

[5] 'I have always held the view, and I have always expressed the view, that it would have been better if the Government of Wales Act had incorporated primary legislative powers': House of Lords Select Committee on the Constitution, *Devolution: Inter-institutional Relations in the United Kingdom Evidence complete to 10 July 2002*, Session 2001–02, HL Paper 147, (London: The Stationery Office, 2002), Evidence of Mr Morgan, 27 May 2002, Q. 826.

[6] Wyn Jones, R., and Scully, R., *Agenda* Winter 2002, (Cardiff: Institute of Welsh Affairs), pp. 23–24.

[7] Hain, P., Secretary of State for Wales, *Evidence to the Richard Commission*, 13 March 2003, available at http://www.richardcommission.gov.uk/content/evidence/oral/sosw/index-e.htm

would bring to the people of Wales — a 'practical delivery benchmark test'. He has held to the same line in public speeches in Wales.[8]

Even if Hain is privately more sympathetic to the case for primary legislative powers than his public utterances might suggest, he will have an uphill task persuading his colleagues in the UK Government. There is no interest amongst other members of the Cabinet. Devolution is a done deal, especially in the mind of the Prime Minister. It was one of the achievements of Labour's first term, as part of their wider constitutional reform programme. Tony Blair has no desire to revisit devolution in Wales, and has never displayed any sense of the political dynamic which devolution set in train. Lord Falconer is likely to be more sympathetic than was John Prescott, his predecessor as Cabinet Minister in overall charge of devolution policy. Falconer is also more likely to ask, now that both the Wales Office and the Scotland Office are part of his department, why Wales is treated so differently from Scotland. As chair of the Cabinet Committee on Devolution Policy he can ensure that the Richard report gets a proper hearing. But he cannot determine the outcome, and he cannot overrule the Welsh Secretary on matters of devolution policy in Wales.

The official stance of the UK Government is that the current arrangements for devolution in Wales are working well.[9] For the Government to change its mind, Peter Hain and Lord Falconer both need to be strongly convinced of the case for change, and willing to risk some political capital in arguing the case with their colleagues. The Prime Minister is at best indifferent, and the rest of the cabinet are unlikely to be any more supportive.

Any number of scaremongering arguments may be deployed. Cabinet colleagues will warn of the risk of an English backlash; of the Scottish Parliament in turn demanding more powers; of the devolution project running away with them. Welsh Labour MPs at Westminster will be a vocal lobby against any change, fearing for their seats if (following the Scottish precedent) the number of Welsh MPs seems likely to be reduced following the grant of legislative powers.

Increasing the Size of the National Assembly

It will be salt in the wound if the Richard Commission proposes an expansion in the size of the Assembly to match an increase in its powers. The Commission is charged with reviewing the size of the Assembly and its voting system, as well as its powers. The existing Assembly members are already spread thin, and serve on more committees than their counterparts in Scotland. The evidence points towards an expanded Assembly if it is to have

---

[8] See for example 'The Future Relationship between Wales, Whitehall and Westminster', Speech to Institute of Welsh Affairs and Constitution Unit conference, Cardiff, 7 July 2003.

[9] Hain, P., Secretary of State for Wales, *Evidence to the Richard Commission*, 13 March 2003.

expanded powers, but there is no consensus on the size of the increase, the voting system, or the balance between constituency and list members in a larger Assembly.

The difficulty facing the Richard Commission is that there is no single option round which reformers might coalesce. The ancillary part of the Commission's terms of reference, on the size of the Assembly and its voting system, may yet prove more troublesome than the first. It may also prove more of a gift to opponents who want to undermine the Commission's recommendations. There is no perfect voting system, and it is easy to pick holes in any of the options which the Commission put forward.

This then is the hostile climate at Westminster. The expectation in Cardiff may be that if the Richard Commission recommends more powers, London will deliver. Rhodri Morgan's cabinet colleagues in Cardiff are thought to support the case for primary powers, as does the new Labour group in the Assembly. But seen from London that looks much more problematic. Rhodri Morgan will need to judge very carefully when to submit his request, and take advice from Peter Hain about the timing. He will almost certainly be advised to bide his time. In what will probably be the last session before the next general election, the 2004–05 legislative programme will not include a new Wales Act. Rhodri Morgan must wait until after the election, and aim for legislation early in the next Parliament.

Laying the Ground within the Labour Party

He must also lay the ground carefully with the Labour party, in Wales and in the UK. In 2004 the countdown to the next UK general election begins. The timing already looks impossibly tight to get something into the next manifesto. In March the UK Labour party's National Policy Forum will finalise the policy papers to go before party conference in September. Labour's draft policy paper on *Democracy, Political Engagement, Citizenship and Equalities* contains only one passing reference to devolution in its 20 pages. So far as the UK Labour party is concerned, the Richard Commission and any inquiry into the powers of the National Assembly might not exist.

Rhodri Morgan needs first to get a commitment from the Welsh Labour Party, but here the timing is also impossibly tight. The Welsh Labour Party holds its annual conference in the spring, with the next scheduled for late March 2004. The party wants to allow two months for internal consultation before holding any public debate on the Richard report. That suggests they might hold a special conference on the Richard report in the summer, but too late to feed into the UK Labour party's National Policy Forum, which in turn feeds into the Labour manifesto.

The fallback position would be to aim for something in Labour's Welsh manifesto. Like the other main political parties, Labour now produces slightly different manifestos in Scotland and Wales at a UK general election. Rhodri Morgan could insist on some reference to the Richard report in the Welsh Labour manifesto. And if the UK Labour party remains inert or the Welsh Labour party continues to be lukewarm, the compromise pledge could be to hold a referendum before granting further powers to the National Assembly. That could offer advantages to both sides. It gives opponents another hope that the proposals might be defeated. For Rhodri, it is at least a step forward; and a referendum on the powers of the National Assembly is something only the UK Parliament can authorise.[10] It buys further time to negotiate with the UK Government on the details of the Richard package. If the referendum result is positive, it would also (as in 1998) make for a much easier passage for any subsequent bill, and undermine resistance from Welsh Labour MPs and the Opposition.

Will the Welsh Assembly Ever Get Legislative Powers?

It is time to sum up, and to assess the prospects of the National Assembly being granted legislative powers in the next Parliament and beyond. The case on its merits still seems strong. The grant of only executive powers was a compromise to bridge the divisions within the Welsh Labour party. It has been made to work, just, but a succession of official inquiries have shown how difficult it is to make the present arrangements work satisfactorily. With the successful example of the Scottish Parliament before us, it is increasingly hard to understand why Wales should be left for ever struggling with second best.

Everything still turns on the debates inside the Welsh Labour Party. The Richard Commission was always a device to enable the Welsh Labour Party to move forward. Rhodri Morgan has to win the debate there before he can make any further move. He may find his hand forced if Labour lose their majority (of one) in the Assembly, and are forced to negotiate a new coalition with the Liberal Democrats. But to show how high the obstacles still are, it is worth setting out the steps which need to be gone through to gain legislative powers for Wales in the next Parliament:

- Richard report recommends primary legislative powers for the Assembly
- Welsh Labour Party agrees to support Richard recommendations
- Commitment in Labour's Welsh manifesto to implement Richard findings
- Labour wins next UK general election
- UK Government agrees to find Parliamentary time for new Wales Bill.

---

[10] Although the Assembly has a general power to hold referendums under the Government of Wales Act 1998, it is precluded by s. 36 (1) from holding referendums on matters lying outside its own fields of competence.

If the UK Government resists, the issue could be deployed in the next Assembly elections in 2007. But by then the Richard report will be four years old, and risks having passed its sell-by date; and Labour may not want to highlight the constitutional issue, which is seldom an election winner. Morgan may feel it is more prudent to suggest a referendum, as a way of winning round the Labour party doubters. If he wins the referendum, that will then be a powerful card to play with the British government in demanding a new settlement for Wales.

WHITHER THE ENGLISH REGIONS?

England is the gaping hole in the devolution settlement, and the space where everything is still to play for. It could go either way. England could remain with a highly centralised system of government, still largely run by Whitehall and Westminster, or the regional tier of government which has been developing before and since 1997 could evolve into full scale political devolution, with the creation of elected regional assemblies following the first referendums in October 2004.

Chapter 5 shows how UK Government policy since the 1997 Labour manifesto has been to move towards elected assemblies, but in a gradual process. So the first Blair Government set up Regional Development Agencies as agencies of central government, with budgets, targets and performance set by ministers, but with a secondary line of accountability in the region to non-statutory Regional Chambers. The 2001 manifesto repeated the pledge to allow the people, region by region, to decide in a referendum if they want directly-elected regional government. John Prescott's long-awaited White Paper on regional government finally appeared in May 2002.[11] It proposes slimline, strategic regional assemblies with relatively small budgets and few executive powers.

This raises a big question whether, come the referendum, voters will be willing to vote for bodies with such slender powers. Recognising that some regions might not be ready, or might vote against an elected Assembly, the White Paper contained a chapter with suggestions for possible strengthening of the existing Regional Chambers. The scope for further evolution of Regional Chambers is discussed first, before assessing the likely outcome in the forthcoming referendums on elected Regional Assemblies, and the prospects for any elected Assemblies established thereafter.

[11] Cabinet Office and Department of Transport, Local Government and the Regions, *Your Region, Your Choice: Revitalising the English Regions*, Cm 5511, (London: The Stationery Office, 2002).

Further Development of Regional Chambers

With only three out of the eight regions of England due to hold referendums in the first wave, Regional Chambers look set to continue in the other five regions for several years at least, and possibly indefinitely. If the referendums are lost Regional Chambers may continue in all eight regions. The White Paper was therefore realistic in devoting a separate chapter to strengthening existing regional arrangements, but chapter 2 of the White Paper is very short of new ideas. For the most part it proposes changes which are already in place or in train, and the rest are marginal or incremental improvements.

The White Paper summarised its proposals for strengthening Regional Chambers as follows (Figure 11.1):

Figure 11.1: The Role of Regional Chambers

A Stronger Role for Regional Chambers

The chambers have a valuable role to play in the regions alongside the Regional Development Agencies and Government Offices. Their responsibilities are being strengthened to include in the future:

- Continuing scrutiny of the relevant Regional Development Agency
- Co-ordination and integration of regional strategies
- A formal role as the regional planning body
- A new relationship with the Regional Directors of Government Offices and senior officers in other government-funded bodies in the region, who will be ready to discuss their work
- Input to the spending review process, through the relevant Government Office.

The first four suggestions are already in place in most regions. The fifth suggestion, of input to UK Government spending reviews, is unlikely to have much impact. If the government were serious in wanting to strengthen the existing Regional Chambers, it could put them on a statutory basis and give them statutory powers, to give some force to the strategies they must produce or help to implement, and give them additional funding. It could also give chambers the right to appoint members to other regional bodies, and develop closer relationships, or even merger, with bodies such as the Regional Cultural Consortiums, Sustainable Development Round Tables and Public Health Observatories.[12]

Paradoxically, an increase in funding and powers might destroy the secret of the partnerships which the chambers have helped to foster. Opposition by

---

[12] Sandford, M., *Further Steps for Regional Chambers* (London: The Constitution Unit, 2001), paras 77–80.

local authority members to the involvement of the other partners is ebbing away. But it is possible that local authority members have been willing to accept the regional stakeholders as equal partners precisely because there is little to play for in Regional Chambers, which have no powers of delivery, very little money, and rely heavily on voluntary co-operation. The involvement of the regional stakeholders has been the main success story of the Regional Chambers, but to develop more effective regional policy-making with wider participation they may have to move beyond the present stakeholder and consensus-based model, which has very little visibility beyond the charmed circle of those involved. The present system seems too depoliticised to last in the longer term. It requires institutions with more clout to overcome disagreements and deliver, and that in turn requires the legitimacy of direct election.

Prospects for the Referendums on Elected Regional Assemblies

In June 2003 John Prescott announced that the first referendums would be held in the North East, North West and Yorkshire and the Humber in autumn 2004. These three regions were selected following a six-month 'soundings' exercise by the UK Government to judge which regions had the strongest interest in holding a referendum. What are the prospects of those referendums being won?

The soundings produced a wave of opinion polls commissioned by organisations sending in views, summarised in *Your Region, Your Say.*[13] The most comprehensive was commissioned by the County Councils Network and conducted by ICM in January 2003.[14] It showed that in all regions around 60 per cent of respondents wanted a referendum, and suggested that in most regions the referendums would be won by 2:1 (national average 44 per cent Yes, 21 per cent No, 35 per cent Don't Know). The three vanguard regions of the North East, North West and Yorkshire and the Humber were most likely to vote Yes. But more worrying for the Yes campaigners, awareness of UK Government policy on regional assemblies was very low, and turnout was likely to be very low. ICM's speculative prediction was for a turnout of less than 30 per cent.

The referendums will be won by whichever side can mobilise more of this meagre vote in what will be an all-postal ballot. The CCN / ICM survey suggested those most likely to vote are also more likely to vote Yes. Despite the wish of the Yes campaign in the North East to keep the politicians in the background, the only organisations capable of mobilising votes on a large scale are those of the political parties. In the North East that means

[13] Office of the Deputy Prime Minister, *Your Region, Your Say* (London: The Stationery Office, 2003). Available at http://www.odpm.gov.uk/stellent/groups/odpm_regions/documents/pdf/odpm_regions_pdf_023485.pdf

[14] Available on-line at http://www.lga.gov.uk/ccn/research.htm.

predominantly the Labour party. In the North West the Labour party is more divided, and some prominent Labour MPs and Councillors will campaign against, alongside the Tories. The No campaigners will exploit the arguments about an additional layer of bureaucracy, increase in cost, and alienation from politics in general.

To counter the charge that regional government is an unnecessary additional tier, the UK Government has insisted that regional assemblies will be accompanied by unitary local government. The Electoral Commission's Boundary Committee for England is to publish by end 2003 alternative sets of proposals for introducing unitary local government in the three vanguard regions. Two-tier areas in those regions will have a second referendum question on the options for creating unitary authorities in the remaining counties. It could be a major source of dissension which could yet derail the referendum campaign, especially in the North West where the counties of Cheshire, Lancashire and Cumbria still reject unitary local government. In Durham and Northumberland the principle is accepted, but argument remains over whether the counties or the districts would disappear. Comfortingly for the Yes campaigners, local government reform did not seem to be much of an issue for respondents in the opinion surveys, and the historic counties have less resonance in the North which already has predominantly unitary local government.

The best guess for the outcome of the referendums has to be the polling forecast given above, of a 2:1 vote for a regional assembly in the North East, but on a low turnout, and with less certainty about the result in the North West and Yorkshire and the Humber. It is just conceivable, if the referendums look like being lost, that the government will pull the plug rather than face an embarrassing defeat in what will then be the run-up to the next general election. But deferment could be even more embarrassing. More likely would be a distancing of the national Labour party, and in particular the Prime Minister, from the regional campaigns, leaving John Prescott to carry the can if things go horribly wrong.

Are Elected Regional Assemblies Doomed to Failure?

Prescott has promised that if the referendums are won, the first assemblies might be up and running early in the next Parliament. In practice it will be half way through the Parliament, 2007 at the earliest, if they follow the same fast track timetable as devolution in Scotland and Wales. The legislation will take a year, and it will take a year after that before the first elections are held, possibly at the same time as the next Scottish and Welsh elections in May 2007.

How long after that will the honeymoon last? In Scotland and Wales disillusion set in pretty quickly, with a sharp drop in the public's perception of the importance of the devolved institutions and of their impact within only a year or two of their birth. In the English regions the drop could be even sharper, because the gap between expectation and reality will be infinitely greater. It is just as well that the English don't appear to have high hopes of the new regional assemblies (see Figure 9.4 in chapter 9). To win the referendums and the first elections politicians will be forced to give the impression that regional assemblies can make a difference, when the harsh reality is that they will have almost no effective power. The range of functions on offer is the best that Prescott has been able to wring out of his reluctant colleagues in Whitehall, and no-one could pretend that regional assemblies are going to have much impact, certainly not in the short term.

The model chosen for the new assemblies is the Greater London Authority. As chapter 6 on London shows, by setting the assemblies up as slimline, strategic bodies, with tiny budgets and no executive powers, in the eyes of the public they are doomed to fail. The London Mayor's only visible impact has been in fields (transport, the police) where he has executive powers which are not on offer to regional assemblies. Their main function is to write strategies, ten of them, on technocratic subjects (regional spatial strategy, regional waste strategy, biodiversity strategy) which will mean nothing to the general public.[15] There is no evidence so far from the GLA that writing strategies has much impact on the policies of the front line agencies that deliver public services. Neither the GLA nor regional assemblies have any powers or sanctions over bodies that do not deliver their part of the strategy. The assemblies' budgets will be tiny, with almost all their spending devoted to economic development and housing investment. The budget of the North East Assembly will be about thirty times smaller than that of the National Assembly for Wales. Although in both cases the budget is delivered as a block grant, regional assemblies will enjoy significantly less autonomy, because they will be required to set out their key objectives in a number of high level targets, to be agreed with the Treasury.

A final reason for disillusionment is that the politicians will be back in charge. Functional regionalism of the kind exemplified in the Regional Chambers allows a new range of actors into the political process, from business, the voluntary sector and wider civil society. Because they have no statutory powers, no budgets and no staff, they have to operate a consensual kind of politics which works through negotiated agreements and partnership. There is little appreciation of politics as a means of managing conflict or mediating between competing interests, and ultimately imposing decisions with winners and losers. Regional campaigners will seek to promote an

---

[15] For a comparison of the powers of the GLA and the powers proposed for elected Regional Assemblies, and a breakdown of the latter into strategic, executive and 'influencing' functions, see Sandford, M., *A Commentary on the Regional Government White Paper, Your Region, Your Choice* (London: The Constitution Unit, 2002), pp. 8–10. See also chapter 6.

imagined regional community which floats above local divisions, and an imagined new political class. In practice the members of the new assemblies will come from the existing local politicians, plus a few MPs, as they did in Scotland, Wales and the GLA. Because much of the discontent which feeds into the demand for regionalism is part of a more general discontent with conventional politics and politicians, there will be serious disillusionment when it is discovered that the professional politicians have hijacked the regional project. Of one thing we can be reasonably sure: turnout in the first assembly elections will be disappointingly low, and in the second round of elections lower still.

Or Can Regional Assemblies Only Grow?

The White Paper holds out a promise of 'further proposals for the decentralisation of responsibilities to assemblies as time goes on'.[16] To the core functions around economic development, strategic land use planning, transport planning and housing investment, have been added a dash of culture, tourism, museums and libraries, rural regeneration, and sport and the arts. This ragbag of additional items adds little to policy coherence and owes everything to political bargaining. But such an eclectic range of functions helps to make the case for further functions to be added in due course, as other functions come up for review and are looking for a home.

Regional campaigners can draw some hope from the experience in Europe, where functional regionalism has led on to political regionalism, and once established, elected regional assemblies have seen further powers accrue to them. This has been the case in France and Italy, which have both seen proposals for expanding the powers of regional assemblies in recent years. But France also suggests the possible limitations of a model built around economic development as the central function. French regional assemblies began (in 1986) with a strong focus on economic development, but they remain functionally limited, squeezed between two powerful tiers of local government and a powerful central state bureaucracy. Whitehall will continue to resist any serious encroachments on its own powers and budgets. Local government will do likewise. The best hope for regional assemblies lies in inheriting functions from public bodies and quangos, rather than taking them directly from central or local government;[17] or in adopting new functions which lack an institutional home, as the GLA has done with recycling, renewable energy and public health.

---

[16] Cabinet Office and Department of Transport, Local Government and the Regions, 2002, Overview para 18.

[17] A current example is DEFRA's rural delivery review, led by Lord Haskins, which may lead to the breakup of English Nature, the Countryside Agency and the Forestry Commission, with the potential for some of their functions to be given to Regional Development Agencies or regional assemblies. See *The Guardian*, 12 November 2003.

These would be incremental additions which might gradually mount up, but would still leave regional assemblies looking relatively weak in terms of budgets and public profile. That would only change if the regional tier were given responsibility for a major public service such as the health service, the police, or part of education (e.g. further and higher education). One test of the likelihood of this ever happening lies in the UK Government's willingness to use the boundaries of regional assemblies in any future reorganisation of these major public services. The Department of Health signally failed to do that when Regional Health Authorities were reorganised in 2001. The Home Office could do that following the 2003 Green Paper on the future organisation of the police, which proposes regional federations of the existing county-wide police forces.[18] But current government policy seems to favour a more fragmented structure of directly-elected specific-purpose bodies for foundation hospitals and for police authorities, rather than regrouping these functions round the new regional tier.

Regionalism, Equity and Diversity

Campaigners for regional assemblies argue that they are needed to combat not just a democratic deficit but also an economic deficit. The North-South divide has grown worse since 1997, and the Treasury is increasingly concerned to redress the poor productivity of England's poorest regions. But the new regional policy could exacerbate rather than alleviate regional imbalances, because it is designed to raise the economic potential of all regions rather than improve the North relative to the South.[19]

Regional assemblies could lead to greater inequity, not less; and the more power that is devolved, the greater the inequity could be. This has led some to re-assert the social democratic case for a strong central state; and others to assert the need for a re-statement of what the minimum level of state provision should be in all the regions.[20] The debate is at least as old as that between the Girondins and the Jacobins. What is missing is any acknowledgement within the government that devolution and diversity versus equity and uniformity might involve competing values. It is understandable that campaigners will want to argue that regions can have their cake and eat it — that they can have greater autonomy and diversity with no reduction in equity. It is less forgivable on the part of the government, whose job it is to hold the ring and to explain and defend both sets of values.

---

[18] Home Office, *Policing, Building Safer Communities Together*, 4 November 2003, available at www.policereform.gov.uk.

[19] Morgan, K., 'The English Question: Regional Perspectives on a Fractured Nation', *Regional Studies*, 36 (7), 2002, p 800.

[20] An example of the former is Walker, D., *In praise of centralism* (London: The Catalyst Forum, 2002).

THE CONSERVATISM OF THE CENTRE

Conservatism in Whitehall

The third major item of unfinished devolution business is the insufficient adaptation at the centre. As chapter 7 reminds us, the changes in Whitehall have been minimalist in the extreme. This stems more from conservatism on the part of Ministers than officials. The Cabinet Office suggested amalgamation of the Scotland Office and Wales Office in their briefs for the incoming administration after the 2001 election. The Lords Constitution Committee made the same suggestion in their January 2003 report. The case is a positive and negative one. There is no longer enough work to justify retaining separate posts in Cabinet, as Helen Liddell herself was privately well aware. More positively, combining the posts would enable the government to take a more synoptic view of devolution and to think more strategically about its future in a way which is made impossible with the present fragmented structure.

The creation of the new Department for Constitutional Affairs in June 2003 presented an opportunity to merge the two offices, but the Prime Minister cannot break away from the pre-devolution idea of a Scottish Secretary speaking for Scotland and a Welsh Secretary speaking for Wales.[21] As a result responsibility for devolution in Whitehall continues to be badly fragmented. With the part-time Scottish Secretary, the part-time Welsh Secretary, the Northern Ireland Secretary, and John Prescott in charge of regional government in England, there are still four Cabinet ministers with responsibility for different aspects of devolution. Lord Falconer is described as the Minister in overall charge of devolution policy and the devolution settlement, but he is the most junior member of the Cabinet, he has no power to direct the others, and it seems highly unlikely that he can give a lead in shaping the devolution settlement, even though he is nominally responsible for doing so.[22]

Conservatism at Westminster

These fragmented and pre-devolution structures are mirrored by the continuation of equally fragmented structures at Westminster. The Scottish and Welsh Secretaries continue to have separate question times, and continue to be shadowed by separate Scottish and Welsh Select Committees, with separate Grand Committees continuing as well. If, as the Lords Constitution

---

[21] See his reply to Charles Kennedy MP, HC Deb, 18 June 2003, col. 365, and Lord Falconer explaining the Prime Minister's reasoning to the Select Committee on the Lord Chancellor's Department, HC 903–i, 30 June 2003.

[22] Hazell, R., 'Merger, What Merger? Scotland, Wales and the Department for Constitutional Affairs', *Public Law*, Winter 2003, pp. 650–655, (2003).

Committee recommended, we had a single cabinet minister responsible for intergovernmental relations the Westminster structures would be merged as well.

The Commons Procedure Committee made some modest suggestions along these lines back in 1999, which the UK Government declined. Without a lead from the Government nothing will happen. It is a fiction to say these are matters for the House to decide: no reform to Parliament can succeed without Government support.[23] That lead must now come from Peter Hain, the new Leader of the House. Because of his other responsibilities as part-time Welsh Secretary he has less time for his duties as Leader of the House, and parliamentary reform is likely to have a lower priority than under his predecessor. This particular reform is also likely to have less appeal. The Welsh Labour MPs on the Welsh Select Committee and Welsh Grand Committee form an important part of the Welsh Secretary's power-base, so they are a vested interest which is likely to be left alone.

As chapter 8 has shown, Westminster remains untouched by devolution. With the abandonment of any elected element for the Lords, has also gone the vision that the second chamber might adopt a quasi-federal role and start to represent the nations and regions of the UK. The Commons seems rigidly stuck with all its pre-devolution structures, however redundant they may be. The territorial Select Committees and Grand Committees are not going to vote themselves out of existence, and offer a refuge for Scottish and Welsh MPs whose role is otherwise on the wane. The Commons Procedure Committee and the Lords Constitution Committee both called for some rationalisation but no one paid any heed. The anachronistic pre-devolution structures seem likely to linger on for some time to come.

PROSPECTS FOR THE FUTURE

Devolution may remain as an incomplete project for some time to come. The case for further change may be strong, but the forces of inertia may yet prove stronger. The balance of forces has been laid out in relation to each item of unfinished business. This concluding section assesses the consequences for the devolution settlement if no further change is forthcoming. It looks first at England, then at Wales, and lastly at Westminster and Whitehall.

England: Incomplete, But Stable

In England the choice lies with the people, delivered in the referendums in the three vanguard regions in autumn 2004. The likelihood is that the North

---

[23] See Kennon, A., *The Commons: Reform or Modernisation* (London: The Constitution Unit, 2001), p 2, which sets out the four distinct stages where government support is required for any reform to succeed.

East will vote Yes; in the North West, and Yorkshire and the Humber the result is less certain. If all three regions vote No, devolution in England is dead for five years at least, probably for a lot longer. The UK would be 15 per cent devolved, 85 per cent ruled from the centre. The English would have opted out. They might resent certain aspects of devolution, such as the more generous financing of the Celtic nations, but they could not resent the fact of devolution, because those most interested would have had their chance. If the Northern regions vote No, it seems unlikely that other regions of England will demand the chance to vote Yes.

Whether the English might choose to opt in at some later date if they initially vote No is very hard to guess. They could quite rationally vote No on the basis of the current prospectus, because the initial basket of powers on offer is so slender that it is hard to believe regional assemblies can make much difference. Voting Yes will be an act of faith to get regional government launched, in the hope that once launched, regional assemblies will gradually be given further powers. In that respect it will not be much different from the birth of devolution in Wales. Wales showed that even with a low turnout in the referendum and a wafer thin majority, once an assembly is launched the people can become quite strongly attached to it, even if unimpressed by its initial performance.[24]

Wales: Incomplete, Sub-Optimal, Potentially Unstable

Wales also shows that once an Assembly is launched with unsatisfactory powers, it becomes a running sore that cannot simply be plastered over. In the first five years of devolution three official enquiries have looked at different aspects of the problem of primary legislation for Wales. The present system can be made to work, just, but it is completely reliant on a fount of goodwill in Whitehall and Westminster. The time will come when there are different administrations in London and Cardiff. That fount of goodwill could then dry up, and the National Assembly will be stymied. To ask then for legislative autonomy to get round the blockage will be too late. That is why the devolution settlement in Wales is unstable. It is a contingent settlement, excessively dependent on political goodwill between London and Cardiff to make it work. The moment that goodwill is removed, the settlement faces breakdown.

To deliver a stable settlement in Wales calls for brave political leadership: first from the Richard Commission, then from Rhodri Morgan in turning round the Wales Labour party, and then from Peter Hain in persuading the UK Labour party and his colleagues in the UK Cabinet. The Welsh section in this chapter showed how high those hurdles are. The only comfort for

---

[24] See Curtice, J., 'The People's Verdict' in Hazell, R., (ed) *The State and the Nations: The First Year of Devolution in the UK* (Exeter: Imprint Academic, 2001), pp 228–229; and chapter 9.

Morgan is that, when asked about the different options, the people of Wales have indicated with growing confidence that they would prefer an Assembly with legislative powers.[25] That is Morgan's trump card, to appeal direct to the people of Wales. But it is a card which formally rests in the hands of the UK Government, because only Westminster can authorise a referendum on the issue. It will require political gamesmanship of a high order for Morgan to finesse the referendum card out of the UK Government and into the hands of the people of Wales.

The Centre: Incomplete, Stable, But Distinctly Sub-Optimal

Consideration of the Richard report will be the first test of the capacity of the British government to consider a big devolution issue. It is not well configured to do so. The opportunity was missed in the June 2003 reshuffle to take a more synoptic view of devolution, by bringing together in a single post responsibility for devolution in Scotland and Wales. The new Secretary of State for Constitutional Affairs might yet fulfil that role, as the minister responsible for the devolution settlements and overall UK Government policy on devolution. But the clear signs are that Lord Falconer will not want to tread on the toes of his territorial Secretaries of State, who will have a free hand in their respective fiefdoms.[26] Despite the potential for a more synoptic approach following the incorporation of the Scotland and Wales Offices into the Department for Constitutional Affairs, in practice responsibility for devolution continues to be badly fragmented. There is no capacity to think about devolution in the round, to understand the dynamics of devolution, to think and prepare ahead for how the devolution settlement is likely to evolve.

The present arrangements are decidedly sub-optimal, but seem stubbornly resistant to change. The logic of the evolving devolution settlement may suggest that the next step is merger of the part-time territorial Secretaries of State, as the Conservatives appear to have done in Michael Howard's slimmed-down shadow cabinet.[27] But on the Labour side the politics may for some time dictate otherwise. Three separate sources of pressure reinforce the Blair Government's instinct to cling to the old ways. First, the outcry in Labour Wales in summer 2003 at the possible loss of their Secretary of State showed how the Welsh still feel dependent on a godfather figure in London, even if the Scots do not. Second, Westminster buttresses Whitehall in

---

[25] Curtice, J., 'Hopes Dashed and Fears Assuaged' in Trench, A., (ed.) *The State of the Nations 2001: The Second Year of Devolution* (Exeter: Imprint Academic, 2002), Figure 10.1 on p 228, showing survey data for 1997, 1999 and 2001.

[26] Hazell, 2003, p. 652.

[27] In the shadow cabinet of just 12 members announced in November 2003, David Curry MP is Shadow Secretary of State for Local and Devolved Government, leading a team of five junior ministers, for local government, the regions, Northern Ireland, Scotland and Wales.

clinging to pre-devolution structures, with the Commons retaining the full range of separate territorial committees as if devolution had never happened. Third, the Scottish and Welsh Select Committees and Grand Committees provide tailor-made fora for special pleading by special territorial interests, to which the Secretaries of State are ready to respond because the Scottish and Welsh Labour MPs form part of their power base. The whips also look on the Scottish and Welsh Labour MPs as reliable lobby fodder. It may not be until a change to a Conservative UK Government which is less reliant on support in Scotland and Wales that the Whitehall structures finally change, and the Westminster structures with them.

BIBLIOGRAPHY

Official Documents

Cabinet Office and Department for Transport, Local Government and the Regions, *Your Region, Your Choice: Revitalising the English Regions*, Cm 5511, (London: The Stationery Office, 2002).

Department for Constitutional Affairs, *Constitutional Reform: A New Supreme Court for the United Kingdom*, CP 11/03, (London: The Stationery Office, 2003).

Home Office, *Policing: Building Safer Communities Together* (London: The Stationery Office, 2003). Available at www.policereform.gov.uk.

House of Lords Constitution Committee, *Devolution: Inter-Institutional Relations in the UK*, Evidence volume, HL 147, (London: The Stationery Office, 2002).

House of Lords Select Committee on the Constitution, *Devolution: Inter-Institutional Relations in the UK*, Session 2002–03, Second Report, HL Paper 28, (London: The Stationery Office, 2003).

Office of the Deputy Prime Minister, *Your Region, Your Say* (London: The Stationery Office, 2003). Available at http://www.odpm.gov.uk/stellent/groups/odpm_regions/documents/pdf/odpm_regions_pdf_023485.pdf.

Select Committee on the Lord Chancellor's Department (now the Constitutional Affairs Committee), *Department for Constitutional Affairs*, Uncorrected oral evidence, HC 903–i, 30 June 2003.

Welsh Affairs Select Committee, *The Primary Legislative Process as it affects Wales*, Session 2002–03, Fourth Report, HC 79, (London: The Stationery Office, 2003).

Secondary Sources

Curtice, J., 'The People's Verdict' in Hazell, R., (ed.) *The State and the Nations: The First Year of Devolution in the UK* (Exeter: Imprint Academic, 2001).

Curtice, J., 'Hopes Dashed and Fears Assuaged' in Trench, A., (ed.) *The State of the Nations 2001: The Second Year of Devolution* (Exeter: Imprint Academic, 2002).

Hazell, R., 'Merger, What Merger? Scotland, Wales and the Department for Constitutional Affairs', *Public Law*, Winter 2003, pp. 650–655, (2003).

Wyn Jones, R., and Scully, R., 'Let's Make it Work', *Agenda* Winter 2002, (Institute of Welsh Affairs).

Kennon, A., *The Commons: Reform or Modernisation* (London: The Constitution Unit, 2001).

Morgan, K., 'The English Question: Regional Perspectives on a Fractured Nation', *Regional Studies*, vol. 36 (7), pp. 797–810, (2002).

Sandford, M., *A Commentary on the Regional Government White Paper, Your Region, Your Choice* (London: The Constitution Unit, 2002).

Sandford, M., *Further Steps for Regional Chambers* (London: The Constitution Unit, 2001).

Walker, D., *In praise of centralism*, (London: The Catalyst Forum, 2002).

Index

Working Families Tax Credit 152, 238, 241

Y

Yorkshire and the Humber (see Regional Assemblies)
Yorkshire Post 134